THE CHALLENGE
OF RADICAL
POLITICAL
ECONOMY

THE CHALLENGE OF RADICAL POLITICAL ECONOMY

*An Introduction to the Alternatives
to Neo-Classical Economics*

MALCOLM C. SAWYER

*Professor of Economics
University of York*

Harvester Wheatsheaf

New York   London   Toronto   Sydney   Tokyo

First published 1989 by
Harvester Wheatsheaf,
66 Wood Lane End, Hemel Hempstead,
Hertfordshire, HP2 4RG
A division of
Simon & Schuster International Group

Printed and bound in Great Britain by
Billing and Sons Ltd, Worcester

British Library Cataloguing in Publication Data

Sawyer, Malcolm C. (Malcolm Charles), *1945–*
    The challenge of radical political economy:
    an introduction to the alternatives to
    neo–classical economics
    1. Economics. Radical theories, 1900–1981
    I. Title
    335

    ISBN 0–7450–0194–7
    ISBN 0–7450–0404–0 pbk

---

1 2 3 4 5   93 92 91 90 89

To: Jan, Matthew, Ben and William

CONTENTS

PART 5 THE STATE

CHAPTER 10 THE POLITICAL ECONOMY OF THE STATE

**PART 6 UNEMPLOYMENT, GROWTH AND
        DISPARITIES**

CHAPTER 11 UNEMPLOYMENT AND INFLATION

PREFACE

This book has been written to serve as a test suitable for use by second- and third-year undergraduates on courses with titles such as radical economics, post-Keynesian economics. It also seeks to provide a synthetic treatment of those economic analyses which are not based on a neo-classical approach, ranging over post-Keynesian, Marxian, Sraffian, and institutional paradigms. One of the stimuli for writing this book came from being asked to give a series of lectures on Alternative Perspectives in Economics to second-year undergraduates at the University of York. The structure and aims of that series of lectures are strongly reflected here – in particular the organisation by theme rather than by school of thought.

This book has been written in the belief that there was a need for a broadly based text on the alternatives to neo-classical economics. Nevertheless, there are a number of books which I would regard as complementary to this one, notably Aaronovitch and Smith (1981), Bowles and Edwards (1985), Green and Sutcliffe (1987), Sherman (1987b) and on the macroeconomics side Eichner (1987), Reynolds (1987) and Sawyer (1982a).

I am grateful to Geoff Hodgson who read and commented on a number of chapters. Philip Arestis read all the chapters and his comments (and our general discussions) have been a great help and stimulus for which I am most grateful.

Part One

INTRODUCTION TO RADICAL POLITICAL ECONOMY

Chapter 1
RADICAL POLITICAL ECONOMY

1.1 INTRODUCTION

The central purpose of this book is to provide a synthetic and sympathetic treatment of radical political economy. The approaches to economic analysis which are included within the label of radical political economy have, like any other approach, distinctive views of the nature of economic analysis and focus on a range of questions which their practitioners believe to be of importance. The intention is to focus on the positive and constructive aspects of radical political economy, in the search for understanding and explanation of the economies of the real world. Whilst there are places at which critical remarks are made of the orthodox neo-classical economics, the central aim of this book is to be constructive rather than merely critical.

There is no precise definition of radical political economy, and some would see the common feature of the approaches which we discuss in this book as opposition to neo-classical economics. To some degree, the view of radical political economy will only become fully clear by reading the contents of the book. However, it is useful to provide an initial definition.[1] Radical political economy is a multi-paradigm study of the economy which emphasises features such as the distribution of income, the dynamic rather than static nature of capitalist economies, capital accumulation and the generation and uses of an economic surplus. The themes of radical political economy are discussed further in this chapter. The multi-paradigm aspect means that a variety of different approaches are drawn upon, of which the four main ones are post-Keynesian, Marxian, institutional and Sraffian.[2] These four approaches are discussed shortly. These approaches do, in our view, have a range of common features which enable them to be brought together, although inevitably there are differences as well (and some of those differences have led to fierce debates).

1.2 SCHOOLS OF THOUGHT WITHIN RADICAL POLITICAL ECONOMY

In this section, we briefly outline the four schools of thought included under the broad umbrella of radical political economy. The first school examined is generally now labelled post-Keynesian.[3] This stream has some allegiance to the work of Keynes, but it needs to be distinguished from Keynesian economics which many post-Keynesians view with distaste. The post-Keynesian approach has been described by a leading post-Keynesian in the following terms:

> The characteristics of the historical and humanistic models employed by post-Keynesians may be summarised in the following three propositions:
> 1) The economy is a historical process
> 2) in a world where uncertainty is unavoidable, expectations have an unavoidable and significant effect on economic outcomes; and,
> 3) economic and political institutions play a significant role in shaping economic events. (Davidson, 1981)

The first proposition can be elaborated in several ways but two points are highlighted here. First, what has happened in the past and our perceptions of those events help shape the decisions taken in the present, but those decisions also reflect our expectations for the future. As time proceeds, people's experiences and perceptions of the environment change and that leads them to behave in ways which are different from past behaviour. The economic and political environment itself will change, for that environment is formed in part by the way in which people behave. Second, history is a one-way street. As the economy and society evolve, the basic structure of the economy as well as beliefs and expectations are likely to change. In that case, knowledge on the ways in which a particular economy operated at a specific time may be of little value in explaining or predicting the operations of another economy at a different time. The Marxian approach takes this one step further, by thinking in terms of distinct stages of history, where each stage of history is quite different from the other stages. For example, feudalism generally and gradually gave way to capitalism, and within the capitalist era there has been much debate over whether there has been an evolution from a competitive to a monopolistic stage (see section 5.5). When there are distinct stages of history, then there are inevitable debates over the dating of stages and what the precise nature of each stage is. But more importantly there is a need for an explanation of how and why one era leads into another. To continue the example of competitive capitalism evolving into a monopolistic era, the questions which would arise are when the evolution took place, what its significance is and what forces were at work within the competitive era which led to that evolution.

The second proposition relates to what could be called genuine uncertainty, where a distinction is drawn between risk and uncertainty.[4] *Risk* refers to the case where although the precise outcome of a course of action is not known, the probabilities of different outcomes occurring are known, examples of which are the tossing of an unbiased coin and the rolling of a die. *Uncertainty* refers to the case where not only is the precise outcome unknown but also the probabilities of different outcomes are not known. If risk is the case considered, then an individual can make precise calculations of the expected value (in a statistical sense) of the possible outcomes arising from a particular action, and then choose the course of action which would yield the range of outcomes which have the best expected value. But the presence of genuine uncertainty precludes the possibility of precise calculations, and it is likely that individuals and organisations will fall back on rules of thumb, hunches, etc., in making decisions.

Many of these notions were succinctly expressed in Keynes (1937), which has formed the basis for an important strand of argument in post-Keynesian economics. Keynes argued that the prospects for many future possibilities were uncertain and 'there is no scientific basis on which to form any capable probability whatever. We simply do not know.' He continued by arguing that 'a practical theory of the future ... has certain marked characteristics. In particular, being based on so flimsy a foundation, it is subject to sudden and violent changes.' Keynes attacked the neo-classical approach as 'being one of these pretty, polite techniques which tries to deal with the present by abstracting from the fact that we know very little about the future'. If the future is very much like the past, then past events may give a reasonably good guide to the probabilities of future events. But once we recognise that the economy and society are changing, the past is of much less use for forecasting the future.

The third proposition given above clearly means that the institutional arrangements of a society must be taken into account when the operation of its economy is analysed. As a general proposition institutional factors such as the organisation of firms (e.g. size, who has effective control), of workers (e.g. whether unionised or not), the relationship between firms, workers and the government, the legal framework within which firms and workers operate, would be some of the relevant factors. In this context, the institutional arrangements are to be interpreted widely. Some of these arrangements are reflected in our discussions below, but perhaps most strongly in Chapters 2, 4, 5 and 6.

The importance of institutions leads to consideration of the institutional approach, which is the second approach influencing the current work. A leading institutional economist has described the approach in the following manner:

> Institutional economics assert the primacy of the problem of the organization and control of the economic system, that is, its structure of power. Thus, whereas orthodox economists tend strongly to identify the economy solely with the market, institutional economists argue that the market is itself an institution, comprised of a host of subsidiary institutions and interactive with other institutional complexes in society. In short, the economy is more than the market mechanism: it includes the institutions which form, structure and operate through, or channel the operation of the market. The fundamental institutionalist position is that it is not the market but the organizational structure of the larger economy which effectively allocates resources. (Samuels, 1987)

The market can be seen as concerned with the exchange of goods and services, usually directly for money but indirectly for other goods and services (including labour). At one level, the size of firms and the structure of the industry (including for example relationships between firms) along with the legal background covering the sales of goods and services and of labour will influence the prices at which exchanges take place. At another level, a great deal of economic activity takes place *within* economic institutions, whether they be firms, unions, households, government, etc. This point is elaborated at length in connection with firms in Chapter 4. Thus, for example, decisions on the mix of products to be produced are made within a firm, though those decisions may be influenced by the prices which the firm expects to receive for each product. Further, the organisation of production takes place within a firm, and the efficiency of production is a major element of the overall efficiency of the economy. As will be seen in Chapter 2, the radical political economy approach places considerable emphasis on the organisation of the production process whereas the neo-classical approach stresses exchange rather than production.

Neo-classical economics is to a large degree institution-free in the sense that it is intended to have universal applicability and it has not sought to reflect particular institutional arrangements in its theories. In recent years there have been attempts to extend neo-classical economics to encompass institutional arrangements, but this has generally taken the form of viewing the institutional arrangements as reflecting the optimising choices of individuals; that is, the institutional arrangments reflect individual choice. In contrast, institutional economics would stress the impact of existing institutions on individual behaviour, and the gradual evolution of institutions, but without any implication that institutions are in any sense optimally designed. An example relating to firms can illustrate this general point. An institutional approach would observe the existing organisational nature of firms in an economy, and then discuss how that nature influences the behaviour of those who work for the firm and of the firm as an organisation. Thus, as reflected in the managerial theories of the firm, the separation of ownership and control leads to different behaviour and performance by a corporation. In contrast, a nco-classical approach would view the divorce between ownership and control as derived from the division of labour whereby it was not necessary that the function of ownership and of management were vested in the same people, but without implication for the performance of the corporation.

The third approach considered is the Marxian one, where the term 'Marxian' is used to cover authors whose work has to some degree been acknowledged to be influenced by Marx. Some of the features of this approach have been touched on above, including the idea of stages of history and the evolutionary nature of economies. A central element in any Marxian analysis is the importance of social classes and the conflict of interests between classes. In capitalist economies, the two major social classes are seen to be those based on capital and on labour respectively. Under capitalism, economic power lies with capital, and this view will be reflected below, particularly in the discussion of the labour process (Chapter 2) and in the nature of firms (Chapter 4).

Most economies are capable of generating a surplus of production over consumption requirements, and this is particularly so under industrialised economies. The question then arises as to who receives that surplus and to what use that surplus is put. The Marxian view (which will be much further explored in Chapter 7) is that under capitalism the surplus is largely captured by capitalists as a result of their control of the means of production. Associated with this is the view that capitalism involves the exploitation being received by the capitalists, and this is also explored in more detail below.

Capitalism is a dynamic economic system, which has developed standards of living and technological advances which were previously undreamt of. But capitalism does not evolve smoothly or uniformly and it is subject to cycles of economic activity and to periodic crises, and uneven development whereby some regions prosper at the expense of others. The Marxian and other approaches in these regards are explored in Chapters 11 to 13.

The final stream of thought which has an influence in this book is generally labelled Sraffian or neo-Ricardian. The work of Sraffa (1960) revived interest in the work of Ricardo and was designed as 'a prelude to a critique of economic theory', meaning neo-classical economic theory. The general approach which developed from this work is generally referred to as Sraffian or neo-Ricardian and is discussed in Chapter 8. This approach can be seen as providing a framework within which a number of questions can be discussed without reference to the neo-classical general equilibrium approach. These questions include the relationship between wages, prices and the rate of profits. It has also served to cast doubt on the logical validity of some aspects of an aggregate interpretation of neo-classical economics; in particular, it pointed to the difficulties of the concept of aggregate capital and the required negative relationship between the rate of profit (interest) and the aggregate capital stock (section 8.9). This, as discussed below, served to undermine the aggregate interpretation of the marginal productivity theory of distribution.

These preliminary remarks indicate that there are at least four streams of thought (institutional, Marxian, post-Keynesian and Sraffian) which are reflected in this book. To some degree their common element is their opposition to neo-classical economics, and as such it could be argued that they do not collectively constitute a coherent approach. It is not claimed that this book has forged a coherent approach out of these four streams of thought. However, in the author's view there are many respects in which they are complementary with one another (although there are areas where they are clearly in conflict). A partial reflection of this view is that the discussion in this book is generally organised in terms of topics rather than by school of thought. Further, within each topic a variety of different approaches are discussed, and the reader is left to judge how consistent these approaches are with each other.

In a book of this length it is not possible to provide a comprehensive treatment of the alternatives to neo-classical economics. There are some topics (e.g. international trade) which have not been included and some approaches to the topics discussed are omitted. The book should be seen as a reflection of the author's view of what questions and approaches to those questions are important, within the constraints imposed by length, for understanding capitalist economies. This should not be taken as indicating agreement with all of the approaches discussed below; indeed that would not be possible without a strong degree of internal contradiction. The intention has been to include theories and approaches which have played a significant role in debates within radical political economy.

There is one alternative approach to neo-classical economics which is not covered in this book, namely the Austrian approach.[5] The major reason for this omission (apart from the inevitable space constraint) is that the Austrian approach is rather 'out on a limb' as compared with the other approaches. This arises from an adoption of a rather different methodology and focusing on rather different questions. Indeed the Austrian approach shares with neo-classical economics a generally favourable attitude towards capitalism, and particularly towards the benefits of competition (though the Austrian and neo-classical views of competition are rather different).

There is one aspect stressed by the Austrian approach which does find some reflection in the present text, namely the treatment of uncertainty. This can be briefly summarised as that the world in which we live is an uncertain one in which the future cannot be accurately forecast. Individuals will make mistakes through this uncertainty and will adapt to it in various ways. Specifically, the model of utility maximisation by well-informed individuals is seen as inappropriate. Some authors within the post-Keynesian approach (drawing on some of the work of Keynes, 1937) also stress this uncertainty, as indicated above, and for that reason their work falls within the compass of this book.

1.3 GENERAL THEMES OF RADICAL POLITICAL ECONOMY

The heading of the chapters of this book provide a good indication of the topics and subjects of interest in the study of radical political economy. Some would see the term 'political economy' as the nineteenth-century forerunner of economics. But many others would see the term as having a meaning rather different from that of economics. Indeed, when economics is used to mean neo-classical economics, and political economy as the type of approaches examined in this book, then the material covered below would show that there is indeed a sharp difference between (neo-classical) economics and political economy. This difference extends to the topics of importance and the mode of analysis.

One part of the subject matter of political economy is the study of the use and creation of resources. As such this would include a study of the labour process (which covers the use of labour time and work effort), and the labour market (Chapters 2 and 3), and the ways in which production is organised and reorganised (which is covered in Chapters 4, 5 and 6). It would also cover the study of the levels of employment and the creation of new resources (investment) which are discussed in Chapters 11, 12 and 13. But there would be a stress on the creation of new resources, on the study of growth and development. In addition, radical political economy would study the distribution of income (the benefits of production) as indicated in Chapter 9, and the relationship between prices, wages and profits as in Chapter 8. The activities of the State have always had important impacts on the economy, and the explanations of State activity are discussed in Chapter 10.

Although there are differences of emphasis, radical political economy shares with neo-classical economics a focus on the use of resources. The sharper differences arise from the way in which the analysis is undertaken. But, as suggested by the use of the adjective 'political', the study of political economy does not envisage a sharp division between the study of economics and the studies of political and social forces. Indeed, these forces are important in influencing people's behaviour, including their economic behaviour.

The approach of this book has been described as radical political economy. In part, this helps to ensure that political economy is not seen as a synonym for economic analysis. In recent years, the term 'political economy' has been used to suggest that the economic analysis is being used to assess or influence economic policy. The term 'radical' can also be interpreted in its original meaning as 'to re-examine the roots', for radical political economy is to be seen as seeking to change the foundations of economic analysis as conventionally practised.

This book is only concerned with the operation of developed capitalist economies – that is, economies in which there is extensive private ownership of the means of production with high levels of *per capita* income and industrialisation. This does not mean that the schools of thought discussed have nothing to say about other economies. Indeed, these schools of thought have sometimes been considered to have more to say about economies which are regarded as undeveloped (at least in terms of *per capita* income). Further, many of the basic ideas would find application in economies other than developed capitalist economies. However, whilst there may be underlying ideas applicable to different types of economies, the exact way in which the ideas are applied will be different. It was indicated above that institutional arrangements in an economy are important for its operation. For example, within Marxian economies, the concept of social class is an important one. But the application of that basic idea will depend on the type of society to which it is being applied. In feudal societies, it would be landlord–serf class division; in capitalist societies the division between capitalists and workers is the important one. This is one illustration of the general proposition that there may be important differences between different types of economies. Whereas neo-classical economics has often made claim to universal applicability, the approaches considered here do not usually make such a claim. For example, Robbins (1932) identifies neo-classical economics with the study of the uses of scarce means and then 'scarcity of means to satisfy ends of varying importance is an almost ubiquitous condition of human behaviour. Here, then, is the unity of subject of Economic Science, the forms assumed by human behaviour in disposing of scarce means.' It will be seen below that radical political economy is concerned with many issues, including the creation of resources, besides the use of resources (which are not always scarce), whereas neo-classical economics is not. Further, the power structure, level of development, institutional arrangements, etc., of a society are important elements in the operation of that society's economy.

The first theme emerges from this view – namely, the analysis of capitalist economy must take into account the specific features of such an economy. These features would include the institutional arrangements, the legal framework and the beliefs and perceptions of the individuals and organisations within that economy. There will inevitably be disagreements over what the important features are and how to characterise those features. It will be seen in Chapter 6, for example, that there are many different views on the control of large corporations in existing developed capitalist economies (e.g. whether corporations are largely manager-controlled or owner-controlled) and on the degree of rivalry and competition between firms. The features of capitalist economies may differ across countries and over time. The British economy in the 1980s would seem to differ in a number of important respects from the British economy in the 1930s and from the Japanese economy in the 1980s. The institutional arrangements (e.g. role of trade unions, size of large corporations, role of State) are different in many ways and could be expected to fundamentally influence the operation of the economy. Indeed, a major contribution of radical political economy analysis arises from discussion of the ways in which institutional arrangements differ between countries and over time, and how those different arrangements can influence the behaviour and performance of the economies concerned. One example of this would be that the relationships between the industrial and financial sectors of developed economies are observed to differ considerably as between, for example, United Kingdom, the United States, Germany and Japan. It is often argued that the relationship between the financial and industrial sectors is a much closer one in the last two countries mentioned than in the first two. These differences can then influence the ways in which investment is financed (e.g. through internal or external finance), the time horizon over which decisions are made (e.g. short term or long term), and thereby the volume and type of investment can be influenced. In turn, the nature of investment will mould the development of the economy.

The second major theme is the notion of a surplus.

> Marx, like his classical predecessors, conceived the economic process as involving the creation as a *surplus* product, over and above the need of input replacement and workers' consumption, that was appropriated as profit, interest and rent. Bohm-Bawerk and Wicksteed [and neo-classical economics], by contrast, conceived that process as involving production through the mutual co-operation of various 'factors', there being *no* element of asymmetry as between labour and other 'factors'. (Steedman, 1981)

The concept of surplus is discussed here, and the asymmetry between labour and other factors of production is returned to below.

The existence of a surplus of the output of an economy over the acceptable level of consumption allows for the possibility of investment, which may add to the productive resources available (e.g. machinery) or may be largely unproductive (e.g. the building of pyramids in Ancient Egypt). It is clearly a prerequisite for investment, and economies at low levels of development struggle to find the necessary surplus. The surplus can (and often has been) used for other purposes; for example, the rich and powerful in many societies control much of the surplus and use it to support conspicuous consumption, the building of palaces and cathedrals, etc. Some groups (classes) control the use of the surplus. In slave societies control clearly resides with the slave-owners, whereas in feudal times, the control would lay with feudal barons, landlords, etc. Under capitalism, most of the surplus accrues as profits, and the idea that profits arise from a surplus is extensively explored in Part Four. In this case, profits are not associated with any ideas of abstinence or marginal productivity of capital as in the neo-classical approach (as will be much further discussed in section 9.5). In the neo-classical approach, the rate of profit can be seen as set by the interaction between the demand and supply of capital. On the one side, capital equipment is seen as raising production levels by the marginal product of 'capital'. On the supply of finance side, the individuals supplying finance are abstaining from consumption. The rate of profit is then seen as the interaction between the productivity of 'capital' and the disutility of abstaining from consumption. 'Capital' is on a par with labour – both add to output (provided that the relevant marginal product is positive) and both involve a disutility (abstinence from consumption and working, respectively). In this discussion inverted commas have been placed round 'capital' because of difficulties with the concept of capital which are explored below (section 8.9). It will also be seen below (section 9.5) that the 'disutility' of working is regarded as being of a quite different order of magnitude to the 'disutility' involved in abstaining from consumption. The crucial point to note here is that when the concept of a surplus is used, then profits (and rent) are seen as arising from the existence of the surplus. Control over the surplus allows the owners of capital to extract a surplus. The factors that determine the size and nature of the surplus are seen differently by different authors in ways which are discussed in Chapter 9.

It is often argued in defence of increased profits by firms that extra profits provide the finance for investment, and this illustrates the link between profits as a surplus and investment as resting on a surplus of output over consumption. For it is often implicitly assumed that whilst an increase in wages would lead to an increase in consumer expenditure, an increase in profits leads to an increase in investment. The reasons why increased profits are thought to lead to increased investment are not crucial here, but would include retained profits providing the finance for investment and higher profitability being an incentive for higher investment. The links between investment, profitability and growth are considered below (sections 12.4, 12.5).

The link between surplus and growth becomes clear in the relatively early stages of industrial development. Here one relevant surplus is the agricultural surplus, that is the ability of the agricultural sector to produce more food than is consumed by the workers and others involved in the agricultural sector. For a surplus of production in the agricultural sector is required to feed non-agricultural workers. When productivity is low so that average productivity of an agricultural worker equals average consumption of such a worker, then no surplus is available to feed other workers. However, some agricultural surplus generally exists but may be used to feed the landowners, priests, etc. Thus, industrial development requires not only an agricultural surplus, but also the economic and social arrangements which ensure that the surplus is used to feed the industrial workers (rather than, say, be used by landlords for overindulgence).

Industrialisation requires an agricultural surplus and also a surplus of output over consumption, i.e. savings which can release resources for investment, though the question remains over whether and how those resources will be used. These propositions are general ones, and can be seen as particularly relevant for countries seeking to undertake industrialisation. For example, the Soviet Union in the 1920s aimed for rapid industrialisation, and the policy adopted was the extraction of the required surplus from the peasant agricultural sector (see, e.g. Nove, 1972 ch. 5).

This brief discussion serves to indicate that one key difference between capitalist and socialist economies is which groups of people have control over the surplus, who make investment decisions and in whose interests those decisions are made (cf. Kalecki, 1970). In capitalist economies, decisions on investment and accumulation are largely in the hands of capitalists, who will make decisions on investment depending on factors such as profitability and the state of competition. In socialist economies, when they are centrally planned, investment decisions will be largely made by the central planners. The extent to which total output exceeds consumption and the division of that surplus between different types of investment and expenditure on defence, education, etc., will also be determined by the central planners (who will make mistakes, sometimes be unable to implement the plans and find their plans circumscribed by a variety of political and social pressures).

A further line of thought here is that investment and growth cannot be analysed independently of the type of society being discussed. One expression of this view is that 'the rate of growth at a given time is a phenomenon rooted in the past economic, social and technological developments' (Kalecki, 1971a). This line of thought indicates that the future course of economic development has to build on past developments, and also that the form and pace of economic development is strongly influenced by the economic and social arrangements of a society.

The third theme arises from the second, namely that growth and development are important subjects in radical political economy, and this importance arises from three considerations. First, the idea that economic growth involves the creation (through investment, research and development, training and education, etc.) of additional resources is given prominence in the improvement of human economic welfare. In contrast, the focus of neo-classical economics in this regard is on improving allocative efficiency in the use of existing resources (cf. discussion below).

Second, growth and development do not usually involve more of the same (as would be implied by neo-classical growth theory) but involve the development of new products, new processes of production and new forms of work organisation. Growth involves change in many different ways. New industries grow, old industries decay; some regions prosper whilst others do not. Change involves upheaval and the destruction of established ways of life. Jobs and skills are destroyed whilst new jobs are created and demands for new skills arise. Some communities may prosper but others are virtually destroyed as the industries on which they depend decay.

From the point of view of economic theory, seeing growth and development as a process of change and upheaval does tend to suggest that analysing growth as an equilibrium process which tends to suggest tranquillity may not be very fruitful.[6] Further, adopting an approach which involves an examination of a balanced growth path tends to rule out consideration of unbalanced growth. However, casual observation of the world suggests that growth is unbalanced, by which is meant that some sectors are expanding very rapidly at a rate which could not be sustained for ever.

Third, there is a link between profits, investment and growth (which is explored further in Chapter 12). This can be expressed in a crude form as follows. Profits are the major form of savings, from which investment is financed; growth requires a growth of the capital stock which is net investment. Thus growth requires savings, which arise out of profits. But the other way round, profits require growth in that if there were no growth, then there would be no outlet for savings, and no need for profits out of which savings are made.

The fourth theme in radical political economy is the importance of social class, and this is particularly so in the Marxian approach. The relevance of social class arises when individuals are members of a social class who have substantial interests in common and pursue those interests collectively to some degree. The interests of the social classes are often in conflict with each other, and this will be apparent below in, for example, discussion of the labour process and income distribution. The concept of social class is particularly important in Marxian analysis, where class interests and the conflict between them are important driving forces behind the evolution of the economy. Even where social classes are not explicitly considered, the conflicting interests of different groups are seen as relevant, e.g. owners v. workers, managers v. owners.

In neo-classical economics, the concept of social classes is redundant, with the level of analysis being that of the individual. Individuals with similar characteristics (e.g. similar tastes) may be grouped together, but that is merely a convenience for the analysis. An individual i may be placed as part of group x, but there is no way that membership of group x affects the behaviour of individual i.

The fifth theme is the importance of income distribution, which relates to the division between major types of income (notably labour income and property income) and to the size distribution of income between individuals. The distribution of income (in both senses) is important in its own right. But it is also important for the impact which the distribution of income has on the operation of the economy. The factor distribution of income, especially the share and rate of profits, is likely to influence the determination of savings, investment and growth; and this will be particularly important in the discussion below. But a further importance of inequality comes from consideration of the ways in which health care and education are allocated between individuals and classes. These allocations are important in their own right for the inequality of life chances in society, but, through their impact on the productive capacity of workers, will also influence the growth potential of the economy.

Capitalism is viewed as an economic system which generates and sustains inequalities. There are many dimensions to inequality, and these would include inequality between and within social classes, between regions and countries. The discussion of inequalities is spread throughout the book. In Chapters 2 and 3 inequalities within the labour force are touched upon, whilst in Chapter 9 the distribution of income between social classes is discussed. In Chapter 13 regional and international inequalities are discussed in terms of the mechanisms which generate such inequalities. In that chapter the question of whether market mechanisms tend to reduce or to sustain inequalities is also addressed.

The fourth and fifth themes are reflected in a contrast between neo-classical economics and classical economic analysis (which overlaps considerably with our view of radical political economy).

> In general, the central feature of neo-classical analysis is that the problem of distribution, conceived in terms of a society of atomistic individuals, is solved entirely within the sphere of exchange as related both to exchange of factor services and to exchange of products. Underlying this analysis is the conception of a society *without* classes, defined either in terms of appropriation of the product according to divisions in property ownership, as in Classical economic analysis, or in terms of a social-production relation (the capital–labor relation) based on control of labor in production, as in Marxian theory. (Harris, 1978)

The sixth theme is linked to the preceding ones, and this is the existence and exercise of power.[7] In Chapter 2 on the labour process, the stress is on the power arising from their ownership of the means of production held by capitalists over workers. The discussion of the role of the State likewise must involve the power exercised by the State (through the legal system for example) over its citizens, and also the power exercised by powerful groups in society over the State.

1.4 THE SCOPE OF ECONOMICS AND POLITICAL ECONOMY

In this section, the scope of economic analysis as seen by neo-classical economics and by radical political economy is considered in turn. One conclusion of this discussion is that there is not any agreement between neo-classical economics and radical political economy as to the appropriate scope and subject matter of economic analysis.

A frequently used definition of the scope of economics is that given by Robbins (1932). This is that 'economics is the science which studies human behaviour as a relationship between ends and scarce means which have alternative uses'. Robbins continued by arguing that

> the conception [of economics] we have adopted may be described as *analytical*. It does not attempt to pick out certain *kinds* of behaviour, but

focuses attention on a particular *aspect* of behaviour, the form imposed by the influence of scarcity. It follows from this, therefore, that in so far as it presents this aspect, any kind of human behaviour falls within the scope of economic generalisations. We do not say that the production of potatoes is economic activity and the production of philosophy is not. We say rather that, in so far as either kind of activity involves the relinquishment of other desired alternatives, it has its economic aspects. There are no limitations on the subject-matter of economic Science save this. .... it follows that economics is entirely neutral between ends; that, in so far as the achievement of *any* end is dependent on scarce means, it is germane to the preoccupations of the economist. Economics is not concerned with ends as such.

Robbins, in effect, placed further restriction on economic analysis when he wrote that 'in the last analysis Economics does depend, if not for its existence, at least for its significance, on an ultimate valuation – the affirmation that rationality and ability to choose with knowledge is desirable'.

This view of the scope and nature of economics is one to which neo-classical economics still adheres. The organising feature of economic analysis is then the study of the use of scarce means to satisfying competing ends.

The economic problem [scarce means, insatiable ends] in this sense is universal: it transcends time and space, and political or social organization. ... From the universality of the economic problem, it also follows that if the theory of the firm proves to be a useful and recognizable portion of the theory of allocation (and distribution) in a Western or capitalist context, so it must in a communist context: there must be a Soviet analogy. (Archibald, 1971)

Further, rational behaviour on the part of individuals is largely taken for granted.[8] This means that all neo-classical economics begins from the assumption of rational behaviour, with little attempt to justify such a starting point on the basis of empirical evidence.

The analysis of the use of scarce resources is undertaken within the framework of exchange in that the way by which the allocation of resources is improved is through the process of exchange. The view that individual A will exchange with individual B if and only if both are made better off, for otherwise the exchange will not take place, features strongly. Indeed, one of the distinctions which can be drawn between neo-classical economics and the radical political economy approaches is that the former is largely concerned with exchange whereas the latter is much more interested in the process of production and reproduction.[9,10] 'The essential novelty in the work of these economists [introducers of marginalism such as Jevons and Menger] was that instead of basing their economics on production and distribution, they based it on exchange' (Hicks 1976). This is illustrated by the fact that many propositions in neo-classical economics are illustrated by a model involving only exchange between two individuals without any reference to the process of production, which suggests that exchange rather than production is central. Further, even when a production function is introduced which links inputs with output, such a function can be seen as governing the terms on which inputs can be exchanged for outputs without reference to social and institutional conditions under which that exchange takes place.

In many respects, this definition of the scope of economics places considerable limitations on the scope of economics. It limits economics to the study of 'rational action', which besides the obvious exclusion of non-rational action at the level of the individual,[11] also creates difficulties for the analysis of organisations for, as discussed below (section 4.3), there are difficulties in specifying the objectives of an organisation and whether any such objectives are 'rational' (see note 11). Robbins's definition relates to the use of existing resources, whereas our interest extends to the under- or non-utilisation of resources (e.g. unemployment of labour) and to the creation of resources (e.g. investment). This view of the scope of economics builds in a presumption of full employment, for if resources are scarce then they will surely be fully utilised. It would appear to be irrational (at least at the level of society as a whole) to have unutilised resources in the face of unsatisfied needs and demands. But the presumption of full employment conflicts sharply with simple observation of the real world. This was pointedly expressed by Joan Robinson in the following way: 'It was just a coincidence that the book [of Robbins] appeared [1932] when means for any end at all had rarely been less scarce' (Robinson, 1971), with high levels of unemployment throughout the capitalist world following sharp drops in output.

This definition of economics given by Robbins also tends to focus attention on microeconomics (individual decision-making) and ignores macroeconomic aspects. Macroeconomics analysis is concerned with the overall (aggregate) use of resources (especially labour) and the ways in which macro-forces influence individual behaviour. For example, in Keynesian economics, the level of economic activity (and hence employment) is largely set by the level of aggregate demand. Low levels of aggregate demand lead to high levels of unemployment. Individuals who are unemployed are not unemployed because they have chosen to be, but rather because the macroeconomic forces dictate that a certain number of people are to be unemployed. Indeed, it could be argued on Robbins's definition of economics that macroeconomics (at least of the Keynesian variety) is *not* economics in that it does not use a means/end framework, and does not focus on the scarcity of labour and capital equipment but rather often arrives at the conclusion that there will be insufficient aggregate demand to employ the available labour and capital equipment.[12]

There is, however, one sense in which the Robbins definition of economics is rather wide. The width of the definition depends on which decisions one is prepared to take as subject to rational decision-making within the framework of the use of scarce resources to meet competing ends. The key role of utility analysis in neo-classical economics serves in effect to define the boundaries of economics as seen through neo-classical eyes. On the one hand, any decision which can be analysed in terms of utility maximisation subject to constraints can be included in (neo-classical) economic analysis. Thus subjects such as crime, marriage and religious persuasion can be placed within economic analysis provided that one is prepared to analyse them in terms of utility maximisation subject to constraints.[13] A decision on, for example, participation in crime can be viewed as use of (scarce) time with benefits (from crime) and costs (possibility of detection and punishment). The decision on whether to participate in crime can then be seen as maximising one's utility subject to the time available, where that time can be spent in lawful pursuits or in unlawful pursuits. Both lawful and unlawful pursuits convert time into income according to a particular production function, e.g. that time spent on lawful pursuit generates income according to the time worked. In this way such a decision can be analysed in the framework of utility maximisation subject to constraints. This general approach would provide a very broad definition of economics for it is then difficult to think of any decisions which are necessarily excluded. Whether it is useful to analyse such decisions in this way is, of course, a separate and vital question.

It is also apparent from Robbins's definition above that nothing can be said about the ends which people pursue, i.e. nothing can be said about people's tastes and preferences. Thus a desire to break a piece of pottery is on a par with a desire to create a piece of pottery. This can be seen as part of an attempt to turn economics into a 'neutral science', for nothing is to be said about the desirability of tastes and preferences, nor about the resulting actions.

On the other hand, neo-classical economics says nothing on the formation of an individual's utility function, or expressed alternatively says nothing on the shaping of tastes and preferences. The origin of an individual's utility function is in many respects the key question. If it is assumed that an individual in effect is born with their utility function (i.e. with their tastes and preferences already formed) then the utility function could be taken as a given, and the analysis proceed (and perhaps leave to the study of human biology the question of the determination of an individual's tastes and preferences). But casual observation of differences in tastes and preferences between societies, between classes and over time would suggest that such an assumption is unwarranted. It would also mean that any literature on bringing up children would be irrelevant since the 'tastes and preferences' of children would be determined at birth.

The alternative (and more attractive) option is to consider that there are many influences at work on an individual's tastes and preferences. Thus the family, class and society into which an individual is born are important factors influencing the individual, and her tastes, preferences, etc. But the use of utility analysis (and the assumption of given tastes and preferences) means that the study of the formation of tastes and preferences is considered outside the scope of economic analysis. The formation of preferences is seen as within the provinces of sociology and social psychology. This suggests that the boundary between economics and other social sciences is drawn in such a way that the other social sciences discuss the origins and nature of individuals' tastes and preferences (widely interpreted), whereas economics studies the implications of the pursuit of those preferences subject to various constraints.

It is not easy to draw the boundaries of radical political economy, and perhaps it is not necessary to try to draw sharp boundaries.

Radical political economy is to be seen as part of the social sciences, trying to understand and explain society, with particular emphasis on the use and creation of resources.[14] In that respect, political economy would draw on other social sciences (e.g. sociology, political theory) and this may be evident in some of the following chapters (e.g. Chapter 10). However, radical political economy specialises on the study of the use and abuse of resources, the creation and destruction of resources, the production and distribution of goods and services and the distribution of material possessions between individuals and social classes.

1.5 METHODOLOGY

The political economy approaches discussed in this book have generally been associated with rather different perspectives (than neo-classical economics) on methodology and the possibility of a 'neutral' approach to economic study.[15]

There would probably be widespread agreement that one appropriate test of a theory is the conformity of the predictions of that theory with the real world. It will be pointed out that there are difficulties in testing economic theories (which would also apply to theories in many other disciplines), for example, the difficulties of undertaking controlled experiments in economics, and there are the problems which arise when the economy undergoes change which invalidates theories which may have been previously useful.

There are, however, a number of areas of dispute. The first concerns the question of how important the test of predictions should be. The view that the validity of predictions is the only relevant test of a theory has often been labelled 'positive economics'. 'The ultimate goal of a positive science is the development of a "theory" or "hypothesis" that yields valid and meaningful (i.e. not truistic) predictions about phenomena not yet observed.' Further, 'the only relevant test of the *validity* of a hypothesis is comparison of its predictions with experience' (Friedman, 1953). This position would lead to the dismissal of a theory on the grounds that it contains no testable predictions, for if the predictions test is taken as the only valid test, then it follows that a theory without predictions cannot be evaluated.

It will be argued below that the radical political economy approach has generally seen the accuracy of predictions as only one among a number of criteria by which a theory should be evaluated. Before that discussion, there are a number of other comments to be made. The positivist approach has tended to suggest that it is relatively straightforward to carry through the testing of theories. But the experience of the past three decades, during which there has been an explosion in the use of applied econometrics, suggests that, at least as far as the econometric approach to testing is concerned, advance along these lines is not easy. Indeed, if it were straight-forward, then, as Hollis and Nell (1974) remark, 'it is hard to see why economic theory is still beset with raging disputes, and why so few general laws are widely accepted or well-confirmed'. The difficulties which arise include the conflicting results obtained from econometric studies, the lack of correspondence between available statistics and the variables of economic theory, and the use of aggregate data (e.g. on the total consumption of a particular product) to test theories of individual behaviour (in this example on consumption).

Economic theories generally make a distinction between endogenous variables (those determined within the theory) and exogenous ones (those taken as constant for the purposes of the theory). The predictions derived from a theory then take the form of a conditional prediction based on 'other things being equal', the famous *ceteris paribus* assumption. Further, most predictions relate to equilibrium outcomes. Thus the testing of a theory often requires that the exogenous variables are either held constant or due allowance is made for changes in them, and that subsidiary assumptions are made (e.g. that equilibrium is attained, that the statistical measures correspond to the economic variables). However, the theory itself indicates which variables are exogenous and the effect which the variables are expected to have. Thus to some degree the theory has to be provisionally accepted before the theory can itself be tested. The test proceeds by taking as exogenous those variables which the theory suggests to be exogenous. Some of the exogenous variables would be regarded as economic ones, but others would be non-economic ones. The difficulties which arise have been summarised as follows:

> Since this means being able to assess the influence of the exogenous on the endogenous variables, we need in effect an interdisciplinary

theory, which will be more sophisticated than the theory we are trying to test and which, moreover, will need to be already well-confirmed. In order for the interdisciplinary theory to have already been confirmed, it must already have been successfully tested. (Hollis and Nell, 1974)

This line of argument can be related to the Duhem–Quine thesis.[16] The thrust of this thesis is that in order to test a specific hypothesis, a range of supporting auxiliary hypotheses have to be accepted. As an example, consider a test of the proposition that changes in the money supply lead to changes in the price level. In order to test that proposition, assumptions have to be made concerning the available statistics (e.g. that stocks of money as measured by, say, government statistics conform to the supply of money of the theory under test), the constancy or irrelevance of factors not included in the empirical investigations, the possible time lags between a change in the money supply and the subsequent effect on prices.

Much of empirical work in economics has been concerned with the estimation of the numerical values of key parameters. For example, in the context of the consumption function, the focus is on the size of the marginal propensity to consume, rather than whether the consumption function is valid.[17] This is not universally the case, but has been the general approach. Thus it is not generally the case that one hypothesis is tested against another, or that the validity of that hypothesis is subject to scrutiny.

There has been a close association between neo-classical economics and the positivist view of science. There is no necessary connection between the two, but there are reasons as to why this association is not a chance relationship. It can first be noted that the strong advocacy of the positivist view by authors such as Friedman (1953) was often connected with a defence of perfect competition. This arose, in part, as a counter-blast to the attack on the 'unrealism' of the assumptions of perfect competition, and the advocacy of approaches such as monopolistic competition and full-cost pricing on the basis of their greater 'realism'.

The positivist view also accorded with the notion that a sharp distinction could be drawn between positive economics and normative economics, whereby economists *qua* economists would study positive aspects but have nothing to say on the normative aspects. This is reflected above in the quotation from Robbins, in which he distinguished between ends and means, where economists are meant to forgo saying anything about the desirability or otherwise of the end, being pursued.

It can be further argued that despite a nominal adherence to a positivist approach (testing theories by predictions, rejecting theories which failed that test), in practice, (neo-classical) economists have not actually adhered to that approach. For example, Katouzian (1980) argues that the Phillips curve started as a statistical generalisation from historical experience, for which a theoretical basis was found. When the coincidence of high inflation and high unemployment undermined the Phillips curve, the response was the discovery of

> a theoretical 'solution' to 'explain' even this massive 'anomaly' ... It was soon discovered that the Phillips curve has been shifting 'out-wards'. But the 'solution' is inherently untestable for it depends on a knowledge of the *expected* rate of inflation and the circular concept of the 'natural rate of unemployment'.

McCloskey (1986) has argued that 'economists have two attitudes towards discourse, the official and the unofficial, the explicit and the implicit', and further that economists do not adhere in practice to the positivist methodology ('modernism'). Indeed, one of his sections is headed 'modernism itself is impossible and not adhered to'. In effect McCloskey argues that there are many ways (e.g. argument by analogy) by which economists seek to persuade their fellows of the validity of a particular theory or approach. McCloskey points out that the Keynesian view of macroeconomics was widely accepted many years before any empirical evidence was advanced to support it. As a further example McCloskey (pp. 58 ff.) puts forward eleven reasons why economists find the law of demand persuasive, of which only the first three reasons relate to statistical tests (and those are recognised as not always supporting the law of demand).[18]

This would indicate that the *practice* of economists of whatever school of thought) is rather different from the 'positivist ideal'. It could be further argued that this practice is not all that different from that which would be advocated by radical political economists. Theories and economic models have many purposes other than prediction. These purposes would include seeking to understand and explain why economies behave in the way they do, and the gaining of insights into economic behaviour. A theory may be used to highlight a particular tendency, even when there are many other forces at work.[19]

The positivist methodology as expressed by Friedman and others has argued that the realism or otherwise of assumptions is irrelevant.[20] For example,

> truly important and significant hypotheses will be found to have 'assumptions' that are wildly inaccurate descriptive representations of reality, and, in general, the more significant the theory, the more unrealistic the assumption (in this sense). ... To be important, therefore, a hypothesis must be descriptively false in its assumptions; it takes account of, and accounts for, none of the many other attendant circumstances, since its very success shows them to be irrelevant for the phenomena to be explained. (Friedman, 1953)

It can be argued (cf. Tobin, 1980) that assumptions should not be deliberately unrealistic but reflect our current understanding of the world. Indeed, if information on the operation of the real world is available then it is wasteful to discard such informtion. Instead, the attempt could be made to incorporate the available information into theorising by means of careful selection of assumptions. It may be, of course, that it turns out that our information (and thereby our assumptions) about the world were incorrect. It is rather strange that a discipline such as economics which stresses the efficient use of resources (including information) should not seek to make the best use possible of the available information.[21]

There is no disagreement that theories have to make assumptions which are to some degree unrealistic. However, there would be disagreement over how assumptions should be derived and in what sense assumptions can be unrealistic. The radical political economy approach has largely been to derive assumptions of a theory by observation of reality. It is realised that there will be legitimate debate over what assumptions to make, and different people will derive different observations and assumptions from the same reality. Further, many (often unstated) assumptions are made to the effect that a whole range of phenomena are irrelevant for the task at hand. For example, in theories of the determinants of investment expenditure, assumptions are made about the objectives of the relevant decision-makers (and indeed there are assumptions made on who the relevant decision-makers are). But there are many factors which are implicitly ignored, such as the colour of eyes of the decision-makers, the day of the week, etc. However, there is a substantial difference between assuming that certain factors are unimportant for the matter at hand and therefore ignoring those factors, and knowingly making unrealistic assumptions about factors which are important.

1.6 ECONOMIC ANALYSIS AND IDEOLOGY

The radical political economy approach would generally deny the possibility of developing a neutral objective economics analysis:

> This [neoclassical economics] swept the bourgeois intellectual world after 1870, loudly claiming that it was 'scientific', 'objective' and furthermore, separate from any political persuasion. In particular, most neoclassical economists were keen to disassociate their 'science' from the socialist and radical ideology which had tainted the preceding classical school, and especially, Marxism. The neo-classical economists argued that the same standards of scientific validation which were found in the physical sciences must be applied to economics. Above all, they thought, this meant that economics must free itself from historical particularities and develop principles and categories of a universal character. An attempt was made to develop a systematic analysis which would be applicable to all economic systems, all forms of human society, and all history. They abstracted, therefore, from history itself. (Hodgson, 1982c)

Despite the protestations of the practitioners of neo-classical economics, economic analyses of all schools of thought have broader significance than the development of and then the testing of positive statements about the world. Economic analysis focuses on certain problems, with the implication that those problems (areas of concern) are more important than others. It has been argued above that neo-classical economics has focused on the efficient use of existing resources. In contrast, the political economy approach stresses the creation and utilisation of resources, the generation and use of surplus, etc. Insofar as economic analysis has an influence on policymakers, the agenda which is set by the two approaches will be quite different, with one approach highlighting the use of existing resources and the other focusing on the creation of new resources.

The language in which economic analysis is expressed is not neutral. In the case of neo-classical economics, phrases such as *perfect* competition, *natural* rate of unemployment have obvious connotations. For radical political economy, phrases such as exploitation, surplus, carry certain overtones. It can be argued that such terms can be given precise meanings in economic analysis but even so the terms themselves are far from neutral. In conversation with students and with a lay audience the use of such terms will usually carry obvious implications. The 'natural' rate of unemployment may be given a precise meaning but it does imply that such a rate is natural and unalterable.

Economic analysis also helps in the conditioning of thought. The combination of scarcity and rationality create a presumption for full employment. The research agenda is then to find explanations for deviations from full employment, which have often involved invoking (at some level) lack of rationality or lack of information. The radical political economy approach (see section 11.1) generally holds to the presumption that there will often be unemployment, and part of the research agenda would then be to explain why there is sometimes full employment.

It is further argued that neo-classical economics operates as an apologetics for capitalism and serves to provide a justification for that system. This can take a number of forms. The first is the tendency to take an ahistorical perspective. This involves ignoring any study of pre- or post-capitalist economies, and for taking a single (perfect competition) view of capitalism. In other words, no attention is paid to stages of capitalism. The second is highlighted in debates over profits (cf. Chapter 9) in which the neo-classical theory suggests that profits arise as a reward for waiting whereas the radical political economy tradition often views profits as arising as a surplus and expropriated by the powerful. The neo-classical view suggests a justification for profits (as a reward for waiting), whilst the radical political economy view may hint that profits are an unjustified deduction from wages. Rowthorn (1974) argued in a similar vein that neo-classical economics

> achieves its ideological impact in two distinct ways: through the picture of the world given by its apparently neutral variants, and through the openly apologetic use made of certain of its findings. The apparently neutral variants analyse the capitalist system as if it were an inherently stable and smoothly self-regulating mechanism.

Features of the real world, such as unemployment, can then be ascribed to 'frictions' such as imperfect competition, lack of information, etc. A further example arises from the analysis of the labour market. Inequality in the labour market can either be seen as (partially) related to the presence of non-competitive elements (e.g. government intervention, trade unions) as in the neo-classical approach, or inequality can be seen as endemic to the market system as in the political economy approach.

The apologetic use arises from, for example, the identification of the conclusions of a particular economic analysis with the real world. For example, the utility analysis of savings behaviour concludes that the optimum equilibrium outcome requires that the subjective rate of time preference of an individual is equated with the (market) rate of interest. The identification is then made between the conclusion of that particular analysis and the real world whereby interest payments are viewed as a reward for postponing consumption.

1.7 AN OVERVIEW OF THE BOOK

The purpose of this book is to provide a broad introduction to radical political economy. In doing so, work which would be placed under headings such as post-Keynesian, Marxian, radical, Sraffian and institutionalist, and some which would refuse to be categorised under such headings are drawn upon. Within that range of material, the emphasis is on the positive contribution which can be made to the understanding of the operation of industrialised capitalist economies. But the vigour of radical political economy is also reflected in debates and disputes. These debates are reflected in our discussions below. Whilst the elements which unite political economists are stressed, the disagreements are not overlooked.

There is no obvious sequence in which the topics covered below should be arranged, and as such there is no linear progression through the book leading up to a crescendo. This has meant that there has to an degree of both backward and forward cross-referencing. The book is divided into six parts, of which this chapter forms Part One.

Part Two is concerned with the study of the labour process and labour markets. Starting with labour is some indication of the importance which radical political economy attaches to human labour. The labour process deals with the production process, and particularly with questions such as who exercises control, what factors determine the intensity of work and productivity. The chapter on the labour process (Chapter 2) will illustrate the relevance of power (usually that of capital over labour in the productive process), the stress on production (rather than consumption and exchange) and the notion that labour as a factor of production has to be treated quite differently from other, material, inputs. Chapter 3 discusses the labour market, which is seen as an arena in which there is perpetual excess supply of labour. As a consequence of that and other reasons, the labour market does not involve exchange between equals, but rather the hirers of labour (capitalists) have the upper hand. Discrimination is discussed in this context, with emphases on whose interests are served by discrimination (e.g. racial, sexual), and the question of whether market mechanisms tend to eliminate or to re-inforce discrimination.

Part Three covers the operation of firms and the related question of the nature of competition between firms. In Chapter 4, we review the different ways in which firms have been conceptualised as a backdrop to the subsequent discussion on firm behaviour. Chapter 5 is concerned with the nature of competition between firms. Competition is viewed in terms of rivalry between firms arising from the pursuit of profits and the resulting conflict of interests. However, competition may be mutually destructive for the firms involved, and the firms will seek to reduce rivalry in order to safeguard profits. Thus, collusion and co-operation between firms may result. One particular question which we address is whether the extent and nature of competition between firms has changed over the past century or so. The main theme of Chapter 6 stems from the observation that large firms have come to dominate the modern economy, with most large firms being corporations (which means that they have a large number of owners). The corporate form is often seen as permitting the growth of large firms and thereby encouraging the concentration of industry. Further, the corporate form allows a division between ownership and management, with the possibility that the managers become the effective controllers able to pursue their own interests.

Part Four also consists of three chapters, and deals with the related themes of value, the nature and source of profits, the relationship between wages prices and profits (in a Sraffian setting) and theories of income distribution. In Chapter 7, the discussion focuses on theories of value. The utility approach to value is contrasted with the classical approaches which have often been labelled labour theories of value. The nature and relevance of such theories are discussed. Chapter 8 provides an introduction to Sraffian economics, which is viewed as dealing with questions such as the relationship between wages, prices and profits under conditions of long-run equilibrium. The Sraffian approach is seen as taking a specific view of the productive system. But some of its importance is largely seen in terms of the light it throws on matters such as the measurability of capital, the labour theory of value, etc. Chapter 9 is mainly concerned with theories of the distribution of income between labour income and property income. These theories not only express views on the determinants of the size of profits but also on the nature of profits (i.e. why do profits exist?). This chapter is completed by an examination of the implications of the theories of income distribution for movements in the rate of profit over time.

Part Five has only one chapter which is entitled 'The political economy of the State'. This chapter begins by indicating the scale of State activity (and its rise during this century), and the necessity to have views on the nature of the State. Different views on how the economy works lead to different notions on the role and purpose of the State. The main purpose of this chapter is to explore those different views and notions.

Part Six can be seen as the macroeconomic chapters of the book. Chapter 11 is firstly concerned with explanations of unemployment and excess capacity. Unemployment of labour is seen to arise for two basic reasons. The first is a lack of sufficient aggregate demand in the economy, and the second arises from the view that unemployment serves to discipline workers and to hold real wages in check. The final part of the chapter discusses the conflict theory of inflation (whereby inflation is seen to arise from a basic conflict over income shares), although it is necessary to consider the nature of money and the creation of money as part of the explanation of inflation. Chapter 12 begins by a discussion of the nature of capital equipment and the determinants of investment expenditure. The volume of profits is seen as both determined by and determining the level of investment. Similarly, the rate of technical change is seen to influence the rate of investment, and investment is necessary for the implementation of technical change. This leads into discussion of the idea that there are long waves in economic activity, generated by waves in technical advance. The chapter finishes with the post-Keynesian view on technical change and growth. Chapter 13 is concerned with the notion of cumulative causation and the explanation of persistent disparities between regions and countries. The idea of cumulative causation is that there are economic forces under which the successful continue to prosper and pull ahead of the unsuccessful. This general view has important implications for the economic and political relationships between regions and also between developed industrialised and Third World countries.

NOTES

1. I have adopted a suggestion of Philip Arestis on the definition of radical political economy.
2. For introduction to and books of key articles from these schools of thought see Bowles and Edwards (1989) (two volumes on radical political economy), King (1989) (three volumes on Marxian economics), Samuels (1989) (three volumes on institutional economics), Sawyer (1989) (one volume on post-Keynesian economics) and Steedman (1989) (two volumes on Sraffian economics).
3. The editorial introduction to Sawyer (1989) provides a more extensive discussion of the post-Keynesian approach. The references in that introduction and the selection of readings contained in the book provide extensive further readings.
4. This distinction has become semi-conventional but is not adhered to by all economists. Some would deny the significance of what is defined in the text as uncertainty and treat uncertainty and risk as synonymous.
5. On the Austrian approach see, for example, Shand (1984) for an introduction and Littlechild (1989) for volumes of readings.
6. The use of equilibrium analysis obviously involves the search for equilibrium solutions, which in the context of growth is a search for balanced growth paths. But growth may often be 'unbalanced'; sectors may grow rapidly in a way which cannot be sustained in the long term along a balanced growth path, but such bursts of growth form an important part of growth. For example, the production of home

computers has grown very rapidly in recent years, and would be expected to slow down. Initially slow growth, followed by a burst of growth, then a slower pace of growth and perhaps eventual decline is a familiar pattern for individual products. But this would not be a pattern which could be captured by looking for balanced growth path; for further discussion see Himmelweit (1979).

7. For a book of readings on 'Power in economics', see Rothschild (1971).

8. An editor of the prestigious *American Economic Review* discussed on his retirement as editor his attitudes to different schools of thought in economics. He wrote that 'in evaluating papers, I don't consider them as falling into methodological schools, for example, neo classical or radical; monetarist or Keynesian. I do have a bias in favor of papers that contain some rational explanation of the phenomena being analysed; rational meaning consistent with a set of assumptions about intelligent behavior' (Borts, 1981).

9. Baranzini and Scazzieri (1986b) identify two research 'lines' – exchange and production, where the exchange line would correspond to neo-classical economics and the production line would encompass some of the approaches discussed in this book. They argue that 'the exchange and production lines of research are competing in the sense that, starting from two mutually exclusive "ideal" models of an economic system (a pure allocation model and a pure production model, respectively), they have been gradually extended so as to cover empirical domains that are partially overlapping'.

10. Purdy (1988) discusses the two paradigms, namely those of exchange and of reproduction in the context of the analysis of the labour market.

11. 'Rationality' is often interpreted as saying that the following two properties hold:

   1. If the individual chooses A when B is also available, she will never choose B when A is available.
   2. If the individual chooses A in preference to B, and B in preference to C, then she will choose A in preference to C.

   Two difficulties arise. First, the neo-classical view on rationality extends over all possible choices. There are many possibilities which an individual never chooses, and hence the full range of this concept of rationality cannot be tested. Second, suppose that it is observed that an individual buys A one week in preference to B, but buys B the next week in preference to A. This could be taken to be an example of irrationality. But it may be explicable in terms of taste changes, a desire for variety, or a change in circumstances (e.g. some A is left from the previous week).

12. This may indicate that much of conventional macroeconomics does not fall within this definition of the scope of economics. Indeed there is much discussion over the microeconomic foundations of macroeconomics and the idea that much of Keynesian economics does not have a 'choice-theoretic' foundation. See, for example, Weintraub (1979a), and for counter-argument Skott (1983).

13. For the application of utility analysis to areas which are often seen as outside economic analysis see, for example, Becker (1973), Becker, Landes and Michael (1977) on decisions on marriage, and Becker (1966), Becker and Landes (1974), Ehrlich (1973) on participation in crime decisions.

14. It could be argued that neo-classical economics is not a *social* science – in that it does not deal with the social aspects of production and exchange. Neo-classical economics is individual (rather than class) based, with the only relationships between individuals being those expressed at 'arms-length' through the market.

15. Cole *et al.* (1983) identify three broad approaches to economics which they label subjective preference theory (broadly what we label neo-classical economics), cost-of-production theory of value, and abstract labour theory of value. It is the latter two approaches with which this book is concerned. Cole *et al.* argue that each approach has developed its own methodology, which makes for obvious difficulties in the evaluation of one approach by another. Pheby (1988) provides further discussion on this point.

16. This thesis is derived from the work of the French physicist Duhem (1906) and the American philosopher Quine (1951). For discussion in the context of macroeconomics see Cross (1982), and for an introduction Pheby (1988).

17. See Green (1984) for an extensive discussion on the consumption function, and the argument that estimation of the consumption function has not in practice been concerned with seeking to reject received doctrines.

18. For an attempt to explain the popularity of the Phillips' curve along these lines see Sawyer (1987).

19. The Harrod–Domar growth model is generally seen as having a 'knife-edge' property, in that any deviation of actual growth from the 'warranted' growth path would result in an upwards or downward spiral. Casual observation of the real world would indicate that continuous upward or downward spirals are not observed, and therefore the model fails the predictions test. Nevertheless, this model has continued to be taught for forty years. The reason for this could be that it highlights one aspect of the growth process which economists have perceived to be important, even if there are other aspects.

20. It is (probably) not a necessary part of neo-classical economics to adopt the positivist methodology and the distinction between positive and normative. But the position described in the text is that generally adopted by neo-classical economics and features widely in orthodox economics textbooks.
21. For the view that neo-classical economics fails tests of empirical validation on a broad front see Eichner (1983a), Canterbery and Burkhardt (1983).

Part Two

LABOUR

Chapter 2
THE LABOUR PROCESS

2.1 TECHNICAL AND SOCIAL ASPECTS OF PRODUCTION

An important feature of radical political economy is the attention paid to the conditions under which goods and services are produced. In contrast, neo-classical economics focuses on consumption and exchange of goods and services. Another important feature is the recognition that economic analysis must pay attention to the power relationships between people, and within a firm the power relationships include those between the representatives of capital and labour, and between the controllers and the controlled. Those two important features are strongly reflected in the analysis of the labour process which is the subject matter of this chapter.

The neo-classical analysis of production (if it is worthy of that name) is essentially the analysis of production functions. A production function (say of the form $Y = F(L, K, M)$ where Y is volume of output, L is labour services employed, K is a measure of capital equipment and M is material inputs) indicates the maximum output which can be obtained for each combination of inputs under the prevailing technology. It is then assumed that firms operate with full technical efficiency, so that the maximum output is actually achieved.

The production function builds in four features which are particularly relevant for our discussion. First, the assumption of technical efficiency means that the difficulties of achieving technical efficiency are given no attention; the concern of neo-classical economics is with the achievement of allocative efficiency. Leibenstein (1966) drew attention to variations in the degree of technical efficiency between firms and between countries. Relaxing the assumption of technical efficiency obviously allows the

exploration of the question of why the degree of technical
inefficiency varies (and this is further discussed below).

Second, the production function can be seen as setting the
conditions of exchange between inputs and outputs. In effect, the
production process is then to be viewed as an exchange with nature;
nature (technology) will provide a specific amount of output in
exchange for inputs. This view of the production function reinforces
the point of the concern of neo-classical economics with exchange
rather than production.

Third, a firm is virtually synonymous with its production
function with the firm treated rather like a 'black box' into which
inputs are poured and from which outputs flow (with the
relationship between inputs and outputs set by the production
function). This point will be further elaborated in Chapter 4. For
our purposes here, we note that the term 'black box' is designed to
convey the notion that what happens within the firm during the
process of production is of no consequence. In contrast, this chapter
(in terms of the labour process) and Chapters 4 and 6 (in terms of
effective decision-making) can be viewed as examining what does
happen inside the 'black box'.

Fourth, the production function approach focuses on the
technological limits on production. The conversion of inputs into
output is governed by the technologically determined production
function. If the inputs involved were all inanimate, then it would
usually be possible to formulate with considerable accuracy the
relationship between inputs and outputs. For example, if two
chemicals are added together in specified proportions under
specified conditions, then the final outcome can be accurately forecast. But the process of production involves human beings. The
output from, say, ten hours work can vary enormously depending
on, *inter alia*, the skill of the workers, their morale and commitment,
the degree of control over them, etc. Further, there is always a
social dimension of production. Social relationships between people
at work involve many aspects, not all of which are directly relevant
for our discussion here. The aspect of social relationships which is of
most concern is the power relationships involved, between those
who manage and those who are managed, between the
representatives of capital and the workers, and between different
groups of workers. This is elaborated at some length below,
particularly in the situation, which is the typical one in capitalist

economies, where the work situation involves a hierarchy of control. Further, in a capitalist firm, it is capital which hires labour and places labour in a subordinate position relative to capital, at least during the time for which the labour is hired. Thus in capitalist firms, the power relationship is that capital has some degree of control over labour. How much control and what factors determine the degree of control are discussed below.

The social conditions, and not merely the technical conditions, under which production takes place are important for the level of production achieved and for the well-being of the workers involved. The technical conditions governing, say, the preparation of food may be the same whether that preparation is performed within the home or within a catering establishment. But the social conditions under which the preparation is undertaken are quite different. The organisation of the work and the control of the production process within the home are likely to be quite different as compared with the catering establishment with profit objectives.

Prior to the Industrial Revolution, production was generally undertaken on a small scale, with most people producing the bulk of their own consumption goods and services. There was a limited amount of exchange, and production for most people would be close to subsistence level. There were some relatively large organisations, such as the Catholic Church, some armies and some trading companies, but for the most part there was small-scale production. The Industrial Revolution was associated with a growth in the scale of production (e.g. with the emergence of factory production), the development of capitalist firms in which the owners of capital hired labour and the evolution of markets. The first two developments are featured in this chapter, and the consequence of the evolution of markets for workers is examined in Chapter 3. The problems (so far as the controllers of the firm are concerned) of control over their workforce and ensuring low levels of technical inefficiency may arise in any form of large-scale production. If that is the case, then the problems confronting controllers may be similar whether the firm is a capitalist one (i.e. with private owners), nationalised or whatever. The idea that in industrialised economies managers have effective power and confront similar problems is briefly discussed below (section 6.3) and it carries with it the view that there will be a convergence between capitalist and communist economies as they confront these similar problems. However, our discussion is restricted (for resons of space) to consideration of capitalist firms, and the reader is left to ponder how much of the analysis would carry over to other types of economies.

It will generally be assumed here that work involves effort and is not undertaken for its own sake. Thus, it is taken that workers will, *ceteris paribus*, wish to limit their effort and work intensity. There will, of course, be many factors, of which fear of the sack is one, which can be used to increase work effort. Some occupations (performing artists, sports stars come to mind) involve payment for an activity which others undertake for pleasure. Some people are described as workaholics and others gain pleasure from their work and from the intensity of work. Whilst these people and occupations are of some importance, nevertheless they are likely to form a small minority. Although people may enjoy their work, it may still be the case that working longer hours or more intensively is unwelcome for the worker. The typical case is taken to be where work and effort are unpleasant.

A capitalist firm is predominantly interested in profits. The pursuit of profits leads a firm to strive for higher productivity and lower wages. Once a person is employed, profits for the firm will be higher, the more productive the person is. But, *ceteris paribus*, which here includes the amount of capital equipment and skills of the managers, higher productivity involves a higher intensity of work. This view of a conflict of interest between workers and owners of the firm – the former harmed by a higher intensity of work, the latter benefiting – is at the centre of Marx's analysis of the labour process discussed below.

In this chapter, the central concern is with the labour process, that is what happens inside the workplace. In the next chapter, the central concern will be the operations of the market for labour, though it is not possible to firmly separate the two elements, for events in the labour market condition the labour process and vice versa. In this chapter the discussion begins with the general difficulties of achieving technical efficiency before a more detailed consideration of Leibenstein's approach entitled X-inefficiency. This is followed by the Marxian notion of the labour process and the conflict between capital and labour as being a central feature of the labour process. In turn, this leads to a consideration of the factors which enhance or detract from the ability of capital to maintain a high intensity of work. One of the factors is seen to be the degree of skill and discretion which the workers, individually and collectively, exercise. This leads to the next section which is a discussion of the de-skilling thesis (particularly associated with the work of Braverman, 1974), that there will be a tendency to reduce the exercise of skill as capitalists try to increase their control over the labour process. Some criticisms of the work of Braverman are then considered. The final section considers questions related to the relationship between productivity and worker involvement in decision-making.

2.2 VARIABLE PRODUCTIVITY

It has often been observed that there can be substantial differences in the productivity of labour (e.g. output per hour worked) between regions and between countries, even when similar production techniques and capital equipment are being used.[1] We can observe from our own behaviour and that of other people that the intensity and efficiency with which we work can vary considerably depending on how we feel, our morale, the incentives and punishments involved, etc. There are numerous reasons why there can be differences in measured productivity (e.g. output per person-hour) between factories/plants using essentially the same capital equipment and material inputs (or differences in productivity which remain even when due allowance has been made for differences in equipment and material inputs). But it is useful for our purposes to identify four groups of reasons.

The first group could be labelled morale factors. Leibenstein (1976) starts by quoting from Tolstoy's *War and Peace* that

> Military science assumes the strength of an army to be identical with its numbers. Military science says that the more troops the greater the strength. *Les gros battaillons ont toujours raison* [large battalions are always victorious]. ... In military affairs the strength of an army is the product of its mass and some unknown X. ... That unknown quantity is the spirit of the army. ... The spirit of an army is the factor which multiplied by the mass gives the resulting force. To define and express the significance of this unknown factor – the spirit of an army – is a problem for science.
> This problem is only soluble if we cease arbitrarily to substitute for

the unknown X itself the conditions under which that force becomes apparent – such as the commands of the general, the equipment employed, and so on – mistaking these for the real significance of the factor, and if we recognize this unknown quantity in its entirety as being the greater or lesser desire to fight and to face danger.

There are a range of terms which could be used here – spirit (to use Tolstoy's term) of the workforce, commitment to organisation and its aims (corresponding to Tolstoy's desire to fight and to face danger) and general worker morale. The morale (and the resulting effort, etc.) may be a reflection of many other factors rather than an independent factor. The need to raise the morale of the workforce is often cited by trade unions as a reason for employers to grant a pay increase, with the implication that higher wages would be offset by higher productivity. The way the workforce is treated by management may also influence morale and this line is much further explored in the last section of this chapter.

The second group of reasons could be termed the degree of control exercised over workers. The employers can vary the number of people employed to monitor and control the activities of others (which is discussed by Leibenstein as indicated below). Although employers are always in a position of some control over workers, the degree of that control may vary. For example, the effective control which a firm has over workers is likely to be larger when there is substantial unemployment (thereby weakening a worker's position and alternative employment prospects) than when there is full employment. The Marxian analysis of the labour process can be viewed as looking at factors which will influence the degree of control and the means by which employers can increase their degree of control. For a higher degree of control is seen to lead to higher productivity and thereby higher profits.

The third group could be labelled the skill factor. Usually, it would be assumed that a more highly skilled workforce would be more productive than a less skilled one. It would clearly be relevant to any comparison of the measured productivity between similar plants to take account of differences in the skill of the labour force (and the extent to which their skills are utilised). It can, however, be argued that control by management over a workforce will be enhanced by reducing the skill level. Highly skilled workers often have to exercise a degree of discretion in exactly what they do, and possess knowledge and information which the management does not have. These features would mean that management will often find it more difficult to exercise control over highly skilled workers as compared with low-skill workers, and this provides an incentive for management to favour the use of techniques of production using low-skill labour rather than those using high-skill labour. Further, machinery can be used as method of control over the workforce. For example, the use of production-line techniques subordinates the pace of work to the pace of the machine, leaving workers having to work at the pace of the production line. These points are elaborated below.

The fourth group can be labelled management. The process of production clearly has to be organised; decisions on what to produce, what materials to use, which workers will work where etc., have to be made. Management can be more or less effective, can be more or less hierarchical and dictatorial. These are all factors which may affect labour productivity and also which involve the social nature of production. The efficiency of the managers, the information which they have available, etc., will be factors influencing productivity.

2.3 X-INEFFICIENCY

The concept of X-inefficiency was introduced into the economics literature by Leibenstein (1966), and corresponds to the idea that firms typically operate with some degree of technical inefficiency. Whilst this could be considered a new concept within the context of neo-classical economics, it would be familiar as a concept (though not as a name) to many others. There are extensive literatures on ways by which management can increase worker productivity, of which Taylorism ('scientific management') was one of the early examples and is further discussed below. Different methods of determining pay (e.g. payment by results) have been advocated as leading to higher levels of productivity. At times the precise control of a worker's activities has been advocated whilst at others forms of 'job enhancement' have been advanced as the route to higher productivity. Clearly, such a literature only has a purpose if the achievement of technical efficiency is problematic. It will also seem that it is inherent in the Marxian analysis that labour productivity is not technically determined, but rather depends on the degree of control which the employers can exercise over the workers.

Leibenstein suggested four major reasons why enterprises usually operate with some degree of X- or technical inefficiency. First, the contract for labour does not and cannot completely specify the tasks for which labour is hired. A complete specification of the job to be undertaken by a particular individual worker which took into account every possible eventuality would be very long and time-consuming and costly to draw up. It is likely that there would still be eventualities which were not anticipated at the time the contract was drawn up. Further, the firm may find it useful to maintain some element of flexibility in the way labour is used, which would be ruled out by a fully specified contract. A fully specified contract would have to include not only which range of tasks the employee is to undertake and the hours of work, but also the degree of effort and dedication required. It is easy to envisage how difficult it would be to draw up such a contract for many jobs and also to monitor employees as to whether they were fulfilling it.

Second, not all factors of production are available for purchase in a market, so some of the factors required for technical efficiency may not be available to the enterprise. For example, technical efficiency may require management of at least a particular quality. There may be a shortage of such management and also severe difficulties in assessing the qualities of managers prior to hiring them. Thus a firm may be unable to hire the managers they want because of a shortage of such managers or because they make mistakes when hiring managers through being unable to fully assess them.

Third, the production function (which serves to define technical efficiency) is not something about which firms are completely knowledgeable. Instead, the production function is something which firms discover through experience and trial and error. Thus a firm's previous experience and its willingness to experiment will be factors contributing to its knowledge of the production function which it faces. If a firm does not know its production function, it may have difficulty in reaching it, i.e. in achieving technical efficiency. Even if the firm is on its production function it may not realise it and continue to experiment. This point is heightened by technical change which will be the cause of changes in the production function.

Fourth, there is interdependence between firms, and uncertainty over possible reactions of rivals. This can lead, in Leibenstein's view, to tacit co-operation and imitation between firms, which again may prevent an enterprise reaching the production frontier.

These considerations (and some others) strongly suggest that the achievement of technical efficiency is not straightforward. Further, there may be many factors which influence the extent to which technical efficiency is achieved. Much of the subsequent discussion in this chapter can be seen as addressing the question of what are the important factors determining technical efficiency, though there are other questions to which it is addressed as well.

The controllers of a firm can vary the resources devoted to the monitoring of employees by, for example, varying the number of supervisors employed (and using supervisors to monitor the supervisors). This monitoring can include the attention given to gathering information on prospective employees before they are hired, to monitoring time worked and the effort of employees. But all these forms of monitoring are costly whether in terms of time, money or encroachment on the liberty of employees. There are likely to be forms of monitoring which are counter-productive when workers resent the interference in their work practices and when workers seek ways of 'playing the system'.

The controllers of a firm may opt instead for the use of incentive schemes, promotion prospects, appeal to loyalty to the company, etc., to boost effort and labour productivity. The alternative route is the detailed monitoring of workers' efforts. This monitoring can be enhanced by the use of machinery to pace the work effort. This route is particularly relevant for the discussion of the work of Braverman discussed below.

In principle, the resources devoted to monitoring and control could be determined in exactly the same way as decisions on the use of other resources are made. Hence, if the firm is a static profit maximiser, resources devoted to monitoring would be employed up to the point where marginal cost of those resources is equal to the marginal gain from their use. However, the meaning and desirability of technical efficiency now becomes blurred. Suppose C is the control input and the production function reads $Y = Y(L, C)$ (where for simplicity we assume that inputs other than labour L and control C are held constant). Technical efficiency could be described as $Y = Y^*(L)$ i.e. without control labour is working at full effort, with the level of other inputs held constant. But with no control production would be 12Y($L,0$). The firm may find the 'optimum' C from its point of view is C^* and then output is Y(L,C^*). By construction, this outcome is the one preferred by the firm (for example, L and C could be chosen to maximise profits). However, this outcome still involves technical inefficiency, though the standard of technical efficiency is rather blurred. The following elements of technical inefficiency could be isolated:

1. Workers are subject to a degree of control but still do not work to the fullest possible intensity. In Leibenstein's approach, this will still involve X-inefficiency.
2. There is an expenditure of resources on control which involves inefficiency as compared with a situation where the workers worked at the current intensity without external controls. Since work involves effort and the gains of higher work intensity immediately accrue to capitalists, there is no rationale under the capitalist arrangements for workers to volunteer for higher work intensity unless there is some pay-off for them in terms of higher wages or better working conditions.
3. There may be alternative forms of the organisation of production (e.g. a workers' co-operative) in which control is not exercised in a hierarchical fashion by capital, but rather production is organised in a democratic manner by the workers themselves. These alternative forms of organisation may permit similar levels of work intensity and production than under hierarchical organisation but without the expenditure on control and monitoring which hierarchy involves.

The idea that work involves effort and discomfort also undermines the idea that technical efficiency is necessarily desirable. It is usually the case that improving efficiency appears to be unambiguously a 'good thing'. With inanimate factors of production, it would usually be agreed that their efficient use (technically and allocatively) is desirable. But, as conventionally measured, increased technical efficiency in the use of labour (i.e. higher output per unit of labour time) is not to be judged as unambiguously good. If it arises through the better organisation of work, then an improvement may be involved. But if it arises through increased intensity of labour (due say to increased fear of unemployment), then it is not obviously a socially desirable improvement. For, simply, higher output per measured unit of labour time input resulting from a greater intensity of work is beneficial for those who benefit from the higher output but is detrimental from the point of those who are now working harder.

The extent of monitoring is decided by the controllers of the firm, and these decisions may be influenced by two forces: the urgency of monitoring and the costs to the controllers. The constant monitoring and control of workers by managers involves the managers in considerable unpleasant effort. It can then be argued that managers will only become involved in such efforts when the survival of the firm is at stake. A situation where the survival of the firm is threatened would impel the firm to increase monitoring and to raise productivity. In such circumstances, the workforce may accept the increases in managerial control on the basis that not only the survival of the firm but also their own jobs are at stake. A number of authors (e.g. Williamson, 1964) have pointed to examples of firms which have made major changes in the operation of the firm (e.g. its management structure, its control mechanisms) in response to perceived threats to the existence of the firm. This has been used as general evidence for the proposition that firms are not active profit maximisers (which would here be reflected in not being cost minimisers and productivity maximisers). The threat to the very survival of the firm pushes the controllers to make extensive changes, which could have been made before but were not made. This can be taken as *a priori* evidence of a lack of profit maximisation, since profits were increased after a crisis but could have also been before the crisis.

Leibenstein and others have argued that the conditions in the market where the enterprise sells its output are highly relevant to the degree of X-inefficiency. In a situation of monopoly, for example, the firm is protected from competition and would be able to gain above-average profits. But, the monopolist could in a sense take the above-average profits in the form of lower efficiency and productivity, i.e. lower reported profits. This may not be a conscious decision on the part of the controllers of the monopolist, but rather occurs through the firm 'drifting along'. Whether or not the monopoly opts for higher productivity and higher profits or lower productivity and profits rests on the internal drive of the controllers of the monopoly rather than on any external pressures. It could be added as an aside here that the higher profits of monopoly can be dissipated in other ways, through for example managers paying themselves above the going rate. But in a strongly competitive situation there is considerable pressure on the firm to raise productivity and lower costs in order to make profits which will ensure its survival. A highly competitive situation is here identified with a situation in which it is only just possible for a firm to earn sufficient profits to survive. Thus, Leibenstein argues, competitive situations reduce the degree of X-inefficiency.

2.4 CONFLICT AND THE LABOUR PROCESS

In this section some aspects of the Marxian analysis of the labour process are introduced. Before doing so it is necessary to say something about the use of the term 'capital'. The term 'capital equipment' will be used to mean machinery, factories, etc., rather than following the usual neo-classical usage of capital to describe capital equipment as a factor of production. In that neo-classical usage, the emphasis is placed on capital as pieces of machinery, etc. But within the Marxian tradition, capital is also treated as a social relationship. A piece of capital equipment is owned by people, and others work with it. Under capitalism, the equipment is owned privately (as compared with collectively) and the owners hire the required labour, placing the owners in a position of control over labour (as will be discussed below). Below, the term capital is used as a shorthand for the owners of the means of production (and their representatives) under the specific conditions of capitalism under which there is private ownership of the means of production.

The starting point of the analysis of the labour process has already been indicated above, namely that higher labour intensity and lower wages enhance profits but workers struggle for lower labour intensity and higher wages. Thus at the workplace and in wage negotiations, there is a basic conflict of interest between the owners of capital and their representatives (employers) and labour (employees). Under the capitalist system, capital is in the driving seat for it is capital which hires labour; at the workplace it is capital (and its representatives) which gives the orders and labour which receives the orders. Whilst production has to be organised and decisions taken on who does which jobs, etc., a fundamental feature of capitalism is that it is the owners of capital and their appointed representatives who organise and make decisions. This means that not only is there a power imbalance between labour and capital but also the initiative lies with capital, leaving labour in a reactive and defensive position. For example, it is the owners and managers who can take the initiative in the introduction of new techniques of production. Labour is not in a position to propose the introduction of a new technology which may lead to an improvement in working conditions and productivity, and can only react to the proposals made by capital. Thus the pace and form of change are largely determined by capital, placing labour in a position where it may be able to slow down change but is unable to propose alternative forms of change.

The relative power of capital and labour is not some random event which could easily be reversed, but rather is an inherent part of capitalism. In that system, labour is

> free in the double sense, that as a free man he can dispose of his labour-power and his own commodity, and that on the other hand he has no other commodity for sale, is short of everything necessary for the realization of his labour-power. (Marx, 1976)

Thus workers are free in a contractual sense to choose between different employers. This freedom of exchange is a central element of a market economy and contrasts with a feudal or slave economy in which the worker was not free to choose the employer. Workers do have to have an employer in order to work to be able to live. But workers are also free of any ownership of the means of production, over which capital has a monopoly. In contrast, under the guild system workers owned the necessary tools and means of production; in a peasant subsistence economy, workers who owned land would own the means of production.

Since workers are 'free' from the ownership of the means of production, they are forced to work for capitalists in general, if not for a particular capitalist. The alternative to working in the absence of unemployment insurance is starvation through lack of income. The development of the welfare state may bring significant changes in the relationship between capital and labour (which is discussed further at a number of points below, e.g. sections 10.7, 11.5). Two aspects are worth mentioning here. First, the welfare state means that some income of the working class (e.g. unemployment benefits, provision of health care) is not directly linked with work. Thus there is some break in the link between income and work. This weakens the work ethic in so far as work is no longer viewed as necessary for survival. Second, the threat of the sack and of unemployment may be somewhat lessened. This would imply that the degree of control which capital can exercise over labour through fear of unemployment is reduced. These two features suggest that there will be strong forces limiting the scale of unemployment benefits.

The intensity with which capital can force employees to work will depend on the techniques of control which capital uses and also on the general economic environment within which the firm operates. The features of that economic environment which are relevant for the exercise of control by capital over labour several-fold. The macroeconomic environment, and specifically the level and rate of change of unemployment, will be one such factor. Individual firms can suggest that their own survival (and hence the jobs of their employees) depends on successfully competing in a hostile economic environment. Further, high levels of unemployment provide a pool of alternative labour and reinforce the threat of job loss for the individual. The 'political' climate (e.g. degree of hostility towards trade unions and workers, the willingness of government to use police and army to break strikes) and the related state of industrial relations legislation are relevant in influencing the strength of trade unions. When workers find it more difficult to organise and to take strike and other actions, then the position of workers collectively is undermined, allowing the exercise of control by capital. The degree of solidarity of workers would make control on a divide-and-rule basis more difficult. Solidarity may be reflected in the degree of unionisation and the willingness to take collective action, but can be reduced by distrust between workers. Thus the division of jobs along, say racial and sexual lines, reinforced by and reinforcing racial and sexual discrimination can be one mechanism for reducing worker solidarity. The presence of racial hostility between workers, for example, would allow capital to play one group of workers off against other groups. The nature of work performed is also relevant. Control is difficult to exercise where the pace of work by a particular individual cannot be easily monitored, and where considerable skill and knowledge of the particular task are required.

These general ideas are summarised by Bowles (1985), who provides three propositions central to the Marxian analysis of capitalist production. These are:

1. 'capitalists ... will generally select methods of production which forgo improvements in productive efficiency in favor of maintaining their power over workers'.
2. 'it will generally be in the interest of capitalists to structure pay scales and the organization of the production process to foster divisions among workers'.
3. 'involuntary unemployment is a permanent feature of capitalism central to the perpetuation of its institutional structure and growth process'.

Each of these features bears down on the labour process, and each of them can be seen as direct or indirect mechanisms through which the control exercised by capitalists is enhanced.

2.5 THE DIVISION OF LABOUR

One of the notable features of industrialised societies is that individuals in their working lives *specialise* in a narrow range of tasks. The specialisation involved may be in terms of a particular occupation, or undertaking a limited range of tasks. It can be argued that the range of tasks and skills displayed by people in their non-working time may often be much greater than during their working time. For example, at work an individual may undertake a narrow range of tasks on a production line, whilst outside of work that person uses skills of food preparation, home decoration, child care, driving, etc. The purpose of this section is to consider the significance and impact of such specialisation and of the related division of labour.

Adam Smith in the late eighteenth century pointed to the productivity gains which accrue from the division of labour:

> This great increase in the quantity of work, which in consequence of the division of labour, the same number of people are capable of performing, is owing to three different circumstances; first, to the increase of dexterity in every particular workman; secondly, to the saving of the time which is commonly lost in passing from one species

of work to another; and lastly, to the invention of a great number of machines which facilitate and abridge labour, and enable one man to do the work of many. . . . the greatest improvement in the productive power of labour, and the greater part of the skill, dexterity and judgement, with which it is anywhere directed or applied seem to have been the effects of the division of labour. (Smith, 1904)

The general neo-classical approach to specialisation and its benefits is that each person (or firm, or country) would concentrate on the activities at which they are relatively good. Each individual undertakes the activities in which they have a comparative advantage. Thus on the production side, individuals specialise, but in order to meet their consumption requirements they have to trade with others. The general conclusion reached is that economic welfare would be raised by such specialisation in production together with the exchange of the resulting higher levels of production. A further argument would be that many tasks require training and it is not viable to train everyone to be able to do everything. However, the specialisation within the factory system is rather different. First, it may involve acute specialisation. To pursue Adam Smith's example, the specialisation is not a matter of a person becoming a pin-maker rather than a hat-maker, but a specialisation of tasks such that the process of pin-making is divided into eighteen sub-tasks. In the twentieth century within many lines of production, such division of tasks has proceeded much further. Second, the decision on specialisation is not taken by individuals with that specialisation co-ordinated through the market mechanism with trade between the individuals involved, as suggested above. Instead decisions on the degree of specialisation, and which people undertake which activities, are taken by the controllers of the production process. Third, as stressed by Braverman and discussed below, there is a separation between conception and execution in the sense that the people who perform the tasks are not the same people who design the tasks and who take decisions of who does which tasks. Thus, it is not a matter of an individual deciding to become a pin-maker rather than a hat-maker, but rather of the pin manufacturer deciding how the production of pins is to be organised, and then controlling the subsequent production even though it is the workers who carry out the tasks which have been assigned to them.

The form of specialisation which takes our attention here is the specialisation within a factory and the concentration of individuals on a single (or limited range of) tasks. Thus there is specialisation by individuals on those tasks, but the individuals are capable of undertaking a much wider range of tasks. In Smith's description of the division of labour within a pin factory, the significant aspect is not the identification of eighteen operations but that 'in some manufactories, [they] are all performed by distinct hands, though in others the same man will sometimes perform two or three of them'. Braverman (1974) notes that 'not only are the operations separated from each other, but *they are assigned to different workers*. Here we have not just the analysis of the labor process but the creation of the detail workers.'

Division of labour is seen to bring gains in the measured labour productivity and as such capitalists would be keen to increase the division of labour leading to increased profits. Indeed most discussion on the division of labour focuses on these productivity gains. However, the implications of the division of labour for the social relations between employer and employees are also relevant, and two are mentioned here as of particular importance. First, the knowledge and skill requirements of the workers involved are generally reduced (as each worker is undertaking a more limited range of tasks, and is employing less discretion over when and how particular tasks are performed). This line of argument, and the related argument that such 'de-skilling' enhances management control, is further examined below.

Second, the alienation of workers is increased. Marx was one of the first to focus on this effect of the division of labour, and although there has been considerable discussion of the precise meaning of alienation in the work of Marx,[2] here we concentrate on those which are directly related to the production process. Before industrialisation, people largely provided for themselves on a largely self-sufficiency basis with limited exchange. Following industrialisation, the worker is employed by someone else to produce goods and services (or perhaps more accurately parts of goods and services) which the worker does not typically consume. The worker could be said to be alienated from the product produced. Further, and more importantly, is that

> in working, man does not fulfil himself, but degrades himself. With the development and extension of the division of labour, the worker is forced to do routine and repetitious acts which do not give him any

satisfaction in his work. ... He is mentally degraded by the repetitious and trivial activities performed in factories. (Junankar, 1982, discussing Marx on labour's alienation from work)

As Marx put it,

within the capitalist system all methods for raising the social productivity of labour are put into effect at the cost of the individual worker; that all means for the production undergo a dialectical inversion so that they become means of domination and exploitation of the producers; they distort the workers into a fragment of a man, they degrade him to the level of an appendage of a machine, they destroy the actual content of his labour by turning it into a torment; they alienate from him the intellectual potentialities of the labour process in the same proportion as science is incorporated in it as an independent power; they deform the conditions under which he works, subject him during the labour process to a despotism the more hateful for its meanness; they transform his life-time into working-time, and drag his wife and child beneath the wheels of the juggernaut of capital. (Marx, 1976)

One recurring theme which arises both in discussion of the labour process and of the nature of the firm (cf. section 4.3) is the relative roles of technology and of power in determining what happens within the labour process or within the firm. This can be illustrated here for the division of labour. One view would be that the prevailing technology is such that a particular division of labour (for example, in Smith's argument the subdivision of operations in the pin factory into eighteen component parts) maximises productivity (and minimises costs). Thus the division of labour is essentially technologically determined, and is reached as firms seek to minimise costs. Another view is that the prevailing technology permits a range of possibilities of the ways in which production can be organised, and that capitalists will choose the option which enables them to exercise the degree of control over the labour force which will maximise profits. The division and subdivision of tasks is seen to aid the exercise of control over the speed of production.

In the context of the division of labour, the question is whether in order to reap the benefits of the division of labour, specialisation of tasks is required. Smith argued that the source of increased productivity from division of labour arose from the increased dexterity of each specialised worker, the saving of time which would have otherwise been spent moving from one task to another, and the invention of labour-replacing machinery. As Marglin (1974) argues, the dexterity argument is not very persuasive when applied to tasks which require little skill and, as indicated below, the division of labour tends to reduce skill requirements. The time-saving argument may require that on any particular day an individual would concentrate on one task and move on to another task the next day, but it does not necessarily mean that the individual always undertakes the same limited task. The third argument is also suspect. If those involved with production are to develop new methods of production, then those involved with the whole process are more likely to realise the needs and potential for new methods than those involved with one narrow task.

Marglin (1974) argues that

> neither of the two decisive steps in depriving the workers of control of product and process – (1) the development of the minute division of labor that characterized the putting-out system and (2) the development of centralized organization that characterizes the factory system – took place primarily for reasons of technical superiority. Rather than providing more output for the same inputs, these innovations in work organization were introduced so that the capitalist got himself a larger share of the pie at the expense of the worker. . . . The social function of hierarchical work organization is not technical efficiency, but accumulation.

Marglin argues that the division of labour as observed by Adam Smith did not arise as a result of a search for technologically superior organisation of work, but rather from a search 'for an organization which guaranteed to the entrepreneur an essential role in the production process, as integrator of the separate efforts of his workers into a marketable product.'

At least three effects of the increased division of labour can be identified. First, the skill and craft requirements of labour are reduced. An individual who had previously undertaken a range of tasks is now limited to one task. This has the effect of reducing labour costs from the following consideration: 'In a society based upon the purchase and sale of labor power, dividing the craft cheapens its individual parts' (Braverman, 1974). In effect the argument is that any individual employed to do a range of tasks is more highly skilled and will be more highly paid; an individual employed to undertake one task can be less skilled and paid less. The replacement of individuals performing a range of tasks by individuals performing a single task each could be expected to lower the costs of labour.

Second, there is an increased control by capital over the labour process. When an individual is employed on a range of tasks and/or to use knowledge and experience then that individual has some discretion as to what exactly (s)he does.

> But if the capitalist builds upon this distinctive quality [its intelligent and purposive character] and potential of human labor power, it is also this quality, by its very indeterminacy, which places before him his greatest challenge and problem. The coin of labor has its obverse side: in purchasing labor power that can do much, he is at the same time purchasing an undefined quality and quantity. What he buys is infinite in *potential*, but in its *realization* it is limited by the subjective state of the workers, by their previous history, by the general social conditions under which they work as well as the particular conditions of the enterprise, and by the technical setting of their labor. The work actually performed will be affected by these and many other factors, including the organization of the process and the forms of supervision over it, if any. (Braverman, 1974)

In some respects, this point is similar to that made by Leibenstein which was discussed above, but he saw this leading to the question of how many resources would be devoted to monitoring and control. For Braverman it is more a question of how increased division of labour interacts with the exercise of control.

Third, 'having been forced to sell their labor power to another [i.e. capitalists], the workers also surrender their interest in the labor process, which has now been "alienated". *The labor process has become the responsibility of the capitalist*' (Braverman, 1974). This is all summed up in the following:

> The worker may break the process down, but he never voluntarily converts himself into a lifelong detail worker. This is the contribution of the capitalist, who sees no reason why, if so much is to be gained from the first step – analysis – and something more gained from the second – breakdown among workers – he should not take the second step as well as the first step. ... He can now count his gains in a double sense, not only in productivity but in management control, since that which mortally injures the worker is in this case advantageous to him. (Braverman, 1974)

2.6 BRAVERMAN AND THE DE-SKILLING ARGUMENT

The discussion in this chapter so far has indicated the conflict of interest between employees and employer, and the difficulties which the employers face when trying to secure high levels of productivity. Further, we have touched upon the division of labour, particularly that which occurs within a workplace. Braverman (1974) brought these ideas together with an emphasis on employers using 'scientific management' to overcome control problems and to extend the division of labour. In this section, we focus on the argument of Braverman that control by management is enhanced by increased division of labour and by the use of machine pacing. The work of Braverman stimulated much research, some seeking to apply his ideas to specific industries and others developing criticisms of his approach. Some of the critiques of Braverman are examined in the next section.

Much of Braverman's discussion is focused on 'Taylorism', which is a management control strategy developed in the first decade of this century by F. W. Taylor. Its central idea is that the separation between mental and manual labour, and the tasks undertaken by labour (particularly manual) can be subjected to precise measurement. Taylorism rests on the study of each element of the production process and the setting of performance norms for each task. Braverman lists three principles from the work of Taylor, who is often seen as the 'father' of scientific management. These principles are:

1. 'The first principle we may call the *dissociation of the labor process from the skills of the workers*. The labor process is to be rendered independent of craft, tradition, and the workers' knowledge. Henceforth it is to depend not at all upon the abilities of workers, but entirely upon the practices of management.'
2. 'This [second principle] should be called the principle of the *separation of conception from execution*, rather than by its more common name of the separation of mental and manual labor.'
3. 'the third [principle] is the *use of this monopoly over knowledge to control each step of the labor process and its mode of execution*'.

The implementation of these principles can perhaps be most easily seen in the context of the use of the production line in, for example, the manufacture of cars. The tasks undertaken by any individual manual worker are narrowly defined, and often have only a low skill requirement, with little training needed. The speed with which the task is undertaken is dictated by the pace of the production line, which is under the control of management. The rate at which tasks can be undertaken and the related pay scales may be determined by the measurement schemes favoured by Taylor. The planning of the tasks is undertaken by management but the tasks themselves are carried out by the workers (i.e. the second principle discussed above).

At a general level, the importance of the view advanced by Braverman (and reflected in the work of others) is that the increased division of labour and the further use of machinery reflect the response of management to the difficulties of exercising control over the workers. Often, the division of labour is discussed in technical terms, suggesting that further division of labour increases productivity. In contrast, Braverman's approach places emphasis on social factors and the need and desire for control rather than technical factors. The desire for control may be a reflection of a power-drive, but would be seen largely as part of the search for profits. The essential argument is then that the search for higher profits leading to a drive to exercise control over workers leads to an intensification of labour and to a detailed division of labour involving de-skilling.

The setting of performance norms is not without its problems for management. The norms for a task requiring physical strength can be set with reference to what can be achieved by a particular strong and fit person over a relatively short period of time. Such a norm would clearly be unattainable for most workers or over a longer period of time.

> To this phrase ['a fair day's work'] he [Taylor] gave a crude physiological interpretation: all the worker can do without injury to his health, at a pace that can be sustained throughout a working lifetime. (In practice, he tended to define this level of activity at an extreme limit, choosing a pace that only a few could maintain, and then only under strain.) (Braverman, 1974)

In general, performance norms cannot be set by theoretical calculation but by observation of what workers can actually achieve. The worker chosen for observation may be particularly adept or suited to the task for which the performance norm is being set. But once workers realise the purpose for which observation of their current performance is to be used, they can be expected to respond accordingly. Thus during observation for the setting of performance norms, it can be anticipated that workers will slow down the pace at which they work so that norms are set at relatively easily achievable levels.

The use of 'scientific management' and the increased division of labour is seen to increase managerial control in two ways. First, and most clearly, performance norms are set and monitored so that how intensively a worker (or group of workers) are working can be judged. The questions which arise here are whether the subdivision of tasks and the monitoring of workers can be widely applied; this point is returned to below. Second, a skilled worker has knowledge and discretion, which makes control by management difficult. The knowledge of the skilled worker on the tasks which (s)he undertakes may be greater than the knowledge of management. When a range of tasks are undertaken, the worker has some discretion as to when and how the tasks are undertaken. The subdivision of tasks reduces the skill required and exercised by workers but at the same time enhances the control of management. The knowledge of the worker is reduced to that of the single task undertaken rather than of a range of tasks.

The thrust of this argument of Braverman is that there is a tendency for the division of labour (in respect of tasks within a particular factory) to increase over time. The increased division of labour has the effect of cheapening labour (through the lowering of skill requirements) and raising productivity, enhancing capitalist control over the production process and leading to worker alienation. But since these changes are in the interests of capitalists, they will be pushed through even though they harm the workers in a number of ways. The reduction of tasks undertaken by a single individual reduces the skill (widely interpreted) which the worker uses, which is often summarised as de-skilling.

It may appear paradoxical at first sight to argue that there has been a reduction of the exercise of skill over say the past 100 to 150 years. For this idea stands in contrast to the more familiar one that advances in technology raises skill and educational requirements of the workforce. The reduction of skills among the workers as indicated above arises in part from the application of scientific ideas, increased mechanisation, etc. There are, of course, others who are applying and developing those ideas. Thus the educational requirements of those developing technology may rise. There are clearly substantial problems of empirically verifying these ideas – for example, exactly how would the skill requirements of the average employee in say 1850 be compared with those in 1990? It is difficult enough to define precisely and then quantify the skill content of any particular job. However, within a particular industry it may be possible to make comparisons over time in the skill requirements, and such comparisons have often revealed elements of de-skilling.

A further aspect of Braverman's approach is a concern with *differences* in skill levels as much as with the *average* level. 'The question is precisely whether the scientific and "educated" content of labor tends toward *averaging*, or, on the contrary, toward *polarization*' (Braverman, 1974). For example, the skills required by those who are responsible for developing a new machine incorporating the latest technology are likely to be high and varied. On the other hand, the skill level of those who will operate the machine when it is introduced may be rather low. In effect, Braverman argues that the skills required by the operatives may tend to decline over time, whereas the skills of the managerial elite increase, leading to a polarisation between the two.

The work of Braverman stimulated a wide range of studies on the labour process, and particularly on its historical evolution. A range of studies have found elements of de-skilling, though many of the studies have sought to refine Braverman's approach or have been critical of some parts of it. The introduction to one book of studies (Zimbalist, 1979a) which cover the labour process in a range of American industries summarises:

> the general story told by Braverman, as well as by the present essays, is one of progressive job fragmentation, degradation, and deskilling. This ongoing tendency toward job impoverishment and 'worker alienation' is confronted by another tendency – a labor force with higher education levels and higher expectations for rewarding work. The outcome of this confrontation is often high labor turnover, high absenteeism, and lackadaisical work which, in turn, imply low productivity and low quality. (Zimbalist, 1979b)

A study of the evolution of clerical work, which though broadly agreeing with Braverman's approach argues that the concept of de-skilling is in need of refinement, concludes in the following way:

> We have suggested that the value of the clerk to the employer once resided both in a detailed knowledge of clerical work procedures (the clerical 'craft') and also in the fact that, to varying degrees, clerical workers have exercised control on behalf of capital. ... The clerk now typically performs more exclusively the function of (deskilled) labour, being increasingly peripheral to the performance of the computer and having little or no responsibility for the co-ordination and completion of the many separate work tasks in the process as a whole. (Crompton and Reid 1982)

There has also been a dramatic change in the sexual composition in the clerical workforce (from the latter part of the nineteenth century to the present day), 'from a male-dominated area of employment to one dominated by female labour' (Crompton and Reid, 1982). Thus reduction in skill requirements and responsibility exercised have gone alongside a shift from male to female labour.

Kraft and Dubnoff (1986) conclude that in the computer software production process,

> conception and execution have been polarized. ... Software work has been fragmented, a remarkable development given the occupation's relative youth and the fact that intellectual skills are at the core of its labor process. In effect, the making of computer programs has been subjected to a process of intellectual industrial engineering, a scientific management of mind work. In every important respect these techniques are identical to those applied in the production of cars and cornflakes. ... A division of programming labor has been accompanied by a fragmentation of work and a hierarchy of control and rewards.

There may be many forces at work which influence the ways in which labour processes evolve, and not just the drive by capitalists for profits and control. The introduction to one symposium on the labour process (*Cambridge Journal of Economics*, vol. 3) concludes that 'our research suggests that three basic sets of relationships influence the development of the labour process: relationships between capital and labour, among capitalists, and among groups of workers' (Elbaum *et al.*, 1979). The attempts by capitalists to change work practices frequently meet with resistance from workers, which may have some success in amending the nature of change. A study of the Lancashire textile industry in the nineteenth century finds that:

the relations of production and the development of the forces of production interacted in a dialectical manner, primarily because there was a continual process of conflict, compromise and even co-operation between capitalists and workers, and the form and content of the components of technical change – mechanisation, division of labour and intensification of labour. (Lazonick, 1979)

The work of Braverman (1974) raises a range of interesting questions, of which two are raised here. The first question is the extent of the implementation of the ideas of Taylorism, and whether those ideas were relevant to a specific phase of capitalism as it grappled with a particular set of problems, or whether those ideas are generally applicable to capitalism (and more generally to industrialised societies).[3] The discussion later in this chapter and in some parts of the next indicates that Taylorism (and the concept of Fordism) may not always be the most effective (profitable) form of control and may be associated with one phase of capitalism.

The second question is the strength of the tendency towards the de-skilling of the workforce. It could be viewed as a general tendency within capitalism, which would suggest that there will be a general decline over time of the skill used by workers in their working life. This has been the general perception of the de-skilling thesis. But, de-skilling could be seen as one among a number of tendencies present. There are many examples of reorganisation of production which has the effect of reducing the skill requirements. But the general educational skills possessed by the workforce would appear to have grown over the past century (e.g. literacy and numeracy levels have risen). Many jobs which are now undertaken (e.g. scientists) clearly require the exercise of considerable skill and training. But, as seen above, there are others in which the skill content has been reduced.

2.7 CRITIQUES OF BRAVERMAN

This section has the purpose of indicating some of the criticisms which have been directed at the work of Braverman, in a manner which will form the basis for the discussion in the next section.[4]

The first critique concerns the prominence given to Taylorism and 'scientific management' in the attempt by management to secure control over labour. Many other techniques of management control have been tried, under headings such as 'job enrichment', 'human relations'. The techniques of Taylorism could be seen as appropriate in particular industries and at specific historical periods, but may not be universally applicable.[5] However, these other techniques may be viewed as alternatives to Taylorism as a means of direct control (and as such are explored below) or could be seen as the means by which management seeks to make Taylorism acceptable to the workers and lower resistance to it. 'Accordingly, other management theorists, such as Mayo and Herzberg, are for Braverman essentially ideologists, since the changes they prescribe, such as job enrichment, are cosmetic and function simply to "habituate the worker" to deskilled jobs' (Wood, 1982b).

The second line of criticism is that Braverman did not give sufficient weight to worker resistance, and portrayed management as having a free hand:

> It is argued that his thesis relies too heavily on an assumed universal and unproblematic adoption by management of Taylor's 'scientific management', and that he neglects the ways in which workers may resist managerial initiatives and managements may opt for strategies which provide workers with some autonomy. (Wood, 1982b)

The desire by managers to introduce 'scientific management' does not necessarily mean that they achieve their objectives. Indeed, Braverman's discussion of Taylorism largely relies on Taylor's own account rather than the extent to which 'scientific management' was actually instituted.

There are many factors which help to determine the extent to which managers can raise labour intensity. The adoption of a particular technique of control (in this case Taylorism) may reduce the influence of workers on the intensity of labour and the organisation of work (indeed that may be a major reason for its adoption). But the resistance of workers remains, and the effectiveness of that resistance would still remain influenced by factors such as unemployment and cohesion of the workforce, as discussed above.

The third critique is that Braverman adopts a rather romantic attachment to the craft system, and focuses on the replacement of the craftsman (rarely craftswoman) by the introduction of machinery and the related de-skilling. This highlights a comparison

between the replacement of craft-based industries in which workers
would use considerable skill and expertise with production-line
industries in which the workers are subordinated to the pace of the
machine. However, much labour had not been undertaken by
craftsmen, but rather had been low-skill drudgery. 'There is clearly
a romanticism underlying Braverman's work, for not only did such
workers not constitute the majority of workers in the nineteenth
century, but also the majority of workers until only a century ago
lacked basic skills such as literacy' (Wood, 1982b).

2.8 'HEARTS AND MINDS' AND LABOUR PRODUCTIVITY

The title of this section is taken from the article by Weisskopf,
Bowles and Gordon (1983), which is concerned with investigating
the slow-down in productivity growth in the American economy
from the mid-1960s onwards. Their central proposition is that
'declining work intensity and lagging business innovation since the
1960s . . . provide crucial missing clues to the productivity mystery'.
They further argue that

> journalists, business observers and historians frequently argue that
> two other serious problems began to afflict the U.S. economy after
> the mid-1960s. Friction began to mount at the workplace, leading to
> an erosion of worker co-operation and worker effort; and
> corporations turned increasingly toward shorter-term investment
> policies, resulting in more sluggish business attempts to improve
> productive efficiency. (Weisskopf *et al.*, 1983).

The role of business innovation in the growth process is discussed in
some detail in Chapter 12. In this section, attention focuses on the
first part of their proposition, which is considered in general terms,
rather than as an explanation of the slow-down in productivity in
the USA.

One of the central propositions which emerged from the
discussion on the labour process was that labour productivity would
depend, *inter alia*, on the intensity of work, and in turn the intensity
depends on the pressures on workers. Among other factors
influencing productivity we would expect capital intensity and

management efficiency. There are two major modifications which could be made to this basic argument.[6]

The first modification is that the pressure of unemployment depends on the existence and stringency of the social security system. The threat posed to a worker by the prospect of unemployment would be expected to be somewhat less when there is a well-developed social security system (with the provision for the unemployed being particularly significant) than otherwise.

The second modification is that unemployment is not the only control device, and the general morale of the workforce is also important. The quote from Leibenstein given above (section 2.2) suggests the importance of morale in productivity, though it is not a line which he pursues. The Taylorist principles discussed above are very much in line with the notion of managers exercising direct control over workers. But, as Hodgson (1982b) has argued, 'in recent years, management theorists, including the so-called "human relations" school, have rejected the Taylorist approach. If nothing else, Taylorism fails to deliver the goods: it does not seem to increase productivity beyond a certain point.' The morale and commitment of workers can clearly influence their productivity, which leads to consideration of the factors which can affect morale and commitment. One set of factors arises from the extent of worker involvement in the organisation of the production process.

The function of the management of a firm could be viewed largely in terms of the co-ordination of numerous activities. But in most organisations, especially capitalist firms which is our main concern here, administration and management also involve control. But administration and decision-making are two distinct functions, even though they are frequently combined.[7] But this does not mean that they must inevitably be combined. It can be observed that the vast majority of capitalist firms are organised along hierarchical lines, and the implication drawn that hierarchical forms of organisation are efficient since such forms are observed to survive. However, that argument would appear to associate profitability (or at least survival) with efficiency, but for reasons seen above that association cannot be made.[8] Further, the external environment may favour hierarchical firms over other forms. For example, the workers' co-operatives and firms involving worker participation are often more efficient than traditional capitalist firms (as discussed below). It could also be said that it is difficult for the unorthodox non-hierarchical firm to survive in a sea of hierarchy, and in particular workers' co-operatives have persistently encountered problems in raising finance. Finally, the law governing companies is not neutral in this respect.[9] The law generally empowers owners rather than workers; one clear example being that it is owners and not workers who make decisions over a take-over bid (and thereby the future direction of the company concerned). It is usual that directors of a corporation are provided with considerable power, and the important point here is that such power is concentrated on a few people, which encourages a hierarchical structure.

It is useful to distinguish conceptually between two forms of worker participation though, in practice, a specific form of worker participation may involve a mixture of the two. One form could be described as a form of management control, whereas the other form would be where workers become the effective controllers of the firm. An example of the first form would be when workers are permitted to decide how production within a workshop is to be organised but with management determining employment levels and output targets. Thus the precise form of organisation of production would be decided by the workers rather than management but within parameters determined by the management. This would be very much in line with the 'human relations' school view on management.[10] Friedman (1977) distinguishes between 'direct control' and 'relative autonomy' as means by which employers exercise control over workers. The form of worker involvement being considered in this paragraph corresponds to the 'relative autonomy' form of control.

When worker involvement is used as a form of control, there are limits to that involvement. One of the limits will be that the worker involvement should not be sufficient to challenge managerial authority. One of the experiments surveyed by Blumberg (1968, pp. 96–9) illustrates this limitation. Following a consultant's report designed to raise productivity, six young female manual workers were allowed to decide upon and vary the speed of the production line in their section of a toy factory, though against the advice of foreman and engineer. As a consequence, productivity rose substantially. But

> these semi-skilled operators, their production at record levels, began to earn more than many of the highly skilled workers in the plant, and the latter complained vociferously. ... The impertinent success of the

workers had undermined the prestige of the engineers by calling their competence into question, and had rudely challenged the whole system of managerial prerogatives. (Blumberg, 1968)

Eventually the experiment was terminated, and production fell back to its original level.

When workers have control over the objectives of the firm, this will usually involve some form of workers' co-operatives, though devices such as worker co-determination can provide workers with an input into the effective decision-making processes, etc. The control of interest would range over investment and employment decisions (and other decisions such as marketing which have implications for investment and employment) as well as the organisation of the production process.

At a theoretical level, the arguments can be reviewed as follows. At one end of the argument are those who maintain that hierarchy linked with private property are necessary for productive efficiency. Alchian and Demsetz (1972) argue that 'team production' is more productive than production by single individuals because of the advantages of specialisation, gains from division of labour, etc., But the full benefits of 'team production' are only realised when there is someone who both monitors the effort of others and receives 'residual income'. For with team production there are opportunities for any single individual to slack.

> The specialist *who receives the residual rewards* will be the monitor of the members of the team (i.e. will manage the use of cooperative inputs). The monitor earns his residual through the reduction of shirking that he brings about, not only by the prices that he agrees to pay the owners of the inputs, but also by observing and directing the actions or uses of these inputs. (Alchian and Demsetz, 1972)

Thus, they argue, there has to be someone who not only acts as a 'monitor' but also receives the 'residual' as an incentive to act as an effective 'monitor'. It soon follows from such arguments that a capitalist firm in which ownership and control are vested in the same person would be productively efficient since the owner controls ('monitors') and receives the residual income (profits). But a key element here is that a single individual owns and controls the firm. It would follow also that organisations such as workers' co-operatives or non-profit organisations would not be productively efficient, through the absence of a single individual who is the controlling residual claimant. In the case of workers' co-operatives, workers hire finance capital and collectively have the claim on residual income. Non-profit organisations clearly have objectives other than profits and are only required to break even. It would also follow that large corporations in which there are a large number of shareholders and where there may be some divorce between ownership and control would also not be productively efficient[11] (for further discussion see section 6.3 below).

At the other end of the argument are those who point to the advantages of worker involvement. This involvement may have three types of results which could be judged beneficial in productivity terms. First, the hierarchical system requires resources to be expended on control. Some employees have the role of checking on the performance of others and some types of machinery may be preferred to others when they make control and checking easier. When there is a 'self-control' system rather than a hierarchical system, resources devoted to control and monitoring are saved. Second, workers have detailed knowledge of parts of the production system with which they are directly concerned, which they may conceal from management as such knowledge helps them to reduce the intensity of work. There may also be suspicion by the workers of the use to which the management would put such knowledge. Companies do use a variety of devices (of which a suggestion box or forms of worker consultation would be examples) to try to draw on the detailed knowledge of the workers. But there are many examples where such knowledge is successfully concealed. Workers may have a knowledge of the volume of output which they could produce but keep such information from the managers, especially when such knowledge would be used to set production norms or to fix payment schedules when workers' earnings are based on output. Workers have obvious incentives to provide 'information' to managers which will reduce their effort and increase their income. Control involves the controllers and the controlled, and the controlled will often have reasons to conceal information from the controllers where that information could be used to the disadvantage of the controlled.

Third, morale and worker involvement can be enhanced by the participation of workers, which may lead to higher productivity. A number of authors have concluded that participation (of varying types) enhances productivity. For example, 'it has long been established that democratic or participatory methods of work organization lead to productivity levels above those found under authoritarian work regimes' (Drago, 1984). Again,

> there is hardly a study in the entire literature which fails to demonstrate that satisfaction in work is enhanced or that other generally acknowledged beneficial consequences accrue from a genuine increase in workers' decision-making power. Such consistency of findings, I submit, is rare in social research. (Blumberg, 1968)

One way by which workers may be able to influence decision-making in a firm is through the activities of trade unions. The distinction has been drawn between 'exit' effects and 'voice' effects which workers can have on the operation of firms.[12] The 'exit' mechanism (sometimes called the exit-and-entry mechanism) is essentially that a worker who believes that better work conditions and wages are available elsewhere leaves his or her current firm for a 'better' firm. In the conventional analysis of the markets, this exit mechanism is the key to the efficient operation of markets. Wages would be expected to be bid up in firms with poor conditions as workers leave for firms with good conditions. A firm losing workers would have to respond by raising wages or improving working conditions. The radical political economy view would be that competitive labour markets operate rather like the secondary labour markets discussed in the next chapter and would not lead to desirable outcomes. The 'voice' effect is simply that trade unions and collective bargaining provide mechanisms through which the experience and views of workers can have an influence on the organisation of work. It is plausible to argue that there will be many occasions on which workers and managers can agree on new arrangements which are in the interests of both sides. The 'exit' mechanism may signal that a worker is dissatisfied with an employer (though they may leave for other reasons), but it does not signal the nature of the dissatisfaction. Labour turnover, which the 'exit' mechanism involves, is also costly for both workers and employers, and may be reduced by use of the 'voice' mechanism. In labour markets which operate like a 'spot market' (in which workers are hired for a short period of time only and in which wages fluctuate as demand conditions vary) there is no mechanism by which the 'voice' effect can operate. In labour markets where firms hire workers for a significant period of time the relationship between employer and employee may permit the 'voice' effect to operate. In the next chapter the differences between spot markets (secondary labour markets) and those in which workers are hired for extended periods of time (primary labour markets) are extensively discussed.

The 'voice' effect of trade unions would be expected to lead to a range of improvements, though the nature and extent of such improvements would depend on the response of management. In so far as mutually acceptable changes in work organisation were achieved, then this should be reflected in higher levels of productivity. Freeman and Medoff (1984) conclude a survey of a range of American studies by saying that

> the new quantitative studies indicate that productivity is generally higher in unionized establishments than in otherwise comparable establishments that are nonunion, but that the relationship is far from immutable and has notable exceptions. Higher productivity appears to run hand in hand with good industrial relations and to be spurred by competition in the product market, while lower productivity under unionism appears to exist under the opposite circumstances.

It has to noted, though, there are many routes other than 'voice' effects through which unionisation could lead to higher productivity – for example, if unions secure higher wages for their members, the management may respond to higher wages by introducing more capital equipment or by seeking to hire better 'quality' workers. Allen (1988) surveys studies of the impact of unionisation on productivity changes in manufacturing industries. He remarks that these studies and his own work indicate 'that unions have had no impact on productivity *change* in manufacturing' (italics added), though in his own study on the construction industry over the period 1972–82, unions are associated with slower growth of productivity which may be explicable by the deterioration in labour-management relations during the 1970s.

The effect of trade unions on level and change in productivity (as well as a variety of other issues) would be expected to depend on both the legal framework and the management response. It has been argued above that within capitalist firms (and more generally), workers are placed in a subordinate role. Trade unions may be able to establish themselves, but workers and unions remain in an essentially defensive position. In other words, management have, for example, the initiative to propose new techniques of production to which unions respond. Unions may seek to extract higher wages in return for new techniques, but are in this essentially defensive position. Indeed, Manning (1987) argues that unions may have an adverse effect on jobs as a result of being placed in a defensive role. The response to that view is not to seek to reduce the power of unions, but rather to change their role to one in which unions are able to take initiatives to propose desirable change.

The discussion on worker participation has largely been concerned with the impact on measured productivity (e.g. output per person-hour). However, consideration of worker participation usually also involves issues such as job satisfaction and working conditions. In the conventional treatment, an individual's utility is adversely affected by the number of hours of work since work time detracts from leisure time. But there is no allowance for differences between jobs in terms of the amount of satisfaction or dissatisfaction involved nor in terms of work intensity. However, if job satisfaction and work intensity are important elements in the determination of worker well-being, then considerations of economic efficiency should take them into account. Similarly the safety of working conditions is of considerable importance to workers, and their involvement in decision-making is likely to mean that more regard is paid to the safety aspects.

An increase in effective worker participation will, in general, decrease the power of managers. This increase in worker participation and power may arise through an increase in trade union influence. In Britain and other countries, there have been attempts in recent years to reduce trade union power. At the political level, this has been undertaken through changes in industrial relations legislation. At the workplace, this has been exhibited in the use of phrases such as 'the right of managers to manage' and more relevantly in corresponding changes which have swung the balance of power towards the manager and away from workers.

2.9 CONCLUDING REMARKS

The major concern of this chapter has been to discuss technical and social relationships inside the workplace, and the significance of those relationships for productivity, and this discussion is complemented by consideration of the labour market (Chapter 3) and of the firm (especially Chapters 4 and 6). Out of the many issues raised in this chapter, we would stress two. The first is that the ways in which production is organised is an important ingredient in the determination of labour productivity. We have examined arguments on hierarchical versus participation forms of control, and on different management techniques which can be used. The second is that decisions made by management on capital equipment to be used and on which types of labour to employ are not merely based on narrow cost calculations. It is rather the case that concerns over control of the production system, discipline of workers, etc., will also be relevant. Thus, for example, machinery may be adopted for its ability to control the work speed of the workers.

NOTES

1. See, however, Nichols (1986) for the expression of doubts on the validity of many of these studies, especially those in which the productivity of British workers has been compared unfavourably with the productivity of other workers.

2. There is a considerable literature on the concept of alienation, which is capable of many meanings. In this book we only deal with alienation arising from the process of production. For wider discussion see Catephores (1987) (and references cited there).

3. 'We need only recall that Lenin himself repeatedly urged the study of Frederick W. Taylor's "scientific management", with an eye toward utilizing it in Soviet industry. ... In practice, Soviet industrialization imitated the capitalist model; and as industrialization advanced the structure lost its provisional character and the Soviet Union settled down to an organization of labor differing only in details from that of the capitalist countries, so that the Soviet working population bears all the stigmata of the Western working classes' (Braverman, 1974).

4. For critiques and further discussion of Braverman's approach in addition to those mentioned in the text see, for example, Cutler (1978), Elger (1979), Littler and Salaman (1982), Thompson (1983), Thompson (1984), Wood (1982a, 1985).

5. 'Marxists have generally treated the Direct Control strategy as *the* theory and practice of capitalist control over the labour process.' (Friedman, 1977). Taylorism would be a direct control strategy.

6. The first of these is particularly developed by Weisskopf (1987), whereas the second is part of the argument of Weisskopf *et al.* (1983).

7. 'Management under the capitalist mode of production has always involved two rather different, but closely related functions. ... First, there is the co-ordination of the various activities undertaken by the firm. ... Second, there is the exercise of authority over workers' (Friedman, 1977).

8. In the different but related context of the effect of trade unions (to which reference will be made below), Freeman and Medoff (1984) suggest that 'someone who favors ... a thriving market economy' should also favour a 'strong union movement', but that 'someone who wants a thriving, profitable company' should 'oppose the unionization of his or her firm'.

9. I have taken this argument from an unpublished paper by Roger Sugden.

10. 'It is true that participation has lately [*circa* 1968] become quite fashionable in management and business school thinking in the United States, having replaced the human relations approach which was considered too manipulative and thus self-defeating; and the new fad has given rise to concepts and approaches such as bottom up (!) authority styles, theory 'Y', T-groups and an assorted alphabet soup of participative and pseudo-participative techniques' (Blumberg, 1968).

11. One statement of this by an author in this Austrian tradition is: 'a successful corporation is ultimately never controlled by hired managers' (Mises, 1949).

12. Hirschman (1970) argues that there are two basic mechanisms for dealing with social and economic difficulties – the market mechanism of exit and entry and the political mechanism. Freeman and Medoff (1984) apply this distinction to the labour process.

Chapter 3

LABOUR MARKETS

3.1 INTRODUCTION

The previous chapter has focused on the labour process and relations within the workplace although there was recognition of the influence of factors external to the workplace on those relationships. A major external factor would be the nature and operation of labour markets; in particular, the level of and change in the rate of unemployment would aid managerial control over the labour process. In this chapter, attention is focused on labour markets, with some regard to the interaction between labour markets and the labour process. In the first main section the ways in which the labour market is conceptualised in neo-classical economics and in radical political economy is outlined. This will form the backdrop to a discussion in the second section of the ideas of dual or segmented labour markets. The central idea is that there are different labour markets which behave in fundamentally different ways and which are such that participants in the primary labour markets have higher income and status than those in other markets. The third section discusses the notion of internal labour markets, whereby each firm is seen as often relying on promotion to fill posts rather than hiring anew from the external labour market. The fourth section considers some of the evidence presented in support of the idea of segmented labour markets.

The manner in which labour markets operate is unlikely to remain unchanged over time (or between countries). In the fifth section, the ways in which the American and other labour markets have evolved over time are discussed, particularly considering the role of technology and the organisation of work. In the sixth section, the question of the interaction between labour markets and the generation and perpetuation of inequality is considered. The seventh section discusses discrimination (whether racial, sexual, religious, etc.). The segmented labour market approach was originally developed as part of an analysis of racial discrimination. Groups which are discriminated against are predominantly working in the secondary labour markets. But that view raises the prior question of why certain groups are discriminated against, and the subsequent question of the mechanisms which reinforce that discrimination.

3.2 CONCEPTIONS OF THE LABOUR MARKET

Theories of the labour market not only provide explanations and predictions about labour market behaviour, but also serve to condition our thinking. It is therefore useful to consider the general thrust of both the neo-classical economics approach and the radical political economy approach, so that we may be aware of that conditioning. It should also be said that there is some problem of terminology here. In many respects, the purchase and sale of labour time is dissimilar from the purchase and sale of, say, wheat. Using the term 'market' in connection with both labour time and wheat may indicate an essential similarity between the two, which is indeed the neo-classical approach. But an important element of the radical political economy approach is a stress on the differences between human labour and other factors of production (for further discussion see, for example, Purdy, 1988, especially ch. 5). The term 'labour market' is in such wide use that it is not practical to introduce a new term, though it should be remembered that labour markets may be unlike other markets.

There are six general features of the neo-classical approach which are especially relevant here. In each case, the general feature of the neo-classical approach is considered, and then contrasted with the radical political economy approaches. The first feature is that labour is inherently scarce in supply, which fits in with the organising feature of neo-classical economics as the study of alternative uses of scarce means (cf. section 1.4), with labour as the scarce means here. In other words, the supply of labour cannot be readily expanded, from which it readily follows that there will be a strong tendency towards full employment of the available labour. In the neo-classical approach, this full employment can be achieved by flexible real wages which bring the demand for and the supply of labour into balance with each other. In such an equilibrium, those willing to work at the going wage are in employment, which is essentially full employment.

It may seem a little bizarre to say that the supply of labour can be readily expanded, as the number of people of working age is basically fixed for a considerable time ahead. Any change in the birth rate now would only have an effect on the labour force in fifteen to twenty years time. However, it is the supply of labour to the capitalist economies (and within economies, supply to the capitalist sectors) which is relevant here. There are numerous ways by which that supply can be varied and three routes stand out. The first is that within a country, the capitalist economy may cover only a part of the economy. For example, in nineteenth-century Britain there was a capitalist (largely manufacturing) sector existing along-side a non-capitalist (largely agricultural) sector. The capitalist sector could pull workers from the non-capitalist sector when demand for labour was relatively high and push workers back when demand was low. The second route is the migration of labour from one country to another. In nineteenth- and early twentieth-century America and parts of Western Europe in the period of mid-1950s to mid-1970s, for example, immigration was an important source of extra labour. The third route is from the home. The age of entry into and departure from the labour force clearly does change. The participation rate of people can change, and a significant change in the recent past has been the rise of the participation rates of women. In each case, extra supply of labour can be obtained when demand is strong by 'pulling' people into the labour force. Conversely, when the overall demand for labour is low, unemployment can to some degree be hidden by the re-absorption of workers back into the home.

The view that labour is generally not scarce so far as the capitalist sector is concerned has at least three significant impacts. First, unemployment of labour (whether recorded in the statistics, hidden in the home or in the non-capitalist economy) is the norm. Thus, whereas the neo-classical approach tends to see full employment as the norm with departures from that norm requiring explanation, radical political economy tends to see unemployment as the norm with periods of full employment requiring explanation. Second, the expansion of the economy is not generally constrained by the labour supply. The constraining factor is then seen as demand rather than supply. These two consequences are more fully explored in Chapter 12. Third, unemployment and the threat of unemployment have a coercive effect on workers. The fear of losing one's job is one of the mechanisms which help to raise the intensity of labour and productivity. The need to work in order to earn a living places the worker in a fundamentally weaker position than the employer.

The second general feature of the neo-classical approach is that supply and demand are distinct categories (and this applies not only to the labour market) with the adjustment of any imbalance between demand and supply taking place through a change in price (wage). Demand and supply are, in a well-known phrase, the two blades of the scissors. Demand and supply are essentially on a par with each other in the sense that they have a roughly equal effect on the operation of the labour market. On some occasions demand may exceed supply, which puts the suppliers in the relatively stronger position, whilst on other occasions supply exceeds demand, placing the demanders in the stronger position. The alternative approaches depart from this by stressing the disparity of power which generally exists between employer and employee. In the previous chapter, it was argued that it is employer who hires the employee and the employer is thereby placed in a position of power over the employee. Further, as seen immediately above, if unemployment is the norm then the labour market position of workers is weakened and that of the employers strengthened. The implications of that point for the possibility of sustained full employment brought about by government intervention are discussed in Chapter 12.

The third feature of the neo-classical approach, following on from the second, is to stress the allocative role of the price mechanism. Labour would be re-allocated by the response of employers and workers to the price signals, with a movement of labour from low-paying to high-paying sectors. Wages in areas of high demand would rise, thereby attracting labour into those areas, whilst wages would fall (relatively) in areas of low demand which labour would be leaving. The radical political economy approaches would suggest many other mechanisms by which the re-allocation of labour takes place. It can be argued that there is relatively little flexibility in relative wages, and that the re-allocation of labour takes place through job availability. In other words, a sector with a high level of demand for labour can largely attract the required labour without substantial increase in wages, whereas a sector with a low level of demand dismisses workers (rather than offering them a lower wage). The sectors with high levels of demand can draw labour from sectors with low levels of demand and from among the unemployed. But there are other mechanisms available to firms to adjust supply to demand. For example, the educational and skill qualifications required can be varied. When demand for labour is high, employers can adjust downwards the qualifications which they demand for any particular job.

The fourth feature is the conclusion that the payment (wage) of any particular type of labour will be equal to the marginal product of that type of labour. At the level of the firm, the wage of each type of labour is taken as given, and the amount of employment is adjusted to bring the marginal product of each type of labour into equality with the corresponding wage. The marginal productivity theory can be criticised on many grounds, such as the acute difficulties which surround the measurement of the (marginal) contribution of any particular type of labour.[1] The marginal productivity theory as applied to 'capital' and profits is examined in Chapter 8 and here some different lines of argument are examined. The marginal productivity theory assumes that the definition of each type of labour is unproblematic, and in particular that it can be made without reference to the wage paid. But if the intensity of labour depends on factors such as worker morale, then the productivity of labour (and thereby the marginal productivity) would come to depend on factors such as morale. Further, morale itself may depend on the wage which is paid, and hence productivity would then depend on the wage paid.

An aspect of this is the labelling of some jobs as skilled and others as unskilled. It is assumed that skilled workers will have higher marginal productivity than unskilled workers, and this is the explanation of skilled workers receiving a higher wage than unskilled workers. It can first be noted that the marginal productivity of any factor is said to depend on the extent to which that factor is employed. The major point to be made here is that groups of workers may be regarded as skilled (unskilled) because their wages are relatively high (low). Then the causation would run from high (low) wages to a job being classified as skilled (unskilled).

The fifth feature, which is linked in some respects to the fourth, is that education (as an investment in human capital) and experience is thought to enhance productivity. The route is education and experience raises (marginal) productivity, and thereby raises real wages. An alternative view is that education and experience are used by employers as a screening device by which they select from the supply of labour available to them, which generally exceeds their demand for labour. In the context of a basic scarcity of jobs, employers use a variety of devices in order to decide whom to employ and whom not to employ. One of those devices is often to give preference to the more educated over the less educated. It may then be observed that the more educated have better employment prospects (in terms of both earnings and probability of being employed), but this is seen as a consequence of the use of education as a screening mechanism rather than supporting the notion that education adds to human capital and productivity.[2]

The sixth feature is that the neo-classical approach does not distinguish between factors of production in any fundamental way. Factors of production are generally seen as productive, i.e. more of a factor employed leads to a higher level of output. But there are ways in which it is necessary to bring in some of the essential features of labour (cf. section 7.5). It was implicit in the discussion of the last chapter that the productivity of labour can vary, depending on the morale of workers, the pressures applied, etc., and this is a unique feature of labour. Thus labour differs from other factors of production in being human. This implies that the productivity of labour is not technologically determined in the way that the productivity of other factors such as machinery would be. Further, the conditions under which labour works are relevant for human welfare whereas the conditions under which other factors are employed are not.

The neo-classical view of the labour market suggests a degree of harmony between the demanders and suppliers of labour. Any conflict is resolved by movements in the real wage which reconciles demand and supply in equilibrium, which is itself a situation of full employment. Although there are differences between post-Keynesian and Marxian treatments of the labour market, nevertheless each of them represents significant departures from the harmonious view of the labour market. The labour process of the previous chapter emphasised conflict between employees and employers, and as will be seen later this extends into the labour market.

3.3 SEGMENTED LABOUR MARKETS

The starting point of the idea of segmented labour markets is that
not only are there different types of labour (and hence different
labour markets) but that mobility of labour between the different
markets is very limited. Further, there are significant differences in
the ways in which different labour markets operate, and it is
strongly implied that the conditions (for workers) in some of the
markets are much worse than the conditions in others.[3] In this
section we begin with the simplest statement of the segmented
labour market approach – namely the dual labour market case –
followed by consideration of some complications and empirical
evidence.

The idea of a dual labour market would seem to have made its
first appearance in connection with developing countries, where
there is a mixture of rural and urban, agricultural and industrial,
traditional and modern sectors. The modern sector of the economy
is seen as largely urban and industrial. The major characteristics of
the modern sector are that production is undertaken within firms
rather than within households, and that labour is hired for its
contribution to profits. Thus a decision of hiring a worker is
strongly influenced by the contribution of that worker to
production and to profits. The traditional sector is seen as largely
rural and agricultural, with the major characteristic that production
is organised within (extended) families. Social convention
determines the contribution of each individual within the extended
family to the process of production often by reference to age and
sex. Thus certain tasks can be assigned to women, others to
children, and a range undertaken by men. Similarly, the income
which each individual receives is set by convention (and may be
received in kind rather than in money), rather than linked to some
notion of (marginal) contribution to production. The purposes of
distinguishing between the two sectors (modern and traditional)
would include the view that wages (income) are allocated on
different principles in the two sectors and that the organisation of
production is quite different. There may also be limited mobility
between the two sectors. The general view would be that there was
disguised unemployment in the traditional sector, so that the
modern sector, which offers higher pay, can where necessary draw
labour from the traditional sector.

This idea of a dual labour market can be relatively easily extended to developed economies. There are substantial disparities between sectors and between tasks in developed economies (as between the modern and traditional sectors in developing economies), which makes it worth while to distinguish two (or more) distinct sectors. The sectors are distinct in operating in substantially different ways, and such that the movement of labour from one sector to another is severely limited. The initial division considered is that between a primary sector and a secondary sector.

The primary sector of the labour markets within developed capitalist economies can be characterised in many ways, but would include the following:[4]

1. Production is undertaken by large firms who employ capital-intensive methods.
2. Workers have relatively high levels of skill, and are often organised in trade unions.
3. The workers are employed on a long-term basis in that most workers have the expectation and experience of being employed by the same company for a number of years.

The secondary sector can be characterised in terms of the reverse features, so that it has the following elements:

1. Small firms, employing labour-intensive methods of production.
2. Workers with low levels of skill and unorganised in trade unions.
3. Workers employed on a short-term (spot market) basis so that most workers do not have the expectation of long-term employment.

These characteristics which help to define primary and secondary markets are interrelated. For example, in the primary market, the large firm and long-term contract characteristics will make trade union organisation easier. Skills are acquired in many ways, but some of them are learnt whilst at work. Workers employed on a short-term basis have little incentive to acquire 'on-the-job' skills; hence there is likely to be some association between high levels of skill and long-term contracts.

At any particular time, the essential defining characteristic of primary and secondary labour markets is in terms of jobs and occupations. Any specific job or occupation would be classified as being in either the secondary or primary sectors. But (as indicated just above) firms and industries can be thought of in terms of primary or secondary sectors. Firms will usually operate in both sectors to some extent, though belonging predominantly to one of the sectors. A firm which is an extensive employer of casual labour who utilise few skills will nevertheless require some 'core' employees. These 'core' employees may be involved with managing the casual labour. But it is difficult to envisage a firm without some 'core' employees to ensure some stability and continuity for the firm. Conversely, a firm which largely employs workers on a long-term basis may still employ some workers from the secondary sector for specific tasks. For example, in British universities, academics have in the past been employed on long-term contracts but some other employees of the universities are employed on a casual basis. When we talk of a secondary sector (or market) firm, all we mean is that a substantial majority of the firm's employees are drawn from the secondary sector. It may also be the case that when a firm employs predominantly from the primary (secondary) sector, then the manner in which it employs workers from the secondary (primary) sector may be affected. For example, a firm which employs predominantly from the primary sector may offer more stable employment to the workers drawn from the secondary sector.

The existence of two (or more) distinct labour markets may as such be of little interest unless there are substantial differences between the way in which the markets operate. The importance of the dual (segmented) labour market is three-fold. First, the movement of a worker between the primary and the secondary labour markets is viewed as difficult (particularly from secondary to primary) in the segmented labour market approach. Once a worker has entered one particular type of labour market, there are a number of factors reinforcing their position. For example, workers entering the primary labour market receive training whereas workers in the secondary labour market do not. This makes it difficult for secondary-market workers to compete with primary-market workers for jobs in the primary market.

Second, the existence of different labour markets is not merely a recognition that there are different types of labour, but involves a definite ranking whereby the primary labour market is 'superior' to the secondary labour market. This superiority would include, so far as the workers are concerned, better wages and working conditions, and continuity of employment.

Third, the different types of labour markets operated in different ways, and this is explored further below. The secondary labour market will be seen to operate rather like a competitive 'spot' market in which labour is hired for a brief period of time. As the demand and supply situation changes, so will the level of employment and wages. In contrast, in the primary labour market, employment is offered on a long-term contract basis, and employment and wages will be relatively little affected by changes in the demand and supply situation.

The idea that there is not a single market for homogeneous labour has, of course, a long history. It is often summarised by the phrase 'non-competing groups'. But this idea can be easily absorbed by conventional neo-classical theory in the sense that rather than treating labour as homogeneous, it is treated as consisting of a number of different types. For each type of labour, there is a demand and supply schedule, and the interaction of the two schedules determines the wage and employment of that type of labour. The demand and supply for different types of labour are likely to be interconnected with one another. Further, there are empirical difficulties in drawing the boundaries between the different types of labour. The segmented labour market idea is much more than this. The different segments behave in quite different ways (as indicated above), and movement between the segments is difficult. Further, the different segments do not have parity with one another, but rather some segments are distinctly superior (in terms of working conditions, wages, etc.) to others.

The idea of dual labour markets, as its title indicates, focuses on two distinct markets. In its application to industrialised countries, the dual labour market links the secondary workforce with poverty and disadvantaged groups and the primary workforce with relative affluence. However, the segmented labour market idea conceives of a number of distinct labour markets. One grouping which has been widely used is a three-way division, and our discussion of this follows Edwards (1979) closely. These three types are labelled the secondary market, the subordinate primary market, and the independent primary market, and in associated empirical work each of the three segments has been found to be of roughly equal size.

The secondary market is

the preserve of casual labor – 'casual', that is, not in the sweat required of the workers but rather in the lack of any worker rights or elaborate employer-imposed work structures. Here labor power comes closest to being treated simply as a commodity unfettered and unencumbered by any job structure, union, or other institutional constraints. (Edwards, 1979)

Work in this sector requires virtually no previous training and little education apart from basic literacy. Any skills required are quickly learnt and hence experience adds little to a worker's productivity. Similarly, education would do little to enhance a worker's productivity since any skills thereby acquired are not required for work in this sector. It could be said that many workers will be 'over-qualified' for work in this sector with their education far in excess of any which is called upon. It would then be expected that the education and experience of a worker would not add to either their productivity or their earnings. Edwards reports that such expectations are indeed borne out by empirical work.

It would also be expected that employment in the secondary market would be associated with frequent job changes. From the employer's side, any individual worker is dispensable as they do not possess any specialised skills and knowledge, and a newly hired worker is much the same as one who has worked for the firm for a long period of time. From the worker's side the job is usually routine and monotonous, etc., so that a job change may be an escape from boredom. But even when there is not frequent job changes, nevertheless it is the 'lack of job security and the ever-present possibility of immediate replacement by others from the reserve army that marks a secondary job. ... All secondary workers, however, experience the lack of job protection and the immediate possibility of replacement' (Edwards, 1979). In a later section we will explore the links between the secondary labour market and discrimination.

Primary market jobs offer workers some job security, relatively stable employment and higher wages. Further, the movement of a worker from such a job is likely to be to another job representing advancement or promotion, whereas in the secondary market leaving a job is likely to involve a move into the unemployed or to another job of the same status. The primary market is divided by Edwards into the subordinate primary and the independent primary:

The subordinate primary market, then, contains the jobs of the old industrial working class, reinforced by the lower-level jobs of unionized clerical employees. In these routinized, typically machine-operative positions, workers find that by staying on the job ladder they can progress to significantly higher wages and perhaps to better jobs. Schooling pays off, especially, it appears, at the level of high school and the first few years of college. Cyclical unemployment is a not-uncommon feature in subordinate primary work, particularly in production or blue-collar positions. (Edwards, 1979)

In the independent primary market, the jobs are skilled ones requiring relatively high levels of schooling or advanced training, with formal education (or craft union membership or licensing) as an essential requisite for employment. In this sector, additional schooling and experience yield substantial benefits to both worker and employer. Earnings and perceived productivity are enhanced by education and experience. The relevance of experience for an employee's productivity means that employers seek to extend the length of employment to gain the benefits of that experience.

Independent primary jobs, especially the professional and craft positions, have professional and occupational standards that govern performance, and so mobility and turnover tend to be both high and associated with advancement. Except for craft work, these jobs carry slight overall chances of lay-offs. Most strikingly, all independent primary jobs foster occupational consciousness; that is, they provide the basis for job-holders to define their own identities in terms of their particular occupation. (Edwards, 1979)

One of the ways in which the different segments of the labour market differ is in terms of the type of control mechanisms which are used by employers. Edwards (1979) makes a broad identification between segments and control types in the following manner:

1. Secondary segment and 'simple control'.
2. Subordinate primary and 'technical control'.
3. Independent primary and 'bureaucratic control'.

However, 'the relationship between types of control and labor market segments is not perfect or exhaustive', but this link does suggest that there is a relationship between the form of control used in the labour process and the nature of the labour market. In this context, 'simple control' can be thought of as the direct control exercised by an entrepreneur in a small firm, often based on face-to-face contact and the exercise of control. The other types of control are associated with large firms, where the methods of organisation are more deliberate.

> Two possibilities existed: more formal, consciously contrived controls could be embedded in either the physical structure of the labor process (producing 'technical' control) or in its social structure (producing 'bureaucratic' control). In time, employers used both, for they found that the new systems made control more institutional and hence less visible to workers, and they also provided a mean for capitalists to control the 'intermediate layers', those extended lines of supervision and power. (Edwards, 1979)

3.4 INTERNAL LABOUR MARKETS

The idea of the internal labour market has been described by its originators as

> an administrative unit, such as a manufacturing plant, within which the pricing and allocation of labor is governed by a set of administrative rules and procedures. The internal labor market, governed by administrative rules, is to be distinguished from the *external labor market* of conventional economic theory where pricing, allocating, and training decisions are controlled directly by economic variables. (Doeringer and Piore, 1971)

Thus the contrast is drawn between administration and markets in the determination of wages and of decisions on, for example, who is appointed to a particular job.[5] There are links between the primary labour markets and internal labour markets in that many workers in the primary labour markets will be employed by firms operating an internal labour market.

One concept of the firm (often labelled the Coasian view, after Coase, 1937, and discussed further in Chapter 4) is that a firm is an area of the economy within which the market mechanism does not operate as an allocator of resources. Instead, resources are allocated within the firm by the administrative decisions of the controllers. The internal labour market is an extension of that idea in two respects. First, it argues that wages are set by administrative decisions (including collective bargaining) rather than by the market. Doeringer and Piore (1971) state that 'in the internal labor market, wages are administratively determined either by the formal procedures of job evaluation, community surveys, merit rating, and industrial engineering studies, or through less highly structured procedures which nonetheless appear to be similar in character and in effect'. The question inevitably arises as to whether these administrative decisions are merely the implementation of wages which are set by the market (so that the administrators have no discretion over the wage which they set for a particular job) or rather that they do have some significant range of discretion.[6] The internal labour market advocates would point to a number of reasons for there being some discretion. These would include the indeterminacy of the marginal product of many types of labour, the ability of firms to raise the productivity of workers through training, etc. Doeringer and Piore argue that

> the competitive forces emphasized in neoclassical theory place certain constraints upon the wage structure, but, in general, do not establish a unique wage rate for each job. Enterprises with internal markets are able to meet labor market competition through recruitment, screening, and training expenditures as well as through wage and employment adjustments so that a number of different wage structures are consistent with the same labor market conditions.

Second, appointment to a job within the firm is often on the basis of internal promotion rather than external appointment. There have to be entry points ('ports of entry') into the firm and the internal labour market, but otherwise jobs are filled by internal promotion or transfer. These jobs are then protected to some degree from the direct influence of the external market forces. A limiting case of the internal labour market would be when people are hired at the completion of their formal education for a junior position within the firm, and the firm only hires from the external market for those junior positions. The more senior positions within the firm are filled by internal promotion, and the employees see their future within the firm.

The workers in the internal labour market have some rights and privileges which others do not have, and in that sense there is an echo of the primary sector arguments above. The internal labour force has exclusive rights to jobs which are filled internally and the presumption of continuity of employment.

The internal labour markets are seen as arising from the combination of a number of factors.[7] In the main they arise from considering each firm as being in some respects unique and idiosyncratic. A firm gains from having long-stay employees who have become familiar with its operations, its customers, etc. The firm may also have requirements for particular skills which are acquired within the firm. In some circumstances, when a worker leaves a firm, both sides lose. The training and experience of the worker which are only relevant to his or her current firm are lost when the worker leaves.

The internal labour market is seen as having a number of advantages for those involved. For the employee there is the prospect of internal promotion and continuity of employment and for the employer the internal labour market is a device for reducing labour turnover which has costs for the firm. One further reason arises from the difficulties which an employer and an employee have in gaining information about each other. For example, a firm hiring in the external labour market may find difficulties in assessing the potential employee. The firm is still faced with the problem of assessing the potential employee at the port of entry (and if that does lead to long-term employment there are substantial costs of making a mistake). But internal promotion does mean that the firm has considerable knowledge of those being considered.

In internal labour markets there is the presumption that long-term employment and wages are set by administrative decision and as such do not change frequently and often follow certain rules. The contrast can be drawn between such a market and a spot market for labour. In markets such as those for stocks and shares and for some commodities, prices change by the second. The purchase or sale of, say, a company equity does not carry with it any presumption of any future purchase or sale. In contrast, in the internal labour market, wages only change infrequently and then according to certain rules and conventions. Purchase of labour power today does carry a strong presumption of purchase tomorrow. This presumption may be aided by legal constraints on the dismissal of workers. But it is seen here as arising predominantly from the mutual interests of the employers and employees.

The general idea of internal labour markets can be viewed in different ways. One view would be to see internal labour markets as applicable for (parts of) the primary labour markets. The internal labour market is then a reflection of the relatively privileged status of primary workers, with secondary workers employed in competitive markets. Another view would be to interpret the internal labour market in terms of neo-classical theory and of human capital in particular.[8] The argument would run that individual workers receive on-the-job training from the firm and also learn by experience particular skills relevant to the firm. These skills can be widely interpreted to include knowledge of the idiosyncrasies of the firm and its environment. The firm then has an incentive to reduce labour turnover when the firm has borne some of the costs of training and the acquisition of skills, the benefits of which would be lost if the worker leaves the firm. Some of the features of the internal labour market (such as regular pay rises, pension arrangements) may help in the reduction of labour turnover.

There are some macroeconomic consequences of the internal labour market, which have been used in the Keynesian literature to help explain elements of wage rigidity and some stability of employment in the face of aggregate demand fluctuations. Let us express this in its extreme form. The internal labour market creates the presumption that a firm will continue to employ its current workforce and to maintain their level of real wages. If that presumption is borne out, then the response to a change in the level of demand for the firm's output will be met by a variation in the intensity of work and average hours worked and not by changes in either employment or wages. This would mean that changes in aggregate demand would be largely met by changes in output, in the intensity of work and in the productivity of labour, but relatively little change in employment or in real wages.

This line of argument needs to be modified in a number of ways. It could be expected that the argument in the previous paragraph would hold for relatively small fluctuations in demand. Indeed, a firm will expect that its demand will fluctuate to some degree and may gear its employment level to the expected average level of demand. Fluctuations in demand which are within the range anticipated would then not lead to the firm revising its expectations on the average level of demand, and hence it would not change its employment level and policy. However, a dramatic change in demand (and particularly a sharp fall) would lead the firm to change its view; indeed it may have to, since the fall in demand with unchanged employment and wage levels would threaten profitability.

Internal labour markets do not cover all of the economy, and two implications can be drawn out of that remark. First, it is a recognition that some sectors of the economy (roughly speaking the secondary markets) do not operate along those lines. In those sectors, wages and employment can be expected to fluctuate in line with demand. Second, firms which use the internal labour market approach for their own employees may nevertheless also use subcontracting. Fluctuations in demand could then be met by variations in the use of subcontracting. In either case, there is a tendency towards the creation of a core labour force whose employment is relative secure and a peripheral labour force whose employment prospects are insecure.

The question can be raised as to why internal labour markets have arisen. One answer to which Doeringer and Piore (1971) adhere is that the evolution of the internal labour markets reflects technological necessity. They argue that

> internal labor markets appear to be generated by a series of factors not envisioned in conventional economic theory: (1) skill specificity, (2) on-the-job training and (3) customary law. ... Three kinds of cost considerations appear to militate in favor of internal markets: (1) the value of such markets to the labor force, (2) the cost of labor turnover to the employer and the role of such markets in the reduction of turnover, (3) the technical efficiencies of an internal labor market in the recruitment, screening and training of labor.

The requirement by a firm for a more skilled labour force which understands the specific requirements of that firm and its technology would lead to the development of a primary workforce with its high skill and earnings level and stability of employment. The secondary sector is then in effect left behind by technology; its prospects depending on the future course of technology. Another answer is that capitalist firms make use of different control mechanisms (as suggested in Chapter 2). This can be linked with the history of the US labour market as suggested by Gordon *et al.* (1982) and which is discussed below.

3.5 SOME EVIDENCE ON SEGMENTED LABOUR MARKETS

It is not possible to provide a full survey of evidence relating to segmented labour markets in the space available, and this section concentrates on highlighting a few important studies. It should be said first that the empirical evaluation of the segmented labour market approach faces two particular difficulties. The first is that the approach suggests difficulties of movement between segments, although the approach is often portrayed in terms of distinct segments between which there is no movement. It is then necessary to have some criteria against which actual mobility is compared. The second difficulty is that the segmented market idea has been a general framework providing a range of (possibly conflicting) hypotheses rather than a single precisely formulated hypothesis. Two authors sympathetic to the segmentation approach write that 'labour market segmentation does not constitute a single, unified alternative to neo-classical theory. Segmentation proponents differ in the number and type of distinct segments they propose' (Rumberger and Carnoy, 1980). In particular, there are differences in the characterisation of the different segments of the labour market.

Oster (1979) sought to identify the core and periphery industries from the basis that

> proponents of the *theory of the dual economy* have suggested that the American economy is composed of two distinct industrial groups: a *core* of powerful, concentrated, unionized, capital intensive, technologically progressive industries, and a *periphery* composed of industries marked by the absence of these features.

Information on twenty-five variables (ranging over matters such as capital intensity, unionisation, average size of plant, employment record) for eighty-three industries (at the three-digit level of disaggregation) was used with the technique of factor analysis. This enabled Oster to identify three factors (which could be tentatively identified with dual economy, sex and race) which could be used to categorise each industry as either core or peripheral. On this basis, fifty-five industries were identified as peripheral and twenty-eight as core.

This work enables the different segments of the economy to be identified based on their industrial and labour market characteristics. Based on a similar approach, Gordon *et al.* (1982) estimated the size of segmented labour markets in 1950 and 1970, drawing on the three-way division of independent primary, subordinate primary and secondary sectors. The details of their findings are given in Table 3.1. It can be seen from the table that the three segments are of roughly equal size, with the independent primary segment

Table 3.1 Size of segmented labour markets.

	Male		Female		Total	
	N	%	N	%	N	%
1950						
Independent primary	10.6	34.0	2.1	14.6	12.7	27.8
salaried	2.9	9.2	1.3	9.1	4.2	9.1
craft	5.4	17.4	.5	3.5	5.9	13.0
control workers	2.3	7.4	.3	2.0	2.6	5.7
Subordinate primary	10.2	32.8	6.8	46.6	17.0	37.2
Secondary	10.4	33.2	5.6	38.9	16.0	35.0
1970						
Independent primary	17.3	42.7	5.1	18.2	22.4	32.8
salaried	7.1	17.4	3.5	12.8	10.6	15.5
craft	6.2	15.4	.9	3.1	7.1	10.4
control workers	4.0	9.9	.6	2.3	4.7	6.9
Subordinate primary	10.0	24.8	11.1	40.0	21.1	31.0
Secondary	13.1	32.5	11.6	41.8	24.7	36.2

Notes: Non-agricultural employment only. N (numbers) in millions.
Source: Gordon *et al.* (1982).

growing at the expense of the subordinate primary over the period 1950 to 1970.

The next question is whether the labour market behaviour differs between the segments. Rumberger and Carnoy (1980) define three occupational segments – secondary, primary subordinate, and primary independent – based on information on specific training requirements of jobs and 'on how workers in each job relate to other workers (e.g. supervising, serving)'. They also use industrial characteristics, categorising each industry in terms of private competitive, private non-competitive, public and self-employed. Their work is based on a 1/1000 sample of the US population in 1970, and compares employment positions in 1965 and 1970. They conclude that

> within the USA there is considerable stability over a five-year period in the types of jobs and the types of industries people work in; that there are large earnings differences between different occupational segments and between private competitive and non-competitive industries; and that the relationship between education, work experience and earnings differs between types of jobs but *not* between types of industries. This relationship also differs by race and sex. . . . jobs within one segment differ from jobs within another segment along a number of different dimensions, including wages, promotion

opportunities, returns to education and training, and employment security. (Rumberger and Carnoy, 1980)

Reich (1984) talks of a first generation of studies on segmented labour markets which sought 'to test three hypotheses of dual labour market theory: the existence of distinct labour segments; differing behavioural patterns within each segment; and restrictions on intra-segment mobility'. All these studies contained serious limitations so that their results could only be considered inconclusive. A second generation of studies were 'more restricted and static than the first generation' and focused on the 'single issue [of] the existence of a dual industrial structure and its relation to unequal labour market outcomes at a given point in time'. However, 'they generally confirm that industrial structure variables are correlated with labour market variables'.

The approach of Gordon *et al.* (1982) leads to five testable hypotheses, which are evaluated by Reich (1984). These hypotheses relate to the post-war American economy during the period of the long boom up to 1973 and are as follows:

1. Value-added per production worker in the core industries increases relative to that in the peripheral industries.
2. Production workers' earnings in core industries relative to those in the periphery rise with the capital/labour ratio and with union power.
3. Employment grew more rapidly in core industries than in the peripheral ones during the long boom.
4. The ratio of production workers to total employees in the core declines relative to that ratio in the periphery.
5. The incidence of quits per worker falls in core industries relative to the incidence in the periphery.

Reich (1984) and Gordon *et al.* (1982) produce a range of evidence in support of these propositions. In the inter-war period, the ratio of the value-added per production worker in core and periphery manufacturing started below unity in 1919, but rose to 1.10 in 1923 with little increase thereafter, and the ratio of wages in core and periphery between 1914 and 1930 was generally close to 1.20. But in the post-war period, the ratio of value-added as between the core and periphery rose from 1.14 in 1947 through 1.42 in 1958 to reach 1.56 in 1977. The ratio of core to periphery industries for lay-offs (using annual data) has a downward trend and is always less than unity. The rate of unionisation among production workers in core and periphery manufacturing is as follows:

	Core	*Periphery*	*Ratio*
1958	76.6	58.4	1.31
1968/72	70.0	52.3	1.34
1973/75	56.7	39.7	1.43

Some of the decline in unionisation arose from differences in survey concepts. There is evidence of widening disparities in the experience of unemployment as suggested by Table 3.2. It can be seen that the unemployment rate of white males tended to decline (relative to the average rate of unemployment) whereas the experience of other groups was either no improvement or a distinct deterioration (non-white females).

3.6 EVOLUTION IN THE LABOUR MARKET

Three important general ideas which feature in approaches which we are examining in this book are the following:

1. Economies evolve over time.
2. There are periodic crises under capitalism.
3. Institutional, social and political settings are important.

These three ideas are reflected in Gordon *et al.* (1982),[9] though it is

Table 3.2 Unemployment rates (%) among different groups in the USA

Year	*All workers*	*White males*	*Non-white males*	*White females*	*Non-white females*
1949	5.9	5.6	9.6	5.7	7.9
1954	5.5	4.8	10.3	5.6	9.3
1959	5.5	4.6	11.5	5.3	9.4
1964	5.2	4.1	8.9	5.5	10.6
1971	5.9	4.9	9.1	6.3	10.8
1974	5.6	4.3	9.1	6.1	10.7
1979	5.8	4.4	10.3	5.9	12.3

Note: The years are chosen for approximately the same level of aggregate unemployment rate.
Source: Gordon *et al.* (1982).

convenient to delay discussion of the periodic crisis aspect until
Chapter 12. The evolution which is crucial here is that of the labour
process and labour markets. Gordon *et al.* identify three overlapping
stages for the American economy, which they label initial
proletarianisation, homogenisation, and segmentation. The period of
initial proletarianisation lasted from the 1820s to the 1890s and
during this period,

> wage labor became the dominant manner of organizing production;
> ... most typically, the growth of wage labor did not produce
> fundamental changes in the actual organization of work. The labor
> market was still rudimentary. Competition played only a small role in
> determining wages, and older workers passed skills on directly to
> younger workers. (Gordon *et al.*, 1982)

This was followed by the homogenisation period, lasting from the
1870s to the onset of the Second World War, during which the
organisation of work and the structure of labour markets were
profoundly transformed.

> More and more jobs in the capitalist sector of the economy were
> reduced to a common, semi-skilled operative denominator, and
> control over the labor process became concentrated among employers
> and their foremen, who used direct supervision or machine pacing to
> 'drive' their workers. The labor market became increasingly
> generalized and much more competitive. Skills were much less
> controlled by workers. (Gordon *et al.*, 1982)

It was during this period that Taylorism was developed, which was
discussed in the previous chapter.

Finally, there has been the segmentation period, lasting from the
1920s to the present. During this period the three distinct labour
markets discussed in the previous section evolved.

> The origins of segmentation date back to the explorations of the 1920s
> and 1930s; a new system of control in the labor process and
> corresponding labor market structures became consolidated after
> World War II; and these systems began to decay during the 1970s.

This decay causes economic disruption in ways similar to those
proposed by the regulation approach outlined below.

The effect of this segmentation of the labour market is seen as
instrumental in preventing the formation of a strong labour
movement in the USA. Further, the specific history of the United

States (slavery, waves of immigration) has helped to create differences within the labour force which are exacerbated by the segmented labour markets. Thus the experience of slavery creates a history of racism between workers, which interacts with the segmented labour markets which can sustain that discrimination (and this is further discussed below).

A similar line of argument has been advanced by the French 'regulation' school (notably Aglietta, 1979). Regulation has been defined as 'the way in which a system as a whole functions, the conjunction of economic mechanisms associated with a given set of social relationships, of institutional forms and structures' (Boyer, 1979). Such forms and structures change only slowly so that 'the stability of regulation acquires a certain inertia in structure and in institutional forms'. The regulation approach then involves the idea of stability of economic structure and institutional arrangements, so that periods of history can be identified with particular regulations. However, the economic structure changes, and prolonged economic crises arise with the shift from one regulation to another.

The work of Boyer (1979) relates specifically to the determination of wages in France over the past two centuries. He identifies three distinct eras or regulation(s). The *ancienne* regulation, during which there was a 'preponderance of an essentially precapitalist and unproductive agricultural system', lasted roughly up to the middle of the nineteenth century. It was followed by the competitive regulation, lasting around a century with a 'predominance of capitalistic industry'. The 1960s and 1970s are identified by Boyer as the monopolistic regulation. The particular concern of Boyer (1979) is with the process of wage determination in these different eras. The thrust of the argument (for which he produces evidence) is that in the *ancienne* regulation, 'employment and wage levels [moved] in the same direction as each other but in the opposite direction to the cost of living'. In the competitive era wages were sensitive to the level of economic activity and unemployment, and tended to move in line with the cost of living. In the monopolistic regulation, there was an absence of any marked impact of the level of unemployment on the determination of wages determination.

The regulation approach is used by deVroey (1984) to understand the post-1973 recession, and he also provides a summary of the distinctive features of the competitive regulation (mid-nineteenth century to First World War) and the monopoly regulation (post Second World War), with the inter-war period treated as a transition period between the two regimes. Table 3.3 is derived from the tables of de Vroey, and is a highly summarised account of differences between the two regulations.

Table 3.3 Distinctive features of the two regimes of accumulation.

	Competitive regulation (approx. pre-First World War)	*Monopoly regulation (approx. post-Second World War)*
Feature of the wage relation	Commodities involved in the reproduction of labour forces essentially non-capitalist	Mass consumption of standardised commodities
	Important role of domestic labour	Diminishing role of domestic labour/increased importance of collective goods and services
	Unemployed are cared for by the family or charity	Provision of social insurance system for unemployed
	Women and children withdrawn from labour force	Women re-integrated into labour force
Prevailing labour process	Introduction of Taylorism	Taylorism replaced by Fordism
Industrial relations	Individual labour contracts law blatantly favours employers	Collective bargaining with some legal reinforcement of workers' rights
	Emergence of trade unions	Integration of trade union movement in state institutions
	Balance of power favours capital; need for social consensus low	Necessity for social consensus
Price formation	Price flexibility	Administered prices with downward rigidities
Monetary system	Metallic basis with convertible paper-money	Unconvertible paper money
	Gold standard	Dollar standard; Bretton Woods system with fixed exchange rates
	Limited role for central banks; fragility of private banking system	Central banks' role increased; nationally integrated private banking system, well protected against loss of confidence
Prevailing doctrine of State	Liberalism	Keynesianism, counter-cyclical and supplementary action by State is legitimised
Extension of markets	Within prevailing national boundaries	Transnationalisation of production and exchange
International power	Britain	United States of America

Source: Derived from de Vroey (1984, Table 1).

One important feature is that the difference between the two regimes are extensive (and not all of them are reported in Table 3.3), ranging over the prevailing type of labour process through to the organisation of the financial system and the modes of government intervention. This discussion illustrates the general notion of periodisation of history with distinct eras between which there are significant differences. As always there are disputes over precise dating (which anyway will differ from country to country) and over the nature of the significant differences. Some of the features described in Table 3.3 have already been discussed (e.g. nature of the labour process). Some others (especially prices, inflation and the monetary system) will be discussed in Chapter 11.

The movement from one era to another does not proceed smoothly but rather is identified with crisis. One of the reasons for crisis is that the general change of production mode requires many other changes, including institutional ones. The institutional arrangements which appear to work well under one form of regulation are unlikely to be suited to another form. But changes in institutional arrangements are likely to come slowly, in part because it will take time before any requirement for change is recognised. The inter-war period, with depression and high levels of unemployment, can be seen as a transitional period (between the competitive and monopoly regulations) during which there was a discordance between the requirements of the forces of production and the institutional and other arrangements. Similarly, the post-1973 generalised recession (with higher unemployment levels and lower growth than during the post-war boom up to 1973), is seen to result from a decay of the institutional structures which underpinned the long post-war boom. This leads to the view that '[a] way out of the crisis would involve the development of a new form of regulation, a new regime of accumulation' (deVroey, 1984).

The evolution from the competitive regulation to the monopoly one was accompanied by a gradual decline in the international power of Britain and the growth of American power. The pre-First World War financial system was labelled a gold standard though it also rested on the dominant role of sterling. The decline of the monopoly regulation is also associated with a decline in the international power of the United States, and of the status of the dollar in international trade.

A particular feature of the monopoly regulation (and the post-war period in general) was the growth of the welfare state in most capitalist economies. This growth was associated with a large shift in perceptions on the role of the State, which became to be widely seen as responsible for the level of unemployment and for the provision of a wide range of social services. The social democrat consensus (e.g. promotion of the welfare state, commitment to macroeconomic demand management) which was a feature of the monopoly regulation (cf. Table 3.3) has recently been undermined in a number of countries (notably the USA and UK). Thus, some of the structural elements which supported the monopoly regulation have been weakened. But a crucial change is seen to be the nature of the production process. The monopoly regulation is identified with Fordism (mass-production techniques)[10] as the typical mode of production. It is argued that Fordism is being superseded by neo-Fordism (sometimes called flexible specialisation).[11] Neo-Fordism is

> based upon new micro-electronic technologies, [and] is characterised by the production of specialised commodities for segmented markets. At its core is an integrated production system, sometimes termed flexible specialisation, which has radically reduced the optimum scale of efficient production by systematically connecting design, manufacturing, stock control, marketing and retailing functions. (Nolan and O'Donnell, 1987)

There is seen to be a combination of changes in the patterns of consumer demand (e.g. a shift from standardised commodities to specialised ones) and in production techniques. As the quote above indicates, microelectronic techniques are viewed as particularly important here. The example of car production comes to mind, with a shift from standardised production (exemplified by Ford's famous statement that the customer can have any colour of car as long as it is black) to specialised production whereby computerisation allows each car produced to be slightly different (e.g. in terms of colour, engine size, number of doors, etc.). Since the Fordist mass-production techniques often involved the submission of workers to the speed of the production line, the flexible specialisation techniques have been seen by some as releasing workers from the tyranny of the production line.[12] The regulation approach would suggest that if indeed neo-Fordism and flexible specialisation are the production techniques of the future, then future prosperity would require appropriate institutional arrangements to be developed and for a set of ideas (comparable to the social democratic consensus referred to above) to evolve.

In the past few years, there has been considerable discussion (especially by right-of-centre governments) on increasing workplace flexibility. In terms of our previous discussion, we can identify a number of different trends. First, there has been the reassertion of the managerial prerogative, and of the control by managers over workers. The flexibility which is then restored is that of managers to vary the working conditions of workers. Second, flexibility may mean the ability of firms to vary wages and employment. This involves an element of a shift back from a primary labour market to secondary labour market in which there is flexibility of employment and wage conditions. Third, flexibility may involve change of the form of control even within the primary sector. In conclusion it should be noted that flexibility appears to be advantageous when the neo-classical competitive approach is adopted. However, other approaches indicate that flexibility (which is capable of many definitions) would provide disadvantages as well as advantages. The ability to vary employment may be useful for employers but imposes considerable costs on employees. The internal labour market literature suggests that long-term contracts which introduce inflexibility of wages and employment have mutual benefits for both employers and employees.

3.7 SEGMENTED LABOUR MARKETS AND INEQUALITY

An important element of theories of the labour market is the implications which they have for economic and social inequality. The question of the impact of the operation of markets on inequality arises here specifically in the context of labour markets, which involves not only the inequality of wages and salaries but also of employment opportunities and unemployment experience. But this is only one aspect of a broader question involving, for example, inequalities between regions and between countries and these broader issues are addressed in Chapter 13.

One difficulty in answering the question of the effect of a market mechanism on inequality is that what is meant by the market mechanism is not a straightforward matter. For some, the market mechanism is identified with a competitive market and any departure in practice from the assumptions of perfect competition would be seen as evidence that the market is not fully in operation. Others would see perfect competition as unattainable and some departure from that model in practice being inevitable.[13] Thus, long-term contracts (as, it is argued, appear in internal labour markets) would be seen as an impediment to the market mechanism in that wages and employment would not be flexible in so far as they are set for a prolonged period by contract. But, within the internal market approach, these contracts would be seen as providing benefits for both employer and employee. We take a broad definition of the market mechanism, which would perhaps be better described as *laissez-faire*. Such a broad definition would include all activities associated with trading and actions designed to secure a better trading position (and to offset advantages gained by others). Thus not only would exchange and production activities be included, but also formation of trade unions, cartels, etc., would also be encompassed. Government action which intervenes in trading would, however, be excluded.

The conventional answer, which has a long history, is that the competitive market mechanism will operate to reduce inequalities. The clearest example of this arises from comparing a monopoly position secured by legal protection with a competitive arrangement. The secure monopoly position would yield excess profits to the monopolist, whereas competition would bid down those profits and yield a less unequal outcome. A perfectly competitive equilibrium outcome would envisage inequality between individuals (and also between regions) as merely reflecting differences in initial endowments. Ryan (1981) describes this as follows:

> in its competitive formulation, the market does no more than produce at the end of the period a reflection of the circumstances of market participants at the beginning of the period. The market cannot be blamed for inequality, low pay and the like – it merely reproduces the inequality which is brought to it, without being in any way part of its creation.

Some within the neo-classical orthodoxy would see the operation of an atomistic competitive market as tending to reduce inequality, and imperfections in the market and the operation of governments as tending to increase or at least maintain inequality. 'Much of the actual inequality derives from imperfections of the market' (Friedman, 1962), and many of those imperfections are seen as generated by (or at least supported by) government. In contrast, the radical political economy approach suggests that the market mechanism will tend to reinforce pre-market inequalities rather than reduce them. People come to the labour market(s) with different skills and this sets pre-market segmentation, and it is this form of segmentation which forms the basis of non-competing groups. As such, the labour market converts an existing inequality of skills into a corresponding inequality of income. The segmented labour market approach focuses on in-market segmentation. This 'represents the continuation of such [pre-market] differentiation of opportunities into the market itself. It occurs when individuals of similar achieved productive potential receive markedly different access to employment or job rewards, including both pay rates and opportunities for training, experience and pay increases' (Ryan, 1981).

Thus, it is argued that individuals with similar skills before they enter the labour market receive different wages and other rewards. The primary labour market tends not only to provide higher wages but also to provide more training. Thus, workers in the primary market may have both higher wages and training (as compared with workers in the secondary labour market). The direction of causation is important here. For the neo-classical approach, causation runs from (pre-entry) training to wages. For the segmentation approach, there is an element of causation running from pre-entry training to wages. But much of the training of workers arises after entry and wages and training go together. Thus a worker fortunate enough to secure entry into the primary sector will have his or her skills enhanced through training and experience, leading to higher wages.

The outcome of this debate is relevant for issues such as the operation of labour markets on discrimination, and particularly whether such operations will tend to diminish or exacerbate discrimination. It is to this issue that we now turn.

3.8 DISCRIMINATION

The full discussion of why people are discriminated against on the basis of race, religion, sex, etc., in terms of jobs, housing, education, etc., would take at least a whole book. The task in this section is more modest: it is to indicate the interaction between discrimination and the workings of the labour market.

In order to make some comparisons between the radical political economy approach to discrimination and the neo-classical one, it is necessary to sketch in the neo-classical version. The original work in the neo-classical area is Becker (1957), and we begin with a consideration of that work for not only was it the first neo-classical attempt to deal with discrimination but it also enables us to focus on the nature of the neo-classical approach in this context. The starting point for the neo-classical approach is the existence of a 'taste for discrimination', which appears to be on a par with other tastes. The discussion above (section 1.4) has indicated that the neo-classical approach cannot say anything about the desirability or otherwise of tastes; in this context it means that the neo-classical approach is not able to condemn discrimination. The idea of a 'taste for discrimination' can be seen from the following passage:

> For example, discrimination and prejudice are not usually said to occur when someone prefers looking at a glamorous Hollywood actress rather than at some other woman; yet they are said to occur when he prefers living next to whites rather than next to Negroes. (Becker, 1957)

However, we can note the presumption that 'someone' is white and male. Then 'if an individual has a "taste for discrimination" he must act *as if* he were willing to pay something, either directly or in the form of reduced income, to be associated with some persons instead of others' (Becker, 1957). It is relevant to note that the analysis is intended to apply to all forms of 'discrimination in the market place because of race, religion, sex, color, social class, personality, or other non-pecuniary consideration' (Becker, 1957).

Becker (1957) considers two groups (labelled W(hite) and N(egro)) which differ in their relative ownership of the factors of production of capital (K) and labour (L) such that the W group owns relatively more capital than labour as compared with the N group. He argues that the effect of discrimination is akin to the effects of trade restrictions in international trade theory. The extent of trade between the groups is less than it would be without discrimination, and thereby there are economic losses from discrimination. However, when the W group discriminates against the N group, the returns to the W labour and to N capital rise and the losses are incurred by the N labour and W capital. The key conclusion here is that the losers from discrimination are the capitalists of the group which undertakes the discrimination with gains being made by the labour of that group. It should be noted that this conclusion is derived for a perfectly competitive economy in which the only difference between the two groups is their relative ownership of the two factors of production (and nothing is said about the absolute levels of capital and labour of the two groups).

The assumption of a perfectly competitive environment has two important implications in this context. First, there is no route through which economic power can be exercised, and by implication the two groups have equal (zero) economic and political power. Second, labour markets are assumed to clear so that there is equality between the supply and demand for each type of labour. Hence there is no unemployment of any type of labour, and therefore no differences in the unemployment experience of the W workers and the N workers. 'Yet racial differences in unemployment are as striking and persistent as racial wage differentials' (Reich, 1981).

An alternative way of arriving at the conclusion that the losers from discrimination are the W capital owners and the N labour suppliers arises from consideration of an employer from the majority group, which we label as X. Such an employer could hire employees either from group X or from the minority group (labelled group Y). The wage of group Y is less that that of group X even though the productivity of the two groups is the same. If the employer hires employees from the group X, then (s)he is incurring higher costs by doing so. An employer who hires solely on the basis of cost would hire group Y workers.

In the long run, discrimination would be predicted by this model to disappear. If there are differences in the degree of discrimination felt by employers then those employers with less taste for discrimination would be able to expand at the expense of those with a greater taste for discrimination. The former group would benefit from hiring more of the discriminated against at lower costs than the latter group; the lower costs and higher profits would then enable the former group to expand production and sales at the expense of the latter group.[14] Further, it would be expected that the wages of group *Y* workers would be bid up by this process and those of group *X* workers bid down, thereby removing the observable discrimination in terms of wages. A feature of this view is that discrimination will be more prevalent (in the sense of being observed in terms of employment and wages) in non-competitive industries than in competitive ones. The non-competitive industries can, in effect, use the potential super-normal profits to indulge in discrimination, which is not possible in the competitive industries where profits are bid down to the normal level.[15]

It is useful to consider some crucial weaknesses in this general approach which will help to highlight the differences between a neo-classical approach and a radical political economy approach. Four weaknesses with the neo-classical approach and associated differences between that approach and radical political economy approach can be identified. The first is that certain tastes and factor ownerships are taken as given, presumably to reflect some pre-existing state of affairs. But, in line with the general neo-classical position, there is no explanation of how those 'tastes' arose nor of the origins of current factor ownerships. For example, there is no explanation asked for or given of why one group should own more capital and property than another group. Further, the 'taste for discrimination' cannot really be taken on a par with the 'taste' for, say, a particular kind of food. Racial discrimination, for example, usually also involves racism, that is the ideology of the superiority of a particular type of people. Racism is often observed to generate in turn racial hatred, racial violence, etc.[16]

> Clearly, discrimination is more a status or caste phenomenon, a concept which makes the theory more general because the physical phenomenon surely cannot be applied to sexual discrimination. Discriminators object to discriminees *partly* because the latter are generally regarded to be 'inferior' people who would lower the status of discriminators. (Marshall, 1974).

A 'taste' explanation of discrimination finds it difficult to explain discrimination by capitalists since the ownership and control of capital does not necessarily involve association with workers including those discriminated against. Further, the 'taste' view suggests segregation between the groups involved, whereas whilst discrimination does involve an element of segregation it also often involves the allocation of the discriminees to lower-status jobs which do involve contact with the discriminators with higher-status jobs.

The second weakness arises from a combination of the use of 'tastes' as an explanation for discrimination and the proposed generality of the theory. For example, Becker's approach is quite general in that although groups W and N are used, which suggests white and negroes, the approach is intended as indicated above to apply also to, *inter alia*, sexual as well as racial discrimination. As Lord (1979) argues, the taste for discrimination

> is taken to originate from the disutility of contact with certain individuals, although it is assumed that some direct contact must be necessary for the development of the desire to discriminate. In addition, this desire to avoid contact is sufficiently strong that individuals are prepared to pay for the privilege. As many writers have pointed out, this hardly conforms to reality; in many societies where discrimination is particularly virulent, blacks are employed as house servants; and it is especially difficult to maintain in the case of women.

It could be further pointed out that when applied to sexual discrimination, some explanation has to be provided on the ownership side, e.g. why do men own capital rather than women; what about the joint ownership of property?

The third weakness also arises from the focus of the neo-classical approach on the role of individual tastes. 'The neo-classical model also fails to distinguish between specific acts of discrimination, when, for example, a worker is not hired or promoted because of race, and institutionalized discrimination, which pervades social and economic institutions' (Marshall, 1974). Discrimination by one individual against another is distasteful, but could be offset by discrimination in favour of that individual by another. A major reason for concern over discrimination (racial, sexual, etc.) is its pervasiveness. For example, to use Becker's analogy above in an amended form, a person who was not considered sufficiently attractive or talented to be a Hollywood star is not thereby excluded from a range of other activities. However, a person from a group which is discriminated against will find that they are excluded from a wide range of opportunities. Further, when the 'taste' for discrimination is widespread, discrimination will not only be practised by individuals but also it becomes embedded in the organisation and behavioural rules of institutions, so that there is institutional racism and sexism. Any individual within the institution may wish not to discriminate, but the rules and perceptions under which the institution operates may still involve discrimination.

Fourth, there would appear to be an element of symmetry in the approach in that if group X dislikes working with group Y and group Y dislikes working with group X, then separation between the groups may be observed but there is no presumption that one group would have higher incomes and better job opportunities than the other. But whilst discrimination in practice involves some separation between groups (particularly that certain types of jobs are predominantly undertaken by particular groups such as when some jobs are identified as 'women's work'), it also involves pervasive disadvantages for those discriminated against. In most capitalist countries (and many others), white male workers have in general labour market advantages over black workers and over female workers. The neo-classical approach would focus on lower wages for the groups discriminated against (although these lower wages would gradually disappear), whereas the radical political economy approach stresses the multi-dimensional aspect of the disadvantages suffered.[17]

There have been other attempts within the neo-classical paradigm to discuss the causes and consequences of discrimination, of which a popular one has drawn on the notion of a cartel among white workers to analyse discrimination.[18] Without going into the details, it is possible to outline the general features and difficulties of such an approach by reference to basic ideas on cartels. The banding together of a group of individuals (or firms) will generally permit them to reach an outcome which at least for the group as a whole is better than the outcome which would result without the cartel. For example, in the context of firms, a cartel which pursues the objective of joint profit maximisation will reach a higher level of joint profits than would be possible without a cartel. Within the cartel, each firm would generally find it advantageous to trim its prices and expand its own output, but such actions would undermine the policies of the cartel. Further some firms may have lower profits within the cartel, even if total profits of the firm taken together are higher. These factors are usually seen as making it difficult to hold a cartel together.

Applying the cartel concept to discrimination faces the difficulty of explaining how a cartel involving millions of people is organised (especially if it is a tacit rather than an explicit cartel). Further, it is usually the case that each individual member of the cartel has an incentive to undermine the cartel. For example, when a cartel results in higher prices and lower outputs, then each individual firm has the incentive to increase its own output to benefit from the higher prices, but in doing so tends to undermine the cartel. In the case of discrimination over employment, employers from the dominant group have an economic incentive to hire workers from other groups, since they are available at lower wages. Within the employers from the dominant group, collective self-interest indicates continuation of discrimination but individual self-interest suggests undermining the effects of discrimination. On this view, the effects (in terms of lower wages and worse employment prospects) of discrimination would gradually disappear.

The radical political economy approach to explaining and understanding discrimination has a number of themes. The first is the need to adopt an historical perspective. For example, the understanding of discrimination against blacks in the United States would need to take account of the long history of slavery, and the dominant position of whites over blacks which that entailed. Slavery is often justified by appeal to ideas of racial superiority of the slave-owners over the slaves. Further, under slavery low-grade jobs are undertaken by the slaves. The abolition of slavery does not immediately change the ideology of racism nor the general range of jobs undertaken by different racial groups. Much post-war immigration into Western European countries has taken the form of immigrant workers drawn into low-paying sectors of the economy (into the secondary labour markets) which had to some degree been deserted by the native workforce, so that immigrant workers are associated with low-prestige jobs and income. Current discrimination against women in the workforce and elsewhere cannot be understood without at least some reference to centuries of patriarchy.

The historical perspective can suffer from an infinite regress problem; that is, current discrimination may be understood in terms of some previous historical situation, but that situation itself may need to be understood in terms of some preceding situation. However, the historical perspective helps to understand why some groups are in advantageous positions and others in disadvantageous ones. One expression of this is

> the recurrent observation that severe ethnic or racial antagonism often can be traced to the point at which groups first find themselves competing in the labour market. Some writers have argued that all discrimination by race or ethnic group can be traced to such a dynamic, in which groups mobilize political and economic resources to further their material interests. The goal of such action is seen to be the exclusion of the competing group from the labour market or, failing this, the creation of a caste system providing the dominant group with preferential treatment. (Mueser, 1987)

Second, discrimination operates to the advantage of employers (and to some degree the advantage of some groups of workers), and with economic gains to the dominant group who have the power to discriminate. Antagonism between groups of workers was suggested above as enabling employers to exercise greater control over the labour process. Mutual support by groups of workers is less likely in the event of industrial disputes. Thus, it is argued, any existing antagonism between workers can be used by the employers to pursue a 'divide and rule' strategy. Further, as jobs are divided and subdivided, it may be beneficial for employers if certain tasks are identified as available only to specific groups (e.g. for a job to be identified as 'women's work').

> As heterogeneity of worker experience *within* productive activity may weaken worker resistance, so heterogeneity of worker characteristics and experiences which are *brought* to productive activity may also weaken resistance. Differences in age, sex, race and nationality, and differences in working backgrounds may discourage resonance and encourage sectionalism, particularly when these sociological or demographic characteristics are matched by different working conditions, status and earnings levels within productive activity – when stratification accompanies social heterogeneity. Top managers *do not create racism and sexism*, but they *do use these divisions* among workers to their advantage. (Friedman, 1977)

The analysis of Reich (1981) develops the view that 'racial divisions weaken worker solidarity and bargaining power;

capitalists gain and most white workers lose'. He contrasts the
neo-classical approach which views white workers as gaining from
discrimination and the 'class conflict analysis' which views black
workers and most white workers as losing from discrimination
(though there may be some groups of white workers, particularly
managerial ones, which gain from discrimination).

> The class conflict analysis of racial inequality identifies specific and
> testable mechanism through which racial inequality works to hurt
> most white workers and benefit capitalists. Unions are weaker and
> the supply of public services to low- and middle-income whites are
> lessened by racial divisions. (Reich, 1981)

He then estimates equations based on these mechanisms for
American data (relating to 1960 and 1970) in terms of differences
between largely urban standard metropolitan statistical areas
(SMSAs), and finds that the empirical findings generally support his
approach. The basis of his model is that unionisation, white
schooling inequality and welfare payment levels are all functionally
related to racial inequality and market control variables, and further
that inequality of white income is related to discrimination,
unionisation and some structural variables. A typical set of results
(which relate to 1960, estimated across 48 of the 50 largest SMSAs
for which data are available) are as follows:

$$UN = -0.491 + 0.787\ BW + 0.601\ PM - 0.838 PG\quad + 0.090\ WY$$
$$(2.68)\qquad (1.95)\qquad (-1.40)\qquad\quad (2.71)$$
$$R^2 = 0.558$$
$$G\ = 0.423 - 0.092\ BW\ - 0.125\ PM + 0.098\ PWC - 0.038\ UN$$
$$(-2.78)\qquad (-4.31)\qquad (2.82)\qquad (-2.49)$$
$$R^2 = 0.697$$

(t-ratios in parenthesis)

where UN is local degree of unionisation, G is the Gini coefficient
of white income (as a measure of income inequality), BW is ratio
of black median income to white median income, PM is
percentage of the workforce in manufacturing, PG the percentage
in government employment, PWC the percentage of the
workforce which is white-collar and WY median white income.

The interpretation of these results is that the degree of
discrimination (measured here inversely by the black/white
income ratio, though Reich uses other measures of discrimination

with similar effect) has a negative effect on the ability of workers to form unions. The extent of inequality among white workers is increased by discrimination as well as by a lower degree of unionisation. In a similar vein, the inequality of white schooling is raised by discrimination whereas welfare payments are lowered. Thus Reich can conclude that relatively poor white workers lose from discrimination (even if some richer workers gain).

One recent study also illustrates the point that the group discriminated against lose out not only in economic terms but in other ways as well. This study based on phone interviews of over 600 people in Illinois, USA, in 1982 concluded that

> reward structures for male and female workers are different even when men and women have similar characteristics and are in similar jobs. We have found that women are at a disadvantage in attaining control over work-related resources. The actual earnings gap in our sample is $11,359. It would be reduced to $6,539 if both men and women achieved work power and rewards as men do. (Ferber, Green and Spaeth, 1986)

The third theme in the radical political economy approach to discrimination is that the interaction between discrimination and segmented labour markets is important. Workers are not entirely allocated between primary and secondary labour markets on some random basis. There is a shortage of jobs in the primary market, which allows the employer to choose which workers to employ. Disadvantaged groups are likely to be discriminated against when the decision is made on entry into the primary market. Disadvantaged groups are likely to have received lower-quality education, which in part is another element of the ubiquity of discrimination. But it may come to be reinforced in that entry into low-skill jobs requires lower-quality education. For example, women have often been denied access to the engineering profession, and that denial of access may be used to 'justify' a poor quality and quantity of science education provided for girls. Hence even if entry into the primary market is based on educational qualifications, there will be implicit discrimination against the disadvantaged groups.

The thrust of the approach developed here is that the market mechanism (with segmented labour markets) tends to reinforce discrimination, and leads to the view the reduction of discrimination requires a range of government interventions (e.g. training programmes, affirmative action). However, if segmented markets are basic to the current stage of capitalist development, then segmentation will remain. If discrimination against those groups which currently suffer from it is successfully eliminated, other groups may take their place. In other words, if a primary market and a secondary market continue, then some workers will suffer from being consigned to the secondary market, whilst others benefit from working in the primary sector.

Two crucial differences arise as between the neo-classical and the radical political economy approaches to discrimination. The first is that the neo-classical approach points to losses which discrimination imposes on everyone but particularly on the discriminators, whereas the radical political economy approach would see those who are discriminated against as being the main losers from discrimination. The second is that the neo-classical approach would see market forces as eroding (the effects of) discrimination, whereas the segmented labour market approach would point to the ways in which market forces help to reinforce discrimination.

3.9 CONCLUDING REMARKS

The intention of this chapter has been to provide a flavour of alternative ways of thinking about labour markets. The underlying premise is that the general vision of the labour market (as discussed in the first major section of this chapter) heavily conditions the economic analysis of the labour market. The segmented labour market analysis points to the divisions within the general labour market, and the differences in experience and behaviour between the different segments. A particularly important difference between the segmented labour market analysis and the neo-classical analysis is the implication for the consequences of the operation of the labour market for inequality and discrimination. The neo-classical approach suggests that the market tends to reduce inequality and discrimination, whilst the segmented labour market analysis suggests that markets may reinforce and support inequality and discrimination.

NOTES

1. The first two instances which come to mind are:

   (a) Situations where two (or more) types of labour are used in fixed proportions. The (marginal) contribution of any one type of labour cannot be evaluated.

   (b) Situations where it is very difficult (expensive) or impossible to measure the contribution.

   The difficulties of measurement would also place considerable obstacles in the way of testing of the marginal productivity theory.

2. This should not be taken as implying that the average level of education in an economy is irrelevant for the productivity of that economy. Clearly, a modern industrial economy could not function without widespread literacy and numeracy. But it may be observed that many jobs do not utilise the education and skills of the person undertaking the job. Further, any correlation between earnings and education cannot be used to infer anything about what benefits would arise if the level of education were increased. For example, it may be estimated for a particular economy at a specific time, that on average an extra year's education leads to a person having annual earnings which are £X higher than otherwise. This cannot be used to infer that the marginal product of a year's education is £X, and that if education were increased, higher productivity would follow. An alternative view is that employers use educational achievement as a screening device, and place more highly educated people in higher-paying jobs.

3. In the neo-classical approach, where there is mobility of labour between different markets, then there would be an 'equalisation of net advantage' between the different markets. This equalisation would mean that (relatively) high wages would be associated with poor (non-wage) conditions, and low wages with good conditions. The segmented labour market approach tends to the view that high wages will be associated with good working conditions in the favoured labour markets, and low wages and poor conditions in the unfavoured markets.

4. One of those heavily involved in the development of the idea of dual labour markets summarised the idea as follows: 'The basic hypothesis of the dual labor market was that the labor market is divided into two essentially distinct segments, termed the *primary* and the *secondary* sectors. The former offers jobs with relatively high wages, good working conditions, chances of advancement, equity and due process in the administration of work rule, and, above all, employment

stability. Jobs in the secondary sector, by contrast, tend to be low-paying, with poorer working conditions and little chance of advancement; to have a highly personalized relationship between workers and supervisors which leaves wide latitude for favoritism and is conducive to harsh and capricious work discipline; and to be characterized by considerable instability in jobs and a high turnover among the labor force' (Piore, 1973).

5. This contrast between administration and markets makes the choice of the term internal labour market an unfortunate one. Hodgson (1988) argues that '"internal labour markets" within firms are not markets in the sense defined above, in that no systematic and institutionalized process involving buying and selling of labour power is normally to be found'.

6. 'It [utility of the internal labor market as an analytical construct] depends rather upon the *rigidity* of the rules which define the boundaries of internal markets and which govern pricing and allocation within them. If the rules are not rigid and respond freely to variations in economic conditions, their independent economic role will be minimal' (Doeringer and Piore, 1971).

7. Besides the two discussed in the text, Doeringer and Piore (1971) also list 'customary law'.

8. Doeringer and Piore (1971) acknowledge the influence of the work of Becker on human capital which is firmly within the neo-classical tradition.

9. For a detailed review and critique of Gordon *et al.* (1982) see Nolan and Edwards (1984).

10. Fordism is '[a] term ... which extends the technique of factory production – based on the assembly line – developed by Ford into a category referring to a general stage in capitalist production' (Thompson, 1983).

11. This has been associated with the work of Piore and Sabel (1984). Others have explored its relevance for political strategies; see, for example, Murray (1985). For some doubts on this approach see Nolan and O'Donnell (1987).

12. There is a tendency 'to idealise modern technology, particularly in its discussion of "human centred" machines and factory systems ... This, despite the mounting evidence from America and Britain suggests that increased flexibility at the level of particular jobs has been accompanied by greater centralisation of control, work intensification and greater job insecurity' (Nolan and O'Donnell, 1987), and reference is made to the work of Shaiken *et al.* (1986) and Kraft and Dubnoff (1986).

13. See, for example, Hodgson (1988, pp. 187–94).

14. 'A business man or an entrepreneur who expresses preferences in his

business activities that are not related to productive efficiency is at a disadvantage compared to other individuals who do not. Such an individual is in effect imposing higher costs on himself than are individuals who do not have such preferences. Hence, in a free market, they will tend to drive him out' (Friedman, 1962).

15. For some critical discussion of the evidence on this see Reich (1981).

16. One neo-classical response to that would be to analyse racial violence, say, in terms of a 'taste' for violence against people of other racial groups, constrained by the 'costs' of such violence such as revenge attacks.

17. Myrdal (1944) was one of the first to compare discrimination against women with discrimination against Negroes. His appendix 5 contains a comparison of the legal and social position of women and Negroes in the Southern United States especially during the nineteenth century.

18. For models in this vein see Krueger (1963), Thurlow (1969), and for a fuller discussion and critique of them see Reich (1981).

Part Three

COMPETITION, RIVALRY AND FIRMS

Chapter 4

THE NATURE OF FIRMS

4.1 CONCEPTS OF FIRMS

This and the next two chapters are all concerned, albeit in different ways, with the way firms operate and the interaction (particularly through competition but also through tacit co-operation) between firms. In this chapter, attention is focused on the question of how different economists have viewed the nature of the firm. In the next chapter, the attention is on the relationship between firms, and in particular the nature and degree of competition between firms. One particular view of the nature of (incorporated) firms is that these firms are largely managerial-controlled. In Chapter 6, the question of whether corporations are managerial-controlled is discussed, and the consequence of the answer to that question for their behaviour and the operation of the economy.

For some economists, the purpose of a theory of the firm is to be able to predict price and output responses by firms to specified changes in the environment in which they operate (e.g. changes in sales tax).[1] But the purpose in these three chapters is much broader in seeking to understand the operations of firms and their general significance for the economy and for society. In developed capitalist economies the decisions on investment, employment, etc., taken by a relatively small number of directors of large corporations have a major impact on the prosperity of communities and of countries. The influences on those decisions are then of crucial relevance.

When economists and others think about the behaviour of firms, they adopt (often implicitly) a particular mental construct of the nature of the firm. For example, for some theorists the typical firm may be taken as controlled by a single owner whereas others would see the typical (large) firm as difficult to control, with a large number of owners and managers with varying interests. It will become clear from the discussion below that the way in which the firm is conceptualised has a strong influence on the conclusions which are drawn from any analysis.

It has become conventional in the study of microeconomics to make a distinction between households and firms. A glance at the real world reveals some organisations which can be labelled households and others as firms. But once the question what is the distinction between household and firm? is asked, some difficulties are encountered. It could be said that firms use inputs to produce output of goods and services which are largely for the use of others. But members of a household produce services (e.g. washing-up, house-cleaning), many of which are for the use of other members of the household. Further, households could be seen as using inputs (e.g. food) to produce output (meals, labour services) which are used by others. Finally, note that within a firm, the goods and services produced in one part of the firm may well be used by other parts of the same firm.

The reader may well respond to this discussion by saying something like 'I may not be able to define an elephant but I know an elephant when I see one.' But in the case of firms, it may not be a straightforward matter in the real world to recognise all firms (is a small shop run by members of one family to be seen as a household or a firm?). Further, in this case (as elsewhere in economics) it is not sufficient to be able to recognise a real-world firm when one is seen, but also to know how to go about thinking about a firm. This raises the question of the correspondence between the theoretical construct of a firm and the reality of actual firms. The analogue would be a zoologist defining a theoretical elephant in terms of a number of key features, and then having to discuss whether an animal which has been observed has the crucial properties. These considerations lead to the question of how to conceptualise a firm.[2]

When inputs and outputs are thought about at a general level without distinguishing between different types of inputs (between, say, labour and materials), then it is difficult to say what the difference between households and firms is. Both can be seen as turning inputs into outputs, some of which are sold to others. The objectives of firms and households may be thought to be different. Firms are often seen as run for profits though, as will be seen below, a number of other objectives of the controllers or owners of firms (e.g. growth) have been proposed. Households could be seen as formed for non-profit objectives such as love and affection between the members. But when the objectives of an organisation are expressed in a rather general form such as maximisation of utility, then it is possible to encompass firms and households under the umbrella of the single objective of utility maximisation. There may still be differences in the key variables which enter the utility functions of the typical firm and the typical household, but there is an overall unity in that maximisation of a utility function is taken as the objective of both firms and households.

The division between work and home, between household and firm, which is usual in developed economies, would seem to be largely a product of economic development and industrialisation. In many societies it would not be meaningful to talk of differences between firm and household. However, in the developed capitalist economies with which this book is concerned, the fact that there are differences does lead to the questions of the nature of those differences and why they arise.

Our discussion is limited to economies which are predominantly capitalist, and within such economies we focus on firms which are privately owned. It is debatable how far other types of firms (e.g. publicly owned firms, workers co-operatives) have to conform within a predominantly capitalist economy to the same behaviour as privately owned firms. Where competition is intense, it can be argued that the ownership and objectives of firms are of little import as the pressures of competition force the same type of actions onto all firms. Whilst there may be similarities between the operation of firms under capitalism and the operation of firms under other economic systems, there are sufficient differences to mean that the discussion of capitalist firms cannot be extended in a straightforward manner into a discussion of other firms.

The preceding discussion indicates that it is not an easy matter to define a firm with any precision. The way in which production is organised and the division between production within the home and outside the home clearly differ considerably between societies. The firms which we are analysing below are privately owned ones operating within a capitalist environment. This will mean, *inter alia*, that the firm must pay at least some attention to profits and will generally be involved in competition with other firms.

For the discussion below, three major ways in which firms have been conceptualised in economic analysis are identified. Each of these ways has become associated with a particular approach to economic theory,[3,4] and these three conceptualisations are now discussed in turn.

4.2 FIRM AS A 'BLACK BOX'

The first view is often called the 'black box' view, and is closely associated with neo-classical economics. It is this concept of the firm which lies behind much that is taught about firms (e.g. theories of perfect competition, monopoly, oligopoly). In this approach, the firm is seen rather like a box into which inputs are entered at one end and out of which outputs are produced at the other end. What happens inside the box is of little importance, and attention is placed on the relationship between inputs and outputs (i.e. the production function). In order to complete this view of the firm, it is necessary to assume something about the motivation of the firm, and that is usually taken to be profit maximisation. However, profit is defined as the excess of revenue over opportunity cost of the inputs used (including any capital inputs), and not as a return to the owners of property (cf. section 9.5).

The firm is then viewed as

> a technical unit in which commodities are produced. Its entrepreneur decides how much of and how one or more commodities will be produced, and gains the profit or bears the loss which results from his decision. An entrepreneur transforms inputs into outputs, subject to the technical rules specified by his production function. The difference between his revenue from the sale of outputs, and the costs of his inputs, is his profit if positive, or his loss if negative. (Henderson and Quandt, 1971)

Apart from noting the close relationship between firm and the production function, it can also be noted that it is the entrepreneur rather than the workers who are said to turn inputs into outputs, and workers are (implicitly) included among the inputs.

It can now be seen why it is difficult to distinguish between firm and household in this framework. If utility maximisation were substituted for profit maximisation in the above, an outline of the 'black-box'/neo-classical view of the household would be obtained.

The only distinction between household and firm then comes down to motivation. But even then, it could be said that profit is taken as a convenient proxy for the utility of the owners of the firm.[5] The 'black-box' view of the firm ignores what happens inside the firm, e.g. the relationship between people; similarly, a 'black box' view of the household ignores relationships between members of the household.

An element of opening up the 'black box' of the firm while remaining within the neo-classical tradition arises from the work of Coase (1937) and Williamson (1975, 1985), leading to a view which can be labelled the Coasian or 'transactions cost' view of the firm. Coase drew a contrast between the co-ordination of economic activity within a society through a decentralised price mechanism and co-ordination by central decision-making. He pointed out that, even within an economy based on the price mechanism, within a firm resources are allocated by the decisions of the controllers of the firm. 'If a workman moves from department Y to department X, he does not go because of a change in relative prices, but because he is ordered to do so' (Coase, 1937). It can then be argued that the efficiency of such an economy would depend on not only the allocative efficiency of firms, and the mechanisms by which resources are allocated and used within firms.

This Coasian view of the firm has led to the transactions cost approach. This can be summarised by saying that when a firm requires a particular input (to help produce its output) then it can choose between buying that input from another firm or producing the input itself. There are a variety of advantages and disadvantages for a firm in using the market (i.e. buying from another firm) and in internal production. Market transactions involve a contract (explicit or implicit) between buyer and seller. Williamson (1975) points to three features which pose difficulties for arriving at mutually acceptable contracts between buyer and seller, which tend to favour internal production by a firm over market transactions.[6] These three features are as follows:

1. Bounded rationality, uncertainty and complexity. The view of bounded rationality stresses that there are limits on the human capacity to receive, store and process information. Uncertainty about the economic environment (e.g. about the quality of a product) and its complexity make decision-making difficult. This line of argument indicates that there are limits to the use of the

market – for example, it would not be possible for an individual to know and make use of all relative prices in arriving at a consumption decision.

2. Opportunism linked with small numbers. Williamson (1975) argues that 'internal organisation enjoys advantages ... over market modes of contracting in circumstances where opportunism and small-numbers conditions are joined'. Among these advantages are that disputes between departments within a firm are easier to resolve than disputes between separate firms, and the ability of a firm to conduct audits into the performance of its own divisions but not to conduct audits into the performance of other firms (e.g. its suppliers). Auditing can be used to reduce the use of opportunism (i.e. where one economic agent takes advantage of whatever opportunities arise even at the expense of others) by one department of a firm.

3. Differential availability of information. The producer of a product will often know much more than the purchaser about the product and how it has been made. For example, a car mechanic will know whether a repair has been correctly made when the customer may not be able to judge. In market transactions, this often leaves the purchaser at a relative disadvantage as compared with the producer. However, in the case of internal production (that is where one part of a firm produces an output which becomes an input in another part of the firm) the user/purchaser and producer are part of the same organisation. This may enable the user to have better information about the product and how it is made, etc., than if a similar product had been purchased from another firm.

One implication of this approach is that the size of the firm is seen as determined by essentially technical (cost) considerations. A transaction is undertaken within the firm if it is less costly than if it were undertaken between firms. The expansion of a firm's operations is further seen as efficiency-improving, because it is presumed that such expansion would only be undertaken if the firm's costs are reduced. More generally, the reason for the emergence of large firms is seen as a consequence of efficiency-improving expansion. The 'transactions costs' of using the market tends to lead to firms evolving to reduce those costs by the use of internal production.[7]

4.3 FIRM AS A COMPLEX SOCIAL ORGANISATION

Virtually all production requires the involvement directly or indirectly of more than one person. A painter may work by his or herself but will buy the necessary materials from others and sell services to others. In such a case, the involvement of others may be through market transactions. But the case of people working in isolation is relatively rare, and production usually requires the immediate co-operation of others. In the discussion of the labour process, attention was paid to the nature of social relationships and power arrangements between employers and employees. The interaction of the people involved can lead to considering a firm as a social organisation with a focus on the relations between the people involved. In contrast to seeing the firm as a black box, this approach pays particular attention to the contents of the black box. In other words, the focus of attention is on the internal workings of a firm, rather than its external circumstances.

The conventional way of modelling firm behaviour is to treat the firm as maximising profits subject to constraints in terms of demand, production function and cost of inputs. But when the firm is treated as a social organisation, two questions arises. First, is it possible to talk of the objectives of an organisation? Second, if the answer to the first question is yes, then what are those objectives?. The answers to these questions will then determine whether it makes any sense to continue to model firms as maximising a single well-defined objective.

Individuals may have objectives, but in what sense do organisations have them? One approach would be to take the objectives of an organisation as in some sense the sum of the objectives of the individuals belonging to that organisation. But that approach faces three difficulties. First, there will generally be a variety of objectives pursued by individuals, and it would be necessary to investigate whose objectives are actually pursued within the organisation. This would involve a consideration of the power structure within the organisation.

Second, a single individual may belong to several organisations – working for a firm, member of a household, member of sports clubs, political parties, religious organisations, etc. As a member of a firm, only part of his or her objectives may be satisfied – e.g. desire for income, work satisfaction. The pursuit of other objectives is made through membership of other organisations.

The third difficulty is that even if the individuals within an organisation have 'rational' objectives, it does not follow that the organisation does so when its objectives are taken to reflect those of the individuals which belong to it. 'Rational' here means only that if an individual prefers A to B, and B to C, then the individual would prefer A to C. The difficulty in ascribing rational objectives to organisations can be illustrated as follows. Suppose that an organisation of three people is operated democratically, and that as between three actions A, B and C, the three individuals would rank them in order of preference as follows:

- Individual 1: A, C, B
- Individual 2: C, B, A
- Individual 3: B, A, C

If the three individuals were to vote on the basis of their preferences, they would vote (on the basis of two votes to one in each case) for B over A, for C over B and for A over C. Thus there is no unique order of preferences between A, B and C.[8]

Individuals may join organisations for specific purposes, such as joining a tennis club to play tennis. Thus, the organisation would be said to have the objective of serving that purpose for which individuals join it, and then it may not be too misleading to say that that purpose was the objective of the organisation. But even then there may be disagreement over how that objective is to be met. However, people generally join a firm to secure work, income, etc., though job satisfaction and prestige can also be relevant. Thus it may be difficult to infer from the objectives of the individuals what the objectives of the firm are.

Broadly, the range of responses to the difficulties just posed can be classified into five categories.

1. The usual response is that firms can be analysed *as if* they had a single well-specified objective. This would mean that a firm would be treated as though it had a single controller whose objectives are paramount. Thus a firm would be treated in the same way whether it was a single individual (as would be the case with a single-person firm) or a large organisation with thousands of employees. A number of justifications can be put forward for

this view, and serves to link in with the general positivist methodology (cf. section 1.5). The initial justification would be that at least as a start, theories can be developed based on relatively simple assumptions, even though those assumptions are known in some sense to be unrealistic.[9] Assuming a single objective function is likely to lead to a simpler analysis than assuming multiple objective functions. The theory can then be tested by a comparison of its predictions with the evidence. If the predictions pass on that test, then there is presumed to be no reason to proceed to a more complicated analysis, though this assumes that there are no gains in terms of explanation and insight to be achieved from a more complex analysis.

2. It can be observed that most firms (particularly large ones) are organised on a hierarchical basis with a number of layers of command. There are examples of productive organisations (e.g. workers' co-operatives, communes) which have striven to avoid the use of hierarchies and chains of command. But in capitalist firms (which are the type of firms under consideration here), hierarchy and command is the general rule.

Two responses to the hierarchical nature of capitalist firms can be highlighted. The first response is to counterpoise those in control (capitalists or their representatives) and those who are controlled (the workers). This view was discussed in Chapter 2 under the heading 'Conflict and the labour process'. There is nothing inherently efficient in that form of organisation, but rather it is seen to reflect the existing power structure in the economy and society generally. A non-hierarchical form of organisation (cf. section 2.8 for evidence) may be more efficient. But a move to a non-hierarchical form of organisation would involve capitalists giving up the power which comes from and is reflected in hierarchy. This is reflected by Bowles (1985) when he states that one of the central propositions in the Marxian analysis of capitalist production is that

> capitalists may often implement methods of production which enhance their power over workers rather than those which raise productive efficiency. For this reason, the technologies in use in a capitalist economy, as well as the direction of technical change, cannot be said to be an efficient solution to the problem of scarcity, but rather, at least in part, an expression of class interest. This proposition is fundamental to the Marxian assertion that the

productive potential of a society ... is inhibited ... by the specifically capitalist institutional structure of the economy.

The second rather different response comes from the Austrian approach, and particularly exemplified in the approach of Alchian and Demsetz (1972) which was briefly discussed in Chapter 2. Team production is viewed as more productive than individual production because of, *inter alia*, benefits of the division of labour. However, there is a strong tendency for individual workers to shirk (to use a term which is frequently encountered in that literature). Thus there is a requirement for a 'monitor' to reduce shirking. The Austrian emphasis on property rights serves to make this monitor a 'residual claimant', who thereby benefits financially from any increase in worker effort (which increases the residual of revenue over costs). Within the context of the firm, this comes down to a stress on a small group being both entitled to profits and to be in control of the organisation.[10]

These two views (Austrian and Marxian) may agree that hierarchical control is generally found under capitalism, but they would sharply disagree over the significance of such control. The Austrian view would see hierarchical control as necessary for technical efficiency. In contrast, the Marxian view would see hierarchical control as a part of capitalism, but that under other economic systems there are possibilities for other methods of work organisation. Further, hierarchical control is not seen as technically efficient, for reasons indicated above (section 2.8).

3. Organisations, like people, may be forced to act in a particular way despite wishing to act differently. Organisations may have different objectives but if they all face much the same constraints they may finish acting in rather similar ways. More formally, it can be said that the constraints on an organisation are so tight that it has little or no discretion in what it does if it wishes to survive. The constraints on firms arise from the demand and cost conditions which they face. But of particular importance here are the constraints which arise from the actions of others. The process of competition is seen as particularly important here, and notions of competition are discussed at length in Chapter 5. For the present purposes the argument can be summarised as follows. Both models of perfect competition and the Marxian concept of competition, even though they involve quite different notions of competition, suggest that an individual firm in a competitive

situation has little discretion in what it can do if it wishes to survive. In particular, there are substantial constraints on what profits a firm can gain, so that the firm has to maximise profits in order to survive. Any firm, for whatever reason, which does not maximise profits will disappear.

The stress on competition takes us full circle in that internal considerations are now seen to be of little relevance and the external forces of competition are of key importance. However, it will be seen in Chapter 5 that the question of the importance of competition is far from settled. It should be noted that the internal structure of the firm may well determine which firms survive. But also the extent to which competition bears down on firms may not be absolute. Whilst long-term survival for a single firm which is not profit-maximising may not be possible, short-term survival may be. But as one non-profit maximiser quits the scene, another may appear.

Friedman's defence of profit maximisation is based on the forces of competition (and also the view that the firm can be seen as having a single objective). He argues:

> Unless the behaviour of businessmen in some way or another approximated the behaviour consistent with the maximisation of returns [i.e. profits], it seems unlikely that they would remain in business for long. Let the apparent immediate determinant of business behaviour be anything at all, habitual reaction, random chance or what not. Whenever this determinant happens to lead to behaviour consistent with rational and informed maximisation of returns, the business will prosper and acquire resources with which to expand; whenever it does not, the business will tend to lose resources and can be kept in existence only by the addition of resources from outside. The process of 'natural selection' thus helps to validate the hypothesis, or, rather given 'natural selection', acceptance of the hypothesis can be based largely on the judgement that it summarizes appropriately the conditions for survival. (Friedman, 1953)

There are two elements in this argument to highlight here. First, the amount of profits governs expansion or contraction of the firm, and the process of the decline of firms which do not maximise profits may be a very prolonged one. Further, that process of expansion or contraction would occur to some degree without competition. Second, the reason how the firms have arrived at a profit-maximising outcome can be relevant. Winter

(1964) argues that if the actions of firms which are consistent with profit maximisation are randomly determined (i.e. a firm arrives at a profit-maximising position by luck and good fortune), why should they be expected to persist? If the actions are habitual, then the habit will persist and though such actions just happened to be profit maximising in one situation it is unlikely that they will be so in other situations.

This general line of argument clearly has strong overtones of the process of Darwinian natural selection. However, the arguments applied in economic theory to justify profit maximisation do not

> fairly reflect Darwin's natural selection theory. Firstly, departure from optimal behaviour does not necessarily lead to failure since neoclassical optimality may be unattainable in principle or not pursued in practice. ... Secondly, neoclassical theory tends to draw selectively on the tenets of Darwin's theory emphasising repetition and similarity at the expense of variation and diversity. (Kay, 1984)

4. It could be acknowledged that firms are indeed organisations, and investigate which groups within a firm hold effective power so far as the key decisions are concerned. For example, decisions on production levels, price, investment, etc., would be seen as key ones, whereas the date of the Christmas party would not be. Thus although a large firm employs many people, only a relatively small number will be involved in those key decisions. Even so, the difficulties of deriving well-defined objectives in such cases (the 'voting paradox' referred to above) still arise. If the group of individuals making decisions were cohesive and of like mind then it could be that they have well-defined objectives.

The concept of an owner-controlled firm would picture that group of people as consisting of a single owner, who makes all the key decisions. But when the number of owners is at all substantial, there are questions of whether all the owners have a common interest. Some owners may be heavily involved in the management of the firm whereas others are more like rentiers receiving income from the firm but with no management involvement. There may well be occasions when the interests of different types of owners are different.

One way of proceeding would be to study the internal power structure of firms to find out which groups were in effective control so far as key decisions were concerned. One school of thought which could be seen in this light is the managerial theory of the firm. Starting with Berle and Means (1933), a number of authors have argued that, in most large corporations which dominate capitalist economies, the effective control is in the hands of management rather than owners. From that proposition, the next step is to model the consequences for the crucial decisions of the firm. This involves a discussion of the interests of managers (in particular whether they differ from those of the owners), how those interests can be represented and the impact of those interests on the key decisions. To take one example, Baumol (1959) argued that managers' interests would involve salaries, prestige, etc., which were related to the size of the firm in terms of sales. Thus he proposed to represent the interests of managers by sales maximisation (which is subject to a profit constraint imposed by owners). The pursuit of sales maximisation would lead to higher output, lower price than a comparable profit-maximising firm (for some further discussion, see the next chapter, and for more extensive discussion Sawyer (1990) and for empirical evidence Sawyer (1985a, ch. 12).

5. The ideas that the firm is an organisation containing many interest groups can lead to the view that the behaviour of the firm is to be understood in terms of the objectives of the different interest groups and the resolution of the conflict between those groups. Cyert and March (1963) argue for considering a firm as having several goals and objectives, with different interest groups within the firm placing different relative weights on the objectives. In their approach, they identify five goals: production, inventory/stocks, sales, market share and profits. It is likely that the sales department will be more interested in sales, because their incomes and prestige are linked to the volume of sales. Similarly, owners are presumed to be more interested in profits and profit-related variables such as the share price than in sales or employment.

The relative size and influence of the different interest groups could be expected to vary across companies. For example, in a high-technology company the research and development department may be relatively large and influential, whilst in a consumer goods firm the sales and advertising department may be relatively influential. One key part of this general view is that the

behaviour of firms will depend on its internal organisation and
structure and the relative power of different interest groups and
the objectives of those groups.

It may be that pursuit of the different goals referred to above
would not be in conflict with one another. For example, it is
likely that there is some range of the expansion of output for
which sales and profits both increase. It is only where the goals
are in conflict with one another which would imply conflict
between departments arising from the different objectives which
the departments/interest groups have. The pursuit of one goal
would then be to the detriment of other goals.

Cyert and March (1963) argue that where an organisation has
multiple goals (or perhaps more accurately groups with
conflicting interests), the notion of maximisation has to be
dropped in favour of the notion of *satisficing*. The main idea of
satisficing is that

> the motive to act stems from drives, and action terminates when
> the drive is satisfied. Moreover, the conditions for satisfying a
> drive are not necessarily fixed, but may be specified by an
> aspiration level that itself adjusts upward or downward on the
> basis of experience. (Simon, 1959)

The notion of satisficing can be linked with the idea of
bounded rationality which was briefly mentioned above: indeed
both ideas are closely associated with the work of Simon. In the
presence of a lack of full information and an inability to process
all the available information, an individual does not know what a
maximising outcome would be. Thus, whilst the individual can
judge whether the existing outcome is satisfactory, he or she
cannot know whether it is a maximising one. Gradually, the
individual acquires further information, which may indicate that
an outcome which was judged satisfactory can be improved upon
(that is, in terms of the quote above from Simon, the aspiration
level adjusts). For further discussion see Hodgson (1988,
especially pp. 78–83).

Cyert and March advance the argument that when there are
several interest groups within an organisation, if each group
strives for a satisfactory level of whatever objective they pursue
(e.g. profits, sales), then a reconciliation between the various
groups is possible. But if each interest group strives to reach a
maximum level of their own goal, there is likely to be a conflict

of interest. There could, for example, be a conflict between increasing sales (say by reducing price) and increasing profits, so that if one group sought to maximise sales and another to maximise profits, then one group's interests could only be pursued at the expense of those of the other group.

Galbraith (1967) argues that

> in the accepted view of the corporation [as typically controlled by its management], profit maximisation involves a substantial contradiction. Those in charge forgo personal reward to enhance it for others. ... The technostructure [managers], as a matter of necessity, bans personal profit-making ... management does not go out ruthlessly to reward itself – a sound management is expected to exercise restraint.

Another important aspect of the view that firms are social organisations is to consider the 'rules' under which the firms operate. These rules would include the legal framework, which serves, *inter alia*, to condition the relationships between a firm and its employees and its customers. The legal structure and social customs would strongly influence the nature of the relationship between managers and workers, and the obvious example would be that the dismissal of a worker is governed by employment law and by custom and practice.

4.4 FIRMS AS 'BLOCS OF CAPITAL'

In this section, we return to the basic Marxian view of the firm as being a capitalist firm, and explore what exactly is meant by that term. There are two aspects – the nature of the firm itself and the environment within which it operates. The firm is a capitalist one if it is owned by private individuals. Thus ownership by the State (e.g. nationalised industries), by the workers (workers' co-operatives) or by consumers (e.g. retail co-operatives, mutual societies) are not included. These other forms of ownership are likely to mean that the objectives of the firms are different and that the drive for profits will be much reduced. But these non-capitalist firms may operate in a largely capitalist environment, and as such their behaviour, objectives, etc., will be heavily conditioned by that environment. Thus, the non-capitalist firms may be forced to behave in ways similar to that of capitalist firms.

The second aspect is the environment within which the firm operates. This environment is one in which profits are required for survival and for growth and where there is competition (actual or potential) between firms. This competition is not of the perfect competitive type, but rather involves rivalry between firms in the pursuit of profits and market shares.[11] An economy in which some privately owned firms received cash transfers from the State or one in which competition between independent firms had been suspended (e.g. in a Fascist state) would require a different analysis.

It is the unco-ordinated nature of the relationship between firms which is significant. As each firm pursues profitability, it is drawn into conflict with other firms that are also pursuing their own profits. In some phases of capitalism, this conflict of interest leads to intense competition between the firms. Each firm is forced to compete if it is to survive. The consequences of this competition (and its nature) are explored in the next chapter. But in other phases of capitalism, the conflict of interest may be met by the firms agreeing not to compete (collusion, formation of cartels) or through merger, thereby reducing the number of independent firms (which would also make successful collusion easier to effect). This unco-ordinated nature of capitalism also means that there are fluctuations in economic activity and periodic crises, which will be examined in later chapters. For capitalist enterprises, there is the ever-present possibility of rivalry; even during periods of agreement between firms there is uncertainty as to whether competition will break out.

A capitalist firm is a firm in which capital hires labour and not, as in a workers' co-operative, where labour hires capital. In a Marxian approach, there are two important features arising from that. First, labour is in a weak position since it has to work and is forced to work for capitalists in general though not for a specific capitalist. This unequal position between labour and capital, and particularly that capital commands labour within the production process, is a key element of the analysis of the labour process in Chapter 2. The 'organization of production in the capitalist firm must reflect essential elements of class struggle' (Gintis, 1976), for the firm is one of the arenas in which the struggle between labour and capital takes place. Second, the capitalist class have a monopoly of access to finance capital. This access includes their own finance and an ability to borrow from others. In effect, this means that labour is denied access to finance capital and thus excludes the self-employment option for labour.

Treating a firm as a bloc of capital serves to indicate that the expansion of a firm requires finance capital as a prerequisite. That finance may come from retained profits or from borrowing, but without it expansion is not possible. It is, of course, also necessary for the firm to hire more people and purchase more material inputs. But it is the finance which is vital for hiring labour, and purchasing material inputs is not possible without the finance. The firm may be able to obtain the finance for expansion from its own profits, which would mean that the more profitable firms would have more scope for expansion. The alternative for the firm is to borrow the required finance, which is likely to be more readily available to the more profitable firms. Thus there is likely to be a strong element of success breeding success. The discussion of investment expenditure (section 12.3) will elaborate on the relevance of profits for the expansion of firms. In Chapter 13, there is a discussion of cumulative causation, where a variety of ways by which success breeds success will be considered.

The central purposes of a capitalist firm are then seen to be the generation of surplus and of capital accumulation. 'Accumulation where capital is privately owned involves competition. Capital accumulation is therefore not the *consequence* of competition, competition is the consequence of capital accumulation when capital operates as distinct blocs in a system of private ownership' (Aaronovitch, 1977). It could be said that the pursuit of profits brings firms into conflict with one another. But the competition between firms forces them to pursue profits more ruthlessly to be able to compete successfully. In that way, the pursuit of profits and competition tends to reinforce one another. However, competition tends to undermine profits, and when that is so, firms put profits first and seek ways of reducing the intensity of competition through collusion, merger, etc.

4.5 CONCLUDING REMARKS

The way in which a firm is conceptualised has a strong influence on theorising about the firm. In the next two chapters, we will concentrate on theories which treat the firm as either a complex social organisation or a bloc of capital (and to some extent, as for example in the theory of Baran and Sweezy, combining the two elements). Adopting these concepts of the firm also means that the purpose of theorising about firm (and firm behaviour) is wider than merely seeking to predict price and quantity changes. Indeed, at a general level, the views that will be adopted on the nature and operation of firms and of the role of competition and the market will strongly influence the view on the desirability or otherwise of the operation of capitalist economies.

NOTES

1. For example, 'Let us ... pose four typical questions and see which of them we might expect to answer with the aid of 'price theory'. (1) What will be the prices of cotton and textiles. (2) What prices will the X corporation charge. (3) How will the prices of cotton textiles be affected by an increase in wage rates. (4) How will the X corporation change its prices when wage rates are increased.
   Conventional price theory is not equipped to answer any but the third question; it may perhaps also suggest a rebuttable answer to the fourth question. But questions 1 and 2 are out of reach.' (Machlup, 1967).
2. 'The model of the firm in that theory [perfect competition] is not ... designed to serve to explain and predict the behaviour of real firms; instead, it is designed to explain and predict changes in prices ... as effects of particular changes in conditions. ... In this causal connection the firm is only a *theoretical link*, a mental construct helping to explain how one gets from the cause to the effect' (Machlup, 1967; italics added). Further, he argued that 'to confuse the firm as a theoretical construct with the firm as an empirical concept, that is, to confuse a *heuristic fiction* with a real organisation like General Motors or Atlantic and Pacific is to commit the "fallacy of misplaced concreteness". This fallacy consists in using theoretic symbols as though they had a direct, observable, concrete meaning.' (italics added)
3. However, whilst the 'black box' view has become associated with the neo-classical approach, two caveats should be entered. First, some essentially neo-classical attempts have been made to investigate the internal structure of firms, e.g. Williamson (1986). Second, the theories of authors such as Kalecki (see Chapter 9) concerning the mark-up of price over costs have not said anything about the internal structure of firms.
4. Bowles (1985) provides an alternative three-way classification of

approaches to the firm, which he labels Walrasian, neo-Hobbesian and Marxian. The Walrasian model corresponds to the 'black box' view discussed in the text, and the Marxian model to the 'blocs of capital' view. The neo-Hobbesian view can be seen as reflected in the approach of Alchian and Demsetz (1972) which is briefly discussed in the text.

5. The model of Scitovsky (1943) is explicitly based on utility maximisation by the owner/ controller.

6. For a discussion see Sawyer (1985a, pp. 198–205), Sawyer (1990), Williamson (1975, 1981).

7. For a critical discussion of the transactions cost approach see Francis *et al.* (1983), Dugger (1983).

8. The argument which has been advanced here in the context of decision-making within an organisation is the same argument advanced by Arrow (1951) concerning the 'impossibility' of deriving a democratic social welfare function; this is often labelled the 'voting paradox'.

9. In this case, it could be argued that it is not so much an unrealistic assumption which is being made, but rather it is being assumed that the internal organisation of a firm does not matter. This would arise if the external pressures on firms were in some meaningful sense much stronger than internal forces. If that were so, then it would only be necessary to look at external forces.

10. For a critique of this approach see Bowles (1985), who labels such an approach as neo-Hobbesian.

11. Many have remarked along with Samuelson (1957) that 'in the competitive model it makes no difference whether capital hires labor or the other way round'. That is so only under a model of perfect competition, but not under Marxian competition. Indeed, Marxian competition, based on the pursuit of profits, is specific to capitalist firms in which capital hires labour. Further, the relationships within the firm (as analysed under the heading of the labour process) crucially involve the power of capital over labour derived, *inter alia*, from, the hiring of labour by capital.

Chapter 5
COMPETITION AND RIVALRY

5.1 INTRODUCTION

All of the different approaches to economics take some view on the nature and degree of competition in capitalist economies. A major purpose of this chapter is to review the different views which have been adopted, particularly within the radical political economy tradition. The ways in which independent firms interact with one another, e.g. whether they compete or whether they collude, have important implications for the nature and evolution of a capitalist econonmy. Thus, the aim is to draw out of the discussion of competition the different views concerning the operations of a capitalist economy.

The term 'competition' is widely used in economic analysis as well as in everyday speech. But several meanings can be attached to the term. This chapter begins with a review of the different meanings which can be given to the word 'competition'. This is followed by a discussion of the Marxian concept of competition, leading to the idea that atomistic competition carries within it the seeds of its own (structural) destruction in that the number of firms tends to decline as a result of the competitive process. Industrialised capitalist economies were seen to be competitive in the nineteenth century, but there have been substantial changes since then, which raises the question as to whether developed capitalist economies can still be characterised as competitive. To some degree, the answer to that question depends on the definition given to competition. In the latter sections of this chapter, theories which go under the heading *monopoly capitalism* are discussed, and then the answers which have been given to be the question of whether capitalist economies should be characterised as competitive are reviewed.

Capitalist economies generally involve some degree of competition between independent firms.[1] How that competition and its consequences for the economy are regarded will have a considerable influence on more general views on the desirability of capitalism and the competitive process. The way in which competition is seen by economists is likely to have a large effect on the conclusions drawn on the operation and desirability of capitalism.

5.2 THE MEANING OF COMPETITION

There are a number of different uses of the term competition. For each definition used, there is a corresponding concept of competition, and of its implications. It is not surprising that the different concepts of competition lead to different conclusions on the consequences of competition. For the discussion below, it is useful to categorise definitions of competition in four ways.

The first definition of competition refers to the concept of perfect competition. An industry is said to be perfectly competitive if there are a large number of small firms producing a homogeneous product with no restrictions on entry into or exit from the industry. In the short run, profit maximisation means that firms are equating price with marginal cost, whilst free entry and exit in the longer term mean that price is equal to average cost. The long-run equality of average and marginal costs also implies that firms operate at the point of minimum average costs. The equilibrium outcome of perfect competition has the property of being Pareto optimal (under assumptions on the absence of economies of scale and of externalities).[2] Thus, under the Pareto criteria, perfectly competitive equilibrium has certain desirable properties.

The contrast is often drawn between perfect competition and monopoly, under which there is a single firm and entry into the industry is effectively blockaded. Under monopoly, price is above marginal cost, and there are super-normal profits in the long term. Price is predicted to be higher and output lower under monopoly than under a comparable situation of perfect competition, and it is argued that there are welfare losses involved with monopoly as compared with perfect competition.[3]

Within the framework which views perfect competition and monopoly as the polar extremes for industrial structure, one industry A would be said to be more competitive than another industry B if industry A was a closer approximation to the model of perfect competition than industry B. The actual measurement of the degree of the closeness or otherwise of an industry to the model of perfect competition is not without its problems.[4]

For the present purposes, it is sufficient to say that regard could be paid to the number of firms, the degree of size inequality of firms and the conditions of entry. The key point here is that the degree of competition in an industry is judged relative to the model of perfect competition.

The teaching of elementary theories of the firm makes much use of the dichotomy of perfect competition and monopoly. But more generally, much work within industrial economics uses the structure–conduct–performance paradigm.[5] Under this paradigm, an industry can be viewed in terms of its structure (number of firms, conditions of entry, etc.) as lying somewhere between perfect competition and monopoly. Then the performance of that industry (for example, profitability, advertising) would lie between that of perfect competition and monopoly in a corresponding manner.

There are two elements of this approach to which attention should be drawn. First, competition is viewed in a structural sense, i.e. in terms of the structure of the industry, by which is meant number of firms, entry conditions, etc. The behaviour and performance of the firms themselves are not seen as directly relevant to the issue, although it is expected that the structure of the industry will influence its performance.

Second, under perfect competition each firm is a price-taker, and the decisions of one firm are seen to have a negligible impact on the industry as a whole and on each firm in particular. Thus each firm operates in a vacuum in that its actions do not impinge on other firms. There is then no reason why a single firm should see itself as being in active competition with others. If one firm improves its position (say by reducing its costs) then in the theory of perfect competition that does not have any measurable effect on other firms who are only concerned with the prices which they face.

The notion of competition involved with perfect competition is seen to relate to the structure of the industry. More firms are taken to indicate more competition and less monopoly. This structural notion of competition can be contrasted with the everyday notion of competition which is a process of striving to outdo others. The perfect competition concept does not involve any rivalry or competing against others, and indeed in equilibrium all firms are in harmony.

The second concept of competition is the classical/Marxian one.[6] This concept involves two aspects. The first is that each firm is seeking to secure as much profits as possible. Since there are limits on the total amount of profits to be shared out among firms, firms are inevitably brought into conflict with one another. Hence the pursuit of profits will be seen to generally involve rivalry. However, collusion between firms can bring higher profits than would be possible under competition (for at worst firms can do at least as well in total profit terms by colluding). Profit seeking is more fundamental than rivalry in the sense it is the former which generates the latter, rather than the reverse. There will, then, be tendencies to suspend or remove rivalry in the interests of higher profits. Second, the pursuit of profits leads firms to seek out opportunities to increase profits by moving into areas of high profitability. The term 'areas' includes the production of different products as well as geographical regions and countries. This movement of firms in the pursuit of profits would tend to reduce the rate of profits in those areas into which firms are moving. This movement could still be worthwhile for the firms since the new areas still yield a higher rate of profit than would expansion in their old areas of operation. Conversely, firms would be moving out of low-profit areas, causing the rate of profit to rise there.

Firms have both profits and depreciation allowances from which investment can be financed. They may also be able to borrow funds from banks and the finance capital markets, etc. The ability to borrow often depends on the existing rate of profits and ownership of capital. The firms are looking for areas of the economy in which to use those funds to maximum advantage. At the same time, the firms are able to gradually relocate their activities, moving out of low-profit areas and into high-profit ones.

This relocation of activities can be said to involve the movement of capital out of areas of low profitability into areas of high profitability. It is a movement of capital in the sense that as capital equipment wears out in the areas of low profitability it is not replaced, and new capital equipment is brought into use in areas of relatively high profitability. Further, the money capital advanced by capitalists gradually moves out of low-profitability areas into high-profitability ones. This movement creates a tendency for the rate of profit to be equalised across sectors. Such a tendency is seen as the result of the combination of the drive by capitalists to raise profits in the context of competition and rivalry between firms.

How should the situation in which the rate of profit has been equalised across sectors be regarded? It could be regarded as a situation which closely approximates reality, and hence is useful for an analysis of the real world. For this argument, bear in mind that the equalisation of the rate of profit comes about through movement of capital from low-profit areas into high-profit ones. The position arising from equalisation of the rate of profit could be seen one towards which the economy gradually moves, and hence represents the long-run equilibrium of the economy. However, that equilibrium may never be reached. Before the tendency for the equalisation of the rate of profit has worked itself out, the economy may have changed. The structure of demand, the available technology and products, etc., may have evolved. Corresponding to these new conditions, there will be a different position with an equalised rate of profit.

The analysis of positions arising from an equalised rate of profit can be undertaken, as indeed it is within Sraffian economics which is discussed in Chapter 8. The position of an equalised rate of profit is seen as one which could only arise in the long term. But the prices derived for such a long-run position can be seen as underlying prices towards which actual prices move. It is also the case that an assumption such as an equalised rate of profit simplifies the analysis considerably (as compared with, say, a range of rates of profit), and the gains from simplicity in terms of insights may be substantial.

Whilst there may be some underlying tendency towards equalisation of the rate of profit, as indicated above, the position in which the rate of profit would be equalised is continually changing. One way in which this could arise is the following. The invention of a new product often creates a monopoly position for the firm introducing that product. This gives rise to a high profit area. Gradually, other firms move into production of that new product or to develop close substitutes. These moves would tend to reduce the rate of profit on the previously new product which is now ageing. In a dynamic economy (which capitalism is generally seen as being), the development of new products is continually taking place. Thus the rate of profit may be declining in some parts of the economy (in this example those producing an ageing product), but high rates of profit will be arising in other parts of the economy (where new products are being developed). Hence, the equalisation of the rate of profit may then be an outcome which is never reached. For although there are forces at work in that direction, there are other forces offsetting them.

The notion of competition here is closely linked with the mobility of capital from areas of low profitability into areas of high profitability. The outcome of competition is then a tendency towards the equalisation of the rate of profit. But there are limits on the mobility of capital, for it is not a simple matter to transform the capital equipment suitable for one industry into equipment suitable for another. The process will take time, and is likely to be affected through the depreciation of capital equipment in low-profit industries, which is not directly replaced. The depreciation funds and profits are used to purchase new capital equipment for use in high-profit industries.

There would appear to be some common features between the neo-classical and the Marxian/classical concepts of competition in that from both of them a long-run equilibrium position in which the rate of profit is equalised across sectors can be derived. But there are some sharp differences. It can be seen from the above that the neo-classical notion involves price-taking behaviour by small firms. The equilibrating mechanism is partly through price changes and partly through entry and exit of firms. In contrast, the classical notion says nothing about the size of firms nor whether they are price-takers, and indeed would generally view firms as price-makers. The crucial element is the mobility of capital seeking out profits, and the consequent movement of capital from low- to high-profit areas of activity.

The third concept of competition corresponds to the everyday usage of the term to imply rivalry and competition of one against another. This has some common elements with the previous classical concept. The rivalry between firms can be (for reasons indicated above) an ever-present possibility between independent firms in the pursuit of profits. But although rivalry is a possibility, it may be in effect suspended at times. There will be times when one firm sees an advantage in actively competing with other firms. When one firm feels itself in a relatively strong position (because it has lower costs than its rivals or a better product), it may be worth while for that firm to use its stronger position to lower prices to expand its market share and profits, i.e. that firm competes more forcibly. But equally there can be periods of time when collusion (tacit or explicit) may appear to be more profitable.

Two opposing forces are at work. On the one hand, collusion between firms will usually enable them to earn higher profits than without collusion. Competition is generally destructive of profits for firms in general even if some particular firms benefit. It is the prospect of profits which is seen to motivate a firm to take a particular course of action, but the result of many firms adopting such a course of action is that the prospective profits do not appear.

> The system of free competition is a rather peculiar one. Its mechanism is one of *fooling* entrepreneurs. It requires the pursuit of maximum profit in order to function, but it destroys profits when they are actually pursued by a large number of people. (Lange, 1937)

On the other hand, firms may be suspicious of one another, and each firm may find it attractive to 'cheat' on any agreement. Each firm is likely to find it profitable (in the immediate term) to produce a little more output than agreed or to charge a lower price than that agreed.

The structure–conduct–performance approach views industries as lying along the spectrum running from perfect competition through to monopoly (cf. note 5). This has often been interpreted as indicating that the degree of competition in an industry is (positively) related to the number of firms in the industry. However, it says nothing about the intensity of rivalry between the firms involved, and the degree of rivalry may not be closely related to the structure of an industry. It is often observed that an industry with two major firms may involve intense rivalry between the firms, although on a structural basis such an industry would be classified as a duopoly, and hence towards the monopoly end of the spectrum. Thus the structural concept of competition (which corresponds to the perfect competitive view) stands in contrast with rivalry and with competition as an ongoing process.

The fourth concept of competition is that derived from the Austrian tradition. It shares some common themes with the second and third concepts in viewing competition as a process, rather than a state (as would be the case under perfect competition). Indeed, it could be argued that the equilibrium position under perfect competition occurs when the process of competition has exhausted itself. But the Austrian approach (as well as the Marxian) would not envisage the process of competition as reaching some final state of equilibrium. The driving force in the Austrian view is the entrepreneur, who is anyone who can spot opportunities for profit and who then takes the initiative to seize those opportunities. For example, a person who sees a consumer requirement for a new product and then organises its production would be regarded as an entrepreneur. The analysis of perfect competition focuses on the disappearance of economic profit (that is, the excess of revenue over opportunity costs). In contrast, the Austrian approach would see the existence of economic profit as necessary to spur entrepreneurs into action.

There are two important distinctions between the Austrian approach and the classical/Marxian one. The first is that in the Austrian approach, profit is a reward for entrepreneurship, for spotting and acting on opportunities, whereas in the Marxian approach profit is derived from exploitation (see section 9.5 below). The second is that the Austrian approach has a rather favourable attitude towards competition, viewing it as the source of economic progress. The Marxian approach would view competition as a necessary part of capitalism (at least in its competitive capitalism stage) which brings change, some of which may be considered desirable but some may cause considerable distress.

5.3 CLASSICAL/MARXIAN COMPETITION FURTHER EXPLORED

The classical/Marxian concept of competition has so far been seen as involving mobility of capital and a tendency towards the equalisation of the rate of profit. In this section, the discussion of competition and firm behaviour is broadened.

Capitalism involves competition both in terms of firms competing with each other for profits and of the mobility of capital in the pursuit of profits. But it is monopolistic in that only the capitalist class has access to finance capital, as briefly discussed in the previous chapter. Further, there are ways in which competition breeds a tendency towards a reduction in the number of firms, which would be a move towards monopoly in a structural sense.

In the structure–conduct–performance approach (as summarised above) competition and monopoly are polar opposites in that more of one necessarily means less of the other. But with the classical/Marxian concept, monopoly (in the sense of fewer firms) is seen as the outcome of competition. A key question (which is addressed below) is whether under the structural conditions of oligopoly and monopoly, there is still competition. This competition may mean the tendency towards equalisation of the rate of profits and/or that even with few firms intense rivalry remains (or may be greater than with many firms).

Under a regime of competition, there are intense pressures bearing down on any individual firm so that there is little discretion available for the firm in what they decide to do. The process of competition is a coercive one which ensures that firms conform, for otherwise they lose profits and do not survive.

> No capitalist voluntarily applies a new method of production, no matter how much more productive it may be or how much it might raise the rate of surplus-value, if it reduces the rate of profit. But every new method of production of this kind makes commodities cheaper. At first, therefore, he can sell them above their price of production, perhaps above their value. ... His production procedure is ahead of the social average. But competition makes the new procedure universal and subjects it to the general law. A fall in the profit rate then ensues – firstly perhaps in this sphere of production, and subsequently equalized with the others – a fall that is completely independent of the capitalists' will. (Marx, 1981)

Further,

> but what appears in the miser as the mania of an individual is in the capitalist the effect of a social mechanism in which he is merely a cog. Moreover, the development of capitalist production makes it necessary constantly to increase the amount of capital laid out in a given industrial undertaking, and competition subordinates every individual capitalist to the immanent laws of capitalist production, as external and coercive laws. It compels him to keep extending his capital, so as to preserve it, and he can only extend it by means of progressive accumulation. (Marx, 1976)

What form do these pressures take? The technological background against which firms operate is important here. Economies of scale would mean larger firms having lower unit costs than small firms. Hence if production takes place subject to economies of scale, there will be an incentive for firms to become large. Further, the form which technical change takes is relevant. When technical change is leading to cost reduction, then firms have an incentive to introduce new techniques which require new types of machinery.

The existence of economies of scale and of cost-reducing technical change places pressures on any single firm to invest. The investment may be the purchase of a greater scale of capital equipment to gain economies of scale or the purchase of new equipment incorporating more advanced techniques of production. In either case, the intention would be for the firm to be able to produce at lower unit costs. The possibility of lower costs is not only an incentive but contributes to the pressures on a firm, as other firms are themselves taking advantage of lower costs. As a consequence, some combination of lower prices and higher profits take place. In either case, the individual firm will be at a disadvantage if it does not keep up with the lower costs. Lower prices elsewhere will take demand away from the firm, whilst higher profits elsewhere will enable other firms to expand at that firm's expense.

Under a system of perfect competition, there are pressures on any single firm of the form that a firm can only gain normal profits and therefore must operate with minimum costs. In the neo-classical framework, operation with minimum (opportunity) cost is equated with technical efficiency. In the classical/Marxian conception of competition, the pressures bearing down on firms are pushing them to expand production and to introduce new techniques of production. Further, whilst there are pressures on firms to reduce costs, this will involve not only new investment but pressures to make workers work more intensively, and lowest costs and technical efficiency cannot then be equated (cf. section 2.3 above).

These pressures on the firm lead to investment by the firm to secure more and newer equipment in the pursuit of lower unit costs. Investment is largely financed by the profits of the firm. This takes a particular view of the finance capital market, namely that internal finance is less costly than external finance, with internal finance arising from profits, and further that the amount of external finance depends on profits. This is further elaborated in the next chapter.

The thrust of this argument is that a firm will plough back as high a proportion of its profits as possible (i.e. after allowing for the consumption expenditure of owners). This can be summarised by saying that the ratio of savings out of profits to profits will be relatively high. Indeed, as a first approximation, it is quite often assumed that all of profits are saved so that the savings ratio out of profits is unity. In Chapter 9, the income distributional consequences of this view are explored. It will be seen there that the view that savings propensity out of profits is high and that out of wages is low (or zero) is often described as the classical savings function. Marx summarised this general approach in the following way: 'Accumulate, accumulate! That is Moses and the prophets! ... Therefore save, save, i.e. reconvert the greatest possible portion of surplus-value or surplus product into capital. Accumulation for the sake of accumulation, production for the sake of production' (Marx, 1976).

There are pressures on each firm to expand and innovate. In turn, the response of each firm to those pressures helps to create pressures on other firms. Each firm strives to become larger in order to exploit the available economies of scale. In any event, profits are accruing to firms, who would be looking for investment opportunities. Both of these arguments suggest that firms will tend to become larger in absolute size. But if most or all firms are striving to exploit economies of scale, it is clearly not possible for all of them to grow relative to the total market. The striving of each firm to grow and increase profits brings them into conflict with one another. Some of the firms will be more efficient, more profitable and luckier than others and those firms will grow whilst the less profitable will decline. The process of competition then leads to an increased disparity of size of firms. The profitable and successful continue to grow whilst the unsuccessful decline. The level of concentration tends to rise, leading to structural oligopoly, and many firms disappear under the pressures of competition.

In the work of Marx, a distinction is drawn between the process of concentration and that of centralisation. The former is the absolute increase of firm size arising from accumulation in the way which we have described above. This process of concentration arises from the internal growth of firms, where firms are growing through the creation of new resources (largely investment). The latter process of centralisation arises through the fusion of previously independent firms, which would usually be described as merger and acquisition. It can alternatively be described as external growth, for the surviving firm which acquires another grows but does not create any new resources in the process.

The processes of concentration and centralisation both involve the disappearance of firms. In the case of centralisation, this arises when firms are acquired and disappear. In the case of concentration, the successful firms grow relatively but the unsuccessful decline and some of them fail and go out of business.

Although there are likely to be some similar forces at work for both concentration and centralisation, it is useful to distinguish between them and to some degree focus on the different forces at work. The process of concentration arises largely through the internal accumulation by firms, and does not necessarily involve the finance capital market. However, the process of centralisation involves either the purchase of one company by another or the fusion of two or more companies to form a new company. The nature of the financial system can make mergers and acquisitions more or less difficult. For example, banks and financial institutions may find it profitable to promote the acquisitions and initiate the process of encouraging one firm to take over another.

There are a number of forces involved in the process of concentration, and the effect of economies of scale has already been discussed. At any particular time, firms will vary in terms of age, size, costs and profitability. There are seen to be cumulative forces at work by which the successful prosper further and the unsuccessful decline. The cumulative force begins with firms with lower costs and higher profits. Those firms can to some degree undercut their rivals by charging lower prices. Further, the higher profits provide a large pool of funds from which future expansion can be financed. The expansion leads to lower costs through the exploitation of economies of scale and introduction of new lower-cost techniques of production.

The drive for increased profits and the search for profitable areas in which to invest profits leads to an expansion of firms. But it will also lead to the capitalist sphere of production being expanded. In the early days of capitalism it was largely confined to a few countries, and within those countries to a few industries. The pursuit of profits and the availability of past profits pushes firms to expand their operations. This drive for expansion would bring firms into conflict with one another, and also the overall expansion would be limited by the availability of markets for the goods and services produced. However, the pursuit of profits also leads capitalist firms to expand into areas which were previously non-capitalist. For the capitalist firms, this has twin benefits. First, areas which had previously not operated under the capitalist mode of production are likely to be highly profitable ones. Traditional techniques of production can be replaced by modern capital-intensive techniques which yield lower costs. There are substantial, perhaps revolutionary, changes in the techniques of production as traditional methods of production are replaced. Second, the non-capitalist areas help to provide a market for goods and services. When producers find difficulty in selling their output in the capitalist countries, they are likely to seek to sell into non-capitalist ones. The search for markets by capitalist firms then is another force leading to the expansion of capitalism.

Firms are continually seeking to expand profits, and in order to do so have to use existing profits to build up the capacity to produce more and to find new markets for their production. The re-investment of profits generates expansion of firms in general and hence of the economic system. Indeed, if there were not expansion and new investment, then there would not be any requirement for profits with which to finance that investment. It will be seen below (section 9.3) that the absence of growth implies the absence of profits. Thus the capitalist system both generates growth and relies on growth for its continuation. Some of the expansion of a firm can come at the expense of other firms. But much expansion of capitalist firms comes from moving into areas which were previously the preserve of non-capitalist modes of production; this is a point to which we return below (section 13.5).

5.4 MONOPOLY CAPITALISM[7]

The line of argument above suggested that the competition and rivalry between firms would lead through the processes of centralisation and concentration to fewer and larger firms. This would be accompanied by the expansion of capitalist firms into areas of non-capitalist production, which involves the capitalist production of goods and services previously undertaken by non-capitalist methods and into geographical areas previously outside the capitalist domain. There is little doubt that, within any developed national economy, the tendency towards fewer and larger firms has been present over the past century.[8] Further, there has been a geographical expansion of capitalism over the past century (though this has been limited by the exclusion of capitalism from the socialist third of the world). Related to both of these features there has been the growth of multinational enterprises.[9] These broad developments vindicate the thrust of the analysis of competition undertaken by Marx, which foresaw the emergence of the domination of the economy by large firms as a result of competition. At least in a structural sense, atomistic competition carries in it the seeds of its own destruction, as atomistic competition is replaced by the structure of oligopoly. This stands in contrast to the neo-classical analysis of perfect competition which does not contain any suggestions that perfect competition will break down and monopolistic competition and oligopoly will develop. In this section, terms such as 'becoming more concentrated' are used to describe this tendency where the number of firms tends to decline and the inequality of size of firm tends to increase whether it comes about, in Marx's terminology, through the processes of concentration or of centralisation.[10]

Although the increased concentration of industry (considered over a span of the last century or so) is not in doubt, its significance is. This section considers those theories (often given the label of theories of monopoly capitalism) which argue that concentrated industries behave differently from atomistic industries. This can range from behaviour which is monopolistic in terms of output restriction and higher prices through to less pressure on firms to invest, which has macroeconomic consequences. In the following section, the view which argues that competition in the sense of rivalry and mobility of capital persists despite (or perhaps because of) higher levels of concentration is considered. Further, the arena of competition has moved from the local area to the regional and national level and now operates for many products at the international level.

The discussion of monopoly capitalism focuses on the decline of atomistic competition and its economic consequences. There is not a single theory of monopoly capitalism, but rather a number of contributions which share a number of common features (and also have differences). In this section, the focus is on the common features without ascribing them to particular authors.

The idea of monopoly capitalism begins from the observation that in developed capitalist economies there are high levels of industrial concentration. However, whilst the theories of monopoly capitalism have generally been developed by people within the Marxist tradition, there are others within that same tradition who strongly disagree with such theories.[11] At a simple level, a central question can be posed as follows. When the economy has moved from an industrial one with a large number of mainly small firms to one where many industries are dominated by a few firms, what are the consequences for the behaviour of firms? In particular, will the domination of industries by a few firms mean that competition and rivalry will be replaced by forms of collusion and understandings between firms designed to reduce rivalry?

Theories of monopoly capitalism are based on the view that there is a general tendency for industrial concentration to increase, at least from low levels up to relatively high levels of concentration. There may be periods of history when concentration does not change much but there will be others when it does increase. But it is not expected that overall concentration would generally decline substantially. The emphasis is on general decline, for there are likely to be industries where concentration does decrease. A notable example of this would be the establishment of a new industry by a single firm introducing a new product and hence establishing a monopoly, followed by other firms entering the industry. But even here it could be expected that the initial decline in concentration would be followed by a rise as some firms succeed and others fail in this new industry. In addition to the reasons given above, a further reason for rising concentration is that firms can gain market power and increased profits through larger size and market shares. Thus firms will have strong incentive to acquire other firms in order to reduce competition and to gain market power.

The high levels of concentration are seen by monopoly capital theorists to lead to elements of monopolistic behaviour. At this point, the theories of monopoly capitalism have some common elements with conventional industrial economics. There are a number of reasons for thinking that prices (relative to costs) would be higher in more concentrated industries (and this is apparent in the formal model of Cowling, 1982, discussed below). It would be easier for firms to agree over prices and to monitor any implicit or explicit agreement when there are a smaller number of firms involved. In an industry with a large number of small firms, the impact of one firm's actions on another will generally be small; but with a small number of firms the impact would be noticeable. Thus, when the number of firms is small, each firm is likely to take into account the impact which its actions have on others and their response. In this way, at least implicit collusion develops. Firms would come to realise that they have some interests in common, and also learn how their rivals react.

When a few firms dominate an industry and extract high profits, other firms would be presumed to be looking to enter that industry. The long-term security of high profits would then depend on effective barriers to entry into the industry. The greater are the current profits, the greater will be the incentive for the existing firms to build barriers to entry. These barriers may take the form of advertising, ownership of suppliers and purchasers, ownership of key patents, etc.

A further aspect is the effect of oligopoly and monopoly on the pace of technological advance. It was seen in the discussion of classical/Marxian competition that the pressure of competition pushed firms into using new lower-cost technology. If the competitive pressures are reduced, then it would follow that the pressures on firms to innovate (whether to reduce costs or to introduce new products) would be reduced. As a consequence, it would be expected that the pace of technical change will be lower under monopoly capitalism than under competitive capitalism, and the rate of investment would also be reduced. Cowling (1982), drawing on the work of Mandel (1968), argues that 'in attempting to secure their monopoly positions, firms will invest in, say, R & D but having done so, they will simply put the invention on the shelf', which may be optimal behaviour for the firms involved though slowing down the rate of technical advance in the economy. 'All this suggests that protective R & D is probably a widespread and protective component of planned excess capacity aimed at maintaining and enhancing positions of monopoly power.'

When there is a tendency for concentration to rise, and when higher levels of concentration lead to higher levels of profits, then it follows that there will be a tendency for profits to rise. It has also been argued above that there would be a reduced incentive for technological change and investment. The rise in profits would tend to lead to a rise in the propensity to save whilst investment expenditure tends to fall. Keynesian considerations would indicate that a high propensity to save and a low tendency to invest would lead to low levels of capacity utilisation, output and employment. This indicates the strong element within the theories of monopoly capitalism which suggests stagnation. A formal model which incorporates some of these ideas is presented and discussed in Chapter 11.

Firms earn an excess of revenue over costs, but the controllers of the firm have to make decisions of the uses of that excess. A (possibly substantial) part will be reported as profits, with some paid out as dividends to shareholders and some reported as retained profits used to finance investment. But other parts of profits may be used to pay top management more or make their working conditions more attractive. Profits can be used to finance advertising and sales promotion. One element of the monopoly capital analysis is then what determines the size of the surplus (of revenue over costs) which a firm gains and to what uses is that surplus put. This then leads into discussion of the surplus in total, and the impact which monopoly capital has on economic variables such as prices, output, investment and growth.

Two particular approaches to monopoly capital are now considered in a little more detail (see also note 7), beginning with the work of Baran and Sweezy (1966) and then considering the work of Cowling (1982). Baran and Sweezy view their work as within the Marxian tradition, though they recognise that Marx

> like the classical economists before him, . . . treated monopolies not as essential elements of capitalism but rather as remnants of the feudal and mercantilist past which had to be abstracted from in order to attain the clearest possible view of the basic structure and tendencies of capitalism.

It could be noted here that the monopolies mentioned in this quote as remnants of the pre-capitalist past were generally protected by statute. In that way, those monopolies correspond closely to the orthodox model of monopoly, i.e. one firm with no threat from new entry into the industry, since entry was not legally permitted. In contrast, the monopoly element of monopoly capital is not a single firm with legal protection but rather dominance of most industries by a few firms (i.e. the structure often described as oligopoly).

Baran and Sweezy argue that

> Marx fully recognized the powerful trend toward the concentration and centralization of capital inherent in a competitive economy; his vision of the future of capitalism certainly included new and purely capitalist forms of monopoly. But he never attempted to investigate what would at the time have been a hypothetical system characterized by the prevalence of large-scale enterprise and monopoly.

A key element in the approach of Baran and Sweezy (and of monopoly capital generally) is that

> we must recognize that competition, which was the predominant form of market relations in nineteenth-century Britain, has ceased to occupy that position, not only in Britain but everywhere else in the capitalist world. Today, the typical economic unit in the capitalist world is not the small firm producing a negligible fraction of a homogeneous output for an anonymous market but a large-scale enterprise producing a significant share of the output of an industry, or even several industries, and able to control its prices, the volume of its production, and the types and amounts of its investments. ... It is ... impermissible to ignore monopoly in constructing our model of the economy and to go on treating competition as the general case. In an attempt to understand capitalism in its monopoly stage, we cannot abstract from monopoly or introduce it as a mere modifying factor; we must put it at the very centre of the analytical effort. (Baran and Sweezy, 1966)

The central theme of Baran and Sweezy (1966) is described by them as 'the generation and absorption of the surplus under conditions of monopoly capitalism'. Our discussion focuses on that central theme, and ignores the other aspects of Baran and Sweezy's analysis. It will be recalled from Chapter 1 that one of the themes of radical political economy is the notion of a surplus, and in that sense (among others) theories of monopoly capital are part of that tradition. As with terms such as competition, it is necessary to be careful with words which are used by different authors to have different meanings. Baran and Sweezy define the economic surplus as 'the difference between what a society produces and the costs of producing it'.[12]

The view of Baran and Sweezy on the nature and operation of modern large corporations can be summarised by saying that firms are controlled by managers but still operated in the interests of the owners. The main discussion on managerial firms is left until the next chapter. The corporate paradigm put forward by Baran and Sweezy can be summarised in terms of three features. First,

> control rests in the hands of management, that is to say, the board of directors plus the chief executive officers. Outside interests are often (but not always) represented on the board to facilitate the harmonization of the interests and policies of the corporation with those of customers, suppliers, bankers, etc.

These arrangements would help to reduce conflict between managers and owners, and to some degree enable the mutual interests of managers and owners to be pursued. Second, 'management is a self-perpetuating group'. One generation of managers is responsible for the selection of the next generation. Each succeeding generation of managers will be selected for their abilities of management but also for their conformity to the perceived interests of the present generation of managers and owners. Third, 'each corporation aims at and normally achieves financial independence through the internal generation of funds which remain at the disposal of management'. The management then has some discretion over the use to which funds are put, and this also prevents the kind of interference in their internal affairs which might arise if the firm were heavily reliant on finance from, say, the banks. These views of Baran and Sweezy could be described as a managerial view of the firm in the sense that managers are seen as being in effective control of the firm. However, it is modified in that there is not a sharp conflict of interests between managers and owners in the manner portrayed by managerial theorists.

Although large corporations are managerially controlled, they are nevertheless pursuing profits, and could be described as profit maximisers. Baran and Sweezy portray the typical oligopoly as usually operating along price leadership lines towards a monopoly (joint profit maximisation) outcome. There is generally a lack of price competition, since such competition is seen as likely to set off a downward price spiral which would damage the profits of all. There will be occasions when a company believes it can permanently benefit from aggressive price tactics [then it] will not hesitate to use them. Such a situation is particularly likely to arise in a new industry where all firms are jockeying for position and no reasonably stable pattern of market sharing has yet taken shape.

There are many theories of pricing under conditions of oligopoly, but there is a general notion embedded within them. This is that oligopolists have some market power, which enables them to gain more profits (than under conditions of atomistic competition). The market power derives from the smallness of number of firms in the industry and their ability to co-ordinate their activities and also from the limitations on entry into the industry. A more formal model on these lines is considered below based on Cowling (1982). It should also be noted that the theory of income distribution of Kalecki (discussed in Chapter 9) rests on the idea that market power (degree of monopoly) is the basic determinant of the mark-up of price over costs.

A distinctive feature of Baran and Sweezy's approach is 'the tendency of surplus to rise'. The surplus at the firm level is the excess of revenue over costs and includes profits and 'unnecessary' costs (which would include advertising and sales promotion expenditure). The basis of their argument is as follows.

> The whole motivation of cost reduction is to increase profits, and the monopolistic structure of markets enables the corporations to appropriate the lion's share of the fruits of increasing productivity directly in the form of higher profits. This means that under monopoly capitalism, declining costs imply continuously widening profit margins. And continuously widening profit margins in turn imply aggregate profits which rise not only absolutely but as a share of national product. If we provisionally equate aggregate profits with society's economic surplus, we can formulate as a law of monopoly capitalism that the surplus tends to rise both absolutely and relatively as the system develops.[13]

Other authors in the monopoly capitalism tradition have seen a tendency for profits' share to rise, though through different mechanisms. For example, Kalecki foresaw industrial concentration tending to rise, and as a consequence market power and price–cost margins (and thereby profits share) tending to rise over time.

Next consider the aggregate demand implications of a rise in the surplus. For ease of exposition, consider the case where initially overall output is unchanged but wages decline and the surplus increases. The level of output will remain unchanged in subsequent periods only if there is sufficient expenditure to buy the output. A high proportion (perhaps all) of wages are spent. The reduction of wages will lead to a reduction in the level of demand unless there is an offsetting rise in expenditure out of the surplus. The surplus can be spent (or to use the phrase of Baran and Sweezy, absorbed) through consumption, investment or waste. The extent of consumption out of the surplus is likely to be relatively low (cf. section 9.3). A rise in the surplus, which in effect is a rise in profitability, will have a stimulating effect on investment. Thus, there will be some rise in spending out of the surplus, but probably not enough to offset the reduction in spending because of the fall in wages. There is also an overall limit on the expenditure on investment, which arises from the growth prospects of the economy. The growth rate of the economy (which will to some degree be influenced by the level of investment) would place a limit on the growth rate of the capital stock, which can be written as I/K where I is net investment and K as measure of the capital stock. A simple manipulation would yield I/Y (where Y is national income) equal to $(I/K)(K/Y)$ and provided that the capital–income (K/Y) ratio does not continually rise, the investment-to-income ratio is restrained by the growth requirements.

One possible avenue for the absorption of the surplus is that it can be wasted, i.e. spent on activities which are not socially useful. The basic idea here is that there are forms of expenditure which like all forms of expenditure create employment but which do not yield socially useful or necessary output. One type of such expenditure to which Baran and Sweezy give a lot of attention is advertising and sales promotion. The argument here is that advertising is a form of expenditure which creates employment and by boosting sales of firms helps to increase profits. But what are the social benefits of advertising? There are private benefits to the advertisers, namely the increase in sales. But there may be little benefit to consumers. There are elements of persuasion in advertising – and what is the benefit of being persuaded to buy something which you would otherwise not want? Further, much advertising is competitive, and the effects of one firm's advertising is offset by other firms' advertising. Each firm advertises because the other firm advertises; co-ordination between them would allow them both to stop advertising and remain with much the same market shares but with increased profits.[14]

Another major way by which the surplus is absorbed is through government expenditure. In effect, government steps in to help spend the rising surplus which occurs under monopoly capitalism. For if the rising surplus is not spent, then there will be insufficient aggregate demand to maintain low levels of unemployment and more particularly to support the realisation of the surplus.

> State and church have always been recognized as co-consumers of surplus, and both classics and Marx considered that in addition to public official and clergy there was an important category of 'unproductive' workers, typified by domestic servants, who received a large part or all of their incomes from capitalists and landlords. (Baran and Sweezy 1966)

Under monopoly capital, there is a much greater 'need' for government expenditure to absorb the surplus, since the surplus is large and growing. However, the forms of 'the uses to which the government puts the surplus which it absorbs are narrowly circumscribed by the nature of monopoly capitalist society and as time goes on become more and more irrational and destructive'. In effect, government expenditure tends to be channelled into areas such as defence expenditure, which are non-competitive with private provision and which are highly profitable for the firms concerned.

The aspects of Cowling (1982) to which attention is given can be usefully discussed in the context of a model of oligopoly which he presents. The details of this model are given in the appendix to this chapter, though it should be noted that the model relates to an industry which produces a homogeneous product though it is intended that the conclusions drawn from this model extend to the more complicated case of differentiated oligopoly. We begin here with the final equation of that model which relates to the industry level and is:

$$(P + F)/S = (a/e) + (1 - a). H/e \qquad (5.1)$$

where P is profits, F fixed costs (and P and F together constitute the surplus of revenue over direct costs), S is sales revenue, e is the elasticity of demand, H is the Herfindahl measure of industrial concentration (which is defined as Σs_i^2 where s_i is the share of firm i; see note 4) and a is a measure of the interaction between firms over quantity decisions. This term a is the industry average of the term

(q_i/Q_i) (dQ_i/dq_i) where q_i is the output of the ith firm and Q_i the output of all firms apart from the ith firm. Thus the term a provides an indication of the (expected) proportionate response in output terms of other firms to a change in the output of one firm. It can be taken to represent the degree of (tacit) co-ordination (over output decisions) between firms.

This result suggests that the immediate factors influencing the share of profits in sales revenue are industrial concentration, the elasticity of demand, the interdependence between firms (as reflected in the a term) and the size of fixed costs. But it would be expected that the elasticity of demand would be influenced by factors such as the degree of advertising, whereas industrial concentration and the interdependence between firms would depend on the past history of the industry (e.g. whether it had a history of fierce competition or of tacit collusion).

Cowling argues that existing firms can protect their position and profits by a number of actions designed to discourage new firms from entering the industry in question. These actions would include the use of advertising to secure the loyalty of consumers, seeking to control distribution outlets and essential suppliers, etc. He also argues that excess capacity by existing firms can be used to frighten off potential entrants. The argument is that a potential entrant observing the existence of excess capacity will realise that the existing firms would respond to entry by lowering price and expanding output, thereby denying profits to any new entrant.

It can be seen by reference to equation (5.1) that market power (as reflected in concentration, elasticity of demand and degree of co-ordination) determines the ratio of profits plus 'fixed' costs to sales, which leads to the question of the determination of the division between profits and 'fixed' costs. In a general way, this depends on the power relationships between owners (to whom part of profits will be paid as dividends) and managers (whose salaries, etc., will be part of 'fixed' costs). A powerful managerial class can raise the 'fixed' costs by increasing their own salaries as well as improving the conditions under which they work. Conversely, a firm in which ownership interests were powerful would raise reported profits at the expense of 'fixed' costs. However, in either case, the firm as an organisation seeks to generate as large a surplus as possible, and then there is a distributional struggle to share out the surplus between profits and 'fixed' costs.

It can be seen that theories of monopoly capitalism acknowledge an element of managerial control, that is owners are not usually in direct control of large corporations. But the managers largely serve the interests of the owners, and still seek to maximise the difference between revenue and costs. However, the power of the managers allows them to cream off some of that difference for their own benefit rather than to be reported as profits.

The basic idea of monopoly capitalism is then that developed capitalist economies are dominated by a relatively small number of large firms, whose decisions on investment, employment, etc., have a profound influence on economic performance. These dominant large firms draw back from mutually destructive competition, and their economic power provides them with considerable political influence.

5.5 COMPETITION RULES?

The applicability of the Marxian notion of competition to modern capitalism has been challenged in two key respects. The managerial and to a lesser extent behavioural theories of the firm challenge the view that firms are operated in the interests of capital. The managerial theories are more extensively discussed in the next chapter, where the counter-evidence to the managerial revolution exponents is considered. The ways in which the managerial theories have developed have played down (to the extent of ignoring) the interactions between firms and thereby the role of competition between firms. Further, some aspect of the managerial theories have expressed the view that there has been a fundamental change in capitalism such that the system is no longer composed of profit-seeking firms operated in the interests of capital. This view takes its extreme form in the 'soulful corporation' (which is briefly discussed in section 6.3). The idea of the 'soulful corporation', as the phrase suggests, is that of a corporation which has a soul and which operates for the greater good, rather than for the good of its owners. The second challenge to the relevance of the Marxian notion of competition comes from the theories of monopoly capitalism. As can be seen from the previous discussion, monopoly capitalism retains the idea that firms are operated in the interests of the owners but within a monopolistic framework.

There is little dispute that concentration measured at a local or national level (and more recently at the international level) has increased substantially over the past century or so. The dispute relates to the significance of such changes. It is also indisputable that there have been substantial reductions in costs and barriers associated with international trade. Transport costs have fallen in real terms; the services required by big business (such as banking, transport, hotel accommodation) are operated on an international basis by other large multinational companies. In the post-war period there has been a general but not universal trend towards lowering of tariffs and protection. There are well-known examples of free trade areas and common markets being established. There has also been a general growth of the operations of multinational enterprises (cf. note 9). The effect of these changes would be to bring firms of different nationalities into contact and competition with each other. The lowering of transport costs and of trade barriers would allow firms to operate more easily in markets which were previously regarded as foreign.

In a previous era, the operations of a firm would largely be confined to a locality or region. But the regional operations of firms gradually gave way to national operations, and regional markets to national markets. The subsequent stage, which has been a central feature of the post-war capitalist economies, has been national operations evolving into international operations, and national markets into international ones. This would mean that the geographical level (region, nation, world) at which concentration and market domination should be calculated changes. Most statistics on concentration relate to the national level, and those statistics could be seen as increasingly irrelevant as national markets give way to international ones. Within the Marxian approach to competition, it is useful to identify two sets of forces at work. The first is the tendency towards centralisation and concentration, and the second is a tendency for firms to expand into new areas in search of profits. Some of this expansion will be to take capitalist firms into areas previously controlled by pre-capitalist modes of production. But much expansion comes from capitalist firms invading the territory of other capitalist firms (from another region, country, etc.). Thus one tendency points towards increasing concentration and market power, whilst the other points in the opposite direction.

This can be illustrated by the following example. Suppose that initially there are two countries A and B which do not trade with each other because of high transport costs and tariffs. Consider a particular commodity (say cars) which is initially produced by three firms in each country. The above arguments would suggest that over time the number of firms would tend to decline but as transport costs and tariffs decline there will be a rise in international trade. The change in effective concentration would then rest on a combination of increasing internal concentration and rising international trade. However, the interpenetration of national markets may well lead to cross-border agreements on price, etc., and multinational mergers.

Under competition there is seen to be a tendency towards equalisation of the rate of profit as capital moves from low-profit areas into high-profit areas. The theories of monopoly capital have been accused of focusing on the degree of concentration in the determination of the degree of monopoly; but a necessary (if sometimes implicit) assumption for the theories of monopoly capitalism is that there are substantial barriers of entry which prevent the mobility of capital. Indeed, Cowling (1982) points to the importance of entry barriers and also the means by which existing firms can help to build up barriers to protect their profits. At an empirical level, the difference between the competition view and the monopoly capital view may not be as sharp as portrayed here. It is well recognised by the classical competition view that the equalisation of the rate of profit is only a tendency which involves a movement of physical capital from one industry to another by depreciation in one industry and the creation of new capital equipment in another. This tendency may take years to work itself out, by which time many other factors will have changed. Conversely, the monopoly capital view could allow that entry does sometimes occur, through, for example, mistakes by the established firms or by entry of multinationals. Thus in the one case it is recognised that profit rates may change only slowly, and in the other case it is seen that profit rates may change somewhat over time.

A further consideration is the question of the forces determining the average rate of profit towards which rates of profit are tending. It would be consistent with the monopoly capitalism approach for there to be some tendency towards equalisation of the rate of profit (which may never be fully achieved) with the average rate of profit

influenced by the interaction of the degree of monopoly and the degree of capital intensity. Thus the average rate of profit is influenced by monopolistic elements, and it would be expected that this average rate of profit would be higher under monopoly capitalism than under competitive capitalism.
expected that this average rate of profit would be higher under monopoly capitalism than under competitive capitalism.

It is perhaps not surprising that one basic criticism of monopoly capital theories is that they place too much emphasis on monopoly and not enough on competition. This operates at least at two levels. First, in terms of empirical observation of the behaviour of firms and industries, there are many examples of competition and rivalry between firms and also many of market power, tacit agreements. The reporting and discussion of observations of firms and industries can place more or less emphasis on competitive elements and the oligopolistic elements. It is relatively easy to measure competition and concentration in a structural sense (e.g. compute the market shares of a few firms). But it is much more difficult to measure matters such as the intensity of rivalry between firms, the mobility of capital in the search for profits.

Second, the short-run static models of oligopoly (as used for example by Cowling, 1982) focus on price and output decisions within the context of predetermined cost conditions. As a consequence, price (relative to costs) is seen as influenced by the extent of agreement among the firms. However, the determination of cost conditions is also important for the firms' profitability. These cost conditions depend on the price of inputs (notably labour), the intensity of labour and the technology employed. The Marxian competitive process involves firms striving to invest in a larger scale of production and in more technologically advanced and more capital-intensive production techniques, all of which help the firm to achieve lower costs. This aspect of the competitive process is overlooked in any short-run static model of oligopoly.

The very expression 'monopoly capitalism' places emphasis on monopoly, and not on competition. Classical economists, and in this context notably Marx, emphasised competition, with elements of monopoly seen as a remnant of the pre-capitalist era. It is recognised within the monopoly capital literature that the industrial structure is characterised by oligopoly (rather than monopoly) and a remaining element of competition between firms. To some degree it is a question of the relative emphasis on the elements of competition (rivalry) and monopoly involved.

It is difficult to give a precise meaning to terms such as intensity of rivalry or competition. In an industry in which the products produced are regarded by the purchasers as very close substitutes, and where price information is easily available and the purchasers are able to switch easily from one supplier to another, each firm would need to keep its price (and perhaps product specification) in line with those of other firms. Each firm would then feel under considerable pressure (which they may seek to resolve through agreements and/or through merger). But the intensity of rivalry in such circumstances is related to the degree and ease of substitution between the products of the industry rather than the number of firms. A key question would be whether over the past century or so the rise in industrial concentration has been more or less offset by an increase in the substitution possibilities between products.

Clifton (1977) is largely concerned to 'argue that the capitalist mode of production has become far *more* competitive through two hundred years of development', and as such could be seen as a critique of one of the central propositions of the monopoly capital school. In the early stages of capitalism, there are remnants of the previous economic conditions, so that competition did not operate to full effect. 'The clear-cut implication [of a quote from Marx's *Capital*, vol. III] is that the adjustment mechanism tending to produce a uniform rate of profit throughout the economy becomes stronger, not weaker, with capitalist development' (Clifton, 1977). Auerbach and Skott (1988) similarly argue that 'the lowering of costs of transport and communication expands the functional sphere of competition', and 'the development and dispersion of the technical prerequisites of business calculation has increasingly permitted the possibility of a more "rational" organisation of the firm's activities in the direction of wealth maximization'.

The thrust of Clifton's argument is that large corporations have adopted strategies, particularly for investment, research and development, to search out the highest rate of return.

> It is the range of competitive strategies available to the large firm and the intensity with which they may be applied to the market in the search for competitive advantage that makes the contemporary capitalist economy dominated by such firms far more competitive than ever before. . . . It is . . . the intensity and scope with which these

competitive strategies may be applied which increase the operational mobility of the large firm's capital in pursuit of its own self-expansion. (Clifton, 1977)

However, questions remain with Clifton's approach. First, why do firms compete with each other? The greater sophistication of modern corporations (as compared with the small firms of the nineteenth century) is likely to lead to at least a greater awareness of their interdependence, if not further attempts to co-ordinate their activities. The lowering of communication costs, which enhances a firm's ability to operate on a world-wide basis, also permits firms to co-ordinate their activities. In mature oligopolistic industries, each firm is fully aware of its rivals and the ways in which they operate, and would seek to make their own business decisions in light of their rivals' reactions. Second, the availability of management techniques, increased information flows, aids to decision-making, etc., should mean that the objectives of a firm can be better achieved. The calculations of a firm can be made more accurately. The question still remains as to the objectives of the firms. However, all concerned in this particular debate would agree that the pursuit of profits is the fundamental objective of a firm.

5.6 CONCLUDING REMARKS

This chapter has been concerned with competition and rivalry, which could be seen as involving the external relations between firms. The next chapter, dealing with managerialism, could be seen as focusing on the internal arrangements within a firm. But it will be seen that at the end of the next chapter we return to the same question as raised here, namely whether competition is still the ruling force of modern capitalism.

APPENDIX

This appendix sets out in formal terms the model of Cowling (1982) (which is based on Cowling and Waterson, 1976) discussed in the text. The simplest expression of this is for an industry in which there are N firms producing an homogeneous product for which the common price is p. The decision facing a firm is seen as maximise the surplus S of revenue over variable costs, i.e.

$$S = p(Q)q - C(q)$$

where q is the firm's own output and Q the output of the industry. The first-order condition gives:

$$dS/dq = p'\cdot(dQ/dq)q + p - dC/dq = 0$$

where p' is the (first) derivative of p with respect to Q, and this can be written as $(p - dC/dq) = -p'\cdot(dQ/dq)q$. Multiplying this equation by q and summing over all firms yields:

$$\Sigma(p - dC/dq)\cdot q = \Sigma(-p' \, Q/p) \, (dQ/dq)(q^2/Q_2)pQ$$

which can be rewritten as:

$$\Sigma\{(p - dC/dq)\Sigma\cdot q\}/p \, Q = (1/e)(dQ/dq)H$$

where e is the price elasticity of demand and H is the Herfindahl measure of industrial concentration.

Under the (common) assumption of constant marginal costs (which are hence equal to average variable costs), the term on the left-hand side of this equation becomes the ratio of the surplus of revenue over variable costs to sales. The surplus is divided between profits and fixed costs, where the fixed costs include items such as (top) managerial remuneration. This can be treated as a formalisation of Kalecki's degree of monopoly approach, which is discussed in Chapter 9, in that it indicates that the average price-cost margin (left-hand side of last equation) is seen as determined by the elasticity of demand, the degree of industrial concentration and the term dQ/dq. The lower limit on the last term is unity which is the case of the Cournot response (that is, that each firm believes that other firms will not change their output in the face of the firm's own output change). This lower limit on dQ/dq provides a lower limit on the price–cost margin. The upper limit on dQ/dq is $1/H$ which arises in the case of joint profit maximisation, and generates the upper limit on the price–cost margin. In this way, dQ/dq can be seen as reflecting the effective degree of collusion between the firms. Further, Cowling argues that the elasticity of demand will be influenced by advertising and sales promotion. This leads to a list of factors determining the price–cost margin which is very similar to the list provided by Kalecki.

NOTES

1. In small capitalist economies where there are substantial barriers to international trade, the degree of competition may be quite small. Under a fascist state, the competition between firms is largely removed.
2. Any standard text on welfare economics discusses the Pareto optimality of perfect competition: see, for example, Ng (1983), Boadway and Bruce (1984).
3. For further discussion on monopoly welfare loss see Sawyer (1985a, ch. 14).
4. The notion of a concentrated industry is that a few firms dominate the industry. But that raises questions of what is meant by few and by domination. In practice, there is usually a wide disparity of size of firms within an industry which makes it difficult to summarise the size distribution of firms in a single indicator which could be labelled degree of concentration. For further discussion see Sawyer (1985a, ch. 3).
5. Structure of an industry is seen to strongly influence (or even determine) the conduct of firms in that industry and more importantly the performance of the industry. The structure of an industry refers to number of firms, inequality of their size, impediments to entry, etc., and performance usually encompasses pricing, profitability, advertising, technical advance.
6. For further discussion on competition see Eatwell (1982), Clifton (1977), Eatwell (1987a), Semmler (1987) and McNulty (1987).
7. For a survey of theories of monopoly capitalism and a discussion of critiques of those theories see Sawyer (1988). The main authors in this tradition are Hilferding (1981), Lenin (1916), Kalecki (1971a), Steindl (1952), Baran and Sweezy (1966), Cowling (1982) and Cowling and Sugden (1987a, b).
8. For a summary on the level and trends in industrial concentration see Sawyer (1985a, ch. 3).
9. For example, Stopford and Dunning (1983) estimate that the largest 500 multinationals accounted for the employment of 26 million employees in 1981, of which over 17 million were in the home country of the enterprise. This can be roughly compared with total OECD employment at the same time of around 300 million. Employment in

multinational enterprises would include some employment outside the OECD area, whilst total OECD employment would cover the public sector and also industries such as agriculture where multinationals do not operate extensively. See also Cowling and Sugden (1987b).

10. The evidence suggests that at a number of times in economic history, the process of centralisation (mergers and acquisitions) has been a particularly important factor in increasing concentration (e.g. Hannah and Kay, 1977).

11. Critics of theories of monopoly capitalism include Fine and Murfin (1984a, b), Semmler (1981), Auerbach and Skott (1988), and Auerbach (1988).

12. See also Baran (1957) for a number of different concepts of surplus; Lippit (1985) provides further discussion, drawing particularly on the work of Baran.

13. This argument has some relationship with the kinked demand curve theory, arising from Sweezy (1939). In effect, a fall in costs in the argument in the text does not result in a fall in price, i.e. prices are downward rigid.

14. Perhaps the only firms who admit that advertising does not raise total sales but redistributes sales among the producers are tobacco companies. A frequent defence by them of their advertising is that it only effects their market shares and does not affect the total consumption of cigarettes.

Chapter 6
CORPORATE CAPITALISM

6.1 THE SIGNIFICANCE OF JOINT STOCK COMPANIES

In industralised capitalist economies, larger firms are mainly joint stock companies with a large number of shareholders sometimes numbered in thousands or more, and at least some element of separation between ownership and management. The question arises as to whether the emergence of the joint stock company ('corporation' will be used as a synonym) involves any basic changes to how capitalist economies operate where the basis of comparison would be entrepreneurial capitalism where firms were small and generally run by their owners. Two possible types of change will be discussed in this chapter. The first is whether the corporate structure lifts constraints on the ability of firms to grow (through, for example, being able to draw on a larger pool of finance for their expansion), thereby encouraging the growth of large firms and of concentration. The second is whether the separation between ownership and management leads to the firm adopting different objectives. If management have effective control of the corporation, they would presumably seek to run the company in their interests rather than in the interests of the owners. The questions which arise here are to what extent there has been a separation of ownership and management and whether there is any conflict between the interests of management and those of the owners.

The development of the corporate structure permits a large number of individual shareholders. The associated development of stock exchanges allows the easy transfer of equity between individuals. Ownership is then dispersed over a number (perhaps large) of individuals and can be readily transferred. The position in a corporation can be contrasted with that of, say, a partnership, where in the latter case ownership and management are embodied in the same people, and the sale by one owner of their ownership interest is not straightforward as it involves not only a sale of ownership interest but also the replacement of a manager.

The general idea that owners (of land, factories or whatever) who appointed agents or managers to look after their property ran the risk that agents act in their own interests rather than those of the owners has a long history. Pollard (1968) in a discussion of the growth of management wrote in the following vein:

> There is here a further factor to be considered, which loomed much larger in eighteenth and early nineteenth century minds than in our own, but which ought on that account not to be entirely neglected. That was the view, based on bitter experience as well as on fashionable reasoning, that a system of large scale management was to be avoided at all costs because managers who had to be given any measure of power or responsibility were not to be trusted.

> Adam Smith, denying in a famous passage the ability of salaried managers to administer honestly and well any but the most routine and easily checked business, argued, as usual, not merely from philosophical principles, but from a wealth of practical experience relating, in particular, to joint stock companies: 'The directors of such companies [he accuses], being managers rather of other people's money than of their own, it cannot well be expected that they should watch over it with the same anxious vigilance with which the partners in a private copartnery frequently watch over their own. ... Negligence and profusion ... must always prevail, more or less, in the management of the affairs of such a company.'

In spite of the problems mentioned by Smith, a major development in the nineteenth century was the growth of joint stock companies. This growth was encouraged by changes in the legal framework and administrative innovations in the area of accountancy (cf. Chandler, 1977, especially pp. 109–20).

> However, it seems clear that before such *ad hoc* partnerships could develop further into a more modern form of corporate enterprise, institutional developments both in company law and in stock exchange practices were necessary. Formally, the required legal changes came in England and Wales between 1844 and 1856 when first joint stock companies and then limited liability companies received the general sanction of parliament. ... The facility of joint stock was more convenient than either a full partnership or the deposit of money with a firm, since the shares were readily transferable and the

rights of control which they carried strengthened the security of the investor. Finally, with the granting of limited liability, the joint stock investor was also relieved of the responsibility for the whole of the debts of the firms in which he held shares. (Hannah, 1983)

One of the eventual results of these changes were the rise of the corporate economy. 'Between 1885 and 1907 the number of firms in domestic manufacturing and distribution with quotations on the London stock exchange grew from only sixty to almost 600, and the provincial stock exchanges were almost of greater importance in relation to home securities than London' (Hannah, 1983).

6.2 MARX, HILFERDING AND MARSHALL ON CORPORATIONS

Marx, writing in the third quarter of the nineteenth century, pointed to two aspects of the rise of joint stock companies which are relevant to our discussion.[1] First, the size and scale of a single firm is rather restricted if the finance capital underpinning that firm can only be supplied by a few individuals known to each other. In order to undertake capitalist production, machinery and property has to be bought or hired, material inputs purchased and labour employed. The finance for production is paid out in the hope that in time the resulting output will be sold at a profit. But the scale of production and the time lag between purchase of inputs and the sale of outputs will be limited by the availability of finance. These limits on finance were overcome historically in two ways. There was the development of the financial system, particularly banks, which would attract funds from savers and then lend finance to companies. Thus banks and other financial institutions in effect drew upon the funds of many individuals to lend to firms. There was also the growth of joint stock companies which also allowed a pooling of finance among a large number of individuals. In Marx's words:

> On the basis of capitalist production, however, extended operations of long duration require greater advances of money capital for a longer time. Production in these branches is therefore dependent on the extent of the money capital which the individual capitalist has at his disposal. This limit is overcome by the credit system and the forms of association related to it, e.g. joint-stock companies. (Marx, 1978)

The emergence of the joint stock company can be seen as an efficiency improvement whereby new activities (production on a larger scale) can be undertaken which were previously not undertaken. It can also be argued that when the shares of a joint stock company can be traded, there are further advantages for individual shareholders. Any individual shareowner who for whatever reason wishes to dispose of his/her shares can do so by selling them. Thus for the individual, shares are a liquid financial asset which can be sold as required to others (though obviously the price may not be to their liking). The flow of funds between households and firms may be thereby enhanced. However, Marx pointed to the further consequences of the emergence of joint stock companies. He summarised these as:

1. Tremendous expansion in the scale of production, and of enterprises, which would be impossible for individual capitals. . . .
2. Capital, which is inherently based on a social mode of production and presupposes a social concentration of means of prodution and labour power, now receives the form of social capital (capital of directly associated individuals) in contrast to private capital, and its enterprises appear as social enterprises as opposed to private ones. This is the abolition of capital as private property within the confines of the capitalist mode of production itself.
3. Transformation of the actual functioning capitalist into a mere manager, in charge of other people's capital, and of the capital owner into a mere owner, a mere money capitalist. Even if the dividends that they draw include both interest and profit of enterprise, i.e. the total profit (for the manager's salary is or should be simply the wage for a certain kind of skilled labour. . .), this total profit is still drawn only in the form of interest, i.e. as a mere reward for capital ownership, which is now completely separated from its function in the actual production process as this function, in the person of the manager, is from capital ownership. . . . This is the abolition of the capitalist mode of production within the capitalist mode of production itself, and hence a self-abolishing contradication, which presents itself *prima facie* as a mere point of transition to a new form of production. (Marx, 1981)

The emergence and growth of the joint stock company (corporation) in place of one-person firms and partnerships were seen by Hilferding (1981) as crucial to the understanding of twentieth-century capitalism, and we focus on the following three important elements of the growth of joint stock companies arising from Hilferding's analysis.

First, the industrial corporation 'converts what had been an occasional accidental occurrence in the individual enterprise into a fundamental principle; namely, the liberation of the industrial capitalist from his function as industrial entrepreneur' (Hilferding, 1981). In other words, it is no longer the case that ownership and management have to be undertaken by the same group of people. The shareowners become more like rentiers than entrepreneurs, with the return on shares more akin to interest payments to rentiers, and the rate of return on shares moves towards the general rate of interest.

Second, the control of a corporation is no longer exercised by all the owners, but rather a relatively small number of owners are able to exercise effective control. 'In practice, the amount of capital necessary to ensure control of a corporation is usually less than this, amounting to a third or a quarter, or even less. Whoever controls the corporation also has control over the outside capital as if it were his own' (Hilferding, 1981). Among the shareholders of a corporation, the distinction can be made between 'insiders' and 'outsiders'. The shareholders who are 'insiders' are those involved with the running of the company, and who exercise some control over the corporation. The 'outsiders' are those who are completely uninvolved in the management of the company, and are the rentiers receiving their dividends.

Third, the restraints from a limited amount of finance for expansion (and to underpin large scale of operation) are largely lifted by the use of the joint-stock form of organisation and other developments in the financial system. The scale of an individual firm's activities is no longer restricted by relying on the financial resources of a few individuals, and a firm can grow with few limits from the financial side, and this will clearly help to speed up the process of centralisation and concentration, leading into monopoly. These changes signify an important change in the nature of the competitive process. The corporation can obtain finance relatively easily to expand, so that it can fully reap available economies of scale, whereas the individual entrepreneur is constrained by availability of finance.

The mobility of capital in the pursuit of profits is seen with the classical and Marxian analysis of competition as leading towards the equalisation of the rate of profit. Hilferding argued that technological developments had reduced the mobility of capital, particularly the ability of capital to move out of areas of low profitability. The increased importance of fixed capital (machinery, buildings, etc.) absolutely and relative to circulating capital (stocks of partially complete production, etc.) reduces the ability to move capital from one activity to another. Further, the increasing scale of production

> requires an ever greater absolute sum of capital in order to expand production itself on a corresponding scale or to establish new enterprises. The sums which are gradually accumulated from surplus value are far from adequate to be transformed into independent capitals. It is conceivable, therefore, that the influx of new capital is insufficient or arrives too late. (Hilferding, 1981).

There are two related effects of these changes in the financial system and the emergence of corporations. First, the growth of firms can be more easily financed, and there is a general speeding up of the processes of concentration and centralisation. This enhances the emergence of a situation of structural oligopoly, by which is meant that the typical industry is dominated by a few firms. Second, there are increasing restrictions on the mobility of capital into areas of high profitability, slowing down the tendency towards the equalisation of the rate of profit. Both of these would point in the direction of a move away from competition in the Marxian sense.

Hilferding argued that there was a third way in which the nature of competition had changed, which was from a struggle between the strong and the weak (in which the weak were relatively quickly destroyed) to a struggle between equals. Such a struggle could be a long drawn-out process imposing substantial costs on the firms involved, with the rates of profit being held down during this struggle.

There is a fourth important change involved. The growth of a small number of banks particularly as owners of industrial firms means that one bank can have an ownership interest in a wide range of firms, including firms potentially in competition with one another. Thus the bank would have an interest in reducing competition between the firms in which it has an ownership stake in order to increase profits. Hilferding argued that banks would then strive to reduce competition, by encouraging cartels, mergers, etc., and the firms themselves would welcome a reduction in competition. Hence, there would be strong forces at work fostering the growth of monopoly.

However, there may be limits to the process of concentration, or at least to the speed of the process.

> The growing concentration also creates obstacles to its own further progress. The larger, stronger, and more similar the enterprises, the less chance there is that any one of them will be able to expand its production by eliminating one of the others through competition. (Hilferding, 1981)

Hilferding stressed the growth of the power of finance capital and particularly of the banking system. In this, Hilferding was strongly influenced by the German and Austrian experiences in the first decade of this century, which have not generally been repeated in other capitalist economies. The ownership of industrial companies was seen by Hilferding to be falling into the hands of the banks, who thereby could exercise control over the industrial companies. The banks would have an interest in co-ordinating the activities of the industrial firms in which they had an ownership interest, thereby exacerbating the trend towards monopolisation.

Marshall provided extensive discussion of the influence on firm size and growth of increasing or decreasing returns to scale and of internal and external economies.[2] Much of that discussion can be represented in terms of the determinants on the cost side of the static size of firms. But he also was concerned with the process of growth, and the influence of talented individuals in the growth of firms. When a talented individual is closely identified with a particular firm, then the life of the firm may parallel the life of that individual.

> But long before this end [monopoly position] is reached, his progress is likely to be arrested by the decay, if not of his facilities, yet of his liking for energetic work. The rise of his firm may be prolonged if he can hand down his business to a successor almost as energetic as himself. But the continued very rapid growth of his firm requires the presence of two conditions which are seldom combined in the same industry. There are many trades in which an individual producer could secure much increased 'internal' economies by a great increase of his output; and there are many in which he could market that output easily; yet there are few in which he could do both. (Marshall, 1920)

The rapid growth of a firm would rely on the exceptional talents of a particular individual. When such an individual had to hand over the business to a successor from the same family, then the chances were that the successor would be less talented, and the rapid growth would slow down.

Marshall saw the growth of firms as rather like the growth of trees, with firms following a life cycle of growth and decline. Many young trees begin to grow, but only a few of them reach their full potential, and even those eventually decline. There is a perpetual renewal as new trees replace the old. The similar decline of old and previously successful firms (often through the death of their founder) means that average firm size and concentration have no basic tendency to increase. However, Marshall foresaw that the development of large joint stock companies (corporations) would transform the situation by enabling a large firm to continue to grow.

> There might have seemed to be nothing to prevent the concentration in the hands of a single firm of the whole production of the world, except in so far as it was closed by tariff barriers. The reason why this result did not follow was simply that no firm ever had a sufficiently long life of unabated energy and power of initiative for the purpose. It is not possible to say how far this position is now changed by the expansion of joint stock companies with a potentially perpetual life: but every recent decade had contained some episodes which suggest that it may probably be greatly changed. (Marshall, 1919)

The discussions by Marx, Hilferding and Marshall on the emergence of the joint stock company indicate that there was an acknowledgement of the impact on the operation and growth of firms which that emergence would have. These impacts were seen as on the size of firms, and the separation of ownership and control. However, it has to be said that the discussion by Marx and Marshall was not central to their analysis, and the main effect was seen as being on the size (absolute and relative) of firms.

6.3 MANAGERIAL CAPITALISM

Study of the corporate economy and managerial capitalism was sparked off by the work of Berle and Means (1932). Their contribution could be seen as two-fold. First, they provided estimates of the extent to which the largest 200 American

companies in the 1920s were managerial-controlled and the extent
to which they were owner-controlled. They brought to the fore the
idea that corporations could be managerial-controlled with the
suggestion that such firms would have different objectives and
behaviour as compared with the individual entrepreneur. The
nature of this evidence is further evaluated below. Second, there
was the idea that the interests of owners and controllers were
different.

> Under the corporate system, control over industrial wealth can be
> and is exercised with a minimum of ownership interest. Conceivably
> it can be exercised without any such interest. Ownership of wealth
> without appreciable control and control of wealth without
> appreciable ownership appear to be the logical outcome of corporate
> development. This separation of functions forces us to recognise
> 'control' as something apart from ownership on the one hand and
> management on the other. (Berle and Means, 1932)

Three sets of ideas which have arisen within the general
managerialist tradition stemming from the work of Berle and Means
are identified here. The overarching theme of the three different
sets of ideas is that the 'divorce' between ownership and control
means that capitalism has changed. When the ownership of a firm is
closely associated with control of that firm, then firms would be
operated in the interests of owners which are usually assumed to be
associated with profits. The pursuit of profits was seen to involve
the fullest exploitation of monopoly power (i.e. charging prices
which maximised profits) and of power over workers (i.e. paying
lowest possible wages). If managers have control of a corporation
(and managers are not owners) then they may exercise that control
for a variety of purposes. But if the divorce of ownership and
control has any significance, managers will not be pursuing profits
as their sole objective.

The first idea which is mentioned rather briefly here is associated
particularly with Burnham (1941). This can be seen as an early
expression of the 'convergence' thesis that there is a tendency for
capitalist and socialist economies to become similar to one another.
One expression of this view is that the form of ownership (whether
private or public) matters little. The argument is that any particular
technology of production has an associated set of management and
administrative problems, so that the problems confronting managers

are largely determined by technology rather than by the nature of the economic system. These management problems are confronted by the managerial class, who adopt solutions which are similar no matter what the form of ownership is. Further, the dominant class in these societies is seen to be a managerial class, which exercises its power through the bureaucracy whether of the private or public sector.[3]

The second set of ideas is the clearest example of the notion that the 'divorce' between ownership and control involves a fundamental change in the nature of capitalism. It is the idea that managers in control would not pursue their own private interests but rather would pursue wider social interests, which has been summarised by the term 'soulful corporation'. Managerial theorists 'have also argued that because the "new managers" have a different relationship to private property, they also have different interests and objectives to the "old capitalists", and therefore pursue significantly different policies' (Nichols, 1969). Mason (1958) summarised this view as follows:

> control has passed from ownership's hands into the hands of management; management personnel is more highly specialized and selected for professional competence; its motivations are substantially different from those of the owner-capitalist; its areas of discretionary action and the character of the limitations that bound that area differ markedly from those relevant to the enterprise of an earlier capitalism.

The managers of a 'soulful corporation' have a wide discretion in their actions, and are no longer compelled to strive after profits. In particular, appeal to the social conscience of the managers can lead to actions which are in the social interest, even where they do not raise profits.

The third set of ideas is more familiar to economists and involves the development of simple models of firms based on the separation of ownership and control and the pursuit of self-interest by managers subject to some constraints placed on their behaviour by owners. This set of ideas encompasses the theories of Baumol (1959), Marris (1964) and Williamson (1964). A full discussion of these theories and relevant evidence is given elsewhere (Sawyer, 1979, 1985a, 1990). For the purposes of our discussion here it is sufficient to take the simplest of these theories (Baumol, 1959) to illustrate some general points.

The starting point of Baumol's theory is the acceptance of the divorce between ownership and control in large corporations. The managers pursue their own interests subject to some limitations placed on them by the owners. The managers are in operational control of the firm, and make decisions on prices, advertising, investment, etc. The residual control of the owners comes from the ultimate ability to sack the managers and to withhold finance from the firm.

The interests of the managers of a large corporation are taken to include salary and other benefits, promotion prospects, prestige and status. Many of these interests would be enhanced by the firm being larger. Salary of managers is seen as related to size of firm, and prestige and promotion prospects are likely to be associated with size and with growth. Thus the size of the firm may serve as a proxy for the interests of the managers, and Baumol argues that the indicator of size is sales. Hence he represents the interests of

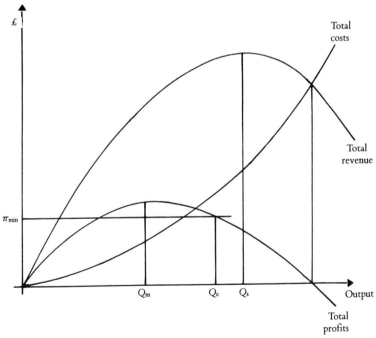

Figure 6.1 Baumol's model of sales revenue maximisation.

managers as the maximisation of sales revenue. Since the managers are in effective control of the firm, the pursuit of sales becomes the objective of the firm.

The owners of the firm place some limits on the pursuit of sales revenue (for if maximisation of sales revenue were taken to the limit, profits could be negative), and this limit is expressed as the imposition of a minimum profit constraint on the managers. This constraint is determined by the need of managers to be able to raise finance in order to pay for the future expansion of sales. This finance may be directly derived from retention of profits or from some external source (e.g. borrowing from banks).

The theory of Baumol is represented diagrammatically in Figure 6.1. The profit-maximising output would be Q_m, whereas the output which maximises sales revenue would be Q_s. The profit constraints (π_{min}) imposed by shareholders on managers leads to output of Q_c, and Baumol argues that this constraint will always be binding on the managers.[4] Over the range of output up to Q_m the interests of managers (sales) and of owners (profits) coincide in that both would be enhanced by higher output. The range of output of interest is that above Q_m, for there the interests of the two groups are in conflict. In effect, the greater the difference between Q_m and Q_c, the greater is the range of conflict between owners and managers. If the owners can impose a 'tight' profit constraint on the managers, then not only is this range of conflict reduced, but also the difference between the price/output behaviour of a profit-maximising and a sales-maximising firm is much reduced.

The central idea of managerial capitalism is the divorce between ownership and management, with managers able to pursue interests in conflict to some degree with those of the owners. Thus, managerial capitalism theorists would anticipate that large corporations would behave in ways which are essentially different from the ways in which owner-controlled firms would behave.

6.4 INVESTMENT AND PROFITS

One view of the operation of large corporations, which has often been associated with a post-Keynesian approach, stresses the role of profits as providing the finance for investment.[5] For a firm, profits are a major source of finance and the ability to borrow further finance is favourably affected by the level of profits. The approach examined in this chapter builds on those observations, with the idea that firms can to some degree adjust their profit margins and total profits in order to provide the required finance. This section begins with the starkest representation of this approach, before introducing some modifications to the argument.

Firms have considerable market power, and adjust prices to seek to achieve their objectives. Mature oligopolistic industries are portrayed as having a firm which acts as a price leader, whose prices are broadly followed by the other firms. From their expectation of the growth of demand, firms seek to invest so that the stock of capital equipment and the capacity to produce grow in line with demand. Some firms may seek to grow faster and others slower than average, but a typical firm can be considered here as one that grows at the average rate. Firms have a preference for internal finance over external finance, and in the simple case considered here seek to finance their investment programme out of their own resources, largely provided by savings out of profits. The preference for internal finance arises from a number of considerations. External finance requires the presentation by the firm of its investment plans to the financial institutions or to the stock market, in order for them to evaluate the plans to be able to make a decision on whether to supply finance. There are significant transaction costs involved in raising external finance (e.g. preparing a prospectus for the stock market, time spent visiting bank manager). Finally, external finance bears a higher rate of interest than internal finance. The cost of internal finance is the opportunity cost of that finance, i.e. the interest rate which could be obtained by lending out the money, where clearly the cost of external finance is the rate of interest charged on borrowing. The interest rate on borrowing exceeds that on lending, and the difference helps to provide financial institutions including banks with profits. Thus external finance for the firm (borrowing) will be more expensive than internal finance (the opportunity cost of which is the lending rate of interest).

When the expected growth rate facing the firm is g, the net investment requirement is gK (where K is a measure of the stock of capital equipment). Denoting profits by P, the retained profits (providing the internal finance) will be rP, where r is the proportion of profits which are retained (and hence a proportion $1-r$ is paid out as dividends to shareholders). When investment expenditure is fully financed out of retained profits, the following applies:

$$gK = rP \tag{6.1}$$

which after dividing both sides by output (Y) can be rearranged as:

$$gv/r = P/Y \tag{6.2}$$

where v is the capital–output ratio. These equations are intended to apply to the typical firm, and then by summation for the whole economy. The interpretation of equation (6.2) is that causation runs from left to right–growth expectations, capital–output ratio and retention ratio determining the profit share. Firms are then portrayed as adjusting prices to generate the required profit share with which investment is financed.

It is perhaps more usual to think that profits (whether actual or expected) stimulate investment (cf. section 12.3). The view of the profits–investment relationship in equation (6.2) reverses that direction of causation and stresses the influence of desired investment expenditure on profitability. Further, equations (6.1) and (6.2) interpreted at the aggregate (rather than the firm) level are that investment (gK) is equal to savings (rP) under the assumptions that a proportion r of profits is saved and there are no other savings.

The above representation of the links between pricing and investment is a rather simple one, and now we turn to a discussion of the more sophisticated approach of Eichner (see Eichner, 1973, 1976, 1985, 1987). This approach relates explicitly to the pricing and investment policies of large corporations (megacorp in Eichner's terminology) operating in oligopolistic industries.

> The megacorp is an organization rather than an individual. ... As an organization, the megacorp's goal is to expand at the highest possible rate. ... It is expansion at the highest rate possible that creates the maximum opportunities for advancement within the organization, and thus personal rewards for those who are part of the firm's decision-making structure. (Eichner, 1985)

Thus the objective of the organisation and its members is summarised as being to maximise growth rate. This maximisation is subject to a number of constraints – among them the need to maintain a certain rate of growth of dividends.

In pursuit of this goal, the megacorp can be expected to follow two behavioral rules. One of these is that it will attempt to maintain, if not actually to enlarge, its share of the market in the industries to which it already belongs while simultaneously undertaking whatever investment is necessary to lower its costs of production. The other behavioral rule is that it will attempt to expand into newer, more rapidly growing industries while simultaneously withdrawing from any older, relatively stagnant industries. (Eichner, 1987)

For a corporation interested in growth, a higher price has two opposing effects. It is assumed that a higher price will raise profits in the short-run cash-flow,[6] and thereby raise the available internal finance. However, a higher price leads to a lower level of demand and to a reduction in the growth of demand. This fall arises from the substitution in demand by consumers for now relatively lower price goods and by an increased probability of entry by new firms which will draw demand away from existing firms. These ideas are represented in Figure 6.2 (though it should be noted that this is not the way by which Eichner illustrates his approach[7]). The curve which is labelled 'Supply of funds' reflects the notion that as the

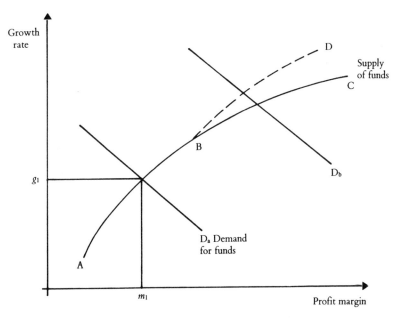

Figure 6.2 Demand and supply of funds.

profit margin is raised, more funds become available to the firm with which investment can be financed. The curve ABC relates to the internal funds, and the difference between that curve and the curve ABD relates to the possibility of securing external finance. The view is built in that internal finance is generally used in preference to external finance, but above the point B the firm considers it worth while to resort to some external finance. The 'Demand for funds' curve refers to the firm's investment requirements, and reflects the notion that higher profit margins (and prices) lower growth and investment.

The demand-for-funds curve D_a generates a maximum growth rate of g_1 with an associated profit margin of m_1. In this case, the firm has no requirement for external finance. A higher demand-for-funds curve such as D_b involves some requirement for external finance. When no use is made of external finance, then once again equations (6.1) and (6.2) apply, although in this more sophisticated version the firm has decided its own growth rate and profit margin rather than taking the growth rate as predetermined. When external finance is involved, then equation (6.1) is modified to give:

$$rP + D = gK \tag{6.3}$$

where D is the external finance. The implication for the profit margin can then be calculated as:

$$P/Y = (gK - D)/Y \tag{6.4}$$

where firms only draw on external finance when it is seen as cheaper than further internal finance.

In terms of this chapter, Eichner's approach is interesting in two respects. First, he argues that the objectives of the corporation can be seen as the pursuit of growth, on the basis that growth of the organisation creates opportunities for the members of the organisation. Thus, in terms of the discussion in Chapter 4, the pursuit of growth serves as a proxy for the interests of the members of the organisation. Second, it stresses the role of profits as a source of finance for investment. In the absence of profits, firms would be unable to grow, but profits are the means to the end of growth of the organisation.

6.5 CRITIQUE OF THE MANAGERIALIST THESIS

There are three key ingredients in the managerial theories of firm
behaviour (which include both the formal theories of authors such as
Baumol (1959) and of Eichner as well as the more general view that
managers are in effective control of large corporations and pursue
objectives which are significantly in conflict with the interests of the
shareholders) relevant for the critiques to be discussed in this
section. First, there is an acceptance of the evidence of Berle and
Means and their successors that there is now a substantial divorce
between ownership and control. Second, this divorce means that
managers are to some significant degree free to pursue their own
interests or some broader social interests which are in conflict with
the profit interests of the shareholders. Third, these managerial
theories place all their emphasis on the objectives of the managers
and do not pay regard to the external conditions of the firm. In
particular, competitive pressures from other firms are in effect
ignored. The second and third ingredients are linked and below they
are considered together. Thus the critiques of the managerial
theories are divided into two groups, namely questioning of the
evidence on the extent of managerial control and a reassertion of
various arguments that firms have to pursue profits in order to
survive and grow.

We begin with an examination of the evidence on the divorce
between ownership and control. It is helpful to distinguish between
two possible interpretations of the term 'managerial revolution'.
The first one, which is the focus of the discussion in this chapter,
refers to the idea of a divorce between ownership and control
whereby crucial decisions on prices, output, investment, dividends,
etc., are taken by people who are managers but who have little
ownership interest in the company. The second refers to the
increased importance of non-manual and particularly supervisory
labour within most sectors of the economy over, say, the past
century.[8] One of the effects of such developments is that there are
more 'layers' of a company through which information has to flow
upwards and commands pass downwards.[9] There may then be
increased problems for the controllers of the firm in the provision of
accurate information and in securing the execution of their
commands. Offsetting those difficulties, there may be gains from

increased division of labour and specialisation within the firm.

Berle and Means (1932) start from the view that 'in most cases, however, if one can determine who does actually have the power to select the directors, one has located the group of individuals who for practical purposes may be regarded as "the control"'. A corporation was seen as under owner-control if there were a clear majority shareholder or if there was a substantial minority shareholder. Minority control

> may be said to exist when an individual or small group hold a sufficient stock interest to be in a position to dominate a corporation *through their stock interest*. Such a group is often said to have 'working control' of the company. In general, their control rests upon their ability to attract from scattered owners proxies sufficient when combined with their substantial minority interest to control a majority of the votes at the annual elections. (Berle and Means, 1932)

An archetypal owner-controlled firm would be one in which a family or small group of people (known to each other) own at least half the shares of the firm and effectively determine the policy of the firm. In contrast, an archetypal management-controlled firm would be one with thousands of shareholders, none of which owned more than a minute proportion of shares, and those involved in the management of the company having no ownership interests. Berle and Means describe their method of classification as follows.

> Corporations which appeared to be owned to the extent of 80 per cent or more by a compact group of individuals were classed as private and those in which the public interest appeared to be larger than 20 per cent but less than 50 per cent were classed as majority owned. ... The dividing line between minority and management control was drawn roughly at 20 per cent, though in a few special instances a small holding was credited with the power of control. It is notable that in none of the companies classed under management control was the dominant stock interest known to be greater than 5 per cent of the voting stock. Cases falling between 20 and 5 per cent were usually classed as joint minority-management control.

Management control arose in the absence of identified owner-control, that is when

> ownership is so widely distributed that no individual or small group has even a minority interest large enough to dominate the affairs of the company. ... In such companies [management control] where does control lie? ... In the election of the board the stockholder

ordinarily has three alternatives. He can refrain from voting, he can attend the annual meeting and personally vote his stock, or he can sign a proxy transferring his voting power to certain individuals selected by the management of the corporation, the proxy committee. As his personal vote will count for little or nothing at the meeting unless he has a very large block of stock, the stockholder is practically reduced to the alternative of not voting at all or else of *handing over his vote to individuals over whom he has no control and in whose selection he did not participate.* ... Where ownership is sufficiently sub-divided, the management can thus become a self-perpetuating body even though its share in the ownership is negligible. This form of control can properly be called 'management control'. (Berle and Means, 1932)

Further, consider a shareholder dissatisfied with the way the firm is operated. The benefits of using the voting power of the shareholding is that the performance of the firm may be improved, with a shareholder receiving the proportion of the benefits of improved performance as determined by the proportion of shares held by the individual. But there are substantial costs of campaigning for a change in the way in which a corporation is managed (apart from any doubts of how effective action for a change in performance would be). A majority of shareholders has to be contacted and convinced of the effectiveness of seeking to change management policy. A shareholder with a small proportion of shares would receive only a small proportion of any benefits and would have little incentive to campaign for a change in performance. It is only when a connected group of shareholders have a substantial proportion of shares that it is worth while for them to exercise control over the managers. The underlying idea is that if share ownership is disperse then it is not worth while for any individual shareholder (or group of shareholders) to exercise control, and by default control passes into the hands of the managers.

The other angle to consider is the source of income of the managers. If the managers own no part of the firm for which they work and their salaries are unrelated to profits, then the managers would have no direct economic incentive to pursue profits. However, it has been observed that there has been a substantial increase in the degree to which managerial income is related to profit performance, so that conflict of interest between shareholders and 'top' managers would be thereby reduced (see e.g. Llewelyn, 1969).

Berle and Means (1932) classified the largest 200 American

companies in 1929 in terms of immediate control as follows:

	By numbers	By wealth
Management control	44%	58%
Legal device	21%	22%
Minority control	23%	14%
Majority ownership	5%	6%
Private ownership	6%	4%
In hands of receiver	1%	negligible

Larner (1966) adopted a similar technique although he took a 10 per cent share interest by a small group as the criterion for owner control. He reported that by 1963 manager-controlled firms accounted for 169 of the largest 200 non-financial American corporations, thereby appearing to confirm the predictions of Berle and Means that management control would increase.

This evidence has been criticised along two lines. First, some doubts have been expressed on the accuracy of Berle and Means's estimates. For example, Burch (1972) and Zeitlin (1974) have pointed out that Berle and Means has reasonably definite and reliable information on at most two-thirds of the companies in their sample. The figures for control type reported above relate to ultimate control. This differs from immediate control in that if, for example, firm A owns firm B then the immediate control of firm B would be owner-controlled (since there is a single owner), but the ultimate control would be the control type of firm A. For the immediate control figures, it can be reported that of the 73 companies classified as under minority control, 44 were reported as 'known to be so controlled' whereas 29 were given as 'thought to be so controlled'. Of the management-controlled firms, 21 were 'known to be so controlled', 44 were 'thought to be so controlled', with 16 under joint control (as defined above). Thus the number of firms known to be under immediate management control was 11 per cent (21 out of 200), which gives a rather different impression to the figure of 44 per cent under management control indicated above, on which much subsequent attention was focused.[10]

Second (and more importantly), the notion of control and the evidence on control is rather naive. It is based on rather mechanical rules, and to some extent counterpoises the interests of owners and managers. This counterpoising of the interests of owners and managers is continued in the managerial theories of the firm, as indicated by the theory of Baumol considered above. The application of mechanical rules (such as 20 per cent or more of shares owned by a small number of individuals taken to represent owner control) overlooks the variety of avenues through which control can be exercised.[11] Thus, it has been argued that

> to locate control in any given corporation, it is not adequate to set up arbitrary statistical criteria such as the percentage of shares which must be owned by the largest holder or the largest twenty holders. Rather a case-by-case approach is necessary. Any individual firm may be related to other corporations, banks, financial institutions, and family owners via complex patterns of shareholdings, interlocking directorates, and kinship networks. (Nyman and Silberston, 1978)

Nyman and Silberston (1978) seek to 'define circumstances in which an individual, or a group of individuals (whether incorporated or not), are probably able to exercise control over a firm, in the sense of being able to select its senior management'. Their criteria include not only the percentage of shares owned by a single individual or group of individuals, but also look at 'the presence on the board of directors of the founder of company, member of his family, or his descendants'. The argument here is that 'if the Chairman is the founder of a company, or if he is a member of the founder's family or one of his descendants, then we may well be able to designate the firm as "family", even if the family are not large current shareholders'. In addition, they look at the background of the Chairman and Managing Director. On the basis of such criteria, they classify 126 firms out of 224 (which were the largest UK firms after the exclusion of foreign-owned companies in the sample) as being owner-controlled.

Cosh and Hughes (1987) examine corporate control in fifty-four companies (half British and half American) which were among the largest hundred companies in their own country. They show that different methods of classifying corporations as owner-controlled or manager-controlled yield substantially different results, which range from three-quarters of corporations being classified as manager-controlled to three-fifths classified as owner-controlled.

In the UK a picture emerges of a board of directors dominated by a majority of insider executives, who typically spent the bulk of their careers in the company they now direct. ... The board of directors as a whole in these giant corporations is in percentage terms an insignificant holder of shares.

But this is not as much support for the managerialist position as it may appear, for

a small number of financial institutions recur as significant owners and controllers of stock. These major institutions are also represented on the boards of industrial companies. They are therefore, by virtue of their position, potentially able to play a key role in the determination of corporate behaviour.

The situation in the United States is not dissimilar, but with directors having greater shareholdings of their own corporation.

The counterpoising of owners and managers (and of their interests) runs into the question of the background and selection of managers. Managers are likely to be chosen not only for their ability to manage, but also on their willingness to promote the interests of the shareholders (or at least the board of directors). Further, it is likely that someone who has reached the heights of top management of a company will generally conform to the ethos of that company and of the economic system in general. It would be rather unlikely that a company would appoint as a top manager an individual who did not accept the general basis on which the company was run.[12] It is even more unlikely that a capitalist company would appoint someone who was a revolutionary Marxist seeking to overthrow the system. Even if there are opportunities for a manager to promote their own interests at the expense of the shareholders, there would be a general promotion of the interests of the company and its shareholders.

The debate over owner-controlled versus management-controlled firms tends to assume that the owners and managers are separate groups and that there is a commonality of interests among the owners. However, whilst some shareholders are rather like rentiers with no management involvement with the company, there are shareholders who are involved in management. However, some of the individuals who are managers and shareholders will have achieved their position as manager because of their shareholding. But in other cases, an individual may be appointed manager and then be paid in the form of shares or given options to purchase shares at below the market price.

One example can be given to illustrate the point that there may be conflict of interests between the rentier or outsider shareholders and the manager–shareholders or insiders. It also illustrates the point that share ownership by an individual does not mean that the company is run in the general interests of the shareholders.

> It seems that Henry Ford II may have recently overstepped the bounds of what was considered reasonable and inspired a stockholders' revolt. Their action cites the equipping of his office with a $250,000 sauna, private gym and full-time masseur, and a private dining-room for him and his guests, staffed with six full-time employees including a Swiss chef. Each lunch that Ford eats was alleged to cost approximately $200 per person. Ford was also accused of having five to six company employees tend his girlfriend's lawn, along with various other indiscretions and misuses of funds. (Cowling, 1982)

This leads on to a consideration of the social and class background of individuals appointed as top-level managers. If the general background of the managers is similar to that of shareholders, then it is plausible to argue that the outlook of managers and owners will be similar. This does not rule out that there can be some conflict of interests between managers and owners, but rather that managers will not undertake courses of action which fundamentally threaten the interests of the owners. Nichols (1969), for example, argues that

> there is a substantial over-representation of directors from the highest social strata (and notably of those whose fathers were in business), that there is also a substantial over-representation of those educated at the traditional elite institutions and that, though it is certainly true that most of them cannot be termed 'capitalists', directors collectively are clearly part of the wealthiest section of British society, and are among the largest (personal) shareholders.

The conclusion of Francis (1980), following interviews with directors of some large companies, is similarly that there is not a sharp conflict of perceived interests. He concludes that

> although our managers did report satisfaction from the growth of their company ... their primary sources of satisfaction do not include the other factors commonly expressed by managerialist writers, such as security, prestige and service to employees, customers and the community. Moreover whatever interests they have in the fast

growth of their company these are not seen to be in conflict with profit-maximising corporate objectives. Profits and growth are both pursued, although growth in profits is given higher priority than growth in sales or assets. (Francis, 1980)

One supporting argument in Baumol's theory was that the income (salaries) of managers were related to the size of firm (especially in terms of sales) rather than with profits. The lack of ownership interest by managers is an implicit assumption in much theorising on management control. Both of these assumptions can be questioned. Salaries may be only loosely related to profits, and in turn salaries may be only a relatively small part of total managerial income.[13] Managers typically own some shares in the company for which they work, and part of their remuneration may be in the form of shares. By various routes, the income of managers can be profits-related, in ways designed to bind the interests of the managers with those of the shareholders.[14]

One conclusion which could be drawn from the above discussion is that the power relationship within firms between managers and shareholders is a complex one, which cannot be simply described as divorce between ownership and control. Further, profits are important to the controllers of large corporations, whether as an end in themselves or as a means to further growth.

6.6 COMPETITIVE PRESSURES?

One view of the large corporation is that in many respects it is a more efficient and less constrained version of an individual capitalist.

We have tried to show that the giant corporation of today is an engine for maximizing profits and accumulating capital to at least as great an extent as the individual enterprise of an earlier period. But it is not merely an enlarged and institutionalized version of the personal capitalist. There are major differences between these types of business enterprise, and at least two of them are of key importance to a general theory of monopoly capitalism: the corporation has a longer time horizon than the individual capitalist, and it is a more rational calculator. (Baran and Sweezy, 1966)

This argues that the modern corporation differs significantly from the individual entrepreneur. However, it argues that the modern corporation is closer to the well-informed maximising agent portrayed in much of economic theory than the individual entrepreneur could be.

Baran and Sweezy (1966), however, see the rise of the modern corporation as leading to a diminution of competition and rivalry. There is 'an attitude of live-and-let-live [by each corporation] toward other members of the corporate world'. But 'by and large, this attitude is reserved for other big corporations, and does not extend to the small businessman'. In general, Baran and Sweezy conclude that 'today there are probably fewer genuine monopolies than there were at the turn of the century, but there is also *infinitely* less cut-throat competition' (italics added). The thrust of the argument of Baran and Sweezy is that large corporations come to realise their mutual dependence, and that competition among a few large corporations would be mutually destructive. But the size of the large corporations does allow them to compete with smaller firms, and where necessary to buy up successful small firms and/or to buy any profitable ideas and products developed by smaller firms.

In Chapter 5 a number of concepts of competition were distinguished, and it is useful to bear those distinctions in mind here. 'The development of oligopolistic markets which has occurred with the concentration of capital is, within the context of neoclassical theory, proof that capitalism has become less competitive over time' (Clifton, 1977). This is clearly the case where competition is synonymous with atomistic competition. But it is not only neo-classical economists who see a rise in industrial concentration as implying a decline in competition, for as indicated immediately above, authors such as Baran and Sweezy share that view.

Clifton (1977) emphasises the distinction between perfect competition, where competition is viewed in the structural sense of a large number of small firms each of which faces a perfectly elastic demand, and competition which involves the mobility of capital and a tendency towards the equalisation of profit. Competition in the former sense has clearly declined, but Clifton argues that 'the requirement of free capital mobility finds its closest approximation in the real world in the corporate structure and competitive strategy of the modern corporation, rather than the atomistic firm of neo-classical theory'. Clifton argues along two lines as to why the mobility of capital and hence competition is greater in the late twentieth century than hitherto (and particularly than in the nineteenth century when atomistic competition appeared to rule). First, 'through organisation and ever improving means of communication and transportation, factor mobility is much more highly developed today than ever before in history'. In the mid-nineteenth century, a firm located in, say, one area of England would find it difficult to communicate with other parts of that country, let alone the rest of the world. The postal system had recently been established, and the telephone and telegraph had yet to be invented. The banking system was largely localised, with the operations of an individual bank largely restricted to one area or region of the country. The ability of a firm in one area of the country to discover profit opportunities in other areas of the country would be limited, as would the possibility of them acting on such information. Simply the firm would not have a suitable form of organisation to support geographically dispersed operations. The accountancy practice and the conduct of audits would not have been sufficiently developed to permit the firm to operate on a large scale. Communications and transport between different areas would be difficult and expensive. The reduction in communication and transport costs (along with various technical developments) has enhanced the possibilities of capital mobility.

Auerbach (1988) argues similarly that

> the inexorable increase in the quantity of business information, the improvement of the quality and comparability of business data with the development of the accounting profession and the adoption of standards of reporting and the general improvement in communications of all kinds – all these factors, coupled with the progressive professionalisation of management have generated a long-term tendency for competitiveness to increase in the capitalist market economy.

All these developments make it possible for a firm to operate on a large scale at geographically dispersed places. Further, it is argued that managers used to identify themselves with a particular industry (e.g. they would think of themselves as 'steelmen' or 'cotton men'), and be reluctant to move into other industries.

> If they [managers] stayed within a specific sphere of activity either out of personal propensity or because of plain ignorance of the opportunities which loomed elsewhere, such behaviour would have a dampening effect on the rate of equalisation of profits and the process of competition. (Auerbach, 1988)

The rise of accountants and managers unattached to a specific industry, interacting with the development of conglomerate firms, has lead to increased mobility between industries of both personnel and capital, and this leads on to the second line of argument of Clifton.

This second line of argument is that 'the conditions of free capital mobility which permit maximum flexibility and intensity for an independent unit of capital to directly search out the highest possible rate of return in the market are most closely approximated in the modern corporation'. Large corporations typically produce several ranges of goods and services, operating in many regions and countries and organised along multi-divisional lines so as to be able to cope with the diversity of their operations. In a multi-divisional corporation, each division would deal with the production of a limited range of goods and services and to operate in a number of regions or countries. The co-ordination of the operations of the divisions is undertaken by the head office, which monitors the work of the divisions and also serves to allocate finance capital between the divisions.

The emergence of large diversified corporations, in Clifton's view, enhances competition in two respects. First, a single corporation may find itself in competition with several other corporations. In one market, it may be in competition with firms $X_1, X_2, \ldots, X_L$, and in another market with firms $Y_1, Y_2, \ldots Y_M$ and in a third market with firms $Z_1, Z_2, \ldots, Z_N$. In contrast, the small firm operating under atomistic competition would only be in competition in one market, rather than as with the large corporation in several markets. Second, the head office of the large corporation allocates finance capital. As such it can scan the profit opportunities of each of its divisions, and also it is geared up to moving into new areas if there are profit opportunities. The large modern corporation is better able (than the small atomistic competitive firm) to assess profit opportunities (with the development of, for example, accountancy techniques, operations research, market research). It is organised so as to be able to move capital from low-profit areas into high-profit areas and to spot and act on profit opportunities outside its current range of activities. In contrast, the nineteenth-century firm would be highly restricted in its activities and in the pursuit of profits. The view of the operation of large corporations also arises in the work of Williamson (1975), in which attention is drawn to the various organisational structures which firms can adopt. He contrasts the unitary form (where the firm is organised centrally as a single unit) and the multi-divisional form (where the firm is organised into product divisions). In the latter form, which is seen as gradually replacing the former, a key function which is retained at the centre is the allocation of finance between divisions. In this respect, finance is allocated within the firm by administrative decision rather than through the financial markets. But also the central allocator of finance is in a position to scan the profit opportunities across a range of activities, and this may lead to greater capital mobility between different areas of activity.

6.7 CONCLUDING REMARKS

There can be little doubting the importance of large corporations in industrialised economies in that a relatively few large corporation account for a large proportion of output. The main question is whether capitalism has changed in terms of monopoly and competition (Chapter 5) and control (this chapter). This is not only of historical interest, but the answer to this question determines the type of analysis which we apply to the late twentieth century. The neo-classical approach is still largely based on the entrepreneurial firm in conditions of perfect competition. In contrast, the radical political economy approach focuses on the role of large corporations, which dominate the industrial landscape. Within these corporations there is some degree of separation between ownership and management, and the power relationships between shareholders and managers influence the performance of the corporation. These corporations often operate on a world-wide basis and in oligopolistic markets. There may be competition between corporations but this will take the form of rivalry in the pursuit of profits and market shares and not of the atomistic competitive variety.

One aspect of these corporations which we have not had space to deal with is their political power. This power in part arises from their sheer size and importance within the economy, so that crucial decisions on investment, employment, regional locations, exports, etc., are taken by a relatively few large corporations. These large corporations operate increasingly on a multinational basis.[15] The transnational basis of their operations enhances their political power, especially where governments are keen to secure investment from multinational enterprises for the employment they can provide. Finally, whilst there are differences within the radical political economy approach on the degree to which late twentieth-century capitalism can be said to be competitive, there is agreement that any competition does not take the form of atomistic competition. As a minimum, this means that no desirable attributes can be extended to an enhancement of competition, and that analysis of modern capitalism must reject any atomistic competitive theories as being irrelevant.

NOTES

1. For further discussion see deVroey (1975).
2. Internal economies are gained by a firm in terms of lower unit costs when the firm's own output expands. External economies arise when the unit costs of each firm are lowered by the expansion of the total industry output.
3. For discussion of Burnham see Nichols (1969, ch. 2).
4. The argument is that if the minimum profit constraint is not binding (i.e. the sales revenue-maximising output is less than the profit-constrained output), then the firm would use the 'excess' profits (those above the minimum constraint) to advertise in order to further stimulate sales.
5. In this section we focus on the work of Eichner. Other authors whose work could be viewed as being in the same vein include Wood (1975), Harcourt and Kenyon (1976), Shapiro (1981), Ong (1981).
6. Eichner argues that demand facing an oligopolistic industry is typically inelastic. Under the assumed conditions of price leadership, inelastic demand means that firms cannot be maximising short-run profits. It also means that sales revenue and profits can be increased by raising price.
7. In particular, Eichner represents the effects of raising price on the supply of finance as an implied rate of interest. The cost of internal finance can then be compared with the cost of external finance. For simplicity in the text only internal finance is considered.
8. In the UK for example, salary earners increased from around 10 per cent of the civilian working population in 1911 to nearly 28 per cent in 1961 (when collection of relevant data stopped). In manufacturing

industries, operatives (manual workers) declined from 79 per cent of employees in 1960 to 71 per cent in 1983. For most of the past century the proportion of self-employed has also been in decline.

9. Marshall described the advantages of the small owner-controlled business in the following way. 'On the other hand the small employer has advantages of his own. The master's eye is everywhere; there is no shirking by his foremen or workmen, no divided responsibility, no sending half-understood messages backwards and forwards from one department to another. He saves much of the book-keeping, and nearly all of the cumbrous system of clerks that are necessary in the business of a large firm; and the gain from this source is of very great importance in trades which use the more valuable metals and other expensive materials' (Marshall, 1920). The obverse of the advantages of small business is the disadvantage of large business especially over problems of co-ordination.

10. Berle and Means (1932) indicate that firm evidence on corporate control was not always available. 'In seeking to classify according to the type of control, reasonably definite and reliable information was obtained for nearly two-thirds of the companies. ... Where reliable information has not been directly available it has been necessary to depend upon newspaper reports.'

11. Leech (1987) adopts another approach. He argues that 'a probabilistic-voting model (whose underling assumptions are essentially the same as those of Berle and Means) has been used to define factual control and to establish a criterion by which to distinguish minority- from management-controlled companies. ... Applying this method to those companies which Berle and Means classified as management controlled (and for which they give detailed data), it is shown that the criterion varies with shareholding dispersion and that in all cases it is much lower than the fixed 20 percent holding they employed. However all these companies remain classified as in the management-controlled group.'

12. An exception to this could arise when the company is in deep crisis and a 'new broom' is thought desirable to shake up the company to overcome the crisis.

13. See Sawyer (1985a, pp. 179–85) for a survey of evidence.

14. Llewellen (1969) finds that the proportion of total post-tax real income of executives paid in the form of salaries and bonuses in 50 of the largest American corporations declined from around two-thirds in the 1940s to around one-half in the 1960s.

15. For some discussion see, e.g., Cowling and Sugden (1987b), Cowling (1985).

Part Four

VALUES, PRICES, WAGES AND PROFITS

Chapter 7
VALUE

7.1 VALUE AND PRICES

Most of this book is concerned with the explanation of behaviour, events and economic variables which are, at least potentially, observable. It could be said that such explanations are superficial in the sense of dealing only with surface relationships, and not exploring more fundamental issues. This chapter is concerned with a rather different matter, which is the question of the reason why goods and services have value, and further the determinants of the magnitude of such value. However, there may be a correspondence between value, which is unobservable, and price, which is observable. Indeed, the cardinal utility approach, which sees value as determined by (marginal) utility, also sees price as equated with marginal utility.[1] The proposition that the price of a product corresponds to (or equals) its value is untestable (since value itself is an unobservable concept); nevertheless the idea can still possess great power. For example, the notion that individuals acquire goods and services to enhance their own utility, and each individual is the best judge of his or her own utility carries with it the connotation that there should be no restrictions on the goods and services available to individuals. Any restriction on which goods or services can be acquired would reduce an individual's welfare by preventing him or her from acquiring some goods and services which he or she is willing and able to purchase. The strong implication of this (taken together with the view that each individual is the best judge of his or her own welfare) is that there should be no censorship on pornography and no legal limitations on, say, the use of (currently illicit) drugs.[2]

Further, such an approach denies any impact of advertising and marketing on people's preferences since the assumption is those preferences are given and not subject to manipulation. Another example, discussed below, is the link between a labour theory of value and the view that labour should receive the full benefits of production. In both these examples, the conclusion drawn may not follow logically from the theories, but rather the conclusions are often associated with the theories.

For the past century or so, the question of the source of value has been dominated by the utility approach,[3] and whilst coverage of the utility approach falls outside the remit of this book, some critical comments are made on it below. But for the century up to 1870, the question of the source of value had been dominated by the labour theory of value, although it will be seen below that the term 'labour theory of value' has a number of interpretations. But, crudely, it could be said that the labour theory of value would see the value (if not the price) of a product as depending on the labour embodied in the product. In the hands of some (e.g. the Ricardian socialists who are discussed below; section 7.2), this led to the proposition that if labour is the *source* of value, then labour should be the recipient of all the value created, and hence nothing should be paid to capitalists. Profits then appear as an unjustified deduction from wages. These type of arguments, and the use of the labour theory of value by Marx are often seen as stimulating the development of an alternative theory of value (i.e. the utility-based theory of value). This utility approach clearly would not carry with it the revolutionary implications which the labour theory of value appeared to have. Further, as will be seen below it also led on to the provision of justifications for profits.

Thus, a major question which has exercised the minds of economists over the past two centuries has been that of why goods and services have value, and there is the associated question of the determination of the degree of value which a good or service possesses. Another and related task has been the search for a 'measuring rod' or an 'invariable standard'. If comparisons of, for example, income are to be made between countries or over time, then some basis of comparison is needed. If there were some units in which income at different times and in different countries could be measured, then the comparison of income would be straightforward. Money is a rather variable 'measuring rod' because of variations in both absolute and relative prices. In the case of neo-classical economics, a substantial part of welfare economics is taken up with making welfare comparisons between different bundles of goods and services. The 'measuring rod' is seen in terms of individual utilities, but the implication of welfare economics is that the comparisons which can be unambiguously made are rather limited. Some limited progress has been made within the Sraffian approach on the search for an 'invariable standard', and this is discussed in the next chapter.

7.2 ORIGINS OF THE LABOUR THEORY OF VALUE

The first part of the discussion of the labour theory of value sketches in briefly the historical development of that theory,[4] which usually begins with Adam Smith.[5] In an 'early and rude state of society which precedes both the accumulation of stock and the appropriation of land', Adam Smith envisaged that the exchange ratio between goods will reflect their relative labour requirements. Thus if it takes (on average) one hour to catch a fish and two hours to capture a rabbit then the exchange ratio will be two fish equal to one rabbit. This 'early and rude' state of society has several important characteristics. Labour is considered as homogeneous and unskilled so that questions of the evaluation of different skills do not arise. There is no significant capital equipment involved. There are, however, inputs other than labour in that labour cannot produce rabbits by itself. Land and rabbits are also involved. But if the land and rabbits were freely available and not subject to private ownership (e.g. commonly owned) then whilst land and rabbit are productive and indeed necessary for production, no payments are made to the owners of land and of rabbits for the simple reason that individual property rights in land and in rabbits had not been established. The other assumption is that there is free exchange, with no impediments to the sale and production of any of the goods and services involved. Thus there would be no monopolies over particular goods or services nor would some groups of individuals be prevented from producing or exchanging specific goods or services. Clearly, if, for example, the rights to fish are limited by, say, royal prerogative, then fish may be able to command a higher price than would be indicated by the relative labour input.

But once the 'early and rude' state has been left behind, the labour theory is not generally seen as a *theory of price*, in that the actual relative prices of commodities are not expected to correspond to the (relative) labour values of the commodities. The nature of the relationship between the values of a commodity based on the labour time embodied in it and the 'prices of production' (which are equilibrium prices based on an equalised rate of profit) is generally referred to as the 'transformation problem', and is examined in some detail in Chapter 8. When capital equipment (which itself will have been produced using labour) is used in production, then it is likely that the ratio of capital equipment and labour input will vary between different products. Variations in that ratio will usually mean that the exchange ratio between goods and services will diverge from the ratio of labour inputs.[6] This will arise whether it is only the direct labour inputs which are included in such a calculation or whether both the direct and indirect labour inputs are included. The term 'indirect labour inputs' means the labour inputs which have been used to produce the materials and capital equipment which are themselves used in the production of the good concerned. The proponents of the labour theory of value (that is, that value depends on direct and indirect labour input) have long realised that price based on costs of production including a rate of profit would diverge from value. Some of the questions which arise are then the following:

1. What is the relationship between price and value? (This is usually referred to as the 'transformation problem', and will be further discussed in the next chapter.)
2. What is the purpose of talking about values, when it would appear that prices differ from them, and it is prices to which individuals respond?
3. If labour input cannot be used as the 'measuring rod', is there an alternative?

For much of the discussion in the nineteenth century, the relative labour values of goods and services were taken as a first approximation for the relative prices. If labour is the major input, and capital equipment is a relatively minor input, then the approximation may be a reasonably good one. How good the approximation is depends on the purpose at hand. If the purpose is the prediction of relative prices, some approximation may be permissible. But if the purpose is to understand why goods and services have prices, then precision would be required.

Adam Smith concluded that 'labour ... is the only universal, as well as the only accurate measure of value, or the only standard by which we can compare the values of different commodities at all times and at all places' (Smith, 1904). This quote could be taken as meaning that the value of a commodity depends on the labour *embodied* in it or as the labour *commanded* by a commodity. Both could be measured in terms of labour time, but the first would measure the time taken in the production of the commodity whereas the second would measure the labour time which the commodity could in effect buy. In the 'early and rude state of society',

> the labour embodied in and the labour commanded by a commodity would come to the same thing. But in a capitalist economy, where 'the whole produce of labour does not always belong to the labourer' the two indices part company unless ... wages move in step with the productivity of labour or, to put it another way, wages constitute a constant fraction of the total value of production. (Deane, 1978)

The next important contributor to this debate was Ricardo, and three elements of his approach are highlighted here. The first element is that a value (or pricing) theory based on the costs of production or on the use of one particular input (usually labour time) can only apply to products which are reproducible. This was probably a much more important limitation in the early nineteenth century when Ricardo was writing than it is now. Then, agriculture and land featured strongly in the economy, and land is generally seen as non-reproducible.[7] In the latter twentieth century, land is less significant, though commodities such as oil remind us of the relevance of non-reproducible products.

The second element is the search for a 'measuring rod' for real income, and in particular a measuring rod which did not bend when the distribution of income (as between wages and profits) varied.

> What Ricardo wanted was a measure of value which would be independent of changes in the division of the social product so that he could use it in a theory of distribution. For if a rise or fall in wages could of itself alter the value of total product it would be impossible to predict the effect on profits. (Deane, 1978)

However, Ricardo did not find a solution which he found to be satisfactory, but a partial solution can be derived within Sraffian economics and this is discussed below (section 8.8).

The third element was the recognition that the relative amounts of labour embodied in products would be only approximately equal to the relative prices of the products.

> The greatest effects which could be produced on the relative prices of these goods from a rise of wages, could not exceed 6 or 7 per cent; for profits could not, probably, under any circumstances admit of a greater general and permanent depression than to that amount. (Ricardo, 1951)

This led Stigler (1958) to label this the 93 per cent labour theory of value. However,

> conscious therefore that he was simplifying, but convinced that he was not straying far from practical reality, Ricardo measured the relative value of a commodity in terms of the quantity (man-hours) of labour embodied in its production. This enabled him to explain profits as a residual after accounting for labour's share in national income net of rents. (Deane, 1978)

The potential political, indeed revolutionary, impact of a theory of value can be seen from the use made by the Ricardian socialists of the labour theory of value. Meek (1967) argued 'that the majority of economists were very much aware of the dangerous use to which a number of radical writers were putting Ricardian concepts'. The Ricardian socialists were radicals in the 1820s and 1830s who were strongly influenced by the ideas of Ricardo. They argued 'that labour is the sole factor of production and that exploitation is an inevitable component of employer–worker relations in an economy based on private ownership' (Burkitt, 1984). Their position was built on three propositions. The first is that labour is the only source of wealth, and conversely that capital does not contribute to wealth creation. A leading Ricardian socialist, Hodgskin, published a book with the title *Labour defended against the Claims of Capital, or the Unproductiveness of Capital Proved by a Labourer.*

The second proposition is that the value of a commodity can be represented as the labour hours embodied in them. When labour is seen as the only source of value, it is a relatively short step to argue that labour ought to receive the entire proceeds of their labour, i.e. all the income, and that capitalists and landlords deserve none of the income. The Ricardian socialists

developed a theory of capitalist exploitation from the proposition that labour is the only source of wealth. . . . Although they differed in detail, they all argued that labour is the sole factor of production and that exploitation is an inevitable component of employer-worker relations in an economy based on private ownership. (Burkitt, 1984)

Some have supposed that the notion of exploitation, and hence of surplus-value, was in some way derived from the proposition that things exchange according to the amounts of labour embodied in them, presumably with the aid of some Lockean 'natural right' doctrine to the effect that labour gives right of ownership over its own produce. . . . Of the Ricardian Socialists this, or something like it, is true. (Dobb, 1973)

Thus this strand of the labour theory of value focused on the rights of labour over the product which labour produced. This represented a serious challenge to the defenders of capitalism, for it raised the question of the justification for any deduction from wages, and in particular for the existence of profits. One frequent justification has been that profits were derived from 'personal abstinence and entrepreneurial flair of the heroic, self-reliant owner manager, who has built up his own capital, risked his own substance, hired his own labour, found his own markets and, in the process, created a new and more productive system' (Marquand, 1988). But the growth of large companies and some separation between owner-ship and management in the second half of the nineteenth century made that justification less appealing. The challenge taken up in the late nineteenth century was to provide a justification for profits based on passive (rather than active entrepreneurial) ownership. This was based on the view that 'capital' is productive (i.e. more capital *equipment* enables a higher level of production) and that profits arise from the productive nature of capital equipment, but these profits are paid to the suppliers of finance capital (which permits the purchase of capital equipment) as a reward for thrift and abstinence. This line of argument is elaborated below (section 9.5).

The third proposition of the Ricardian socialists was that labour becomes a commodity under capitalism, that is labour is bought and sold. This would contrast with some earlier feudal societies in which labour along with many other goods and services were not bought and sold. In feudal times, much work was undertaken to provide for the sustenance of the worker and his family, and other work would have to be undertaken as an obligation to a feudal lord. Under capitalism, the worker is free to sell his or her services in the labour market, whereas under feudalism the worker is compelled to provide labour to the feudal lord. However, under capitalism, there is still the exploitation of the worker since (as outlined above) the worker does not receive the full value of their production.

7.3 SOME DIFFICULTIES WITH THE LABOUR THEORY OF VALUE

In this section, some of the difficulties which arise with the labour theory of value considered as a theory of value are discussed, leaving aside for the moment questions such as the relationship between value and price. The first difficulty arises from the existence of different types of labour with varying skills and talents. The labour theory of value requires some single measure of labour requirement, so that different types of labour have to be expressed in terms of one particular type of labour. This problem is usually conceived in terms of expressing different types of skilled labour in terms of unskilled labour. For differing skills which are acquired through education and training, the problem is resolvable in principle. A particular skilled person's labour is itself more valuable because of the labour which has been expended in providing the education and training on which the skill is based.

The second difficulty concerns the existence of different techniques for production. This may mean that different amounts of labour are required, with different skill levels and with a different time pattern. Marx sought to take account of differences in productive efficiency by using the idea of socially necessary labour and allowing for skill differences which arose from training. However, it is not only a matter of some firms being more efficient than others, but also that there is also usually a range of different techniques of production available to firms. Firms can then to some degree choose which technique of production to use, and that choice would be influenced by considerations of relative costs of the different techniques. The relevant point here is that the labour value of a commodity would then depend on which technique of production was chosen for the production of that commodity.

The third difficulty would appear to be that value depends on what it took to produce it, but does not depend on whether anyone wants what has been produced. However, classical economists recognised the relevance of 'use-value', that is, that a product had to have some use. The 'use-value' sounds rather like an alternative phrase for 'utility', which plays such a central role in neo-classical value theory. But there is a crucial difference between the classical and the neo-classical approach. In the classical approach, a product having use-value is a necessary condition for it having value but the extent of the value depends on the labour input. In the neo-classical approach, the reason why a product has value is that it provides utility, and the extent of the value depends on *marginal* utility. 'Utility then is not the measure of exchangeable value, although it is absolutely essential to it. ... Possessing utility, commodities derive their exchangeable value from two sources: from their scarcity, and from the quantity of labour required to obtain them' (Ricardo, 1951).

The fourth difficulty arises in the case of joint production. To take the oft-quoted example, if wool and mutton are jointly produced in the rearing of sheep, how can the labour used be allocated between wool and mutton? This point becomes particularly relevant when it is recognised that many modern industrial processes produce a number of products. Its relevance is further enhanced when consideration is given to the depreciation of fixed capital equipment (cf. section 8.4).

The fifth difficulty, to which attention has only been drawn in the past fifteen years (starting from Morishima, 1973, pp. 181–2, and Steedman, 1975) is that the labour value of a commodity calculated from embodied labour can be negative even though a positive amount of labour has been used in its production. Thus there is the paradox that a commodity has involved labour in its production but has a calculated negative value.

However, Morishima and Catephores (1978) develop an approach using inequalities rather than equalities which 'can easily accommodate the problem of jointness of production and the problem of choice of techniques'. They use a linear programming technique to generate a valuation which they call 'true values' (as compared with Marx's 'actual values'), where the 'true value' of a commodity is the minimum amount of labour required to produce it. In this way they are able to overcome some of the difficulties indicated in this section, and specifically that labour values as they now define them cannot be negative. The relevance of their approach will also be seen below.

7.4 MARX AND THE LABOUR THEORY OF VALUE

The Marxian labour theory of value is explicitly intended to apply only to capitalism. It is an important feature that capitalists own the means of production and workers are compelled to work. The distinction is made between labour and labour power, where it is labour power which is purchased from the worker by the capitalist. How much labour can be obtained from a particular amount of labour power depends on the intensity of labour and the degree of control exercised in the labour process, as discussed in Chapter 2. There is competition so that there is a uniformity of rates of profits and of wages (discussed further below in section 8.4) across different sectors of the economy. Within the theory, profits do not arise from possession of monopoly power (in the product market) nor from any special ability to buy at low prices and sell at high prices. The interpretation of this can be that (at least in the context of the nineteenth century) monopoly in product markets was unimportant and that the industrial sector was competitive.[8] An alternative interpretation is that profits would arise even in the absence of monopoly (and would be increased by monopoly).

We begin by introducing some definitions. Production requires the use of labour power, materials and capital equipment. All the variables are measured in terms of socially necessary labour time and hence the units of measurement are those of time. The significance of the phrase 'socially necessary' is that the calculations are in terms of the average efficiency currently in use. On one side this means that an inefficient firm or one which is unable to extract as much labour power from its workers as other firms would be using more labour than other firms. But in the calculation of the value of the production of that firm only the socially necessary amount of labour would be taken into account. On the other side, a firm which can use less labour than the socially necessary will be reaping higher profits. Constant capital (c) is defined as the labour value of the materials and the depreciation of capital equipment. Variable capital (v) is the value of the labour input. The labour input can be seen as variable capital in two senses. There can be variation in the amount of labour power which is expended. In other words, the intensity with which workers work can vary; and this was a major theme of Chapter 2. The second sense is that labour creates value, whereas the materials retain their value but do not create further value during the process of production which turns these material inputs and labour power into output.

A distinction is drawn between use-value, exchange-value and value. 'The usefulness of a thing makes it a use-value'. But '[a] use value, or useful article, therefore has value only because abstract labour is objectified or materialized in it'. A thing (e.g. air) can have use-value without having value when it is not the product of human labour. But,

> nothing can be a value without being an object of utility. If the thing is useless, so is the labour contained in it; the labour does not count as labour, and therefore creates no value. ... Exchange-values appear first of all as the quantitative relation, the proportion, in which use-values of one kind exchange for use-values of another kind. (Marx, 1976)

Labour-power is assumed to be bought and sold at its value, that is the amount of labour-time necessary to produce it. 'If it takes 6 hours to produce the average daily means of subsistence of the worker, he must work an average of 6 hours a day to produce his daily labour-power, or to reproduce the value received as a result of its sale' (Marx, 1976). The expression 'average daily means of subsistence' has often been interpreted as Marx saying that wages would be kept at a minimum level necessary for physical survival. However, it is usually taken that the view of subsistence depends on the society and level of development and is culturally determined (for further discussion see Rowthorn, 1980).

Labour has a use-value to capitalists which is greater than its exchange-value. The exchange-value is the cost of labour whereas the use-value is equivalent to the production which the labour produces. The degree of control over the labour process, as discussed in Chapter 2, determines the volume of that production. The greater is the difference between the exchange-value and the use-value, the greater will be the surplus which the capitalist extracts from labour. One way of expressing this general view is as follows:

> The worker, during one part of the labour process, produces only the value of his labour-power, i.e. the value of his means of subsistence. ... During the second period of the labour process, that in which his labour is no longer necessary labour, the worker does indeed expend labour-power, he does work, but his labour is no

longer necessary labour, and he creates no value for himself. He creates surplus-value which, for the capitalist, has all the charms of something created out of nothing. This part of the working day I call surplus labour-time, and to the labour expended during that time I give the name of surplus labour. (Marx, 1976)

The value of the product is given by $c + v + s$, where s is the surplus value, with c and v defined as above. The surplus value is the excess of the use-value of labour over the exchange-value; alternatively expressed, it is the excess of what is produced over the cost of labour embodied in the commodity. The rate of surplus value is defined as s/v, and in terms of the quote from Marx given above is the ratio of the hours worked expropriated by the capitalist to the hours worked which are paid for. A rise in *relative* surplus value results from a fall in v, that is the number of hours required to maintain workers at a constant level of subsistence. This would arise, for example, when technical change enabled the production of workers' consumption goods to be produced at lower cost. A rise in *absolute* surplus value occurs when s increases due to lengthening of the working day. The rate of surplus value shows the extent to which capitalists are able to force workers to produce more than is paid in wages. The higher is s/v, the greater is the share of output taken by capitalists. This leads into the Marxian theory of income distribution which is discussed in Chapter 9.

The size of s/v can be seen as depending on four factors. The first is the length of the working day. If the working day can be lengthened and thereby more produced without any increase in wages, then clearly the rate of surplus value will increase. The second factor is the intensity of work, i.e. the degree of effort which workers have to undertake. The harder workers can be forced to work, the more will be produced, and hence the greater the rate of surplus value. The third is the proportion of the working day required for workers to produce the equivalent of the commodities which are necessary for their subsistence and reproduction. The fourth factor is the productivity of labour as affected by the capital equipment and technology with which it works. A rise in this productivity will raise output (per person at a given work intensity) and in itself raise the rate of surplus value.

The rate of profit (measured in value terms) can be written as $s/(c + v)$, and then rewritten as $(s/v)/(c/v + 1)$. This expresses the rate of profit in terms of the rate of surplus value and the 'organic composition of capital' (c/v). The discussion on movements in the rate of profit is delayed until Chapter 9, where it is placed alongside a more general discussion. But it should be noted here that this rate of profit is measured in value terms, and the question has to be raised as to the correspondence between that rate of profit and one which is measured in terms of prices, and this question is covered in the discussion below.

In the Marxian tradition, profits in a capitalist system are based on exploitation and a surplus. This clearly involves the existence of a surplus, and the control by capitalists of the means of production which enables capitalists to capture the surplus.

> What distinguishes the various economic formations of society – the distinction between for example a society based on slave-labour and a society based on wage-labour – is the form in which this surplus labour is in each case extorted from the immediate producer, the worker. (Marx, 1976)

In feudal and other pre-capitalist societies, the capture of a surplus by the powerful groups in those societies is plain. It may take, for example, the form of the lord of the manor extracting labour from the peasants without payment. It may take the form that the very powerful can command labour and extract surplus with which to have monuments built to themselves. But in capitalist societies, the extraction of a surplus is more subtle. The legal compulsion associated with feudalism is no longer present, and the worker appears to be free. However, the freedom is a limited one; there may be freedom to choose one employer rather than another but the worker has to work in order to survive. The capitalists own the means of production (e.g. capital equipment) and the workers do not. Hence in order to work, workers have to find work with capitalists. Capitalists as a class have a monopoly over the means of production. This is not the monopoly of a single producer in a product market, but rather a class monopoly over the ownership of the means of production and access to finance. This is to say that the monopoly concerned is not the control of the production of a particular commodity by a single individual (or firm) but rather the control by a social class over the means of production. It is implicit in that view that capitalists have common interests and operate (at least to some degree) in pursuit of those interests.

The degree to which a capitalist economy offers freedom

(however that may be defined) will find echoes elsewhere in this book. Whilst we do not enter into the broad debate which a full treatment would entail, nevertheless it does have some important implications in the analysis of the labour market and the labour process. The radical political economy view tends to have two elements. First, workers have a rather limited freedom since they have to work in order to survive. At the workplace, control is ceded to capitalists, and workers have to take orders from owners and managers. Second, the labour market generally suffers from inadequate demand for labour relative to the supply which is available (cf. section 11.1).

The Marxian view could then be summarised by saying that capitalists receive the surplus because they have control over the means of production. Thus, receipt of the surplus depends on economic power, which comes from ownership. The ownership of the means of production and the control of the production process provide the means to extract surplus-value from labour. Further, profits arise from a surplus which itself arises in the process of production. The product market may itself be competitive, and there would still be profits because of the control over the process of production. This view on the nature and source of profits is more fully discussed in Chapter 9, where it is compared with other views on profits.

This Marxian view implies that capitalists do not contribute anything to the process of production but are able to extract profits through ownership of the means of production. In this way, capitalists are little different from, say, feudal barons, for in both cases power enables the extraction of a surplus. The difference lies in that the feudal baron's power arises from political and legal power whereas the capitalist's power arises from economic power. It is power which is less obvious and more discrete, but it is still power nevertheless.

The existence of a surplus of output over wages is not in doubt (although it may not be described in such terms), but the question arises on the relationship between surplus, surplus value and profits. Surplus value is measured in value terms, whereas profits are measured in terms of prices. The 'transformation problem' involved in the relationship between prices and values has been mentioned above, and arises again here in terms of the relationship between surplus value measured in value terms and profits measured in terms of 'prices of production'. A number of authors have used the phrase the fundamental Marxian theorem (hereafter FMT) for the notion that positive surplus value (measured in terms of values) is a necessary and sufficient condition for positive profits (measured in terms of prices of production). There are two aspects of this FMT which are addressed here. First, is the theorem mathematically correct, and second, if it is, what is its significance?

It is perhaps not surprising that the answer to the first question is that it depends on what assumptions are made, and in particular, it does depend on the assumptions made concerning the availability of a range of techniques of production. When there is a single technique of production for each commodity (and hence capitalists have no choice over which technique to use) and in which there is no joint production, then the FMT holds. Further, to refer back to one of the difficulties raised above concerning the labour theory of value, under those conditions labour values are well-defined and never negative. But these technical assumptions can be seen as very restrictive, ruling out joint production, for example. It was mentioned above that joint production involves not only the classic mutton/wool case, but also any case where there is fixed capital equipment (see section 8.4).

Morishima and Catephores (1978) use an inequality approach, with 'true values' rather than 'actual values' as indicated above, which 'enables us to extend the Fundamental Marxian Theorem ... to cover the case of joint products and the choice of techniques'. Under assumptions which they regard as 'plausible, realistic, and basic to all economic analysis', they prove the generalised fundamental Marxian theorem (GFMT), namely that 'positive exploitation is necessary and sufficient for the system to have positive growth capacity as well as to guarantee capitalists positive profits'.[9]

The significance of this line of argument has been questioned by Steedman (1977) among others. It arises from the conclusion that positive profits arise if and only if there is positive surplus value. This could be interpreted (as it often has been) as saying that surplus value (and hence exploitation in the Marxian sense) is the cause of profits. But, in a mathematical sense, it could be equally be said that profits are a cause of surplus value. The mathematical argument can say nothing about which is the cause and which is the effect.

The very fact that the proposition in question 'runs both ways' (r [rate of profit] is positive *if and only if* S [surplus value] is positive) means at once that it does not constitute a theory of why *r* is positive. A theory of *why profits are positive* will at the same time, be a theory of why surplus value is positive. Neo-classical economists do not commonly invoke the concept of surplus labour but they could do so without causing the slightest inconsistency within their theory. ... [A neo-classical economist] might say, 'Time preference is positive; therefore the rate of profit is positive; therefore surplus labour is positive. (Steedman, 1977; italics in original)

Thus the algebra cannot settle the matter, for that does not tell us about the causes of profits.

7.5 DEBATES ON THE LABOUR THEORY OF VALUE

With the revival of interest in Marxian economics during the 1970s and the development of the Sraffian approach (discussed in the next chapter), the nature and relevance of the labour theory of value became the subject of intense debate.[10] It is useful to follow the distinction drawn by Sen (1978) of three distinct though interrelated non-metaphysical interpretations of the labour theory of value, which will also help to indicate the differences drawn on the nature of the labour theory of value.

The first is labelled *descriptive* in the sense of making a statement about the real world which draws attention to some key features of the world. It may, for example, be used to focus on the necessary involvement of people in the process of production. Marx (1976) argued that value is 'a relation between persons disguised as a relation between things'. One purpose of the labour theory of value can then be seen to draw attention to the participation and involvement of people in the process of production. 'For humans in society, labour power is a special category, separate and inexchangeable with any other, *simply because it is human*' (Braverman, 1974). However, when the human involvement in production activities is stressed, 'it is, however, worth underlining that the descriptive features thus focused on is not the so-called "law of value" dealing with the proportionality of prices to values' (Sen, 1978).

The second interpretation is to treat the labour theory of value (LTV) as a *predictive* theory, with the predictions concerning prices. In general, however, this view of the LTV has not been followed in the sense that actual prices are not expected to be proportional to labour values. The relationship ('transformation problem') between labour values and the 'prices of production' is discussed in the next chapter. It is argued by some defenders of the LTV that prices of production are superficial (that is, appear on the surface only) whereas the labour values are more fundamental (see below). It should be noted, however, that both labour values and the prices of production are theoretical constructs to which actual (market) prices will not generally conform. Thus, even prices of production, in which prices are based on the costs of production and the rate of profit, do not necessarily conform with actual market prices. Indeed, some have argued that labour values provide a more accurate guide to actual market prices than prices of production do.

The third view of the labour theory of value can be labelled *normative*, and relates to views taken on the rights of certain classes to particular types of income. Two aspects of this need to be highlighted. One normative aspect would be the interpretation that labour produces the whole product and is thereby entitled to all the benefits. One expression of this view was made by the Ricardian socialists, as briefly mentioned above. Another aspect would be the view that it is factors of production which are productive, i.e. capital machines, raw materials, labour power which contribute to the overall level of production. But income is largely received in capitalist economies on the basis of ownership. It is the capital machine which enhances production level, but it is the owners of that machine who receive the profits. In that way, profits are a reward for ownership and not for adding to production. Labour power is unique (in capitalist societies) in being human and where the owner and the factor of production coincide.

In the debate over the labour theory of value, it is useful to identify the range of opinions by reference to two sets of views which could be identified as the extremes (among those with some sympathy with the work of Marx). At one end of the range are those who would argue that the calculation of labour values was at best an irrelevance and at worst a definite hindrance. Steedman (1981), for example, argues that 'the ineradicable difficulties involved in labour theories of value have always, and quite reasonably, been regarded as barriers to serious consideration of Marx's political economy'. But 'some recent arguments which demonstrate that certain central aspects of Marx's political economy are entirely *independent* of any "labour theory of value"'. Further, 'it is now generally recognized that the demonstration of that irrelevance [of the labour theory of value] is logically impeccable'. The difficulties of the 'labour theory of value' include the possibility of negative labour values. The argument of Steedman is based on a Sraffian approach, and the elaboration of this line of argument must await our discussion of the Sraffian approach in the next chapter (see especially section 8.8).

In one sense, labour is akin to any other input which is used directly or indirectly in the production of every commodity.

> It would be quite possible to go through the whole of Sraffa's book, deleting the word 'labour' and substituting 'horse-power' (assuming that horses are used to produce at least one basic good). The word 'wages' would become 'the food and maintenance distributed to the horses'. Formally, all this would make sense; there is no logical objection. The result could be a 'dated horse-power series' and a 'horse-power theory of value'! ... the unique properties of labour, and labour-power, are important, and should not be neglected. In particular, labour-power is the only commodity which is inseparable from its owner, and under capitalism it is produced under non-capitalist conditions. (Hodgson, 1982c)

At the other end of the range are those who argue that the labour theory of value contains some important insights which would be lost by its abandonment. In considering these arguments, it should be noted that the labour theory of value is generally interpreted in a rather broad sense way. For example,

> the most important role that the LTV plays in Marx's writings is to expose the conflict between classes: between capitalists and workers. ... Similarly, in studying the nature and origin of profits, Marx was using the LTV as a descriptive theory. ... He stressed the fact that profits were not due to the private ownership of the means of production, but due to the existence of surplus labour or surplus value. The importance of the LTV in exposing the 'reality' beneath the 'appearances' is often suggested by Marx. (Junankar, 1982)

There is a distinction to be drawn between prices which appear in the market and values which do not appear but nevertheless are significant. 'Reality is made up of appearances *and* essence. Prices of production belong to the realm of appearance, values to the realm of essence' (Sweezy, 1981). Sweezy acknowledges that total price does not equal total value, and the rate of profit in the price scheme is not equal to the rate of profit in the value scheme. But these are changes of dimension only, not of substance; and there is no reason to suppose that analysing the accumulation process on the basis of values yields results which need to be altered in any significant way by shifting to prices.

He argues that

the key concept and variable in the analysis, the centre of gravity which holds everything in place, is the rate of surplus-value, *and it is precisely the rate of surplus-value which disappears, vanishes without a trace, from an analysis made in terms of prices.*

Much of the argument of authors such as Hodgson and Steedman is that the 'prices of production' and labour values are essentially on a par with each other, and the data required for the calculation of one is the data required for the other. It is the significance of this which Fine and Harris (1979) dispute when they write that

Marx's theory consists of the proposition that this transformation is not an arbitrary, purely mental operation, but parallels the relations of determination which exist in reality. In other words, in reality surplus value is produced but it never appears as such; it appears as profits.

There are three conclusions reached by Marx which are especially significant in distinguishing his work from Classical and neo-Classical political economy and which are uniquely based on this abstraction. First, the determining contradiction in capitalism is the antagonism of the two great classes; second, capitalism is a dynamic system producing constant revolutions in the process of production; third, capitalism involves tensions and displacements between production, exchange and distribution.

Fine and Harris then make clear that each of these topics are to be discussed in value terms, e.g. 'The dynamic nature of capitalism ... is similarly seen as being fundamentally based on the antagonism of capital-in-general with labour. As such it can, again, logically only be analysed in value terms.' In sum, 'there are, then, three particular results obtained by Marx on the basis of value analysis. Neo-Ricardianism, by abandoning such analysis, cannot obtain these results although it may in some cases put forward propositions which appear similar' (Fine and Harris, 1979).

7.6 SUBJECTIVE OR OBJECTIVE?

One sharp contrast which can be drawn between the neo-classical view of value based on utility analysis and the radical political economy approach can be summarised in terms of subjective or objective? The neo-classical view is seen as being subjective since if value is based on utility, then since utility is essentially based on individuals' subjective feelings, tastes and preferences, it can be said that value is subjective. In contrast, in the radical political economy approach, value is seen as based on the costs of production. In the labour theory of value, the emphasis is clearly on labour costs. In the next chapter, it will be seen that the Sraffian approach derives equilibrium 'prices of production' which are based on the costs of production.

The marginalist idea, which is so strongly embedded in neo-classical economics, can be seen as stressing the importance of subjective feelings. Marginal utility represents subjective feelings in two ways. First, and most clearly, the utility represents a person's tastes and feelings. The impression is given that those tastes and feelings are generated by the person themselves. In other words, no attention is paid to the moulding of those tastes through, for example, advertising and socialisation. Second, the margin is a subjective assessment. For example, marginal cost is the difference in costs between one level of output and another level divided by the difference in output (i.e. $(C_2 - C_1)/(Q_2 - Q_1)$) for a small difference in output. At most, only one of the output levels can be actually observed at any particular time. Thus if the firm actually produces output Q_1 with cost C_1, it can only estimate what the costs would have been if the output had been Q_2. In the next time period it may decide to operate at output level Q_2, but there may be many differences (e.g. in input prices, technology) between one time period and the next. Hence, even if Q_1, C_1 is observed by the firm, Q_2, C_2 is not and so the calculation of marginal cost is always based on an estimate of what would have happened. Further, in much theorising, concepts such as marginal cost, marginal revenue are intended as concepts which are (or could be) used by decision-makers. Thus if a firm is making a decision on output, it needs to have estimates of the costs of different levels of output prior to making the decision. So the marginal cost relevant for the decision-maker is the estimate of that cost prior to the decision. When the firm has decided upon a particular level of output it may be able to judge the accuracy or otherwise of its estimate of the level of costs associated with that output, but not on the accuracy of its estimate of marginal cost.

The neo-classical theory of profits and wages can then be described as a subjective theory. It is subjective in being based on tastes (utility) for the derivation of the supply of labour, 'capital', etc., and also subjective in drawing on the concept of the margin. The neo-classical theory of value can be seen as also firmly a subjective theory. On the demand side (for goods and services), the role of subjective assessment of utility is clear in the derivation of demand curves based on utility maximisation. On the supply side, the supply curve for a product is based on the marginal cost of production. But the marginal cost is based on wages, profits and material costs. Material inputs are purchased from other firms, and the material costs are themselves based on wages, profits and other material costs. Eventually, the material costs can be broken down into wages and profits. When the wages and profits depend on disutility, the picture is complete for the determination of value based on subjective elements.

Since price and value are virtually synonymous in the neo-classical approach, it can also be said that this approach has a subjective view of price. The contrast can be drawn between that subjective approach and the objective one of much of the radical political economy tradition. This objective nature will be more clearly seen in the next chapter when the prices of production are discussed, where it will be seen that the data required to calculate prices of production are the technical coefficients (relating inputs to outputs) and the rate of profit (or equivalently the real wage). The Sraffian approach is then seen as a way of determining equilibrium prices without any recourse to the subjective notions of utility, etc. The labour theory of value can be seen as an objective theory of value in that the value of a product depends on the (direct and indirect) labour time spent in its production. Thus, in principle, the value (according to the labour theory of value) of a product could be calculated from a knowledge of objective (measurable) factors.

A further major difference between the classical approach (which is continued in the radical political economy approach) and the neo-classical approach to price and value concerns the roles of production and distribution (on which classical economists and political economists place emphasis) and of exchange (on which neo-classical economists focus), and reference was made to this difference in Chapter 1. When production and distribution are emphasised, then it is perhaps not surprising that the conditions of production (the technical coefficients) and of income distribution (rate of profit or real wage) are relevant for the determination of prices (as occurs with the Sraffian approach). Similarly, when exchange is emphasised, the utility gained from possession of goods and services becomes important and influences price formation.

7.7 VALUE AS A METAPHYSICAL CONCEPT

Many doubts have been raised about the usefulness of any value theory whether of the utility-based or the labour theory of value kind. Joan Robinson, among others, attacked both value theories for being metaphysical. Robinson argued 'utility – a metaphysical concept, a mere word, that has no scientific content, yet one which expresses a point of view' (Robinson, 1962), and she made a similar point regarding the Marxian value theory. When the concept of utility was first used in economic theorising, it was generally seen as potentially measurable. But any ideas of measuring utility have long disappeared, and the cardinal notion of utility has been replaced by the ordinal notion. Nevertheless, it is still asserted in the neo-classical approach that goods and services provide utility, the evidence for which is that people seek to acquire goods and services.

The utility theory can also be seen as involving circular reasoning. An item has value because someone purchases it, and they purchase it because it provides them with utility. But the only way by which we presume that it gives them utility is that they buy it. '*Utility* is a metaphysical concept of impregnable circularity; *utility* is a quality in commodities that makes individuals want to buy them, and the fact that individuals want to buy commodities show that they have *utility*' (Robinson, 1962).

If value is seen as governing price, then the statement can be put that X determines value which sets price, with the positive (testable) aspect that X sets price provided that X can be observed. But the statement 'X determines value' is metaphysical since value itself cannot be observed. The labour theory of value is metaphysical because it denies the second part, i.e. that value sets price. The utility theory is metaphysical in that utility is not measurable, though value and price are closely identified.

A concept which is metaphysical may nevertheless have important practical consequences. For example, a belief in a form of the labour theory of value influenced the Ricardian socialists, and led them to advocate particular courses of action. Thus an understanding of the way economies operate can often require an appreciation of metaphysical concepts which are influencing the manner in which people behave in those economies.

NOTES

1. The ordinal utility approach, which has become the neo-classical orthodoxy, indicates that utility as such is not measurable, but that the price ratio of two products will be equated with the marginal rate of substitution between the products.
2. This is reflected to some degree in the following quote from a text written from a neo-classical position. 'We must avoide the temptation to judge a given form of behaviour as contemptuous, immoral, good or bad. Therefore, in the context of our analysis, the services of a prostitute are treated no differently than the services of the butcher; they are neither good nor bad – they exist and are subject to analysis' (McKenzie and Tullock, 1981).
3. The three originators of the concept of marginal utility are generally acknowledged to be Jevons (1871), Menger (1951) and Walras (1954) in the 1870s.
4. For further discussion on the development of the labour theory of value see, for example, Deane (1978), Dobb (1973) and Meek (1973).
5. The general thinking on value prior to Adam Smith had been rather different. 'For example, in medieval-scholastic doctrine the value of the commodity tended to be identified with the morally right price. In a static, parochialised economic and social order the just price would equal the customary price, reflecting a socially accepted scale of values, and the whole community would know what the fair price *ought* to be' (Deane, 1978).
6. There are conditions under which this divergence would not occur. This could be that the rate of profit (interest) is zero so indirect labour is not weighted more highly than direct labour. The alternative is that the ratio of direct labour to indirect labour (and its time pattern) is the same across all products.

7. It can be argued that land can to some extent be produced, e.g. land reclaimed from the sea or brought into cultivation. But there is a limit on how far that is possible. It is also a matter of degree, and if it is necessary to classify land as reproducible or non-reproducible the latter appears to be a better approximation than the former.

8. The development of capitalism during the late eighteenth century and nineteenth century broke down many elements of monopoly. From the late nineteenth century onwards, there has been a general trend towards larger firms and more concentrated markets. The emergence of structural monopoly is generally acknowledged, but the significance of those changes is a matter of debate, as can be seen from Chapters 5 and 6.

9. The assumptions are as follows:
   (a) Labour is indispensable to provide the subsistence–consumption basket.
   (b) When workers are paid no wages, capitalists are guaranteed positive profits.
   (c) Labour is indispensable for the economy to grow at the capacity growth rate.
   For details see Morishima and Catephores (1978, pp. 45–53).

10. Many of the positions taken in the debate on value theory are represented in Steedman *et al.* (1981).

Chapter 8

AN INTRODUCTION TO SRAFFIAN ECONOMICS

8.1 INTRODUCTION

The work of Sraffa (1960) sparked a revival of interest in the work of Ricardo and the classical economists and also served to establish a new branch of economic theory.[1] This branch has often been labelled neo-Ricardian, though the term Sraffian is preferred since this term indicates the immediate origins of the approach in the work of Sraffa and avoids considerations of the relationship between this approach and the work of Ricardo. There has been a substantial literature developing and exploring the approach of Sraffa, as well as many works using the Sraffian approach from which to criticise both neo-classical and Marxian economic theory.[2] It has provided an alternative vision of the nature of the economic system with an emphasis on the use of surplus and the reproduction of the economic system. But also some of the conclusions drawn from the Sraffian approach have been used as a critique of Marxian labour theory of value (Steedman, 1977, 1981). The purpose of this chapter is only to serve as an introduction to the Sraffian approach. As far as possible simple numerical examples are used to indicate conclusions which are of more general validity. It is also the intention to bring out the differences of approach between the Sraffian framework and that of the neo-classical one. Thus this chapter should be treated as only providing a flavour of the Sraffian approach.[3]

The Sraffian approach has to be seen as seeking to answer a certain range of questions. These questions have been central to economic inquiry for the past two centuries. The range of questions include the following:

1. What is the relationship between the prices of commodities,

price of labour (wages) and the rate of profit?
2. Following from 1, in the event of specified changes (e.g. the inputs required for a particular good are reduced by technical progress), what are the consequent changes of prices?
3. Is there a 'measuring rod' available which will permit the comparison of different bundles of goods and services?

The technique which the Sraffian approach adopts is that of the analysis of long-run equilibrium positions. The outcomes are equilibrium ones in the sense that the price of any input or output is uniform (e.g. there are no variations in the price of an identical product between different areas of the country) and there is a uniform rate of profit across all economic activities. It is long-run in that the process of the equalisation of the rate of profit is anticipated to be one which will in some relevant sense take a long time to work itself out. Indeed, some would see the long-run equilibrium as a position which is never achieved, though at any particular time the economy will be tending towards some long-run equilibrium. However, the long-run equilibrium is seen as likely to change before the economy actually reaches it. Questions such as the determination of the relationship between inputs and outputs, the aggregate level of employment are not addressed by the Sraffian approach. The relationship between inputs and outputs will be summarised in terms of the use of inputs made in the production of outputs, and the relative use of the inputs (per unit of output) will be referred to as the *technical coefficients* of production. These technical coefficients should not be seen as technologically determined. For example, the amount of the labour input required to produce a unit of any particular commodity would not be fully specified by the prevailing technology, but the conditions of control over the labour and the resulting labour intensity as discussed in Chapter 2 would also be relevant.

It has been noted in relation to Sraffa (1960) that the

assumptions [made] do not contain a statement of the institutional structures to which the analysis relates. There is, for example, no assumption pertaining to economic agents. In particular, there is no specification that producers maximise profit, that consumers choose rationally and there is no reference to demand and supply relations. (Bradley and Howard, 1982b)

It will be seen below that consumer demand plays no role (and hence neither does utility optimisation), nor is there any direct reference to any choices which producers may make on the techniques of production to be used. The production side of the economy is described by the technical coefficients which relate inputs with output. The long-run equilibrium condition is the equalisation of the rate of profit, from which it may be inferred that capitalist competition of the Marxian variety is assumed (cf. section 8.4).

8.2 A SIMPLE EXAMPLE

The first stage is undertaken with a simple numerical example, which is used to illustrate the underlying framework of the Sraffian approach. Consider an economy in which there are only three commodities, and in which each of three commodities is used as an input in the production process as well as being produced as an output. These three commodities are labelled as corn, iron and pigs. There is a significant time gap between the entry of the inputs into the productive process and the exit of the outputs, and this gap is labelled a year, so that the process of production does not take place instantaneously (as envisaged in a neo-classical production function). The production of corn requires the input of iron, pigs as well as corn itself. Similarly, the production of iron and corn each require the input of all three commodities. The technical conditions under which production takes place is summarised in Table 8.1, where the numerical example used initially by Sraffa (1960) is reproduced as Example 1. It indicates, for example, that the production of 450 kg of corn at the end of the year requires the input of 240 kg of corn, 1200 kg of iron and 18 pigs at the beginning of the year. Similarly, the production of 2100 kg of iron requires the use of 90 kg of corn, 600 kg of iron and 12 pigs as inputs.

The numbers in Example 1 in Table 8.1 do not arise by accident, but rather have been chosen so that the volume of outputs balances with the volume of inputs. So, for example, this cycle of production uses 60 pigs as inputs and also produces 60 pigs as output. Thus, the productive system described is capable of exact reproduction. It can be seen that each year this economic system produces just enough output of the three commodities to match the inputs which were used as inputs into the productive process. Thus the rather simple economic system described in Example 1 is capable of reproducing itself from year to year.

Table 8.1 Some simple numerical examples.

Example 1

Production process	Inputs			Output
	Corn (kg)	Iron (100 kg)	Pigs (Numbers)	
Corn	240	12	18	450 kg of corn
Iron	90	6	12	21 × 100 kg of iron
Pigs	120	3	30	60 pigs
Input usage	450	21	60	

Example 2

Production process	Inputs			Output
	Corn (kg)	Iron (100 kg)	Pigs (Numbers)	
Corn	240	12	18	480 kg of corn
Iron	90	6	12	21 × 100 kg of iron
Pigs	120	3	30	60 pigs
Input usage	450	21	60	

This simple numerical example illustrates a number of the key features involved in the Sraffian approach. First, the idea that production takes time has been introduced by thinking here in terms of an annual cycle of production. The key notion is that there is a significant length of time elapsing between the entry of inputs into the productive process and the emergence of the output. The full relevance of this will become more apparent below. The use of an agricultural example and an annual production cycle is not purely coincidental as it represents the type of example used in the nineteenth century by Ricardo. There is nothing sacrosanct about an annual cycle based on agriculture but some time gap between the use of inputs and the emergence of output is important. It is convenient to talk of production cycle lasting a 'year' in the exposition, but this should not be thought of as a calendar year of 12 months.

Second, there is a focus on the production side of the economy rather than on consumption. In Table 8.1, the numbers entered refer to the production side (i.e. they relate to the relationship between inputs and output), and it will be seen below that prices derived are influenced by the interaction of the production techniques and the requirement of an equalised rate of profit. This will mean that the prices so determined do not rest on any considerations of marginal utility.

Third, production is regarded as a circular process whereby inputs are used to produce outputs in one period, and those outputs from the inputs for the next period. Indeed, the title of Sraffa (1960) is *The Production of Commodities by Means of Commodities*, and this element of production as a circular process is particularly noticeable from the numerical example. This contrasts with the neo-classical view which sharply distinguishes between inputs and outputs whereby the input–output relationship is technically determined, the resources available provide the inputs, and the output is the purpose of production leading through to consumption. This view of the input–output relationship corresponds to the means–ends dichotomy. In contrast, the Sraffian approach focuses on the process of production and re-production and on the uses of a surplus, which were seen above to be important elements in the radical political economy approach. The simple example given as Example 1 in Table 8.1 relates to an economic system which is capable of reproduction, and in which the means of production are themselves produced and hence over time can be added to, though in this example the system does not expand.

The Sraffian approach focuses on the technical coefficients of production in order to answer a limited range of questions, notably the relationship between wages and rate of profit and between prices and rate of profit. The rate of profit and wages are not immediately introduced for this first example but will arise below. These relationships between prices, wages and the rate of profit are explored in the context of long-run equilibrium under conditions of classical/Marxian competition (cf. discussion in Chapter 5). The operation of the forces of competition means that there is a tendency towards the equalisation of the rate of profit and towards the establishment of a single price for each commodity. The long-run nature of the analysis allows that those tendencies towards uniformity are assumed to have worked themselves out. The crucial aspect of that line of argument is that in each line of activity (i.e. here the production of each commodity) the revenue gained from the sale of a commodity is exactly equal to the costs of the inputs used in the production of that commodity. When the rate of profit and 'capital' are explicitly introduced below, the costs of inputs will include paying for 'capital' at the prevailing rate of profit. But there will not be any 'super-normal' profits available in any line of activity.

The condition of the equality between revenue and costs (as a long-run equilibrium condition) can be applied for the particular numerical example given in Example 1 in Table 8.1. The price of corn is labelled p_1 (per kg), of iron p_2 (per 100 kg) and of pigs p_3 (per pig). The costs of the inputs used in the production of corn would be $240p_1 + 12p_2 + 18p_3$, where the first item is the cost of corn used as input, the second the cost of iron and the third the cost of pigs used. The revenue from the production of corn is $450p_1$. The long-run equilibrium condition that costs equals revenue in the production of corn is:

$$240p_1 + 12p_2 + 18p_3 = 450p_1 \tag{8.1}$$

This procedure can be repeated for the price of iron so that the costs equal to revenue condition there is:

$$90p_1 + 6p_2 + 12p_3 = 21p_2 \tag{8.2}$$

Similarly, the condition for the price of pigs is:

$$120p_1 + 3p_2 + 30p_3 = 60p_3 \tag{8.3}$$

These can be rearranged in a slightly simpler form as:

$$-210p_1 + 12p_2 + 18p_3 = 0 \tag{8.4}$$

$$90p_1 - 15p_2 + 12p_3 = 0 \tag{8.5}$$

$$120p_1 + 3p_2 - 30p_3 = 0 \tag{8.6}$$

It would appear that these are three equations in three unknowns, and hence a solution could be obtained for the three unknown prices. But it can be seen from equations (8.4), (8.5), (8.6) that the addition of equations (8.4) and (8.5) would yield equation (8.6) so that the three equations are not linearly independent. Thus there are only two independent equations, so that it is only possible to solve for two prices. However, it is possible to solve this set of equations for relative prices (say p_1/p_3, p_2/p_3). This is not a surprising outcome in that no information is provided or assumptions made which relate to the absolute price level. The determination of the overall price level is a rather different matter. If a monetarist perspective were adopted, then information on the money stock would be required (along with the volume of production) to be able to solve for the overall price level. A more post-Keynesian approach would see some key price (especially the price of labour, i.e. wages) as set by social and historical factors, and the absolute price level dependent on the level of that key price. It is necessary then to take one good as the numeraire, and for no particular reason pigs are taken as the numeraire. Hence the price of pigs is taken as unity, i.e. $p_3 = 1$, and then equations (8.4), (8.5) can be solved to yield $p_1 = 0.2$ and $p_2 = 2$.

These prices will be referred to below as 'prices of production', which reflects the idea that these prices are based on the costs of production. A distinction will be drawn between these prices of production, which are long-period equilibrium prices, and 'market prices', which would be the actual prices appearing in the real economy. In general there will be a divergence between the two types of prices since usually the economic system would not be in long-period equilibrium. Further, the causes of the divergence between actual market prices and long-period prices of production can be various, but two in particular are mentioned here. First, the divergence arise from disequilibrium; that is to say, market prices may be moving towards or fluctuating around the prices of production, but do not actually equal them because the adjustment process has not worked itself out. Second, the market prices may reflect elements of monopoly or oligopoly so that the equality between costs and revenue may not be achieved in all activities. In particular, those commodities produced under conditions of monopoly would exhibit revenue in excess of costs, and the producers of those commodities would reap the benefits of monopoly.

8.3 A MODIFIED NUMERICAL EXAMPLE

A slight modification is now made to the numerical example given in the first part of Table 8.1, but there are some interesting conclusions arising from this modification. Instead of the output of corn production process being 450 kg, it is changed to 480 kg. The significance of this change is that the production system is now capable of generating a surplus of outputs over inputs, and then the question arises as to who receives the surplus and the uses to which it is put. In this case (given as Example 2 in Table 8.1) the input use of corn remains at 450 kg but the output is 480 kg, leaving an annual surplus of 30 kg. One question which arises is to what use is that surplus put? Is it used to help expand the productive system by using the surplus to have more inputs in the next production cycle (i.e. used as investment), or is it used for consumption? Further, who receives the surplus? Thus it can be seen that the Sraffian approach lies very much in the radical political economy approach with its stress on the importance and role of a surplus.[4] The surplus of output over inputs can be used for a variety of purposes. In the Sraffian approach, the basic alternatives for the use of any surplus are between payment as wages and payment as profits. In the simple examples, there is no labour employed (this is introduced below) and hence no wages are paid. Thus, the surplus is here distributed as profits. Further, the surplus is allocated in proportion to the capital employed, which is in effect the assumption that the rate of profit is equal in all activities.

To introduce a rate of profit requires that a definition is made of the capital stock (so that rate of profit is equal to profit divided by capital stock). This particular model contains only 'circulating capital', which is to say that there is no fixed capital, such as machinery, which lasts for more than one production period. Instead the 'capital' here consists of inputs purchased at the beginning of the production period, from which output will be produced at the end of the production period (and in turn some or all of those outputs will form the inputs of the next production period). At the beginning of the annual production cycle, inputs are purchased and used up during the process of productions. Hence, there is an outlay at the beginning of the period, which constitutes the 'capital'. Thus, in the production of corn, the capital stock is $240p_1 + 12p_2 + 18p_3$. The requirement that the rate of profit is equalised in each line of activity means that the profit in the production of corn has to be $(240p_1 + 12p_2 + 18p_3) r$. The costs in the production of corn are then composed of the cost of the inputs plus the required profits. Similar arguments apply in the case of the production of iron and pigs. Then the requirement that costs equal revenue in each line of activity becomes:

$$(240p_1 + 12p_2 + 18p_3) (1 + r) = 480p_1 \qquad (8.7)$$

$$(90p_1 + 6p_2 + 12p_3) (1 + r) = 21p_2 \qquad (8.8)$$

$$(120p_1 + 3p_2 + 30p_3) (1 + r) = 60p_3 \qquad (8.9)$$

This set of equations is not, unlike the system considered previously, linearly dependent. But there are three equations with four unknowns (three prices and the rate of profit). Hence again it is only possible to solve for relative prices, so as before take $p_3 = 1$. The solution to the set of equations (8.7), (8.8), (8.9) is $p_1 = 0.18556$, $p_2 = 1.99476$, $p_3 = 1$ and $r = 0.030025$.

There are three features of this simple example which should be highlighted. First, the existence of a surplus is linked with the existence of profits. In the first numerical example, there was no surplus and profits were not specifically allowed for. But it would be found that if a rate of profit had been included, it would have taken the value zero.[5] Second, the revised numerical example has three elements – the technical coefficients which summarise the relationship between inputs and outputs, the equalisation of the rate of profit, and the existence of a surplus. Thus, there is no reference to marginal utility, the productivity of capital or abstinence. The Sraffian approach appears to explain the existence and level of profits without recourse to notions of utility, marginal productivity, etc., which play a key role in neo-classical economics. Thus the apparent power of this approach can be glimpsed in that it generates a way of viewing price formation independently of neo-classical notions.

Third, in this second numerical example, there is a surplus in the production of just one commodity, although this permitted profits in all lines of production. Nothing has been said about the use to which this surplus may be put. A static system has been considered (i.e. one which is not growing over time) so that the implicit assumption is that the surplus is consumed though since the surplus was paid out as profits this would entail consumption by profit receivers. The existence of a surplus does, however, permit the expansion of the system. However, the production system which is described in Example 2 of Table 8.1 would need some rearrangement to permit expansion so that there was an expansion across the board.

8.4 GENERAL FEATURES OF THE SRAFFIAN APPROACH

In this section, the vision of the productive system which is involved in the Sraffian approach is discussed. The economic system is seen as composed of a number of productive processes or activities, where the number may be very large. Each activity uses inputs, which can include labour, non-produced inputs (e.g. land), and produced inputs and converts them into outputs. A productive process or activity may have a single output (as in the numerical examples above) or a number of outputs (joint production). The output of commodities may be used for consumption purposes, but in the case of those commodities which are used as produced inputs clearly some of their output has to be reserved for use of inputs in the next round of production.

It can be seen from the above that the main concern of the Sraffian approach is with produced commodities, and in the simple examples used above produced commodities are the only ones considered. Non-produced commodities can be included in a variety of ways. The presence of such commodities (such as common land) may influence the technical coefficients under which the economy operates, but as such would not directly appear and would not have any price attached to them. A commodity such as land could be treated both as an input and an output (e.g. the activity of growing wheat could include land as a necessary input and also as one of the outputs), and thereby included. The restriction which this raises is that in long-run equilibrium the price of land would be constant through time[6] (since as can be seen from the examples given above, the price of a commodity as input is the same as its price as output). Thus the Sraffian system can say little about the price of non-produced commodities.[7] In contrast, the neo-classical analysis can cope easily with non-produced goods. For example, the price of an antique would be seen as determined so as to equate demand with the fixed supply, and the demand in turn would depend on the utility gained by consumers for possessing the antique. In some respects, it could be said that the Sraffian system focuses on produced commodities but finds difficulty in handling non-produced commodities (e.g. land), whereas the neo-classical analysis focuses on the exchange of goods and services and pays little regard to the process of production and hence to produced commodities.

The second numerical example given above (and a more general case considered below) involved capital only as circulating capital. In particular, capital goods such as machines or buildings do not appear, and that would seem to limit the usefulness of the analysis. However, a suitable extension of what is included as inputs and outputs allows that problem to be overcome. A machine of age, say, m years at the beginning of the production process is included among the inputs, and a machine of age $m+1$ years is then included among the outputs of that particular activity. A machine of $m+1$ years will differ from a machine of m years through depreciation, and so on.

The economic system being analysed is assumed to be capable of self-replacement. For example, if in the numerical example given above, the output from the production of corn activity had been (for the stated use of inputs), say, 240 kg of corn then the system would not be capable of sustaining itself. For the production of corn requires 240 kg of corn directly and some corn indirectly through the production of iron and pigs. But the output of corn is only 240 kg, and hence output is less than input. This type of degenerating system is not considered, in part because such a system would eventually disappear as its level of production petered out. The fact that the technical coefficients of an economy would allow that economy to be capable of self-replacement or expansion does not mean that such an economy necessarily does not degenerate. An economy may be poorly organised and fail to achieve its potential, and may thereby degenerate over time.

It has already been noted above that the Sraffian approach relies on a uniformity assumption under which a single price for each good and a single rate of profit is established. This is closely linked with the long-run equilibrium approach which underlies the Sraffian approach. If different prices were charged for the physically identical goods, then buying in a low-price market and selling in a high-price market would be a lucrative undertaking. If, however, apparently identical goods were sold at different prices at different places because of, for example, transport cost differences, then those apparently identical goods should be reclassified as different goods. In other words, a good sold at place X could be considered as different from a physical identical good sold at place Y.

Another aspect of the uniformity assumption is that within each activity, producers operate subject to identical technical coefficients and hence identical costs. Thus the process of competition has worked itself out also in terms of eliminating differences in costs between firms in the same line of business, through the elimination of high-cost producers.

The uniformity assumption is seen as particularly important in connection with the equalisation of the rate of profit, and linked to that the nature of competition, where a tendency towards equalisation of the rate of profit occurs through the process of competition. This competition takes the form of capital moving from low-profit rate areas to high-profit ones. This may involve a geographical migration or a movement from one industry to another. In Chapter 5 it was seen that there is still considerable debate over whether competition of this form still operates in the late twentieth century. From that discussion it can be recalled that a monopoly capitalism or oligopolistic approach would deny any strong tendency towards equalisation of the rate of profit and hence deny the relevance of the analysis based on such equalisation, though it may be possible to modify it to allow for differential rates of profits.

These prices can be seen as 'underlying' prices and terms such as 'centre of gravity' and long-run equilibrium prices are also used. Actual (market) prices would then be expected to fluctuate around and move towards these prices. These prices are based on an equalised rate of profit, both within each industry and between industries. The process by which these prices would be reached is through firms moving from some lines of production (those where costs exceed revenue) into other (those where revenue equals costs). During this process, costs and revenues gradually change until the equality of costs and revenue is reached. This process of the equalisation of profits may last a long time, since it requires movement of the means of production.

The Sraffian approach and the general equilibrium analysis of neo-classical economics share a number of common features. They both make the uniformity assumption (single price, equal rate of profit, identical costs). Further, they both study long-run equilibrium positions. However, in terms of their vision of the economic system they are in sharp disagreement, and the relationship between the two approaches is discussed below in more detail.

In the simple representation of the Sraffian approach given above, each output is produced from inputs, which have themselves been produced in the previous period from other inputs. How far this remains the case when labour is introduced depends on the treatment of labour. For example, if labour is itself treated as being produced (from inputs of food, clothing, etc.) these remarks would remain unchanged. In such a case labour becomes another commodity which is produced as an output and subsequently used as an input. This would amount to treating human labour on a par with the work by other animals, for within this approach an animal (say a cow) would appear as a produced commodity, which itself was used as an input in production (in the case of a cow in that of milk). This approach is akin to assuming that labour is paid a subsistence wage which is by definition just sufficient to produce the required labour. an alternative is to allow wages to be above the subsistence level, and this is equivalent to permitting labour to gain some of the surplus which the economic system is capable of producing.

8.5 A FURTHER EXAMPLE INVOLVING LABOUR

In this section labour is introduced as a non-produced commodity which is used as an input into the productive process, and this permits a focus on the relationship between wages and the rate of profit. A three-commodity model is retained, but the model is now a more general one in the sense of being expressed algebraically rather than an as a numerical example. The necessary information for this example is given in Table 8.2, Example 1. It indicates, for example, that the production of one unit of commodity 2 requires as inputs at the beginning of the production period a_{21} units of

Table 8.2 Algebraic examples involving labour

Example 1

Input				Output
1	2	3	Labour	
a_{11}	a_{12}	a_{13}	b_1	1 unit of commodity 1
a_{21}	a_{22}	a_{23}	b_2	1 unit of commodity 2
a_{31}	a_{32}	a_{33}	b_3	1 unit of commodity 3

Example 2

Input				Output
1	2	3	Labour	
c_{11}	c_{12}	c_{13}	d_1	1 unit of commodity 1
c_{21}	c_{22}	c_{23}	d_2	1 unit of commodity 2
c_{31}	c_{32}	c_{33}	d_3	1 unit of commodity 3

commodity 1, a_{22} units of commodity 2, a_{23} units of commodity 3 and b_2 units of labour. These inputs are used at the beginning of the production period, and the output appears at the end of the production period. In the algebra below, it is assumed following the assumption made by Sraffa (1960) that the produced inputs are paid for at the beginning of the period but that labour is paid retrospectively at the end of the period. This assumption means that labour payments are not advanced at the beginning of the period and hence not to be regarded as part of 'capital'. It can also be interpreted as saying that labour and owners of capital share in the surplus of outputs over inputs. The algebraic difference which this assumption makes is minor.

The uniformity assumption with the equalisation of the rate of profit implies that for each process costs equal revenue, where costs include an allowance for profits. This leads to the following equations:

$$(a_{11}p_1 + a_{12}p_2 + a_{13}p_3)\,(1 + r) + b_1 w = p_1 \tag{8.10}$$

$$(a_{21}p_1 + a_{22}p_2 + a_{23}p_3)\,(1 + r) + b_2 w = p_2 \tag{8.11}$$

$$(a_{31}p_1 + a_{32}p_2 + a_{33}p_3)\,(1 + r) + b_3 w = p_3 \tag{8.12}$$

This set of three equations contains five unknowns, namely three commodity prices (p_1, p_2, p_3), wage of labour (w) and the rate of profit (r). As before, one of the prices is taken as the numeraire in order to determine relative prices (which now includes the wage). Suppose p_3 is taken as unity; there is still one more unknown than the number of equations. It is possible to solve these equations to express three of the variables p_1, p_2, w and r in terms of the fourth one when p_3 is used as the numeraire. In particular, it would be possible to solve for p_1, p_2 and w in terms of r (again with p_3 as the numeraire). The resulting formulations are complex and not of interest in themselves so they are not reported here. In general, it is expected that a price (say p_1) would depend on the technical conditions of production (that is the a and b coefficients) and the rate of profit (and also on the chosen numeraire). In other words, the determinants of price are technical conditions of production and the distribution of income as reflected in the rate of profit. Similarly, the wage would also be expressed as depending on the technical conditions of production and the rate of profits.

From an algebraic point of view, the price taken as the numeraire

(p_3 above) and the variable taken as a given (r above) are arbitrarily determined, and any prices could be used. But there is economic significance attached to the choice. Since our interest (for reasons which will become clear below) is in the wage–rate of profit relationship, one of the commodities is chosen as the numeraire (commodity 3 above). The method above was to use the sequence: determine the distribution of income (wage or rate of profit), then consider the consequences for prices. In that case, the distribution of income is determined *prior* to prices. But the method could have been adopted to fix a further commodity price (besides the numeraire), then calculate the remaining variables including wage and rate of profit.

Many writers within the radical political economy tradition would prefer to focus on the first rather than the second method. Under the first method, the data of the analysis would be the techniques of production in use and the real wage. In particular, it can then be argued that it is possible to say something about the determination of the distribution of income from outside the framework of the input–output relationships. The distribution of income is a particularly important topic within the radical political economy approach, and a specific income distribution (i.e. particular values of w and r) would then have consequences for prices, and indeed along with the technical data determine those prices.

It is useful for a variety of reasons to explore a little further the nature of the relationship between the wage and the rate of profit. This relationship can be shown to be a negative one – that is, a higher rate of profit is associated with a lower wage level. There is nothing within the analysis which would indicate the precise shape of the relationship between w and r and it can be concave, convex or combine elements of both. A possible relationship is drawn in Figure 8.1. When a wage–rate of profit relationship is derived, it has to be based on a specific numeraire. However, the precise shape and position of the wage–rate of profit relationship depends on which commodity is used as the numeraire, though the relationship will always remain a negative one. When the rate of profit is zero, the wage is at its maximum, which in Figure 8.1 is W. Conversely, when wages are zero, the rate of profit is at its maximum which is given as R though the value of R will depend on the numeraire chosen since it is defined as profits divided by a measure of the capital stock, both of which are measured in terms of the chosen numeraire.

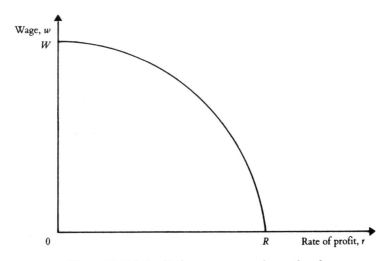

Figure 8.1 Relationship between wage and rate of profit

This relationship between w and r can be interpreted as indicating the basic conflict between workers and capitalists over the distribution of income in that one side's gain is the other side's loss. It is clear that within this framework wages and the rate of profit are negatively related to one another, and this does not rely on some particular configuration of technical coefficients. The discussion below on the measurement of 'capital' will make further use of the $w–r$ relationship.

8.6 THE STANDARD COMMODITY

This section introduces the concept of a standard system, and the related concept of a standard commodity, which has certain properties as an invariable 'measuring rod' (see below). In the process of discussing the standard system, it is also possible to reveal the relationship between growth and profits.

The equations (8.10)–(8.12) above are based on equality of revenue and costs from which prices have been derived, and the corresponding output equations are now derived. A particular configuration of production of commodities is considered which will be called the actual output. The use of commodity 1 in the processes of production (of all the commodities) is $a_{11} Q_1 + a_{21} Q_2 + a_{31} Q_3$, where the first term arises from the use of commodity 1 in the production of itself, the second term from the production of commodity 2 and the third one from the production of commodity 3. This provides:

$$a_{11} Q_1 + a_{21} Q_2 + a_{31} Q_3 + S_1 = Q_1 \qquad (8.13)$$

where S_1 is the surplus of commodity 1 in the sense of the excess of the output of commodity 1 over the use of commodity 1 as an input. Similarly, for commodities 2 and 3 the following can be derived:

$$a_{12} Q_1 + a_{22} Q_2 + a_{32} Q_3 + S_2 = Q_2 \qquad (8.14)$$

$$a_{13} Q_1 + a_{23} Q_2 + a_{33} Q_3 + S_3 = Q_3 \qquad (8.15)$$

where S_2 and S_3 are the surpluses of the production of commodities 2 and 3 over their use as inputs. Writing $G_i = (S_i/(Q_i - S_i))$, which is the ratio of the surplus of each commodity to its use as input, these equations can be rewritten as:

$$(a_{11} Q_1 + a_{21} Q_2 + a_{31} Q_3) (1 + G_1) = Q_1 \qquad (8.16)$$

$$(a_{12} Q_1 + a_{22} Q_2 + a_{32} Q_3) (1 + G_2) = Q_2 \qquad (8.17)$$

$$(a_{13} Q_1 + a_{23} Q_2 + a_{33} Q_3) (1 + G_3) = Q_3 \qquad (8.18)$$

These equations (8.16) to (8.18) are a particular way of describing a production system, which will be described as the 'actual system'. It is possible to construct a hypothetical 'standard system' which is defined as arising when the rates of surplus (i.e. the G_i) are all equal, which would involve a uniform rate of surplus throughout the economic system. In general, the configuration of commodity production would be different under this standard system and the outputs in the standard system are denoted by Q^*_i ($i = 1,2,3$). The equations corresponding to this standard system are then:

$$(a_{11}Q^*_1 + a_{21}Q^*_2 + a_{31}Q^*_3) (1 + G) = Q^*_1 \qquad (8.19)$$

$$(a_{12}Q^*_1 + a_{22}Q^*_2 + a_{32}Q^*_3) (1 + G) = Q^*_2 \qquad (8.20)$$

$$(a_{13}Q^*_1 + a_{23}Q^*_2 + a_{33}Q^*_3) (1 + G) = Q^*_3 \qquad (8.21)$$

These three equations involve four unknowns (G and Q^*_i, $i = 1,2,3$), but since they are homogeneous in the Q^*_i (that is, for example, doubling one solution to these equations for the Q^*_i would yield another solution) it is convenient to treat the unknowns as the relative outputs of commodities (e.g. Q^*_2/Q^*_1). The equations can then be solved for relative quantities and the rate of surplus. An alternative expression is that whilst the relative scale of the standard system is determined, the absolute scale is not.

Now consider the prices of production when the wages are zero and correspondingly the rate of profit is at a maximum and the maximum rate of profit is denoted by R. The set of equations would be:

$$(a_{11}p_1 + a_{12}p_2 + a_{13}p_3)(1 + R) = p_1 \tag{8.22}$$

$$(a_{21}p_1 + a_{22}p_2 + a_{23}p_3)(1 + R) = p_2 \tag{8.23}$$

$$(a_{31}p_1 + a_{32}p_2 + a_{33}p_3)(1 + R) = p_3 \tag{8.24}$$

and these equations are homogeneous of degree zero in prices, and can be solved for relative prices and the maximum rate of profit.

Equations (8.19) to (8.21) can be solved for relative quantities and G. However, the derived equation for G is a cubic so that there are three values of G which are solutions.[8] This equation for G is:

$$(a_{11}a_{22}a_{33} + a_{12}a_{23}a_{31} + a_{13}a_{21}a_{32} - a_{11}a_{32}a_{23} - a_{12}a_{21}a_{33} - a_{13}a_{31}a_{22})(1 + G)^3 - (a_{11}a_{22} + a_{11}a_{33} + a_{22}a_{33} - a_{23}a_{32} - a_{12}a_{21} - a_{13}a_{31})(1 + G)^2 + (a_{11} + a_{22} + a_{33})(1 + G) - 1 = 0 \tag{8.25}$$

Equations (8.22) to (8.24) can similarly be solved for relative prices and R, and a derived cubic equation for R obtained. This equation is:

$$(a_{11}a_{22}a_{33} + a_{12}a_{23}a_{31} + a_{13}a_{21}a_{32} - a_{11}a_{32}a_{23} - a_{12}a_{21}a_{33} - a_{13}a_{31}a_{22})(1 + R)^3 - (a_{11}a_{22} + a_{11}a_{33} + a_{22}a_{33} - a_{23}a_{32} - a_{12}a_{21} - a_{13}a_{31})(1 + R)^2 + (a_{11} + a_{22} + a_{33})(1 + R) - 1 = 0 \tag{8.26}$$

The essential similarity of these two equations yields a significant conclusion. Each system of equations is a cubic in G and R respectively, and so each involves three solutions with each solution for R matched by one for G. But not all of the values of G and R may have an economic meaning (i.e. some values may be negative), but at least one will be positive.[9] The rate of surplus also provides the maximum rate of (balanced) growth for an economic system based on this set of technical coefficients. For each commodity the level of output is $(1 + G)$ times the level of input, so that in the next period the level of inputs could be at most $(1 + G)$ times the level this period. Hence it can be concluded that the maximum rate of profit and rate of growth are equal.

A composite artificial commodity (which has generally been called the standard commodity) can be introduced based on the solution to the equations (8.19) to (8.21). Those solutions provide the relative quantities in which the commodities are combined to provide this composite commodity. The unit of measurement of this standard commodity also has to be set, and following Pasinetti (1977) the total usage of labour is set equal to unity, i.e. $\sum_i b_i Q_i$ in terms of Table 8.2, Example 1, is the total labour requirement and is set equal to unity. This standard commodity can, like any other commodity, be used as the numeraire. It can be recalled that the precise nature of the relationship between w and r depends on the choice of numeraire. However, the relationship becomes a particularly simple one when the standard commodity is used as the numeraire, namely:

$$r = R(1 - w) \tag{8.27}$$

where r is the actual rate of profit, R the maximum rate and w the wage (measured in terms of the standard commodity). But this simple relationship applies not only to the standard system but also to the actual system from which the standard system has been derived, provided *only* that the standard commodity is used as the numeraire. Further, different actual systems would have the same w–r relationship provided that the technical coefficients were the same (thereby generating the same standard system). Thus differences in the composition of output would not lead to differences in the w–r relationship when those relationships are measured in terms of the standard commodity.[10]

Two particular conclusions have been derived from the standard commodity and its properties. The first is that the standard commodity has some elements of being the invariable measuring rod for which Ricardo and others searched. When the numeraire is arbitrarily chosen the study of price movements accompanying a change in the distribution of income is complicated because it is impossible to say whether any particular price variation arises from the features of the commodity whose price is measured or of the commodity used as the numeraire. An invariable measure would be one where the commodity used as the numeraire in such that it is true that, as wages fell, such a commodity would be no less susceptible than any other to rise or fall in price relative to other individual commodities; but we should know for certain that any such fluctuation would originate exclusively in the peculiarities of production of the commodity which was being compared with it, and not in its own. (Sraffa, 1960)

After a century and a half, Sraffa's standard commodity has thus fulfilled Ricardo's dream of an 'invariable measure' of value. It would, of course, be merely fanciful to think that such a commodity might be found in the real world . . . ; yet it can always be constructed from the commodities actually produced, by taking them in the proportions defined by the standard system. (Pasinetti, 1977)

This standard commodity is only an invariable measuring rod in a limited sense, namely it is invariable with respect to variations in the distribution of income, for a specified set of technical coefficients. A single standard system (and corresponding standard commodity) may be derived from a wide range of actual systems, where those actual systems would differ in the composition of commodities produced and in the prices of production which result. But, when the standard commodity is used as the numeraire, the wage–rate of profit relationship is the same for all of those actual systems.

The second conclusion relates to the relationship between prices and the distribution of income. In solving, for example, equations (8.10) to (8.12), after the choice of numeraire and say the wage, the other prices of production and the rate of profit could be solved. In that way, the prices of production and the rate of profit were simultaneously determined. But when the standard commodity is used as numeraire within the actual system, the solution for the equations can proceed in the order of rate of profit (from equation (8.27)) and then for the prices of production. In that limited sense, the rate of profit could be said to be determined prior before prices. For example, Eatwell (1987b) argues that

this is consistent with the classical view that the determination of the distribution of income between wages and profits is logically, *prior to*, and independent of prices. Furthermore, it reveals the origin of surplus in a manner freed from ambiguities engendered by price calculations.

It has been further argued that,

the importance of this theoretical point is that it validates the cost-of-production theory of price advanced by Ricardo and later on by Marx. According to this theory, prices are determined by capitalists by adding together (1) labor costs; (2) capital costs; and (3) a suitable profit markup of $r\%$. These three factors therefore *determine* the prices of production in any industry. (Lichtenstein, 1983)

8.7 BASIC AND NON-BASIC COMMODITIES

A distinction was drawn by Sraffa between basic and non-basic commodities for which a mathematical definition was given.[11] But the distinction can be given an economic interpretation. In effect, the distinction is that basic commodities are those which enter, directly or indirectly, as means of production into all commodities.[12] The basic commodities could be seen as particularly important in that expansion of the economic system will require expansion of the production of basic commodities, whereas it may be able to expand without non-basic commodities expanding. For example, steel would be a basic commodity if it entered directly or indirectly (say through the production of machinery) in the production of all commodities. But candy-floss is likely to be a non-basic commodity since it does not enter into the production of anything else. It is assumed that every economic system includes at least one basic commodity.

There is a link between the standard system and the distinction between basic and non-basic commodities. In particular, it permits an intuitive understanding of that distinction which is not provided by the formal mathematical definition. The standard system may contain fewer commodities (and production processes) than the corresponding actual system. The commodities which do not appear in the standard system are non-basic commodities, whereas those which do are the basic commodities. In other words, the commodities which have a positive value in the standard system (i.e. for which $Q_i^* > 0$) are basic commodities, and those which have a zero value ($Q_j^* = 0$) are the non-basic commodities. The distinction between basic and non-basic commodities arises from the technical properties of the production process, and have no necessary link with the distinction between 'necessary' or subsistence commodities and 'luxury' commodities, which is a distinction related to the consumption side and not the production side.

A basic commodity is one which is technically necessary, directly or indirectly, for the production of all other commodities.

It follows that a zero production of even just one basic commodity necessarily implies zero production of all commodities (basic and non-basic). It also follows that, when any one of the production coefficients for a basic commodity changes, this causes the prices of all commodities (basic and non-basic) to change. It also causes a change of the maximum rate of profit and uniform rate of surplus for the whole system, and a change of the whole [wage-rate of profit] relation. (Pasinetti, 1977)[13]

Thus basic commodities play a much more important role in prices and growth than non-basic commodities.

8.8 PRICES OF PRODUCTION AND LABOUR VALUES

In the previous chapter, discussion touched on the relationship between prices of production and labour values as part of the consideration of (labour) value theory. In this section the relationship between one type of price (prices of production) and labour values is treated more formally, including a discussion of the 'transformation problem'.

To illustrate the nature of the transformation problem, the economic system described by the technical coefficients in Table 8.2 (Example 1) is used. The prices of that system can be derived for the case where there are no profits and hence where the wage payments absorb the entire surplus (or net product). The wage which arises if the wage absorbed the entire net product is denoted by w^*. The resulting price for commodity 1 would be:

$$v_1 = a_{11}v_1 + a_{12}v_2 + a_{13}v_3 + b_1 w^* \tag{8.28}$$

Similarly the corresponding prices of commodities 2 and 3 can be written as:

$$v_2 = a_{21}v_1 + a_{22}v_2 + a_{23}v_3 + b_2 w^* \tag{8.29}$$

$$v_3 = a_{31}v_1 + a_{32}v_2 + a_{33}v_3 + b_3 w^* \tag{8.30}$$

These three equations could be solved to provide a solution for v_i

(i = 1,2,3) in terms of this wage w^*. If we choose w^* as the numeraire and put it equal to unity, then the v_i in these equations also correspond to value defined as the directly and indirectly embodied labour in a commodity. These equations can be compared with equations (8.10) to (8.12), and then it can be seen that the labour values correspond to the prices of production with a zero rate of profit. Further, since there would be no profits and labour would receive the entire output, this economic system would correspond to that advocated by the Ricardian socialists (cf. section 7.2).

An alternative way of expressing values is in terms of constant and variable capital, and surplus value. Recall that variable capital in the Marxian scheme is labour input, which in process 1 is evaluated at $b_1 w$, where w is the (subsistence) wage paid to labour, whilst constant capital is the material inputs which are evaluated at $a_{11}v_1 + a_{12}v_2 + a_{13}v_3$. If we define s as the rate of surplus value (ratio of surplus to variable capital), then surplus value in process one is $b_1 w s$. Then for commodity 1:

$$v_1 = a_{11}v_1 + a_{12}v_2 + a_{13}v_3 + b_1 w + b_1 w s \tag{8.31}$$

Similarly for commodities 2 and 3, we have:

$$v_2 = a_{21}v_1 + a_{22}v_2 + a_{23}v_3 + b_1 w + b_1 w s \tag{8.32}$$

$$v_3 = a_{31}v_1 + a_{32}v_2 + a_{33}v_3 + b_3 w + b_3 w s \tag{8.33}$$

It can now be seen that the relationship between equations (8.28)–(8.30) and equations (8.31)–(8.33) is that $w (1 + s) = w^*$. In other words, the wage received by labour (w) is a proportion $1/(1+s)$ of net output per person, and the remaining portion $(s/(1+s))$ is the rate of surplus value.

A comparison of equations (8.31)–(8.33) with equation (8.10)–(8.12) indicates the following. First, in the 'prices of production' case, profits are distributed in proportion to the 'constant capital'; whereas the surplus is distributed in proportion to 'variable capital' in the 'value' case. Second, the information used to calculate 'prices of production' and to calculate labour values is rather similar, namely the technical coefficients. The transformation problem concerns the movement between values and prices of production. Informally it could be said that inserting zero rate of profit into the prices of production would yield the labour values, which can be seen by a comparison of equations (8.10) to (8.12) with equations

(8.27) to (8.29). Conversely, the introduction of a positive rate of profit into labour values would lead to prices of production. From an algebraic point of view, knowledge of the technical coefficients is required for the calculations of both prices of production and values. The transformation problem can then be seen in a mathematical sense as constructing the route by which the passage from prices of production to values (and vice versa) can be made. For formal statements of the solution to the transformation problem the reader is referred to Pasinetti (1977), Steedman (1977).

In this chapter the main concern has been with prices of production, and in this section introduced (labour) values have been considered. The transformation problem is concerned with the relationship between these two sets of prices. It can also be said that these two sets share the common feature of being equilibrium prices, without any expectation that such prices would actually be observed in the real world. The prices of production are seen as long-run equilibrium prices towards which actual prices may tend and/or around which actual prices would fluctuate. In the case of labour values, as seen in the previous chapter, Marx and others did not expect relative labour values to provide a guide to actual prices. It is useful to distinguish between calculations in terms of the prices of production (hereafter referred to as the price domain) and those in terms of labour values (the value domain). In this section, profits are considered as calculated in the price domain and surplus value as calculated in the value domain.

There have been intense debates over the relationship between calculations undertaken in the price domain and those undertaken in the value domain. These debates have been reviewed in the previous chapter but the formal aspects of those debates can now be briefly reviewed. One part of the debates surrounds the use made by Marx of the value domain and the question of whether there is some sense in which the value domain is more fundamental than the price domain. The suggestion in the treatment of labour values above and the transformation problem is that the value domain and the price domain are on a par with each other. The same type of information (specifically the technical coefficients) is required for the calculation of both the prices of production and the labour values, as can be seen by comparing the equations for prices and for values given above. This view has generally become associated with the Sraffian approach (Steedman, 1977; Hodgson, 1982c). The fundamentalist

Marxian position to the effect that the prices of production are superficial and that labour values expose certain basic features of the capitalist system has been discussed in the previous chapter. A related question is that of the relationship between surplus value and profits. The importance of this relationship arises from the view taken on the nature of profits. When surplus value is seen as arising from exploitation with the productive process, then a link between profits and surplus value would be seen as supporting the view that profits are based on exploitation. In terms of the simple examples which we have used in this chapter, it is indeed possible to prove the fundamental Marxian theorem (FMT; cf. section 7.4) that a positive rate of profits is a necessary and sufficient condition for a positive rate of surplus value. But as indicated, that proof does not survive a move to more complicated cases, though it has been possible to prove an amended version of the FMT.

8.9 THE MEASUREMENT OF 'CAPITAL'

The implications for neo-classical economics of the Sraffian approach are two-fold. The first is that the Sraffian approach provides an analysis of equilibrium prices without recourse to marginalist or utilitarian notions, which is discussed further below. The second is that it is shown that it may not be possible to derive a measure of aggregate 'capital' which has the properties typically given to it in aggregate neo-classical models (such as one-sector growth models). This implication relates to the aggregate version of neo-classical economics, and is avoided by dealing only with the disaggregate version.

A variable described as aggregate capital and often labelled as K is frequently entered into a production function as one of the inputs. In a neo-classical approach, the first derivative of the production function with respect to capital is labelled marginal product of capital and equated with the rate of profit. This procedure involves three assumptions. First, that capital is measurable in a manner which is independent of the rate of profit. The (perfectly competitive) firm is portrayed as adjusting capital so that its marginal product is brought into equality with the externally determined rate of profit. Second, that the (marginal) productivity of capital (which is a higher level of output resulting from the employment of more capital) is paid to the owners of capital. However, the owners supply *finance* capital to a firm, but it is physical capital which is productive in that it is the use of more capital equipment which raises the level of production. Third, as a second-order condition for maximisation, that the marginal product of capital declines as the volume of capital increases. This leads to the view that the demand for capital curve (which is based on the marginal product of capital) is downward-sloping. The Sraffian approach presents a fundamental challenge to these assumptions and hence to the marginal productivity theory as a theory of aggregate income distribution.

Within a production function framework, 'capital' means capital equipment such as machines, buildings, equipment, etc. Thus, if an aggregate measure of capital is required, some method is required which would enable various types of machines, buildings and equipment to be added together to arrive at a single measure.[14] The problem is exacerbated by the existence of machines of different ages and technologies. A machine which is ten years old may no longer be produced as it has been superseded but it still remains in use.[15] How can it be valued?

There are always problems in aggregating together different commodities. Suppose an aggregate measure of fruit production in a country was required; how would the different types of fruit be added together? How would apples and pears be added together? There are alternatives such as weight or number of pieces of fruit which could be used, though for purposes of economic analysis they are likely to be rejected. The way that would usually be chosen is to use some set of prices to arrive at the valuation of the fruit. If the same set of prices were used in each year, it would be possible to compare the value of fruit production in terms of that set of prices. It may well happen that the answer to the question of whether production of fruit is higher in year $t + 1$ than in year t depends on which set of prices is used to make the evaluation.

It would appear at first sight that the same procedure could be used for capital. The market price at some particular time of each type of capital equipment could be used to value that equipment. There are two difficulties with such a procedure. First, there is the evaluation of capital equipment which did not previously exist. If prices at year t are used, how can capitalist equipment new in year $t + 1$ be valued? This problem is not unique to capital equipment but applies whenever new commodities are being introduced. The second, and particularly important, problem arises from the purpose for which the measure of capital is to be used. Within the marginal productivity approach, the measure of capital is used to calculate a marginal product of capital (i.e. difference in output divided by difference in capital) which is said to determine the rate of profit. Is it possible to evaluate a piece of capital equipment without reference to the rate of profit?

How could a piece of capital equipment be valued? The market price for that equipment at a particular time could be used, but that would only push the question back a stage to asking what determines the market price. A backward-looking measure would make reference to the purchase price of the equipment when new. But some allowance would need to be made for events since the equipment was new. The machine itself is likely to have depreciated in effectiveness through use and the passage of time. Prices in general will have changed through the general process of inflation. But also the purchase of the machine may have been a disastrous mistake or a brilliant success. If the equipment was producing a commodity which no one wanted, would the equipment have any worth?

An alternative method for measuring value of the capital equipment is to be forward-looking, in which the value of the equipment; is based on the future profitability of that equipment. As an example, suppose that the use of a particular piece of capital equipment would mean that the stream of future profitability was enhanced by an amount P_t in each future time period t. Using a rate of discount of i, this future stream of profitability would have a value of $\Sigma\ P_t/(1+i)^t$, let us call this V. The rate of profit on this equipment in the first time period would then be P_1/V.

There are a number of difficulties with this approach, and three are highlighted here. First, since the future stream of profits can only be estimated subject to a degree of uncertainty, any estimate of the rate of profit is similarly affected. Second, the approach adopted largely relates to a choice on the value of a *marginal* project. It is not concerned with the rate of profit on other projects. Third, and most importantly here, there will in general be an inconsistency between the rate of profit and the rate of discount. This means that the rate of discount used to derive V will not in general be equal to the consequent rate of profit. Casual observation of the real world suggests that there are spectra of rates of profit and of rates of

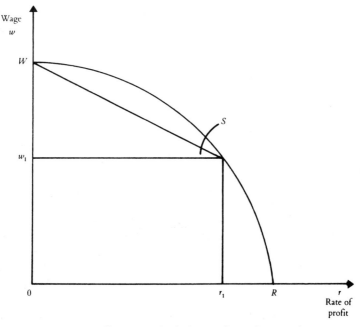

Figure 8.2 Illustration of calculation of capital per worker.

interest, and differences between the average rate of profit and the average rate of interest. In a neo-classical approach it would be anticipated that each firm would employ further capital equipment up to the point where the (marginal) rate of profit was equal to the rate of discount (which is taken to reflect the opportunity cost of finance).

How is capital to be measured within the Sraffian approach? In the examples discussed above, it was seen that capital was taken to be the advance on inputs laid out at the beginning of the production period. In the examples used above, this outlay was on the purchase of inputs which were entirely used up during one cycle of the production process. However, as has been noted above, capital equipment as usually understood can be incorporated within this approach (section 8.4). Thus capital is identified with the outlay on inputs at the beginning of the production cycle.

It is possible to derive a simple expression of the measure of capital and this is aided by Figure 8.2. W is the maximum possible wage (expressed in terms of the chosen numeraire), and must equal the output per person employed (since the maximum wage would arise when all of output is paid out to labour). Suppose the actual wage is w_1 and the corresponding rate of profit is r_1. Since profits and wages add up to the total output, the profit per person employed is $W - w_1$. Call the capital stock per person employed K_1, then by definition $r_1 K_1$ is the profit by person employed, which is $W - w_1$. Rearrangement yields:

$$K_1 = (W - w_1)/r_1 \tag{8.34}$$

In terms of Figure 8.2, the tangent of angle S is equal to $(W - w_1)/r_1$, i.e. $\tan S$ is equal to K_1.

The relationship between wage and rate of profit in Figure 8.2 was derived for a particular technology, which was described in the first part of Table 8.2, and this is labelled the a-technology. Now consider an alternative technology, labelled the c-technology, described in the second part of Table 8.2 (Example 2). We proceed as before and derive the relationship between wage and rate of profit for the c-technology (using the same commodity as the numeraire as for the a-technology case).

It is worth remembering that the w–r relationships for both the a-and the c-technology are derived for long-run equilibrium positions. Further, for movements along the w–r curve, the levels of output of commodities and of inputs (including the physical stock of capital) remain unchanged. But since prices of commodities are themselves dependent on the rate of profit, those prices are varying, as is the measure of the capital stock. This could be seen from the general consideration that as the prices of commodities change, so must the evaluation of the capital stock since commodities make up the capital stock. It can also be seen by reference to Figure 8.2, for clearly different points on the w–r curve would involve different values for the equivalent of $\tan S$ and hence of the capital stock per person employed (and since employment is constant, of the capital stock).

It was noted above that the w–r relationship can be concave or convex, and we consider the case where one of the technologies yields a concave relationship and the other a convex one. This is illustrated in Figure 8.3, where it is seen that there are two intersections between the a-curve and the c-curve. The particular discussion below on the difficulties over the measurement of capital arises from the existence of two or more 'switch-over' points (as

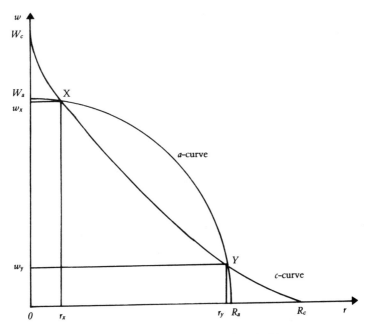

Figure 8.3 Illustration of re-switching problem.

these intersection points may be labelled). In order to illustrate the argument just two possible technologies are used but with the assumption that one of the w–r relationships is concave and the other convex. In reality, there would be many alternative technologies, and the more there are, the greater the probability that there is a mixture of convex and concave relationships between w and r. It will be seen below that the possibility of double intersections between the w–r curves derived from different technologies is an important one; such a possibility may be raised by an increase in the number of technologies from the two considered to many more.

What is the significance of these intersection points? Clearly, at the point of intersection the wage and rate of profit are the same under each of the technologies. As drawn, for a wage above w_x, the c-curve would yield a higher rate of profit than the a-curve. Thus, if a choice could be made between the two technologies then capitalists would prefer the c-technology to the a-technology since a higher rate of profit is involved. However, for a wage lying between w_x

and w_y, the position is reversed in that the rate of profit is higher under the a-technology than under the c-technology. The point labelled X is usually called a *switch* point, as capitalists would wish to switch from the c-technology to the a-technology as the wage is conceptually lowered from above to below w_x. It can also be seen that for wages below w_y the c-technology yields a higher rate of profit than the a-technology. Thus, as conceptually the level of wages is lowered, there would be a switch from the c-technology to the a-technology, and then a re-switching back from the a-technology to the c-technology.

This phenomenon of re-switching raises two interesting conclusions. The first conclusion relates to the measurement of the capital stock. It should be recalled that as the wage and rate of profit vary, so does the measure of the capital stock through price changes. The physical commodities which make up the capital stock remain unchanged, but their valuation changes. At point X in Figure 8.3, where there is an intersection of the two curves, the valuation of the capital stock per person employed is:

For a-technology $K_a = \tan S_a = (W_a - w_x)/r_x$

For c-technology $K_c = \tan S_c = (W_c - w_x)/r_x$

Thus at and near point X, since $W_c > W_a$, $K_c > K_a$. As r is raised near r_x, there is a switch from the c-technology to the a-technology. The valuation of the capital stock in use changes from K_c to K_a, and hence the valuation declines as the rate of profit is increased.

A similar argument can be applied around point Y. There is now a switch from a-technology to c-technology and this involves an increase in the valuation of the capital stock (since again $K_c > K_a$). Hence in this case, a rise in the rate of profit is associated with a rise in the valuation of the capital stock. Thus here the negative relationship between the rate of profit and the capital stock is lost.

Points on the curves drawn in Figures 8.1, 8.2 and 8.3 differ in terms of the wage and rate of profit to which they relate. Although it is not explicitly indicated, they would also differ in the prices of production, for as seen above, when w and r vary, so will the prices of production. However, the points all relate to the same technology and the use of the same inputs to produce the same outputs. Thus the physical capital which is being used is the same for each point on the curve. But because prices vary, so will the evaluation of the capital stock. The relevance of this line of argument is two-fold. The valuation of the capital stock can be seen to vary with the rate of profit even though the physical composition of the capital stock may not vary (as along one of the curves in Figure 8.3). As derived here, it is variations in the rate of profit which lead to variations in the measure of capital.

The second conclusion is that the association between the rate of profit and measure of the capital stock may be positive or negative. In the marginal productivity theory, as indicated above, it is usually assumed that there is a negative relationship between the capital stock and the rate of profit. The Sraffian approach indicates that such a negative relationship does not always arise.

This discussion can also be used to indicate that it may not be possible to compare different technologies in terms of capital intensity. The example illustrated in Figure 8.3 could be taken to refer to a whole economy (which is the way it has so far been treated) or as a particular sector. Thus the technical coefficients in Table 8.2 (on which Figure 8.3 is based) could be taken as referring to the production possibilities for a particular sector of the economy, for example electricity generation. From Figure 8.3, it can be seen that at high and low rates of profit, the *c*-technology would be preferred to the *a*-technology, since the *c*-technology can yield higher wages than the *a*-technology. But for middle range rates of profit the *a*-technology is preferred to the *c*-technology on the same grounds.

The conclusion was reached above that the relationship between a measure of capital and the rate of profit is not necessarily a negative one. It can also be shown that the relationship between labour and the wage is also not necessarily a negative one (Steedman, 1985). Thus the Sraffian approach serves to undermine two of the basic predictions of neo-classical economics, the negative relationships between capital and the rate of profit, and between labour and the real wage.

8.10 FINAL DISCUSSION ON THE SRAFFIAN APPROACH

The determination of prices in the Sraffian approach can be seen to rest on the technical coefficients of production, and as such to stress the role of production. Two particular elements of the neo-classical approach are noticeable by their absence, namely the role of demand for goods and services and that of supply of labour, etc., both of which are viewed as based on utility-maximisation considerations. Thus the Sraffian approach is seen as offering a theory of (equilibrium) price determination which does not require the concept of utility. It could be said that the Sraffian approach suppresses that concept rather than being inconsistent with it.[16] For example, the composition of output (i.e. which commodities are produced) has not been discussed, but rather was taken as given, and we return to another aspect of this below. The clearest point on the suppression of utility analysis arises in connection with the wage–rate of profit relationship. It can be seen by reference to equations (8.10) to (8.12) that the Sraffian system is underdetermined in that even when one price is at unity there is one more variable to be determined than there are equations. The system can be completed in a variety of ways. The approach adopted above (and reflected in Figure 8.1) is to allow that one of the income distribution variables (real wage or rate of profit) be set by forces outside of the pricing system. One possibility would be to treat the real wage as set at a subsistence level (however defined). Another would be to see the real wage set by the 'balance of class forces' in society at large. For example, the strength of trade unions in collective bargaining, the general political climate, etc., would be factors influencing the real wage. It should be remembered that there is a negative relationship between real wage and the rate of profit so that the relative strengths of labour and capital owners are seen as relevant. This view, often summarised by the phrase 'balance of class forces', has been a typical Sraffian formulation. But a neo-classical formulation would be possible as a way of completing the determination of prices from, for example, equations (8.10)–(8.12) in which the disutilities of work and of supplying capital were seen as relevant. For example, the real wage could be pictured to adjust so as to bring into line the requirements of producers for labour with the supply of labour.

There has been considerable discussion on the question of constant returns to scale in the Sraffian approach. It should be first stated that Sraffa himself made no such assumption.[17] To illustrate this, suppose that the production of commodities took place according to Table 8.1 (Example 1) and the prices calculated as in equations (8.1) to (8.3). These calculations make no assumption on the returns to scale. In particular, there is no assumption made or required as to what would happen if, for example, the scale of production were say doubled (i.e. if all inputs were doubled, would the outputs increase by more or less than a factor of two?). The assumption on returns to scale only becomes relevant when there is consideration of variations in the composition of and/or general level of production. Two examples will illustrate this point. The first would arise if, in the context of Table 8.1, the question were asked as to what the predicted effects on prices would be of an increase of output of commodity 1 from 450 to, say, 500. The second example would arise where expansion (or contraction) of an economic system was considered. However, if the assumption of constant returns to scale is made then it is possible to analyse the expansion of the economic system with production subject to the same technical coefficients. Further, in the case of the standard system discussed above where the relative quantities of the commodities are determined, then the economic system can expand at the rate R. The move from the actual system to the standard system incorporated the same technical coefficients for each production activity even though the scale of production of (at least some) commodities differs between the two systems. However, the standard system is a hypothetical construct, rather than an attempt to analyse some real-world changes.

In neo-classical economics, the equilibrium prices balance demand and supply. Further, the price mechanism is seen as a mechanism for the co-ordination of economic activity. Resources are allocated by the price mechanism into areas of high demand (relative to supply) and out of areas of low demand (relative to supply). An increase in the demand for a commodity will raise its prices thereby drawing further resources into the production of that commodity. The Sraffian approach involves the allocation of resources in the sense that there is an underlying view of classical competition through which there is a tendency towards the equalisation of the rate of profit. Capital moves in response to differential profit rates, and as capital moves into a sector, labour and other resources follow. This re-allocation of capital takes considerable time as it involves the run-down of capital equipment in areas of low profitability and the building of different capital equipment in areas of high profitability.

NOTES

1. Sraffa (1960) could also be seen to grow out of Sraffa's work on editing the writings of Ricardo.
2. For a comprehensive collection of articles on Sraffian economics and a survey of the area see Steedman (1989). See also *Cambridge Journal of Economics*, vol. 12, no. 1, for a memorial issue on Sraffa and his work.
3. For further treatment of the Sraffian approach, see, for example, Mainwaring (1984), Lichenstein (1983), Pasinetti (1977), Bradley and Howard (1982b), Harcourt (1982); and for implications for Marxian economics see Steedman (1977).
4. For further discussion on this see Howard (1983, especially Part II).
5. Introducing the rate of profit into the first example would yield the following equations:

$$(240p_1 + 12p_2 + 18p_3) (1 + r) = 450p_1 \qquad (8.1')$$

$$(90p_1 + 6p_2 + 12p_3) (1 + r) = 21p_2 \qquad (8.2')$$

$$(120p_1 + 3p_2 + 30p_3) (1 + r) = 60p_3 \qquad (8.3')$$

Adding those equations together leads to the following:

$$(450p_1 + 21p_2 + 60p_3) r = 0 \qquad (8.3'')$$

and hence prices are zero or the rate of profit is zero.
6. For further discussion on this point see Howard (1987).
7. This is reflected in Steedman (1977) where he writes that 'non-reproducible goods will not be discussed, whether they be land, minerals or "oil-paintings by Rembrandt"'.
8. In the general case of n productive activities the polynomial for G will have order n, yielding n solutions for G (some of which may coincide).
9. The conclusion of at least one positive value for G (and hence for R) follows from the assumption that the economic system is viable. If all the values of G were negative, then the economic system would not be capable of balanced growth or even survival. In each production period with negative values of G the outputs would be less than the inputs.
10. For further discussion on proofs concerning the standard commodity see Pasinetti (1977), Woods (1987).
11. 'In a system of k productive processes and k commodities ... We can say that a commodity or more generally a group of n linked commodities (where n must be smaller than k and may be equal to 1) are *non-basic* if of the k rows (formed by the $2n$ quantities in which they appear in each process) not more than n rows are independent, the

others being linear combinations of these. All commodities which do not satisfy this condition are *basic*' (Sraffa, 1960).

12. An alternative expression is given by Mainwaring (1984). 'If the equations of the system can be re-arranged such that there remains a system capable of self-replacement without need of some commodities as inputs then such commodities may be defined as non-basic'.

13. For further discussion see Pasinetti (1977, pp. 104–11).

14. The recent debates over the measurability of capital and the meaning of any aggregate measure of capital largely started from Robinson (1956). The major part of the debate took place in the second half of the 1960s; for a review of the debate see Harcourt (1972).

15. An old machine may be worth keeping in use provided that the revenue gained from using the machine exceeds its variable costs. A new machine could involve lower variable costs than an old machine, but a firm would incur the purchase costs if a new machine were acquired.

16. For a critique of the Sraffian approach from a neo-classical perspective see Hahn (1982). He argues that 'Sraffa's book contains no formal propositions which I consider to be wrong although here and there it contains remarks which I think to be false.' Further, he argues that 'there is no correct neo-Ricardian [Sraffian] proposition which is not contained in the set of propositions which can be generated by [neo-classical] orthodoxy'.

17. 'If such a supposition [constant returns to scale] is found helpful, there is no harm in the reader's adopting it as a temporary working hypothesis. In fact, however, no such assumption is made' (Sraffa, 1960). However, in contrast, a recent text on (and sympathetic with) the Sraffian approach does assume constant returns to scale (Mainwaring, 1984, see p. xii).

Chapter 9
THEORIES OF INCOME DISTRIBUTION

9.1 INTRODUCTION

The study of radical political economy generally attaches consider-able importance to the distribution of income. This reflects the belief that the distribution of income is an important aspect of economic performance in itself (as many others would view the level of income as an, if not the, important aspect of economic performance). But the importance of the distribution of income (specifically here as between wages and profits) arises from other considerations as well. Profits are seen as the driving motivation of capitalists (cf. Chapter 5), and are a significant factor influencing investment expenditure and thereby the rate of growth of an economy (cf. Chapter 12).

The distribution of income examined in this chapter is that between labour income (often labelled wages) and property income (often referred to as profits). There are many other aspects of income distribution, notably the size-distribution between indiv-iduals (inequality of income) and the distribution of income between social groups, which are also important. Space precludes a discussion of those other aspects, although the material in Chapter 3 is highly relevant for those aspects.

In this chapter the theories of Kalecki, Kaldor and Marx are examined in terms of income distribution. The major purpose of these theories is to explain the division of income between property income and labour income. On occasions, for convenience property income is called profits and labour income wages. After outlining these theories, the nature of profits as implied by the different theories is discussed, and this is followed by an examination of some implications of the theories for movements in the rate of profit and a discussion of a selection of empirical work on movements in the rate of profit.

These theories of income distribution have a number of common features. First, property income is taken to include corporate profits, rent, interest and usually self-employment income, whereas labour income is confined to wages and salaries. These two classes of income exhaust total national income. Second, because the theories are designed in such a way as to ensure that total income is divided between property income and labour with no income left over or unaccounted for, one of the income groups can be viewed as having the prior claim on income, leaving the other income group as having only a residual claim. For example, in Kaldor's theory examined below, profits are seen as having the prior claim with wages as the residual (which reverses the more usual view of wages as having the prior claim with profits residually determined).

In the marginal productivity theory, the payment of each factor is equal to its marginal product. The question arises (usually under heading of 'the adding-up problem') whether the total payments made to factors according to their marginal productivity would add up exactly to the total income available. In the theories discussed below, there is in each case an equation which has the effect that the adding-up problem does not arise in those theories. But it has led to the accusation against the theories of both Kalecki and Kaldor that they are tautologies, that is they are merely manipulations of definitions and identities; this accusation is discussed and refuted below.

Third, the distribution of income is seen as reflecting some aspects of economic power. For example, in the case of the theory of Kalecki, it is the degree of market power that firms wield which is the key ingredient in the determination of the share of profits in total income. The Marxian view stresses the power held by capitalists *vis-à-vis* workers and the ability of capitalists to extract a surplus from the workers.

9.2 DEGREE OF MONOPOLY

The degree of monopoly theory was originated by Kalecki (1938), and subject to considerable modifications by Kalecki himself.[1] The central ideas of the degree of monopoly approach are that the market power of firms determines the mark-up of prices over costs, and that the mark-up thereby determined has interesting implications for the level of real wages and the distribution of income. Kalecki's analysis is firmly set in a world of oligopoly and imperfect competition, and indeed Kalecki stated that his theory would not apply under conditions of perfect competition. Kalecki generally assumed, at least as a first approximation, that average variable costs were constant with respect to output, and hence that marginal costs were also constant. Under perfect competition, the price facing a firm is also constant, and hence the condition of price equal to marginal cost is unlikely to be satisfied. If it is satisfied, then it would hold for all levels of output, so that output level is undetermined. The compatibility of constant unit costs and perfect competition is one reason why Kalecki's approach cannot apply to situations of perfect competition (if any exist). Under conditions of imperfect competition, firms possess a degree of market power, the extent of which varies between firms and industries depending on a variety of factors which are discussed below. Kalecki's approach is relatively informal, but Cowling's approach (as given in the appendix to Chapter 5) provides a formal model which has implications very similar to those of Kalecki's model.

In an industry, the relationship between price and marginal cost is a reflection of the market power of the firms involved, such that greater market power leads to higher price–cost margins.[2] This market power is labelled as X so that price in an industry (p) can be seen as determined according to:

$$p = (1 + m(X))\, mc \tag{9.1}$$

where m is the mark-up of price over marginal cost (mc) and that mark-up depends on market power. In an industry where a range of products is produced, p should be thought of as a price index appropriate to that industry, and similarly mc as an index of costs. This assumption that as a first approximation average direct costs and marginal costs are equal simplifies the algebra considerably. Although Kalecki saw this assumption as a useful approximation to reality (and referred to the considerable evidence that average direct costs are constant with respect to output up to the full capacity), it is an assumption which could be modified without upsetting the key insights of this theory. Direct costs are composed of labour costs and material costs. Thus the sum of average labour costs and material costs can be substituted in equation (9.1) for marginal costs to give:

$$p = (1 + m(X)) (W + M)/Q \tag{9.2}$$

where W is payments to labour, M material costs and Q is output.

The sales revenue of the industry is then pQ which is equal to $(1 + m(X)) (W + M)$, and also the sales revenue of the firm covers wages, material costs and profits so that $pQ = W + M + P$ (where P is described as profits, with further discussion to follow below). Thus profits can be derived as $P = m(X) (W + M)$.

A number of manipulations of the basic equations are possible, each of which illustrates some influence of market power on an aspect of income distribution. The first two implications are for income shares, which are:

$$P/Y = m(1 + j)/(1 + m(1 + j)) \tag{9.3}$$

$$W/Y = 1/(1 + m(1 + j)) \tag{9.4}$$

where $j = M/W$ and Y is value-added. Thus at the industry level the key determinants of profit share in value-added are the market power of firms (reflected in m) and the relationship between material costs and labour costs (j).

The implication for the real product wage can be derived by expanding the sales revenue equation to give $pQ = (1 + m) (wL + nN)$ where w is wage, L is employment of labour, n is material cost index and N the quantity of material inputs. Manipulation yields:

$$w/p = \{1/(1+m)\} (Q/L) - (nN/pL) \tag{9.5}$$

The importance of this equation is that it suggests that the real product wage is strongly influenced by the degree of market power and that the real wage is set in the product market rather than in the labour market. These points are further elaborated in Chapter 12.

The material costs of one industry are composed of purchases from other domestic firms and imports. The purchases from other domestic firms can be viewed as themselves built up from labour costs, material costs and profits. In turn, those material costs can be broken down into purchases from other domestic industries and imports. It is assumed here that carrying this procedure far enough will enable the material costs of an industry to be broken down into labour costs, costs of imported inputs and profits. Thus at the economy level, similar influences will be determining the income shares and the real wage, namely the average degree of market power and the price and volume of material inputs (which at the economy level will be imported inputs).

The share of profits in an economy can also be seen to be influenced by the terms of trade between that economy and the rest of the world. There are two aspects of this. First, the price of imported material inputs (the term j in the equations above) positively influences the profit share, but negatively influences the wage share and the real wage.[3] Thus low prices for commodities and other material inputs favour wages at the expense of profits. Second, foreign competition over goods and services is likely to restrain the mark-up achieved and hence price and the profit share. It is (implicitly) assumed in our exposition of the degree of monopoly approach that a rise in money wages can relatively easily be passed on into prices. But in the presence of foreign rivals this may not be possible, and the degree of foreign competition can thereby influence the mark-up. In these circumstances, a push for higher wages by workers could lead to a rise in both money and real wages, and declining profit margins.

In the above equations P was taken to stand for profits, but it is necessary to say something more about the precise nature of P. The costs of each firm have been divided into variable costs (which were identified with labour and material costs) and fixed costs. Thus the payment of fixed costs would have to be made out of P. These fixed costs would include items such as advertising, managerial salaries and the like. Hence to arrive at the net profits of a firm, fixed costs as just indicated as well as interest payments and depreciation allowances would have to be deducted.

Returning to the determinants of market power, the factors listed by Kalecki were industrial concentration, sales promotion through advertising, etc. (and to a lesser extent the level of overheads and the power of trade unions).[4] The arguments for these factors can be elaborated as follows. The fewer the number of firms in an industry (and the more concentrated are sales among the firms), the more power will the firms have. In part, this comes from applying the idea that price will be higher and output lower under a situation of monopoly than under a comparable situation of perfect competition. The fewer the number of firms, the more closely will an industry resemble monopoly and less perfect competition. Further, the ability and incentive for firms to come to agreements over price (formal or informal) will be greater with fewer firms. The difficulties of firms entering an industry have long been recognised as enabling the existing firms to secure higher profit margins. Product differentiation (aided by advertising), economies of scale, control by existing firms of crucial inputs and/or sales outlets are among the factors determining the difficulties of entry.[5]

An important general feature of Kalecki's approach is that the behaviour of firms in their pricing decisions is seen to have income distribution consequences. Indeed, that insight also applies to any theory of price formation under imperfect competition. As such, the firms are price-makers, and in the process of making prices they are also influencing the relationship between price and costs, which in turn has implications for the profit share and the real wage.

It should also be noted that Kalecki's theory is explicitly a theory of oligopoly where the established firms are protected from potential competitors by barriers to entry. This has two related implications. First, the barriers to entry help to preserve the oligopolistic structure of few large firms and to limit or prevent entry into the industry. Thus, it would be expected that once an oligopolistic structure had become established in an industry it would be relatively stable and not revert back to atomistic competition. Second, the share of profits in an industry depends on market power in that industry, and hence the share of profits would vary between industries as market power varies. It is then likely that the rate of profit would also vary between industries (as the rate of profit is equal to the share of profits multiplied by the capital–output ratio). Thus Kalecki effectively denies that the tendency to the equalisation of profit through the mobility of capital is denied (cf. section 5.5).

9.3 DIFFERENTIAL SAVINGS BEHAVIOUR

The starting point of the differential savings approach is that the tendency to save out of profits is much greater than the tendency to save out of wages. Before exploring the implications for income distribution of that simple proposition, it should first be noted that this idea has many implications other than those for income distribution. For example, it implies that a shift in the distribution of income from profits to wages will reduce savings and thereby increase consumption expenditure. Thus the redistribution of income from profits to wages can have a stimulating impact on the level of aggregate demand (see section 11.3).

The limiting case of differential savings behaviour is when all profits are saved and all wages are spent on consumption. This case is often referred to as the classical savings behaviour, indicating its links with nineteenth-century classical economics. The limiting case indicates one of the lines of reasoning supporting the idea of differential savings behaviour. Wages were viewed as being around a minimum acceptable level, which could be viewed as either a physical subsistence level or a socially determined level. But as a consequence, all wages were spent in order to maintain consumption at the minimum acceptable level. Thus, savings out of wages were taken to be zero. In contrast, profits accrue to capitalists. Their living standards are much higher and they are not compelled to spend all their income. The Marxian view of competition (cf. section 5.3) is that firms are compelled by the forces of competition to invest as much as possible to reduce costs, with investment largely financed out of the firms' own funds. Firms are then pushed towards saving as high a proportion of their profits as possible, which at the limit is all of them. This argument could be modified to allow for some consumption out of profits.

There is a second line of argument supporting the differential savings propensity, namely that as an empirical generalisation the propensity to save out of profits is higher than that out of wages. This is based, in part, on empirical observation that the savings ratio out of profits is higher than that out of wages.[6] Further, profits are subject to 'double savings', namely that a firm makes savings out of profits (i.e. retained profits) and the individuals receiving the profits paid out as dividends also make savings.

This can be summarised by writing savings in terms of wages and profits as:

$$S = s_1 W + s_2 P \tag{9.6}$$

where s_1 and s_2 are the propensities to save out of wages and out of profits respectively.

The author who emphasised the implications of equation (9.6) for income distribution was Kaldor (1955), although the idea of differential savings behaviour has a long history. Kaldor labelled his theory a

Keynesian theory of income distribution, on the grounds that investment was taken as predetermined and savings adjusted to investment through changes in the distribution of income. In developing his theory he made a number of assumptions, which are indicated below. The two crucial ones are that the economy operates at full employment and that investment does not itself depend on profitability. The full employment assumption is discussed further below.

Consider for simplicity a closed economy with no government activity. In such an economy, the macroeconomic condition for equilibrium is the equality of savings and investment, i.e.:

$$I = S \tag{9.7}$$

In this model, there are two categories of income (wages and profits) which add up to total income, i.e.:

$$Y = W + P \tag{9.8}$$

The model is completed by the full-employment assumption, with the full-employment income level taken as Y_f, i.e.

$$Y = Y_f \tag{9.9}$$

The four equations (9.6) to (9.9) constitute the model, with four unknowns (W, P, S and Y) with the level of investment taken as given. The equations can be rearranged to give the share of profits as:

$$P/Y_f = I/(s_2 - s_1) \, Y_f - s_w \tag{9.10}$$

In the limiting case where workers' savings are zero ($s_1 = 0$), profits are determined as:

$$P = I/s_p \tag{9.11}$$

which can be rearranged to give (where c_2 is the propensity to consume out of profits so that $c_2 + s_2 = 1$):

$$P = I + c_2 P \tag{9.12}$$

This gives rise to the well-known dictum that 'workers spend what they earn and capitalists earn what they spend'. The first part of that dictum follows from the assumption that workers do not save. The second part can follow from equation (9.12) since the right-hand side of that equation is the expenditure of capitalists (investment plus capitalists' consumption expenditure). The direction of causation in equation (9.11) and (9.12) is taken to run from right to left. In other words, it is spending which determines profits rather than profits which determine spending.

Kaldor imposes a number of side-conditions on his model. The first two inequality conditions link with the theories of Marx and Kalecki. These conditions are as follows:

1. Real wage cannot fall below a minimum subsistence level w_{min}, i.e. $W/L \geq w_{min}$, which has links with Marx's theory as indicated below. This implies that $P/Y \leq (Y - w_{min}L)/Y$.
2. There is a minimum ratio of profits to net output ps_{min}, i.e. $P/Y \geq ps_{min}$. In Kalecki's theory, the profit–income ratio was determined by the degree of monopoly.
3. There is a minimum rate of profit necessary to ensure that some investment occurs, i.e. $P/vY \geq r_{min}$ where v is the capital–output ratio and r is the minimum acceptable profit rate.
4. The capital–output ratio, v, is *not* influenced by the rate of profit, and in particular it is assumed that v is technologically fixed.

It could be said of each of the first three of these side-conditions that either it operates, in which case it is the force determining the distribution of income, or it is irrelevant. The fourth side-condition could be seen as the most significant one. For this one means that the rate of profit does not influence capital stock and hence investment decisions. If, instead, firms' decisions on investment were influenced by profitability then it would be necessary to re-interpret equations (9.10) and (9.11). This is most easily seen in regard of equation (9.11). Above this was interpreted as indicating that investment decisions determine profits. But if profits themselves influence investment then a two-way relationship between profits and investment is involved in equation (9.11) (for further discussion see section 12.5).

To justify the full-employment assumption, Kaldor argues, in effect, that a form of price flexibility will ensure full employment. For example,

> a rise in investment, and thus in total demand, will raise prices and profit margins, and thus reduce real consumption, whilst a fall in investment, and thus in total demand, causes a fall in prices (relatively to the wage level) and thereby generates a compensating rise in real consumption. Assuming flexible prices (or rather flexible profit margins) the system is stable at full employment. (Kaldor, 1955)

Thus a rise in investment leads to a shift in income towards profits through which savings rise to eventually ensure equilibrium between investment and savings at full employment. The assumption made here is that when, for example, demand and economic activity are at low levels there is a stronger effect on prices than on wages, leading to a rise in the real wage, thereby stimulating demand.[7]

From a mathematical point of view, dropping the full-employment assumption removes equation (9.9), leaving the model under-determined with three equations and four unknowns. However, the degree of monopoly approach can in effect be combined with that of differential savings behaviour to arrive at a complete model. In many respects, such a combined model corresponds to the approach of Kalecki.[8] A model which combines both differential savings and the degree of monopoly is provided in Chapter 11 where the macro-economic implications are more fully discussed.

It will be recalled that Kaldor saw flexibility in the profit margin as maintaining full employment. Kalecki's view was that there would not be a great deal of flexibility of profit margin with respect to changes in the level of demand. Further, the profit margin may tend to increase during recessions, rather than decrease, as would be required by Kaldor's theory.[9]

The charge has been levelled against the theories of both Kaldor and Kalecki to the effect that they are not theories but tautologies, that is they are true by definition.[10] To some degree these charges arose from the manner in which the theories were originally presented, and to some degree from a confusion over the status of particular equations. An example of that confusion is the question of the interpretation of the equation $S = I$ above. This can be treated as an equilibrium condition between desired savings and desired investment, or it could be treated as a statement of an accounting identity which relates to actual savings and actual investment (in the context of a closed private economy). Let us examine this point a little more extensively for Kalecki's theory. The equation $p = (1 + m) \, ac$ can be interpreted in two ways. The treatment above was to see this as an equation determining price, with a view on the factors (market power) which determine the mark-up m. This is then a testable theory based on the prediction that market power and m are positively related. The other interpretation can be more clearly seen if the equation is rearranged to give $m = (p - ac)/p$. This can then be treated as the definition of *m*, and contains no hypothesis. However, the view here is that both Kaldor and Kalecki have presented theories which are not tautologies, and that though there are difficulties in empirically evaluating them, they are potentially refutable. In the case of Kalecki, this could be undertaken, for example, by testing whether the variables (industrial concentration, degree of collusion, barriers to entry) which Kalecki indicated as relevant for the price–cost margin are indeed empirically relevant.[11]

9.4 MARX'S THEORY OF DISTRIBUTION

Many of the elements of Marx's theory of distribution have already been discussed. In this section some earlier discussion is drawn together; but also there are important aspects of Marx's theory which take us further afield than the other theories considered in this chapter. In the previous chapters there has been some discussion of the transformation problem in Marxian economics, which concerned the relationship between (labour) values and prices. This problem raises its head here since much of Marx's discussion which is relevant for the distribution of income is conducted in terms of values. The question then arises as to whether there is a translation from statements about the distribution of income in value terms to statements about the distribution in terms of prices (see section 8.8).

The starting point here is the level of wages. Marx is often represented (as were many of his predecessors) as saying that wages would fluctuate around a subsistence level. In its Malthusian form, the mechanism was that if wages rose above this subsistence level, then population would increase, and conversely wages below the subsistence level would lead to a reduction in the population. In turn, a rising labour supply would depress wages whereas a declining labour supply would tend to push up wages. Marx stressed that labour has to be produced and reproduced. Thus wages have to be sufficient to ensure that the labour supply is maintained and renewed. In the sense of having to be maintained, labour is like any other factor of production, although in many other respects there are crucial differences between labour and other inputs (cf. discussion in Chapter 7).

One of the key questions which arises over what is often called subsistence wages is whether those wages are indeed those which are necessary for subsistence and survival. This could be called an absolute subsistence view. The alternative is that the subsistence level varies over time and society, and contains a strong element of social acceptability. This alternative will be called the relative subsistence view. The absolute subsistence wage would appear to be capable of a concrete definition. For example, the minimum amount of nutrition to support life could be calculated and priced. Similarly, minimum clothing and shelter could be estimated. There has been a long debate in the literature on poverty over absolute and relative notions of poverty, and there is a clear link between poverty and subsistence. The absolute view of poverty is not without its difficulties. It can first be noted that if an absolute level of poverty were adopted then there would be virtually no poverty in developed capitalist economies. For in those economies, most of the people who would be regarded as poor by current standards would have real incomes which are far above the average real income levels of, say, the eighteenth century or of many Third World countries. Further, it can readily be observed that there are many differences in tastes and habits across countries. This would mean that even if the minimum levels of nutrition could be defined (which would presumably depend on the type of work and other activities) the foods which would be available to satisfy those nutritional requirements would vary. Similarly, conditions of shelter (housing) which were acceptable in some societies may not be available in others. For example, societies lay down minimum legal conditions for housing. It is suggested here that the same considerations which apply over the definition of poverty would apply to the definition of subsistence wages. Rowthorn (1980) has argued that Marx gradually changed his view on the nature of subsistence wages, moving from an absolutist position towards a relativist one. Another way of expressing the relativist position is the recognition of the influence of social custom on the prevailing notions of subsistence and poverty.

The notion of a relative subsistence approach appears to be more satisfactory than an absolute subsistence one in that the dramatic rise in real wages over the past two centuries would appear to rule out empirically the validity of the absolute subsistence view. However, the relative subsistence view faces the question of explaining how the social views on subsistence evolve over time and differ across different societies.

The above discussion can be summarised by saying that the real wage of workers is taken as set at a subsistence level, where that level is culturally determined. Further, in this part of the Marxian approach, the real wage as well as other prices, etc., are measured in value terms (rather than prices, cf. section 8.8).

It may be recalled from Chapter 7 that the value of a commodity is made up of material costs, labour costs and surplus value, which can be written as $c + v + s$, where c is constant capital (which corresponds to material costs and depreciation), v is variable capital (which corresponds to cost of labour) and s is surplus value, and this is extracted by capitalists through their ownership of the means of production. The rate of exploitation is defined as s/v, where s is surplus value and v variable capital (labour) input. The rate of profit in value terms is given by $s/(c + v)$. The key element in the distribution of income as between labour and capital is seen to be the rate of exploitation. For that rate simply relates (in value terms) the surplus (seen as the basis of profits) to wages. Thus the share of wages in net income can be simply written as $v/(c + v)$. This requires something to be said about the rate of exploitation. One way of viewing the share of wages in net income is to express it as real wages to average productivity.[12] The relationship between wages and productivity depends in effect on two factors. First, the level of the real wage is set so as to ensure the production and reproduction of labour which could be described as the real wage being set at the subsistence level. Second, the level of labour productivity depends on the ability and power of capitalists to force labour to produce. The intensity of labour depends, as seen in Chapter 2, on the degree of control exercised by capital over labour. The interaction of those two elements is expressed as the rate of exploitation, and the rate of profit follows from that rate of exploitation.

The share of wages in national income can always be expressed in terms of the relationship between real wages and productivity. The focus of the Marxian approach is on the exploitation of labour arising from the control of capital over the production process, and that exploitation sets the relationship between real wages and productivity. In the absence of control over the means of production, the capitalists would not be able to extract surplus (of production over wages) from labour. The Marxian view is that profits arise because of the existence of a surplus taken together with capital's control which enables capital to extract the surplus as profits.

9.5 THE NATURE AND SOURCE OF PROFITS

'Profits' is one of the words which are in use by different schools of
thought, but where each school attaches its own meaning to the
word. In the case of profits, it is useful to distinguish two different
meanings. The first is that profits are the income which accrues to
the owners of property. Thus profits in this sense would include, for
example, rent, self-employment income as well as corporate profits.
However, the term can be used in a narrower sense, referring only
to income from the ownership of capital equipment, with rent
(income from ownership of land) being a separate category. The
other definition is where profits are taken to mean the excess of
revenue over opportunity costs of inputs (including capital equipment). This version of profits is often referred to as super-normal
profits, and is expected to be zero in competitive equilibrium. In our
discussion, we are not concerned with this second definition. The
justification for wages is clear – workers need wages in order to live
and survive and they represent a payment to compensate for the
'disutility' of work. Work is for most people unpleasant, involves
considerable effort and is not undertaken for pleasure. Is there a
corresponding justification for the existence of profits? The challenge thrown down by Marx (and to some degree by the Ricardian
socialists) was that there was no justification for profits comparable
to that for wages, and that profits were a deduction from wages.
There has been no shortage of economists ready to take up that
challenge. In order to discuss the neo–classical view, it is convenient
to state their conclusion first. The equilibrium conditions in the
markets for factors of production are obtained from the equality of
the demand and supply for each factor of production. The demand
side for a factor is closely based on the marginal product function
for that factor. In the case of capital equipment, this leads to a
demand for capital equipment; a further step has to be taken to bring
in profits (as a income category). The capital equipment has to be
bought and owned and hence the demand for capital equipment
generates a demand for funds with that demand for funds ultimately
depending on the (marginal) productivity of capital equipment. The
supply side for a factor is based on the disutility imposed on the
suppliers of that factor. Hence, for labour it is the disutility of
working (e.g. forgoing leisure) whilst for the supply of funds it is the

disutility of forgoing immediate consumption. The supply of funds depends on savings which in turn are seen to depend on the desire for thrift.

The two blades of the demand-and-supply scissors then depend on 'productivity and thrift', i.e. the productivity of capital equipment (marginal product) and the disutility of savings over consumption. The productivity of capital equipment underpins the demand for capital equipment and a payment of profits, whereas the disutility of savings provides a necessity for the payment of profits as compensation for waiting. The gradual emergence of this view is generally dated in the last third of the nineteenth century, and associated with authors such as Bohm-Bawerk. In part, it could be seen as an outgrowth of the marginal utility school (with the emphasis on the disutility of waiting and thrift) and more generally the development of marginal analysis. But, it can also be seen as an attempt to undermine Marxian analysis and the revolutionary implications of that analysis.

Bohm-Bawerk (1975) was one of the key participants in the development of a justification for profits based on a clear role of the source and nature of profits. In effect he argued that production takes time and requires that inputs are used before output is produced. The average length of time which elapses between the use of inputs and the appearance of output is the period of production (cf. section 8.2). Bohm-Bawerk postulated that the longer the period of production, the greater would be the volume of output (for given inputs). A longer period of production meant that the average 'capital' stock was larger and there was more output. This could be summarised by saying that 'capital' is productive in the sense of adding to output. At the same time, those who advance the finance capital have a longer wait between the supply of the finance and the return of it.

The radical political economy approach has criticised this general justification for profits in at least three ways. The first line of attack is that the neo-classical approach has muddled together the productivity of capital equipment with the payment to individuals. The marginal productivity of capital refers to the productivity of capital equipment. It arises when the use of more capital equipment with the same amount of labour raises the level of production. It is not denied that capital equipment is productive in the sense that people working with more capital equipment generally produce more than people working with less equipment. The crucial question is who receives the benefits of the productive nature of capital equipment. The (implicit) answer from neo-classical economics is that the owners of the capital equipment have some entitlement to those benefits since it is they who have refrained from consumption in order to provide the savings which have financed investment in capital equipment. But to a large extent, wealth may be inherited and the wealth itself accumulated from the proceeds of previous exploitation.

The second line of attack concerns the logical coherence of the concept of 'capital', and the related question of whether the marginal product of capital can be defined independently of the rate of profit. This was discussed in Chapter 8 and here we merely summarise the implications of that discussion. There are numerous types of capital equipment, undertaking different types of production and also varying in age and technology employed. Is it possible to derive an aggregate which could be labelled 'capital'? The answer which was derived in Chapter 8 is that it is possible to do so, but that such a measure cannot fulfil the role necessary for an aggregate marginal productivity theory. The measure of 'capital' will be dependent on the rate of profit. The marginal product of such 'capital' would be $(Y_2 - Y_1)/(K_2 - K_1)$, where $Y_i (i = 1,2)$ refers to the level of output and $K_i (i = 1,2)$ refers to this measure of 'capital'. The dependence of K on the rate of profit means that it cannot be said that the marginal product is a determinant of the rate of profit. Further, the marginal product of 'capital' so calculated can be negative. This line of argument undermines the concept of an aggregate measure of 'capital'.

The third line of criticism focuses on the implication that the disutility of labour is on a par with the disutility of waiting. The disutility of labour underlies the supply-of-labour curve, and similarly the disutility of waiting lies behind the supply-of-finance curve. The neo-classical tradition stresses the common features of inputs (e.g. they are productive and involve a disutility in supply) at the expense of focusing on their differences. The argument here is that the 'disutility' of work is on quite a different plane to any 'disutility' of waiting. Work is for most working people unpleasant, requires the subjection of one's time to the wishes of others and occupies much of the waking day. In contrast, waiting involves at most a deferment of gratification. For those with high income and consumption levels, the costs of some postponement of further consumption are likely to be rather small.

The source of profits in the Marxian scheme is clear, and has been touched on in Chapter 7, and in this chapter. For the discussion here, the source of profits in the Marxian approach can be summarised in terms of two basic factors. First, the possibility of profits arises from the existence of a surplus. In the absence of a surplus, there will be no profits. Second, profits are received by capitalists because of their ownership and control of the means of production. However, in the degree of monopoly approach, profits arise because firms possess market power – in the absence of market power, profits disappear. This could be seen to be a reflection of two forces. First, profits have to be realised. In other words, firms have to be able to sell their output at a price above costs before profits are gained. Second, the firms have to possess the necessary market power to raise price above costs. In the absence of market power, profits would then not arise. Thus the contrast can be drawn between the Marxian and the Kaleckian view. The former locates the source of profits in the productive process and profits would arise even under competitive conditions. The latter approach locates the source of profits in the exchange process and profits only arise through the absence of competitive conditions. Finally, in the differential savings approach, it could be said that the key role ascribed to profits is as a source of savings. The difference between profits and wages would disappear in that approach if the propensities to save were the same.

9.6 MOVEMENTS IN THE RATE OF PROFIT

Movements in the rate of profit are seen as important for a variety of reasons. At one level, the rate of profit may be seen as important for its influence on important economic aggregates such as investment (cf. section 12.3), with investment expenditure being important as a part of aggregate demand and as a foundation for future growth. At another level, movements in the rate of profit are seen as important as an indicator of the health of the capitalist system viewed from the perspective of the capitalists. A long-term decline in the rate of profit, for example, is seen as likely to lead to a series of reactions by capitalists, particularly in the political sphere (e.g.

pressure on governments to reduce profits tax, subsidise investment, measures to control wages, etc.) to restore profitability.

In the Marxian approach, the rate of profit is defined as $s/(c + v)$, where s is the surplus value, c constant capital and v variable capital (labour). It should be noted that this rate of profit is measured in terms of labour-time (i.e. in the value domain). The Marxian rate of profit can be rewritten as $(s/v)/(c/v + 1)$, and points to the influence of the rate of surplus value (s/v) and a measure of capital intensity (c/v) (organic composition of capital) for the rate of profit. As such, the movements in the rate of profit can be discussed in terms of those two ratios. The oft-quoted tendency of the rate of profit to decline (Marx, 1981) can be easily represented in terms of those two ratios. Marx viewed technical change as tending to lead to capital equipment replacing labour in production and a rising organic composition of capital (roughly speaking capital–output ratio). This would mean that there is a tendency for the ratio c/v to rise over time and this would *ceteris paribus*, lead to a declining rate of profit. The other tendency points in the opposite direction and this is the tendency for the rate of exploitation to rise, which is reflected in a rising ratio of s/v, which Marx argued, corresponds to increased exploitation. The overall tendency for the rate of profit would then depend on the balance between the rising capital intensity of production and the rising degree of exploitation. Marx predicted a tendency for the rate of profit to fall. In simple terms, the argument was that there is no upper limit to the degree of capital intensity but there is an upper limit to the share of profits in output (since that share could not exceed unity and there would be a lower ceiling since some wages would need to be paid to ensure the physical survival of the workforce).

The tendency towards a declining rate of profit may not be exhibited in the movement of the actual reported rate of profit for two rather different sets of reasons. First, in Marx's approach, the calculations were undertaken in terms of (labour) values. A declining rate of profit in the value domain may not correspond to a declining rate of profit in the price domain, and it is the latter domain to which measured profit rates usually relate. The relationship between values and prices of production has been discussed in the preceding chapters. Further, statistics on the rate of profit are calculated in terms of market prices though profits are usually measured in terms of current market prices, whereas the stock of capital equipment is often measured in a variety of prices (e.g. current replacement prices, historic price of acquisition less depreciation). Thus the observed rate of profit does not necessarily correspond to the rate of profit calculated in value terms nor to one calculated in 'prices of production' terms. Indeed, both values and prices of production are long-run equilibrium concepts which would be generally unobservable. Second, capitalists respond to the evidence of declining profit rates in a variety of ways. Profits are the motivating force of capitalists in production and employment, and the prospects of profits provide the incentive for investment. Thus, the evidence of declining profitability would reduce the expansion of capital equipment and the rising capital intensity. It would also reduce the level of aggregate demand and thereby reduce the level of output, depressing further profitability. The actions of capitalists would then slow down and perhaps reverse the tendency for the rate of profit to decline, although this could itself generate a crisis by depressing output and profits.

The case where the falling rate of profit may not have these effects would be where there was intense competition between firms sufficient to maintain investment levels. Each firm may be reluctant to invest in the face of declining profitability. But each firm, seeing other firms continuing to invest, will itself continue to invest in order to stay in the competitive race. In effect, each firm is locked in by the actions of others, and in turn the actions of each individual impinge on other firms.

The rate of profit can be written in terms of the following identity, where all the variables are measured in terms of market prices:

$$P/K = (P/Y)\,(Y/Y^*)\,(Y^*/K) \tag{9.13}$$

where Y^* is a measure of capacity output. This equation is only an identity and its usefulness arises if something useful can be said about the three factors which have been selected. These three factors are the share of profits (P/Y), capacity utilisation (Y/Y^*), and inverse of the capital–output ratio (Y^*/K). One of the useful aspects of this identity is that it permits discussion of differing views of the determinants of trends (long-term and over the cycle) of the rate of profit.[13] Within the radical political economy tradition, at least three views can be distinguished. First, as indicated by the preceding discussion, there is the view of Marx and others that there is a tendency for a 'rising organic composition' of capital. This would be reflected in equation (9.13) by a tendency of the capital–output ratio to rise over time, which would, *ceteris paribus*, lead to a decline in the rate of profit. It should, however, be noted that equation (9.13) measures the variables in terms of market prices, whereas Marx's discussion was conducted in terms of labour values. It is possible that a say downward trend in the rate of profit measured in value terms would not be reflected in a downward trend in the rate of profit measured in market prices.

The second view focuses on the profit share term (P/Y). The approach of Kalecki discussed earlier in this chapter would suggest that the degree of market power would be the key ingredient in the determination of the profit share. Thus variations in the degree of market power would lead to variations in the profit share. Indeed, Kalecki believed that there would be a tendency for industrial concentration to rise, leading to increasing market power and hence a rising profit share. This would generate a tendency for the rate of profit to rise over time, provided that the capital–output ratio itself is not rising fast enough (through the impact of labour-replacing technical change) to offset the rising share of profits.

Within the degree of monopoly pricing as outlined above, workers appear to have no effect on the profit (and wage) share. Workers may be able to raise money wages, but such a rise is offset by a rise in prices. A view, particularly associated with Glyn and Sutcliffe (1972), adopts a rather different perspective. In conditions of low levels of unemployment (which had been typical of the latter parts of the long post-war boom up to 1973), workers have a strengthened and enhanced position (cf. section 11.5), which enables them to push up money wages as they strive to increase their real wages. Glyn and Sutcliffe (1972) argued that the extent of international competition had increased during the 1950s and 1960s through the growth of international trade (linked with the lowering of trade barriers) and the spread of multinationals, and this increased international competition placed downward pressure on prices. This limited the ability of firms to pass on money-wage increases as price increases; thus real wages rise (faster than productivity) and the profit share declines. The downward pressure on prices would be relaxed by a move from a fixed exchange rate to flexible exchange rates which occurred with the breakdown of the Bretton Woods fixed exchange rate system in 1971, i.e. around the time Glyn and

Sutcliffe were writing. For if prices in one country rise persistently faster than those in other countries, the exchange rate of that country may be expected to fall to offset the higher rate of inflation (though flexible exchange rates have frequently behaved in ways which appear bizarre to economists). Further, the growth of international trade and the lowering of trade barriers does not necessarily increase competition, for the spread of multinational enterprises means that a great deal of international trade takes place between subsidiaries of the same company.

The third aspect, which is often labelled the realisation problem, focuses on possible inadequacies of aggregate demand. Thus firms are not able to realise the full potential profits because they are unable to sell all their output. In terms of the identity of equation (9.13), the level of aggregate demand would be reflected in the capacity utilisation term (i.e. Y/Y^*). Over the course of a business cycle, when aggregate demand is high, the capacity utilisation term is high (and the share of profits may be higher than average) so that the rate of profit would be high during the upswing of a trade cycle. Conversely, the rate of profit would fall with low levels of aggregate demand. However, the variations in the rate of capacity utilisation over the course of the business cycle will also depend on the rate of investment which brings new capital equipment into operation.

In the long term, it is usually anticipated that firms would generally hold some surplus capacity. There are two types of reasons for this. The first will become more apparent in Chapter 12, but the outline can be given here. Capacity utilisation depends on the level of aggregate demand, with one component of demand being investment. In turn, investment demand depends (positively) on the rate of capacity utilisation. There is then an equilibrium level of capacity utilisation, and there is no particular reason to think that such a level of capacity utilisation involves full-capacity working. The second set of reasons is that firms find it worth while to hold some surplus capacity on average. It provides firms with the means to meet an upswing in demand, thereby reducing the possibilities for other firms (especially foreign firms) to eat into their market shares. Further, the established firms can use surplus capacity as a warning to potential entrants that entry will be met by a reduction in price and expansion of output. In that manner, entry into an industry can be made unattractive, thereby enhancing the position of the established firms.

Firms determine capacity through their investment decisions, and though it has been argued that firms will hold some spare capacity (and the degree of capacity utilisation fluctuates) there would appear to be no reasons why firms would allow capacity utilisation to have any distinct trend. Thus over the long haul it is generally expected that there would not be any strong tendency for capacity utilisation to increase or decrease.

9.7 EXPLAINING MOVEMENTS IN THE RATE OF PROFIT

There has been a continuing debate on what have been the trends in the rate of profit in advanced capitalist economies. Much of that debate concerns questions of the precise measurement of profits, the appropriate measures of capital, the relevant sectors of the economy for which the rate of profit is calculated, etc. Space precludes a discussion of these studies. However, a 'tentative synthesis' for the American economy proposed by Dumenil, Glick and Rangel (1987) can be used. They identify six stages in the movement of profitability:

(1) Before World War I, a slow decline.
(2) The fall into the recession of 1921 and the recovery of the 1922–29 period which never restored pre World War I levels.
(3) A new fall during the great depression which is fully offset by an eventual take off in the late 1930s.
(4) A huge recovery of profitability during World War II . . .
(5) The 1948–1958 decline and the 'bulge' of the 1960s.
(6) The recent decline following 1966.

The rate of profit on equity for US manufacturing is reported as falling from an average level of 21.9 per cent in the period 1948 to 1967 to an average of 16.7 per cent in the period 1970 to 1984, touching a low of 12 per cent in 1983. Adjustments for variations in capacity utilisation do not change the basic picture, though the decline from the first to the second period is now rather larger.

Armstrong, Glyn and Harrison (1984) provide a range of data on profitability for the seven major capitalist economies on an annual basis from 1951 to 1981. Their figures show a general downward movement in the rate of profit in most of these countries. In the United States, the net profit rate in the business sector is recorded at an average of 19 per cent in the period 1951–55, 19.1 per cent in the period 1961–65, and then falls steadily to an average of 12.7 per cent in the five years to 1981. The comparable figures (on an weighted average basis) for the other six major economies are 14.8 per cent, 14.1 per cent, falling to 10 per cent.

These falls in the rate of profit would be expected to have substantial economic and political effects, and attempts by capitalists to restore profitability. A decline in the share of profits would be matched by an increase in wage share, and the net effect of those changes would be a rise in aggregate demand (since spending out of wages is greater than spending out of profits). But a decline in the rate of profit, in the expectation of future profitability and in profits as a pool of finance would all point in the direction of a reduction in investment expenditure. The decline in investment would eventually hit the growth potential of an economy. Attempts to offset declining rate of profit through raising prices would have a clear inflationary effect. The political effects could well be more important. Business would pressure governments to adopt policies to restore profitability. These policies could include a reduction of taxes on profits and the subsidisation of investment. Further, there are a range of policies to restrain real wages (e.g. incomes policies, industrial relations legislation, raising level of unemployment) in the hope of restoring profits. The world-wide economic disruption of the 1970s was associated with a decline in the rate of profit, but that leaves open the key question of cause and effect.

The higher levels of unemployment and the government offensives against organised labour which have been particularly evident in the United Kingdom and the United States do appear to have had some impact on the rate of profit. The OECD *Economic Outlook* for December 1987 reports that

> profitability in OECD countries has been improving since 1983, largely reflecting wage moderation during the cyclical recovery of output in 1983–85, and the fall of commodity prices and the associated terms-of-trade gains in 1985–86. ... By historical standards, the levels of profit shares remain high, while profit rate developments have become more varied.

In the United Kingdom, the *Bank of England Quarterly Bulletin* of August 1988 provides data on rates of profits in the seven largest OECD economies, which show a general upward movement in the rate of profit from the early 1980s up to 1987. The upward movement is particularly pronounced in the United Kingdom with the rate of profit in 1987 (on three different measures) above the corresponding rate of profit in 1973 and approaching the level of 1964. At the time of writing it is not possible to say whether these recent increases in the rate of profit represent a recovery in capacity utilisation during the mid-1980s or the move to a higher and possibly rising rate of profit, though it is noteworthy that a substantial part of the rise of the rate of profit can be attributed to a rise in profit margins. It can also be noted that the rise in the rate of profit during the 1980s has been particularly substantial in the United Kingdom where there has been probably the greatest political offensive against the trade union movement.

Weisskopf (1979) examines both the trend and cyclical movements in the rate of profit in terms of the identity given above as equation (9.13) for the American economy over the period 1949 to 1975. There can be debates over how the rate of profit should be calculated, e.g. net or gross of depreciation, and Weisskopf opts for the pre-tax net rate of profit (on net capital stock). Over this period, there was a general downward trend in the rate of profit, equal to an annual (proportionate) rate of decline of 1.20 per cent. His calculations indicate that capacity utilisation and the capital–capacity output ratio barely changed, and each would have generated increases of 0.02 per cent per annum in the rate of profit. This leaves a decline of 1.24 per cent in the share of profit as the cause of the decline in the rate of profit. Henley (1987) updates the calculations of Weisskopf to the end of 1982, and finds that the experience of the period 1975 to 1982 is somewhat different from that of the period 1949 to 1975. The decline in the rate of profit continued but 'as far as the period 1975–82 is concerned, realisation conditions [i.e. movements in Y/Y^*] play by far the largest part in explaining profit rate decline'.

The identity given in equation (9.13) can be expanded slightly to give:

$$P/Y = (P/S)(S/Y)(Y/Y^*)(Y^*/K) \qquad (9.14)$$

where S is the surplus generated by enterprises, out of which not only profits but also fixed costs, depreciation, etc., are paid. The degree of monopoly approach given above refers to the determination of S/Y, and clearly the link between the rate of profit and S/Y may be obscured by changes in (P/S). Attention here is given to two particular elements which would lead to changes in P/S. First, a rise in the number and/or power of the managerial class would lead to a decline in P/S as the managers receive a higher proportion of the surplus. Indeed Henley reports salaried staff more than doubling (absolutely and relative to production workers) in American manufacturing over the post-war period up to 1983. Further, Henley reports a general rise in the ratio of S/Y but substantial rises in salary payments and in supplemental labour costs (fringe benefits) lead to a decline in profit share.

Second, a rising capital–capacity output ratio would imply rising depreciation charges, and these would constitute 'fixed' costs to be deducted from surplus before arriving at net profits. But it can be noted that Weisskopf found little trend in the capital–output ratio although Henley does report a rising capital–output ratio for the 1975–82 period (which contributes 0.22 per cent per annum trend decline in the rate of profit over the full period 1949 to 1982).

Cowling (1982) raises the question of 'what was it that precipitated the decline [in the rate of profit in Britain] in the mid-1960s, and what combination of circumstances prevented a subsequent recovery', with data presented for the period up to 1977. Over this period, the degree of industrial concentration rose, in particular because of merger activity. This would be expected to lead to a rise in the degree of monopoly, and a rise in the share of 'surplus'. Cowling (1982, Table 7.3) draws on figures from the British Census of Production to show that the price–cost margin within manufacturing industry did indeed tend to rise over the period examined (1948–75). This would tend to generate a rising rate of profit. But there are tendencies in the opposite direction. In effect, Cowling argues that the ratio P/S tended to decline. The first reason for this is that 'more and more of the profits generated were being appropriated within the corporation by the managerial hierarchy'. In other words, the managers become more powerful at the expense of the dispersed shareholders and are able to take a higher proportion of the available surplus. The second is 'the tendency for overhead costs to increase in importance for technological or control reasons'. This would include the requirements for more effort and expenditure on the control of the workforce to ensure high levels of productivity. Further, there was a tendency for the rate of capacity utilisation to decline. For example, capacity utilisation was always recorded as being over 90 per cent from 1955 (when the data series began) until

1971, and then from 1971 to 1978 (when data end) capacity utilisation only exceeds 90 per cent once and falls to near 80 per cent in 1975. There is a link between the degree of monopoly and the capacity utilisation. An increase in the degree of monopoly, raising the share of the surplus, tends to depress aggregate demand (cf. section 11.3) and hence lower capacity utilisation.

Weisskopf (1979) also presents calculations of movements of the relevant variables during different phases of the business cycle, and these are reported in Table 9.1. Phase A is the early stage of expansion, phase B the later stages of expansion and phase C the contractionary period. The unimportance of capital–capacity output ratio is evident, with the share of profits being the main proximate cause of variations in the rate of profits. This evidence is consistent with the view that declines in the rate and share of profits precede (and may cause) cyclical declines in economic activity.

Sherman (1987a) divides the business cycle into nine stages (following the tradition of Wesley Mitchell), where stage 1 is the initial trough, stage 5 is the cycle peak and stage 9 the final trough. Thus stages 2, 3 and 4 are the expansionary stages, and stage 6, 7 and 8 the contractionary ones. His calculations for the six business cycles covering the period 1949–80 for the United States are summarised in Table 9.2. The first two lines (for national income and capacity utilisation) record the course of the business cycle. It can be seen from the third line that investment grows faster than national income in the upswing (from stage 1 to stage 5) and declines more than national income in the downswing (stage 5 to stage 9), which is consistent with the active role of investment over the business cycle

Table 9.1 Rates of change of economic variables over phases of trade cycle.

	Phase A	Phase B	Phase C
Rate of profit	+26.8	–10.1	–25.3
Share of profits	+17.0	– 8.8	–15.6
Capacity utilisation	+10.8	+ 0.5	–11.9
Capital–capacity ouput ratio	– 1.1	– 1.8	+ 2.1

Notes: Figures are annualised percentage rate of change and refer to American trade cycles over the period 1949 to 1975. For discussion, see text.
Source: Weisskopf (1979).

(cf. section 12.4 below). It is the statistics on profits which are particularly relevant here. It can be seen that here profits and profit rate both peak before the business cycle itself. Thus these figures would be consistent with the view that declining profits bring the cycle to an end. Finally, it can be seen that wage share only begins to rise about half-way through the upswing but continues to rise in the first half of the downswing.

Bowles, Gordon and Weisskopf (1986) seek to 'explain trends in the United States corporate profitability since World War II through an analysis of the rise and subsequent demise of a post-war social structure of accumulation (SSA)'. Their analysis can be related to our discussion above. From equation (9.3) and the subsequent discussion, it can be seen that the market power of firms (which is influenced by the competitive stance of foreign firms), and the terms of trade influence the share of profits. A militant workforce may be able to secure both money wage and real wage increase when the firms are restrained in their ability to put up prices (see Kalecki, 1971b). Conversely, an acquiescent workforce places much less pressure on profit margins. Further, from equation (9.11) the favourable impact of capacity utilisation on the rate of profit can be seen. Bowles, Gordon and Weisskopf (1986) focus on 'three axes of domination' which feed through the factors we have just discussed (and others) to influence the rate of profit. These three axes are 'capital–labor accord, Pax Americana, and the capital–citizen accord'. The capital–labor accord

Table 9.2 Cyclical behaviour of key economic variables: United States, 1949–80.

Stages	Trough 1–2	2–3	3–4	Peak 4–5	5–6	6–7	Trough 7–8	8–9
National income	.54	.51	.31	.20	– .22	– .60	– .32	– .08
Capacity utilization	.63	.49	.09	.01	– .92	–1.60	–1.04	–1.20
Investment	.25	.66	.52	.46	– .11	– .91	– .74	– .87
Profits	.97	.56	.12	–.08	– .94	–1.47	– .51	.44
Profit rate on capital	.78	.28	–.20	–.40	–1.15	–1.67	– .71	.20
Wage share	– .18	– .01	.09	.10	.27	.28	.07	– .07
Unemployment	–1.36	–1.79	–.59	–.19	3.28	5.18	5.18	4.55

Notes: Figures refer to change from stage to stage of the business cycle, calculated at a quarterly rate, as a percentage of the cycle average. Investment is gross private domestic non-residential investment.
Source: Sherman (1987a, Tables 1 and 2).

involved an explicit and implicit *quid pro quo*, assuring management control over enterprise decision-making (with union submission and cooperation) in exchange for the promise to workers of real compensation rising along with labor productivity, improved working conditions and greater job security – in short, a share in capitalist prosperity.

The degree of power exercised by capital over labour is measured by two variables, namely a cost of job loss (raising the threat of unemployment on workers), and an (inverse) index of worker resistance. Pax Americana 'provided favorable terms for United States capitalists in their interaction with foreign suppliers of both wage goods and intermediate goods and with foreign buyers of United States produced goods'. This dimension is measured by an adjusted terms-of-trade variable and an index of American military power. The capital–citizen accord relates to 'a set of political arrangements which regulated the inherent conflict between capitalists' quest for profits and people's demands for economic security and the social accountability of business'. A few key indicators are used to measure this, and these are an index of the intensity of government regulation of business and an estimate of the percentage of taxes borne by capital.

Their econometric evidence, relating to the United States over the period 1951–79, supports their line of argument on the determinants of the rate of profit. This evidence also permits estimates to made of the causes of the decline in profitability. It is calculated that

> the major source of profitability decline from 1959–1966 to 1966–1973 was the erosion of the labor accord – and decline of the cost of job loss in particular. From 1966–1973 to 1973–79, by contrast, declines in the utilization variables and in the international strength of United States capital were the major factors contributing to the fall in the profit rate. (Bowles, Gordon and Weisskopf, 1986)

This selective discussion on movements in the rate of profit has concentrated on recent studies for the United Kingdom and the United States. Work on other countries includes Webber and Rigby (1986) (Canada), Reati (1986) (West Germany), and Wolff (1986) and Naples (1986) are further studies on the United States.

9.8 CONCLUDING REMARKS

This chapter has considered three important views on the distribution of income. Each of them has implications for movements in the rate of profit, which many would see as influencing the level of investment in a capitalist economy, and thereby the level and growth of national income. In Chapter 12, some of the macroeconomic implications of these views on the distribution of income will be more fully considered.

NOTES

1. For further discussion see Sawyer (1985b, ch. 2), and for a detailed consideration of the evolution of Kalecki's thinking on the degree of monopoly see Kriesler (1987).
2. This exposition is intended to capture the essence of Kalecki's approach, but does not follow the precise formulation used by Kalecki, which developed over time, It should be noted that the mark-up is taken to reflect the degree of monopoly, whereas the mark-up is often identified with the degree of monopoly.
3. From equation (9.3) by differentiation, the following can be obtained:

$$d(P/Y)/d_j = m/\{1 + m(1+j)\}^2 \qquad \text{which is positive}$$

$$d(W/Y)/dj = - m/\{1 + m(1+j)\}^2 \qquad \text{which is negative}$$

$$d(w/p)dn = - (N/pL) \qquad \text{which is also negative}$$

4. For a more formal presentation, see Cowling (1982), Sawyer (1985b) and the appendix to Chapter 5.
5. These points are explored at length in most books on theories of the firm and industrial economics. See, for example, Sawyer, (1979, ch. 5) and Sawyer (1985a, ch. 12).
6. For some evidence that savings out of profits is higher than savings out of wages see Sawyer (1982a).
7. Note that the stabilising factor here is that real wages rise in depression and fall in booms. This is the exact opposite of the stabilising force at work under neo-classical economics. In the latter, depression and unemployment are taken to imply that real wages are 'too high', reducing the demand for labour. The economy would then move back to full employment if real wages fell, stimulating the demand for labour.

8. See Kalecki (1971a, ch. 5, 6 and 7), Sawyer (1985b, pp. 79–83), Cowling (1981).
9. See, for example, Cowling (1983).
10. For example, Ferguson (1969), Bauer (1942) make the tautology charge against Kalecki. For further discussion see Sawyer (1985b, ch. 2).
11. For surveys see, for example, Weiss (1971), Sawyer (1985a, ch. 6), and specifically in the Kaleckian tradition see Reynolds (1984).
12. This could be taken to refer to the wages paid to those in work relative to output divided by number of workers. But in a system which involves social security (or equivalent) under which there is a transfer of income from the currently employed workers to the currently unemployed workers and former workers (i.e. the retired) it could also be thought of as wages per member of working class to output divided by number in working class. Here member of working class means currently employed as well as unemployed and retired workers.
13. This discussion is heavily influenced by Weisskopf (1979), to which reference should be made for a more detailed consideration.

Part Five

THE STATE

Chapter 10
THE POLITICAL ECONOMY OF THE STATE

10.1 INTRODUCTION

One of the most dramatic changes which has occurred in industrial-ised capitalist economies during the twentieth century has been the growth in terms of both scale and range of State activity. Whilst there has been this growth, the rate of growth has varied considerably between countries and over time (as is, to some degree, indicated in Table 10.1 below). The general trend during this century has been for the role of the State to change from one which largely involved defence, law and order, etc., into an involvement with extensive income transfers (i.e. through the Welfare State), the provision of services such as education and the ownership of production facilities (nationalised industries). Although there have been attempts to 'roll back the State' in some countries (notably the UK during the 1980s), the general trend during the twentieth century has been for the expansion of State activity. Indeed, judged by crude indicators such as the ratio of public expenditure to national income (see Table 10.1), this trend has continued into the 1980s.

This expansion of State activity has often been advocated by centre/centre-left political parties, which for convenience are label-led the social democrat tradition.[1] This social democrat tradition has largely seen the State as progressive and benign, and that State activity could achieve much that was not possible through the market mechanism. In effect, the market was seen to fail to deliver adequate performance in a number of crucial areas (e.g. provision of health care, of education), and State activity then became necessary. One notable sphere of 'market failure' is the achievement of full employment, and the social democrat tradition came to see the manipulation of aggregate demand through State fiscal and monetary policies (i.e. the adoption of Keynesian demand-management policies) as being able to achieve full employment. In a rather rough-and-ready manner, the view of the State adopted by the social democratic tradition has a correspondence to the view of the State adopted in mainstream economics, and this is further discussed below.

In political terms, the opposition to this social democratic consensus has come from right and left. On the right, Hayek (1944) advanced the view that the expansion of State activity was, according to its title, 'the road to serfdom'. The basis of the argument is that State activity combines legal coercion with a monopoly supply. For example, the British National Health Service would combine the legal coercion of tax payments to fund it and a single supplier of health care. Hayek's argument was that each extension of State activity was a step down a slippery slope with the power of the State over individual behaviour being further enhanced. From the perspective of this book, a major aspect of this approach is the counterpoising of the market and the State, with the former seen to promote individual freedom and also economic efficiency, and the latter viewed as restricting (at least eventually) liberty and undermining economic efficiency. Some aspects of this are discussed below when the approach of the so-called New Right to the State is considered. The appropriate role of the State is then seen to be a minimal one, often restricted to the provision of defence and the legal framework.

On the left the view of the State was strongly influenced by the Marxian approach to the effect that the activities of the State are strongly influenced and constrained by the requirements of the economically powerful (and the degree of influence has been widely discussed within the Marxian tradition). Further, in capitalist economies, it is the capitalist class (the private owners of the means of production) which is economically powerful. Thus State activity will be undertaken largely in the interests of capitalists. This raises questions such as the role of workers and trade unions, and whether they have power to influence State activity. Further, the question (discussed in Chapter 6) arises as to whether the industrialised economies of the OECD area can still be reasonably described as capitalist, in light of the rise of a managerial class and a shift of control from owners to managers.

Whereas the New Right largely contrasts the role of the market and that of the State, the radical political economy approaches see them intertwined in a variety of ways. It is useful to distinguish three strands of argument. The first, which can be labelled the developmental State, sees the State as playing an essential role in the process of industrialisation and development. Miliband (1969), for example, argues that

> state intervention in every aspect of economic life is nothing new in the history of capitalism. On the contrary, state intervention presided at its birth or at least guided and helped its early steps, not only in such obvious cases as Germany and Japan but in every other capitalist country as well, and it has never ceased to be of crucial importance in the workings of capitalism, even in the country [i.e. the United States of America] most dedicated to *laissez faire* and rugged individualism.

Similarly, Pollin and Alarcon (1988) argue that countries such as Taiwan and South Korea, which are held up as examples of countries which have successfully industrialised through reliance on market capitalism have, in fact, relied heavily on State intervention.[2]

The second aspect is that the State sets the legal framework within which markets operate and economic activity is organised. The law does not only govern the rules of exchange, but has an impact on the relative position of the two sides of the market. An obvious example is that the law on the organisation and rights of trade unions will have a major impact on the relative economic power of workers and employers. Similarly, the sale of goods and services can be governed by laws on minimum quality, on collusion between producers, etc. The institutional arrangements (including the legal ones) under which markets operate are created by human agencies, and there is no natural set of institutional arrangements. Thus, the State (along with other bodies) helps to determine which particular set of arrangements apply, and thereby to strongly influence the balance of power between the two sides of the market and the final outcome of the operation of markets.

The third aspect is that capitalists have requirements which cannot be met without State involvement. The transport of goods requires the provision of roads, but the private provision of roads is generally unprofitable (not least because of the difficulties of charging for use). There are many other examples along similar lines. This general line of argument will be examined further below, where the State is to some degree seen as supplying the needs of capital which capital itself cannot provide.

The first main section of this chapter provides some brief indications of the scale and nature of State activity in developed capitalist economies. The following sections discuss a variety of theories of the State. These theories are theories of the underlying causes of State activity and why the State undertakes certain tasks and not others. These theories of the cause of State activity carry clear suggestions of the answer to the question of in whose interests the State operates.

It is not a straightforward matter to define the State. It can be defined in terms of institutions, which would comprise legislative bodies including parliamentary assemblies, executive bodies including government departments, and judicial bodies responsible for enforcing the law.[3] These state institutions exist at different levels – national, regional and local (and supra-nationally to some degree). However, there are a range of institutions which fall on the borders of this definition: for example, QUANGOs (quasi non-governmental organisations) funded by government to undertake specific tasks but not subject to direct control of government. Nationalised industries and some other firms are owned by the State (central and local) but trade in many ways like private firms.

The State can also be defined in terms of its functions. The unique functions of the State include the ability to pass and enforce laws, the maintenance of law and order, to levy taxes, etc. It is, of course, the case that the State in most industrialised capitalist economies undertakes a range of functions (e.g. provider of education, of health care services) which could be (and have been) carried out by other organisations (e.g. private firms). But the central defining function would remain the ability to levy taxes and pass and enforce laws. There are clear examples where the power of the government to enforce laws and levy taxes breaks down, but in this chapter the discussion is confined to the operation of the State where there is not an immediate threat to its survival in its existing form (that is, no threat of revolutionary overthrow of the government or of a breakdown of law and order). It is, of course, the case that even outside cases where the breakdown of law and order is imminent, the government finds difficulty in enforcing some laws, and taxes are evaded. However, the range of State activities extends far beyond the passage of laws and the levying of taxation.

In contemporary terms, two areas of state intervention are of particular importance. First, there is the range of public services such as education, public health, pensions, income maintenance and housing. Second, following the widespread adoption of Keynesian economic management policies, the modern State has become more closely involved in regulating the operation of the economy. State intervention in this area ranges from facilitating industrial development through subsidies and tax concessions, to direct involvement in the productive process through public ownership of certain industries. (Ham and Hill, 1984).

10.2 THE SCALE AND NATURE OF STATE ACTIVITY

There are numerous ways of summarising the scale of State activity in advanced capitalist economies. Table 10.1 provides some illustrative figures for a range of developed capitalist economies in the late 1980s, with some figures from the three preceding decades for comparison. The first section illustrates the general growth of public expenditure through most of the post-war era. In relation to national income (GDP), public expenditure has increased in each of the decades and for each of the countries for which statistics are reported in the table. In particular, despite the demise of the social democrat consensus during the 1980s, public expenditure has tended to continue to increase relative to GDP. Some of the increase can be ascribed to higher social security payments arising from higher levels of unemployment, and some to higher interest payments on a rising national debt. This is to some degree indicated in the second section of the table. It can be seen that government expenditure on goods and services has only increased by two percentage points of GDP from the mid-1950s to the mid-1980s. The major increases can be seen to arise from the growth of transfer payments, which include both social security and interest payments by the government. During much of the post-war period there was a general downward trend in defence expenditure (relative to GDP). Data for fifteen countries reported in Smith (1977) reveal an almost universal decline in defence expenditure (relative to national income) between 1954 and 1964 and between 1964 and 1973. In the case of the United States, defence expenditure was equivalent to 11.0 per cent of GDP in 1955, declining to 7.5 per cent in 1965 and then rising to

Table 10.1 Selected figures on public expenditure for industrailised capitalist economies.

(i) International comparisons

	Country public expenditure as a percentage of GDP (market prices)			
	mid-1950s	mid-1960s	mid-1970s	mid-1980s
France	33.1	38.3	42.4	52.5
Germany	32.4	36.6	47.1	47.3
Sweden	(26.7)	36.5	49.6	63.9
United Kingdom	31.7	35.3	45.5	47.0
United States	25.9	28.5	33.4	36.5
Largest seven economies	26.9	30.3	36.3	39.4
OECD	27.0	30.0	36.7	40.5

Notes: Variables measured at current market prices. Largest seven economies are Canada, France, Germany, Italy, Japan, United Kingdom and United States. Figures relate to years ending in 4, 5 and 6 of the relevant decades, except for the 1950s which relate to 1955–57. The figure for Sweden for the mid-1950s excludes investment expenditure. Those referring to more than one country are weighted (by GDP) averages.

(ii) Composition of public expenditure (percentages of GDP at market prices)

OECD averages	mid-1950s	mid-1960s	mid-1970s	mid-1980s
Government final consumption expenditure	15.2	15.5	16.8	17.3
Other current expenditure (mainly transfers)	8.6	11.1	16.7	20.8
Capital expenditure	3.1	3.6	3.1	2.4

(iii) Evolution of public expenditure

	United Kingdom: Total government expenditure as a % of GNP (factor cost)						
Year				Total			
1905	12.3	**1910**	12.7	**1915**	35.0	**1920**	26.2
1925	23.7	**1930**	26.1	**1935**	24.4	**1940**	60.1
1945	66.0	**1950**	39.0	**1955**	36.6		

Note: The figures in (iii) are not directly comparable with those in (i) and (ii) since (iii) use GNP at factor cost whilst (i) and (ii) use GDP at market prices as the denominator.
Sources: For (i) and (ii) OECD (1972), OECD *Economic Outlook*, various issues; and for (iii) Peacock and Wiseman (1961).

9.6 per cent in 1968 under the impact of the Vietnam war. The figure then declined to 4.7 per cent in 1980, but rose back to 6.4 per cent in 1985.[4] Finally in Table 10.1, some figures illustrating the growth of public expenditure in this century in the UK are given. The influence of the two world wars are apparent, not only in the very much higher public expenditure during the war, but the shift upwards in the general level of expenditure from before to after each of the wars.

These public expenditure statistics tend to understate the growth of State activity in at least two ways. First, they do not reflect the State ownership of production facilities. In many industrialised countries, the public utilities (electricity, water, gas, post, telephones) are under public ownership and where these utilities are in private ownership are usually subject to public regulation. Although in some countries (notably the UK) there has been a policy of privatisation during the 1980s, there has been a substantial rise in the degree of public ownership during this century. Second, governments have accepted responsibility for the performance of the economy, and this has led to considerable increase in the influence of the State over the economy. Fiscal and monetary policies are used to seek to influence the level of economic activity, rate of inflation, etc. Further, there are a variety of ways in which governments intervene in the operation of industries, e.g. through monopoly and merger policy, through restructuring of industries.

10.3 STATE ACTIVITY IN CONVENTIONAL ECONOMICS

This section seeks to briefly elaborate the way in which State activity is analysed within conventional economics, with attention paid to the nature of the State as conceptualised in neo-classical analysis. This conceptualisation is that the State is generally seen as operating in the public interest, though this would presumably be limited to countries in which there was liberal democracy with an extensive franchise. The public interest is often discussed in terms of some apparently clearly defined objectives such as the maximisation of social welfare. Welfare economics does, of course, discuss the difficulties of the formulation of a social welfare function, that is how the utility functions of individuals might be combined to provide an index of social welfare. It is perhaps in the area of welfare economics (and the application of welfare economics) that concepts of the State are most intimately involved. Ng (1983), for example, sees welfare economics as serving 'as a foundation to many applied (relatively speaking) branches of economics such as public finance, cost benefit analysis, and the economics of government

policy in many areas including international trade, industry and
welfare (social security etc.)'.

Despite the close links between certain areas of conventional
economics and the role of the State, the nature of the State is not
given a great deal of attention. However, it can be inferred that the
view of the State and its activities which is implicit in most conventional economics is a rather simplistic one. At one level it could be
said that the State is treated like other economic agents (households,
firms) with a well-defined set of objectives which it pursues subject
to the constraints which it faces. In that way questions of decision-
making within the State and conflicts between decision-makers are
side-stepped (as also happens with analysis of the firm as seen above,
section 4.3). At another level, the State is generally seen as pursuing
the social interest. Hence the objectives pursued by those in control
of the State are treated as synonymous with the social interest.
Further, the social interest is, in effect, seen as representing the
interests of individuals in which each individual's interests are given
an equal weight (for in a liberal democracy each individual has a
vote of equal weight). Thus there is an assumed equality of political
power between individuals, rather than a disparity of political
power (arising from a disparity of economic power).

The general approach of welfare economics (which is the area of
neo-classical economics where the State is clearly involved) has
been to portray perfect competitive equilibrium as an ideal but one
which may not always be achievable. For example,

> let us now look more closely at what assumptions *are* necessary for this
> proposition [that if the distribution of factor ownership is right, a
> free-market economy can maximise social welfare] to hold. There are
> four. Where these assumptions do not hold, a pure free-market
> economy is not optimal, and government intervention is normally
> suggested [by whom is not stated]. (Layard and Walters, 1978)

The four assumptions, which are rightly described as sweeping,
are no increasing returns, no technical external effects, no market
failure connected with uncertainty, and factor ownership is deemed
acceptable. The pervasiveness of external effects, uncertainty and
increasing returns might suggest a rather large role for government
intervention. However, Layard and Walters (1978) note that

> in any particular case one must of course consider also whether
> governmental institutions in fact have the capacity to do better than

the free market. To say the latter is nonoptimal when compared to an ideal standard does not of itself prove that anything better can be arranged.

However, the overall impression is that

through most of this literature there also runs the strong presumption that free enterprise and the operation of the market will tend to maximize efficiency; thus a necessary condition for state intervention to be desirable becomes the failure of the market. (Aaronovitch and Smith, 1981)

The features of the approach of mainstream economics which are important for the discussion here are as follows:

1. The social interest and social welfare can be measured using the techniques developed by economists. In particular, each individual is assumed to possess a utility function, and seeks to achieve as high a level of utility as possible. Social welfare is based on individual welfare (as reflected in the level of utility). But, the summation of individual welfare to measure social welfare cannot be carried through since utility is not measurable in a cardinal manner, and the utility of different individuals are not comparable.
2. There are no insuperable difficulties for the government to obtain the relevant information. This would mean, for example, that the government would be fully aware of any situation of market failure and would be able to fully assess the range of options and choose the one which would be in the social interest.
3. The normative aspect is that market failure *should* be corrected if there is a gain in social welfare. The use of terms such as welfare carry the connotation that more welfare is better than less. Thus an analysis which points to a way by which social welfare can be improved carries with it the implication that the improvement in social welfare should be implemented.
4. There is a tendency to move from the normative to the positive, that is to say that governments do intervene to correct cases of market failure. Indeed, if the analysis is not used in either a positive or normative way it is difficult to see the purpose of the analysis.

One feature of this general approach to which attention should be drawn is the narrow dividing line between normative and positive aspects, and this can be illustrated by reference to the notion of market failure. For an example, consider the case of an industry which produces subject to increasing returns to scale. In such a case, productive efficiency would appear to require a single producer (and competition between firms may eventually produce a single firm), but a monopoly price appears to generate some loss of consumer welfare (as compared with lower prices). This suggests that the social interest (identified with the sum of individual welfare) requires a price lower than the monopoly one to be charged. This soon leads to a consideration of the forms of government intervention which would generate a lower than monopoly level price, such as the regulation of price, nationalisation with marginal cost pricing.

If 'welfare economics is the branch of study which endeavours to formulate propositions by which we can say that the social welfare in one economic situation is higher or lower than in another' (Ng, 1983), then it would appear a short step to saying that a government interested in the pursuit of social welfare *does* seek to move to an economic situation with a higher level of social welfare. Thus cost–benefit analysis can be advocated as a technique for the evaluation of a proposed public-sector project on the basis that the project *should* be undertaken if the (social) benefits exceed (social) costs, when the benefits and costs are evaluated in accordance with the recommendations of the welfare economists. But cost–benefit analysis can be used in a positive manner, i.e. the (potentially testable) proposition that governments do carry out projects when social net benefits are positive. Indeed, it can be observed that governments do adopt procedures such as cost–benefit analysis (or at least the civil servants carry out cost–benefit analysis, though it may be argued that the cost–benefit studies are carried out in order to provide support for a decision which has already been made on other grounds).

The use of the idea of 'public goods' (as contrasted with 'private goods') is a related attempt to explain the range of activities undertaken by government in that it is argued that the market will fail to provide public goods in the way in which private goods are provided. Thus, public goods could be seen as a further case of where market failure arises. Public goods are defined as goods (and services) with the following properties:

1. They are non-excludable (it is difficult or impossible to exclude

an individual from consuming the good or service).
2. They are non-rivalrous (one person's consumption does not detract from another's consumption).

The examples given of public goods are usually goods and services such as the provision of lighthouse facilities, national defence. These public goods contrast with private goods which have the converse properties and are the subject of most microeconomic analysis. The very term 'public goods' suggests that these goods and services should be (or are) provided by the public sector. At a minimum, it can be said that most goods and services provided by governments (e.g. education, health, income maintenance) in developed capitalist economies are not public goods in the technical sense as defined above, and that the notion of public goods does not provide an adequate explanation for the size and growth of the public sector, though Ng (1983) argues that 'public goods are an (increasingly) important part of the economy'. A particular example of this line of argument is State involvement in the provision of education. Foley (1978) argues that neo-classical theory 'cannot explain why the State is so deeply involved in education in all modern capitalist countries'. There may be some externality from education but 'this argument is not adequate to explain the actual role of the State in education because at most it suggests a subsidy to education as a privately produced commodity, not a full-scale State-regulated or administered educational system'. Indeed 'it is somewhat easier to see why the State is so centrally involved in education in capitalist society' when it is approached from a Marxist perspective. The process of education involves not only teaching of literacy and numeracy but also is part of the process of socialisation and the reproduction of the dominant ideology. Since one requirement for the continuation of capitalism is the reproduction of both the workforce and the capitalist ideology, it is not surprising that the State is heavily involved in the education process.

In macroeconomics, there is discussion of the impact of the level of public expenditure and taxation on the level of economic activity, and the relative efficacy of monetary and fiscal policy in the achievement of the objectives of government macroeconomic policy. Indeed, the role of the State within much of macroeconomic analysis (particularly that of the Keynesian variety) could be described as the 'puller of levers', that is adjustments to public expenditure, taxation, interest rates, etc., to generate desired changes in the economy. A Keynesian macroeconomic view may emphasise the role of aggregate demand, and the government ability to control that demand through public expenditure and taxation. A monetarist view would stress the importance of money. But in either case, the government is portrayed as being able to pull certain levers (government expenditure, money supply) with predictable effects on the economy. The levers can be pulled to achieve the objectives of low level of unemployment, reduce inflation, etc. Following the work of Tinbergen (1952) and others, it was argued that governments had to have at their disposal at least as many instruments of policy (e.g. money supply, public expenditure) as targets of policy (e.g. full employment). This general approach emphasises the technocratic approach (that is, a focus on the relationship between instruments and targets) with little discussion of how the targets of economic policy evolve over time. Hence the source of the objectives of macroeconomic policy is little discussed. For example, the discussion may assume that full employment is one of the objectives of government policy and then fiscal and monetary policy discussed in terms of their relative efficiency in the achievement of that objective. But it is rare to find a discussion of how and why full employment comes to be adopted (if it is) as an objective of government policy.[5]

Most macroeconomics textbooks discuss the determinants of economic variables such as unemployent, output and inflation, including the influence of government activity on those variables. It can be inferred that those variables have been among the major objectives of government policy over, say, the past twenty years, for otherwise it is difficult to see why the discussion takes this form. Although it is not often explicitly stated, there is probably broad agreement in mainstream macroeconomic analysis that the targets of macroeconomic policy have been 'the attainment of (i) a high and stable level of employment, (ii) a stable general price level; (iii) a growing level of real income (i.e. economic growth); (iv) balance of payments equilibrium; and (v) certain distribution aims' (Vane and Thompson, 1985), though as they recognise, these aims may conflict. But it is noticeable that in general there is very little discussion of the origin of these policy objectives, whose interests are served by their achievement, and whether these policy objectives have been seriously pursued. In the case of the UK, the policy of a 'high and stable level of employment' was formally expressed in 1944 in Ministry of Reconstruction (1944), largely abandoned during the 1970s (as described in Deacon, 1981) and formally abandoned in the 1980s (as seen in Department of Employment, 1985, which argued that 'government cannot do what the nation will not. It cannot on its own create jobs.').

Another approach to macroeconomic policy formulation is

the *optimizing approach* to economics [which] assumes that it is conceptually possible to specify *the social welfare function*. Once this is determined, and the preference pattern of society determined with respect to all possible outcomes of inflation and unemployment is known, the task of policy is simply to select whatever attainable combination will maximize welfare. (Greenway and Shaw, 1988)

The use of the Phillips curve as a trade-off between inflation and unemployment is an illustration of the general point. A Phillips curve is drawn in Figure 10.1, reflecting the idea that the rate of inflation is negatively related to the level of unemployment. In most macroeconomic analysis it has been assumed that both inflation and unemployment are socially undesirable. As such it would be possible to draw indifference curves between the two 'bads' of inflation and unemployment, which is illustrated by curve I in Figure 10.1. The point of tangency between the two curves at point X would be the social optimum with wage inflation $\dot{w}^*$ and unemployment u^*. This leaves the role of the economist to discover the nature of the trade-off between inflation and unemployment (i.e. the precise shape of the Phillips curve). This brief example illustrates a number of points.[6] First, there is the apparent division between the positive aspects (that is, the Phillips curve which purports to describe a crucial feature of the economy) and the normative (that is, the indifference curves between inflation and unemployment). Second, it is implicitly assumed that there is a general social consensus over the dislike of unemployment and inflation, whereas it could be argued that some groups in society suffer much more from unemployment than others (and conversely that some suffer from inflation much more than others). Third, there is generally little discussion over how unemployment and inflation come to be regarded as key objectives of government macroeconomic policy.

Although governments in many capitalist countries declared full employment as a major objective of policy around the end of the

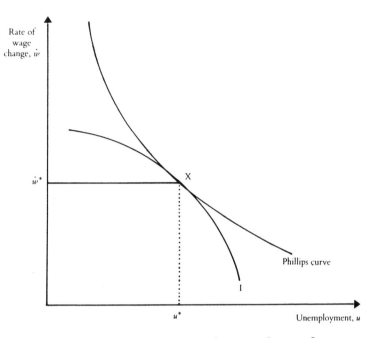

Figure 10.1 'Trade-off' between unemployment and wage inflation.

Second World War, the evidence of the past fifteen years must raise considerable doubts on some combination of their commitment to full employment and their ability to achieve it. Within the orthodox approach to macroeconomics, it is difficult to see why government and society would not have full employment as an objective of policy, though the approach of monetarists and neo-classical macroeconomists would indicate that the capitalist economy left to its own devices would generate full employment. The radical political economy tradition would doubt that capitalist economies would operate at full employment. It would argue (cf. section 11.5), following Kalecki (1943), that full employment does not usually arise under *laissez-faire* capitalism, so that prolonged full employment would require sustained government intervention. This intervention would encroach on private activities, and be resisted by private enterprise (and this is touched on again below). Further, as Kalecki (1943) argued, 'the assumption that a government will maintain full employment in a capitalist economy if it knows how to do it is fallacious'. For the experience of full employment would generate dramatic changes in the balance of power between labour and capital, enhancing the power of labour. 'Indeed, under a regime of permanent full employment, "the sack" would cease to play its role as a disciplinary measure. The social position of the boss would be undermined and the self assurance and class consciousness of the working class would grow' (Kalecki, 1943). These types of change would then generate political pressures from capitalists to raise unemployment. The pressures for unemployment may not be directly expressed in those terms, but that in terms of expression of concern over inflation, with the 'overheating' of the economy and of the rights of managers to manage. But these can all be seen as a cover for higher levels of unemployment which will help to restrain the power of workers. Thus whilst workers gain from prolonged periods of low levels of unemployment, capitalists may not, leading to political pressures for unemployment.

In an extension of that argument, Foley (1978) argues that 'the major effect of these [welfare and unemployment compensation] programs in a Marxist perspective is to maintain a reserve of unemployed, not to eliminate unemployment'. For these programmes help to 'assure on average the survival and political docility of workers disemployed in large numbers in the periodic crises and recessions which are characteristic of capitalist development'.

10.4 VIEWS OF THE NEW RIGHT

The concept of a disinterested State operating in the social interest, which is widely used in the mainstream economic analysis, has been criticised from many directions. The discussion in the next section concentrates on Marxian and related views on the nature of the State, but in this section the views of what can be called the New Right are briefly reviewed, with attention given to two aspects of their views.

The first aspect concerns the view in the macroeconomic sphere that there is little that governments can do which is beneficial, and their interventions into the operation of markets will usually be harmful. This view is particularly associated with monetarism and the New Classical Macroeconomics.[7] The basic proposition on which this is based is that the private enterprise economy will, left itself, generate full employment (often expressed as operating at the 'natural rate of unemployment'). Of course, if that proposition is accepted, then it trivially follows that government action cannot ultimately raise the level of employment (and may indeed reduce it). Indeed, there is a close link between the views on the impact of the State on the level of unemployment and the conclusions drawn from the analysis of the level of unemployment which would result from a *laissez-faire* (minimal government involvement) economy. Monetarism (of various brands) has essentially concluded that a *laissez-faire* economy would operate with full employment of labour and capital equipment. Hence, in that approach, there would be no role for government activity to promote full employment. In contrast, within the radical political economy approaches, there are many who would see full employment under *laissez-faire* as an unusual occurrence. This is reflected below in the discussion of authors such as Baran and Sweezy (1966) and Kidron (1968), where they view the purpose of government expenditure as helping to maintain the level of profits (which requires a relatively low level of unemployment), though some types of government expenditure (notably defence) are seen as more acceptable to the capitalist class than others (e.g. social security).

The second aspect of the analysis of the New Right to which some attention is given here is the idea that the State is not operated in the social interests, but rather is managed by politicians and civil servants (bureaucrats) in their own interests. There is a variety of views on what the interests of those groups are, which of the groups has the greater power and what the constraints on the exercise of their power are. However, some of the main examples which have been to the fore can be briefly mentioned. Politicians' interests are seen to be election to office, and for those in office to pursue policies which will ensure re-election. This rather presumes that politicians' interests are the exercise of power without much concern in how and in whose interests that power is exercised. It could be argued that pursuing policies to ensure re-election means that the democratic will of the people determines the policies pursued, in that the way to be re-elected is to pursue policies which people like.[8] There are two particular counter-arguments to this. The first is that many policies have both advantages and disadvantages, which fall on people in different proportions. A policy whose advantages are focused on relatively few people and/or are received by well-organised pressure groups but whose disadvantages are spread thinly over many people are likely to be pursued. For example, a decision to subsidise a particular industry would benefit the owners of firms and the workers in that industry. Further, the industry may be geographically concentrated, and the subsidy would favour a few areas of the country. The cost of the subsidy would be spread over the generality of taxpayers (and some other industries may suffer indirectly). The argument is that the few gainers will be appreciative of the advantages but the many losers be unaware of the disadvantages. The second counter-argument is that at the macroeconomic level, the (temporary) stimulation of the economy prior to an election will bring short-term gains of output and employment increases. This will help to secure re-election of the government (and there has been much work to indicate that economic prosperity does influence the standing of the government). But, the argument runs, the output and employment gains are short-lived, and the longer-run effect is a general rise in the pace of inflation.[9] This general view relies on a certain short-sightedness by the electorate. But it also helps to generate a 'political business cycle' whereby output and employment are stimulated prior to an election. It should be noted that this argument assumes a particular view of how the macroeconomy works, namely that demand stimulation has a short-lived effect on output and employment.

Members of the bureaucracy, it is argued, will have interests in their own salaries, promotion prospects, size of the budget and staff which they control, etc. In effect, directly or indirectly, members of the bureaucracy are interested in the expansion of the bureaucracy, and this builds in a basic tendency for the size of government to expand.

Whilst these arguments have been advanced in recent years by the New Right, some of the arguments can be incorporated within the radical political economy approaches to the State discussed below. It is, rather, that the arguments advanced below are more wide ranging and would treat the arguments of the New Right as of limited importance. The interests of bureaucrats and politicians are only part of the influences on the State, and the power of others (especially the capitalist classes) has to be brought into the picture. The bureaucrats are able to some degree to pursue their own interests, though there is the question of whether bureaucrats can be represented as having some collective (as opposed to individual) interests. But the pursuit by bureaucrats of their own interests is still subject to a variety of external pressures. Foley (1978), which is a paper on a Marxist perspective on State expenditure, argues that

> State policy itself is decided in elections only in rare and marginal instances. Whatever group or fraction holds State power, the great mass of State policy is determined within the administrative apparatus of the State, a bureaucracy in which an intense struggle for influence among emergent interests constantly manifests itself.

The bureaucracy may have its own interests, one of which is an expansion of its own size. The bureaucracy would then become larger than it needs to be (given the functions which it carries out), but the functions which it performs and the policies adopted are determined by a range of influences on the bureaucracy.

Further, one of the first expressions of the idea of 'political business cycle' (with unemployment falling prior to an election, etc.) can be found from within the radical political economy tradition in Kalecki (1943). A political business cycle would be generated from two sets of pressures. 'The pressure of all these forces, and in particular of big business would most probably induce the Government to return to the orthodox policy of cutting down the budget deficit. A slump would follow.' But then, 'in the slump, either under the pressure of the masses, or even without it, public investment financed by borrowing will be undertaken to prevent large-scale unemployment' (Kalecki, 1943). However, as Henley (1988) points out, 'the principal shortcomings of orthodox theories of the electoral business cycle is that they fail to treat the electorate as sectionalised into different groups whose different interests may be at variance with each other'. Indeed, it is the conflict of interests between labour and capital which helps to generate the cycle in Kalecki's analysis.

If the analysis of the new classical macroeconomists (and the New Right generally) is correct, then the health of capitalism would require minimal State involvement (mainly restricted to law and order and defence). In contrast, much radical political economy analysis would suggest that the health of a capitalist economy requires considerable State involvement. Indeed, if the radical political economy view is correct, then the recommendations of the New Right will not be put into practice, despite the sympathy of most New Right economists with capitalism. For simply, developed capitalism would be unable to operate effectively without substantial State involvement. The governments which during the 1980s would appear to have had most sympathy with the analyses of the New Right have been those of the United Kingdom and the United States. Although in the case of the British government, some previously nationalised industries have been privatised, this could be seen as returning profitable activities to the private sector whilst retaining unprofitable activities within the public sector. Further, a reduction of State involvement in some areas (e.g. the sale of local-authority housing) is counterbalanced by a growth of involvement in other areas (e.g. control over the ways in which trade unions operate). The change in the composition of public expenditure away from the welfare state aspects and towards defence would be consistent with the arguments of Kalecki (1943), Baran and Sweezy (1966) and others of the preference of capitalists for certain forms of public expenditure. Changes in the tax system have not so much changed the overall burden of taxation, but rather rearranged it so that the rich benefit at the expense of the poor. Although space precludes a full discussion, the policies of the British and American governments can be viewed as strengthening the power of capital *vis-à-vis* labour, of the rich over the poor. Thus rather than 'rolling back the State', this can be seen as a shift towards the State giving greater support to capital than under the previous post-war regimes which could be included under the heading of the Keynesian/social democrat consensus.[10]

10.5 MARXIAN AND SIMILAR APPROACHES TO THE STATE

The views of the State which are discussed in the remainder of this chapter could be broadly described as influenced by Marxism. As Miliband (1969) notes, 'Marx himself . . . never attempted a system-atic study of the state', though Marx and Engels 'never departed from the view that in capitalist society, the state was above all the coercive instrument of a ruling class, itself defined in terms of its ownership and control of the means of production'. The lack of a systematic study by Marx of the State and the numerous economic and political developments (notably extension of franchise, rise of working-class based political parties) in more than a century since Marx wrote means that there will always be debate over whether any particular view of the State can be treated as Marxian. However, the concern here is not with that question but rather with the range of approaches which acknowledge some influence by Marx.[11]

The quote given above from Miliband introduces a number of themes. The first is the coercive nature of the State, which is recognised by the notion that the passage and encorcement of law and order is a central, indeed defining, function of any State. Thus, any activity of a State carries with it at least the threat of coercion. The second theme is the question of which classes exercise economic and political power in late twentieth-century industrialised societies. A third theme which will be introduced below is the explanation of the expansion of functions performed by the State during the twentieth century, and in particular an apparent shift away from a coercive role to a developmental role. For,

> advanced capitalist countries now have an often substantial 'public sector', through which the state owns and administers a wide range of industries and services, mainly but not exclusively of an 'infra-structural' kind, which are of vast importance to their economic life; and the state also plays in all capitalist economies an ever-greater economic role by way of regulation, control, coordination, 'planning' and so forth. (Miliband, 1969)

At a very general level, the proposition is that the way in which the State operates depends on the power relations in the society. Further, the nature of those power relations depends on the forces of production, so that it arises from economic power. In feudal times, the power resides with the landowners, etc., and the State is operated in the general interests of the landowners (though, of course, landowners differ over what those interests are and there are struggles over who is to exercise power). Although this general proposition is an improvement over the naive view embedded in orthodox economics, it is only a first step which raises a number of questions. The questions which arise include the following:

1. In developed capitalist economies, which groups and classes exercise economic power?

   The analysis of Marx portrays capitalism with two socio-economic classes based on capital and on labour in essential conflict but with capital exercising power over labour. The two important developments during the twentieth century of relevance here are the growth of organised labour (including trade unions and of political parties linked with them) and the rise of a managerial class. The latter has been discussed in Chapter 6, and here it is merely noted that the conclusion is drawn from that chapter that the interests of top-level managers and shareholders are not substantially different from one another. In particular, both groups will be interested in the health of their own company and of the capitalist system in general.[12]

2. How far is political power determined by economic power?

The implicit view of mainstream economic analysis is that there is a separation between economic power and political power. Indeed, the latter is often seen as a partial corrective to the former – as, for example, in anti-monopoly policy where political power is used to reduce the economic power based on monopoly. In contrast, some Marxist writers have taken an approach which can be labelled reductionist, in which all actions of the State are reduced to an expression of the dominance of the capitalist class. In other words, political power is derived from economic power.

3. Since most industrialised capitalist economies have a universal franchise, is it not the the case that the policies of the government have to reflect the democratic will of the electorate?

In particular, this question would suggest that the exercise of political power by the capitalist class is extremely limited. The quote from Foley given above suggests that infrequent voting has a very small impact on the exercise of political power. Miliband (1969, especially chs. 7 and 8) deals with this question at length. He points out that 'as a pressure group *vis-à-vis* the state, business enjoys a vast degree of superiority over all other groups and interests. In part at least, this must be related to the vast ideological, political and, in the broadest sense, cultural influence which it wields on society at large'. Similarly

in all modern capitalist states capitalist class influence on State policy is also fostered by certain widely shared conceptions and beliefs, which tend to coordinate State decisions in a line favorable to the class interests of capital. There is a strong tendency

promoted by educational and journalistic practice and by political
rhetoric to identify the 'national interest' with the interest of
national capital. (Foley, 1978)

4. What functions does the State fulfil, and in particular why do
   powerful groups find that there are activities which the State can
   do which cannot be achieved through other means?

Drawing on the work of Semmler, Gough (1979) proposes a
division of the functions of the State into three areas:

(i) Establishing the conditions, such as transport, energy, infrastructure and so forth.
(ii) Establishing the conditions for the reproduction of labour
power, such as education, health services and so forth.
(iii) Establishing the general conditions for reproduction of capitalist relations, such as general administration, justice, police and
many other aspects of the general framework within which the
reproduction of the capitalist modes takes place.

The State can be seen as having a number of different roles,
and indeed the mix of roles is likely to vary over time and
between countries. But at a general level, it is possible to
distinguish between two broad sets of roles. The first could be
called the coercive role, that is seeking to prevent people do what
they would otherwise do. The second could be called an enabling
role, that is allowing people to achieve outcomes which would
not be otherwise possible. The enabling role view of the State
can take the form of government intervention in the economy to
correct a variety of 'market failures' (the mainstream economics
view discussed above). Another (not necessarily contradictory
view) is that of the State being intimately involved with
industrial development.

The State has always possesed a repressive nature, though
obviously the degree of repression has varied tremendously
between countries and over time. Laws are passed and enforced
which seek to restrict the activities of people. These restrictions
will harm some but benefit others. In many cases, the restrictions
may be widely regarded as justified (e.g. physical assault), but
others will be much more controversial. One of the defining roles
of the State is the ability to pass and enforce laws. Indeed, some
argue that the role of the State should be restricted to setting the
ground rules against which markets operate. But the laws which

are established governing matters such as trade unions, the formation of corporations, the relationships between firms, etc., are not neutral in their impact on the relative power of labour and capital.

On the other side, there are activities which the State is perhaps uniquely able to provide (or at least provides so much more efficiently that private provision is not considered). Much political debate in recent years could be seen in these terms. The welfare state/social democratic consensus had established a wide range of activities as the prerogative of the State – ranging from law, defence through education, health to social security. The New Right has challenged much of that, and particularly pointed to the non-public good nature of these activities, and also the possibility of separating production of these activities from the financing of them.

The analysis of the State cannot be undertaken in a historical vacuum, but rather it is necessary to say something about the social and political background against which any specific State operates. But often it is precisely differences of view about the historical background which leads to differences of analysis of the State. The following differences can be highlighted. First, the relative power of capital and labour, and particularly the question of whether the nature of capitalism has basically changed during the twentieth century such that the power of labour has been much enhanced. Second, the structure and requirements of the industrial sector, and the question of whether the economic system can be accurately described as competitive (in a Marxian sense) or as one of monopoly capitalism (cf. section 5.5). Third, the rise of some form of managerial capitalism may have led to a shift in economic power from owners to managers (cf. sections 6.3, 6.5).

The role of the State at a particular time in a specific country will reflect the history of that country, the relationship between social classes and its position within the world economy. In this chapter, the intention is to outline some basic ideas, rather than apply them (or any others) to any concrete situation. This may help to avoid spurious generalisation, in which an analysis appropriate to one country is applied to other countries where the analysis is inappropriate. However,

when all such national differences and specificities have been duly taken into account, there remains the fact that advanced capitalism has imposed many fundamental uniformities upon the countries which have come under its sway, and greatly served to attenuate, though not to flatten out, the differences between them. As a result, there has come about a remarkable degree of similarity, not only in economic but in social and even in political terms, between these countries. (Miliband, 1969)

The observation that business and capital have substantial influence on the conduct of State activity has to be circumscribed in two ways. The first is that it is tempting to infer from the fact that the State has undertaken some action, that that action was in the interest of capitalists, in the long term if not in the short term. In one direction, there are many influences at work on State policies, and some policies are implemented which are in the interests of workers and against the interests of capitalists. There may also be a range of policies which are in the mutual interests of workers and capital. In another direction, 'there is no magic process by which the state recognizes and responds to the hidden needs of capital; the specific needs must be expressed through the political process' (Aaronovitch and Smith, 1981).

This general line of argument can be illustrated by the Factory Acts passed in the early nineteenth century in the UK. These Acts fixed, for example, legal limits on the working hours of first children and then of women, which in practice led to a reduction of working hours of men as well. The shortening of working hours was advocated by a coalition of working-class organisations and radicals and generally opposed by capitalist industrial interests. Nevertheless, it was passed through a parliament without working-class representation and elected by a very limited franchise. However, it can be argued that this was a case where the collective interests of the capitalist class were served by a reduction in the working day, though individual firms were prevented by competition from reducing hours worked. For in the longer term, improved health among the working class aided by the reduction in working hours would help a rise in productivity and work effort. This should be seen as an example of where any individual capitalist is prevented by competitive pressures from undertaking an action (reducing working hours) which would be in their collective long-term interests. In such a case, it is only through some form of co-operation (directly organised between firms, or indirectly organised by the State) that such a course of action can be followed.

In the context of Marxian theories of the State, the approach which associated the actions of the State with the interests of capital has generally been labelled 'instrumentalism' in which the State is seen as the instrument of capitalists, or 'reductionist' as the actions of the State can be reduced to the interests of capitalists. 'A reductionist Marxism would see the State as no more than the expression of the capitalist class dominance over the working class in modern capitalist society' (Foley, 1978). However, most recent writing in the Marxian tradition has sought to avoid any simple instrumentalist or reductionist explanation of State activity.

The second direction is to recognise that whilst it is sometimes useful to talk of the capitalist class, the government, etc., as though they were a single coherent entity, it is of course the case that each of the groups is composed of individuals. At any particular time, there will usually be differences of view among individuals as to the exact nature of the current position, the way to pursue their mutual interests as well as differences in their interests. The capitalist class can be seen as divided into *fractions*, which is a reflection of different interest groups within that class. For example, the interests of industrial capital and financial capital have often been seen as conflicting (cf. Bhaduri and Steindl, 1983). Other examples would be the conflict of interests between small businesses and large businesses, and between businesses of different industries. Policies adopted by governments such as restrictive-practices legislation, monopoly and merger policy will have differential effects on firms of different sizes, and the implementation of such policies would depend on which particular groups of capitalists held most political power.

The precise nature of the relationship between the economic and political spheres, and between capitalists and the State has been subject to a great deal of debate (see, for example, Miliband, 1969; Poulantzas, 1973, 1977, 1978; Jessop, 1977, 1982). For our purposes, it is sufficient to portray that discussion in the rather simple terms of the two ends of the spectrum of argument. At one end of the spectrum are those who would argue that ultimately the political is subservient to the economic, the State to the capitalist class. In other words, the actions of the State are viewed as serving the interests of the capitalist class. The State carries out functions on behalf of the capitalist class, essentially those functions which individual capitalists cannot carry out. In the phrases of Marx, 'the executive of the modern State is but a committee for managing the common affairs of the whole bourgeoisie'.

At the other end of the spectrum are those who would portray the State has having a considerable degree of autonomy (from the capitalist class) so that the State is able to pursue some policies which are not in the interests (direct or indirect, short-term or long-term) of the capitalist class. This would allow for bureaucrats as well as the working class to exercise some influence over the actions and operations of the State. Practitioners within the State develop their own ethos and many advocates of the welfare state see it as embodying a non-market purpose. For example, 'common to all [of a range of writers] is the view that the purpose of the welfare state is the enhancement of human welfare, the imposition of more enlightened values over those embodied in the capitalist market system' (Gough, 1979).

Another way of representing the range of argument is as follows. One view is that the State operates to support individual capitalists and capitalism as an economic system. Thus, for example, a nationalised health service would be seen as introduced to provide a healthy workforce for business and to buy off working-class agitation by reform. The other view is that the State operates in a way which is fundamentally different from the ways in which the market mechanism works, and is a forerunner of an alternative to market-based capitalism. Within the State (as within the firm, cf. Chapter 4), decisions may be made by reference to objectives other than profits and resources allocated without direct reference to the market. In particular, as will be elaborated below, the Welfare State can be seen as allocating resources on the basis of need or of citizenship rather than on the basis of ability to pay. These conflicting views on the State are reflected in the observation

> left-wing attitudes towards social welfare: agency of repression, or a system from enlarging human needs and mitigating the rigours of the free-market economy? An aid to capital accumulation and profits or a 'social wage' to be defended and enlarged like the money in your pay packet? Capitalist fraud or working-class victory? (Gough, 1979)[13]

The continuation of the capitalist system under conditions of liberal democracy requires that the populace accepts capitalism. Further, capitalism is only viable as an economic system if profitable accumulation is possible. These simple remarks lead to the view that the essential roles of the State have been seen by some to be that of legitimisation and accumulation. The legitimisation role includes conditioning and persuading workers to accept the capitalist system, which may be achieved through the educational system, the media, etc., and by policies designed to limit popular discontent. The process of legitimisation generally involves policies which benefit the working class (or parts of it), and in the view of some 'the best example [of the State's legitimisation function] is the welfare system, which is designed chiefly to keep social peace among unemployed workers' (O'Connor, 1973). Whilst discussion of the Welfare State is returned to below, it should be noted here that this view of the Welfare State (and more generally any apparent advances made by the workers) is interpreted as a necessary concession made by capitalists in order to ensure the continuation of the capitalist system.

The accumulation role is to preserve and reinforce the conditions for profits. The State performs functions which capitalists themselves do not find profitable to perform (e.g. the provision of transport facilities and other infrastructure). The accumulation role can also involve the subsidisation of investment, research and development, etc., the nationalisation of unprofitable industries. Further, this role may require the State to seek to regulate real wages, to protect access to markets (domestic and foreign), aid firms in restructuring, etc.

O'Connor (1973) argues that these two roles are essentially contradictory, in that the legitimisation role generally involves concessions to the working class at the expense of capital, whereas the accumulation role favours profits over wages. 'A capitalist state that openly uses its coercive forces to help one class accumulate capital at the expense of other classes loses its legitimacy and hence undermines the basis of its loyalty and support (O'Connor, 1973).

10.6 THE STATE AND THE ECONOMY

The purpose of this section is to briefly consider the relationship between State and economy. The conventional view of the objectives of economic (especially macroeconomic) policy was given above (section 10.3). The radical political economy approach would place much more emphasis on the objective of profitability. The general objective of capitalists is taken to be profitable accumulation, and in line with the arguments of this chapter, capitalists would press governments to implement policies towards that aim. The other policy objectives may be derivative from that general objective of profitable accumulation (e.g. control of inflation). The determination of the rate of profit was discussed in the previous chapter (section 9.6), and the general importance of profits is further discussed below (section 12.5). In this discussion, the rate of profit will be taken as a summary indicator of the interests of capitalists; in particular, a declining rate of profit signals an unhealthy economic situation from the view point of the capitalists. Marx postulated a general tendency for the rate of profit to decline, though this tendency was the outcome of two contradictory tendencies – rising capital intensity of production, declining wage share. But whatever the reason, a declining rate of profit would generate demands from capitalists for economic policies which will offset and/or reverse the downward trend in profitability. The reduction of taxation on profits is a clear way of offsetting a decline in the rate of profits, and the subsidisation of investment has a similar effect. A whole range of means have been developed by which investment is effectively subsidised, such as regional policies. Incomes policies have been adopted in response to rising inflation, but the control of money wage increases can operate to the detriment of real wages (Tarling and Wilkinson, 1977). The creation of unemployment is likely to restrain real wages and thereby aid profitability, though the associated increased surplus capacity has a detrimental effect on the rate of profit. The threat of unemployment may also raise labour intensity, and thereby productivity and profitability. The nationalisation of unprofitable industries which nevertheless provide vital goods and services (e.g. transport) is another policy which protects profitability.

Another important theme within the radical political economy tradition is that *laissez-faire* capitalism will generally exhibit unemployment and that full employment would require State intervention (cf. section 11.4). The full employment of labour appears a laudable aim (if rarely achieved) but poses considerable difficulties for capitalism. On one side, higher levels of demand and employment would appear to generate more profits (and more income in general) and a higher rate of profits. However, there may be inadequate private-sector aggregate demand to ensure full employment. On the other side, full employment strengthens the position of workers, and, as argued by Kalecki and others (cf. section 11.5), this undermines the economic and social position of capitalists. Thus, it is not clear that capitalists gain from full employment, particularly permanent full employment. Further, full employment requires State manipulation of aggregate demand.

The approach of authors such as Baran and Sweezy (1966) and Kalecki (1972) could be portrayed as saying that there are some forms of public expenditure which are acceptable to capitalists while others are less so. Baran and Sweezy (1966) seek

> to demonstrate, first, that government plays a similar role [in absorbing part of the surplus] but on a larger scale; and second, that the uses to which government puts the surplus which it absorbs are narrowly circumscribed by the nature of monopoly capitalist society and as time goes on become more and more irrational and destructive.

They argue that military expenditure has a number of advantages so far as capitalists are concerned over many other forms of public expenditure. Military expenditure on weapons, etc., is directed to the private sector, and military contracts provide a high rate of profit to the suppliers. Further, it does not break the link between work and income in the way in which social security expenditures can. Kidron (1968) provides a 'strong' version of this argument, derived from the 'permanent thread of over-production' under capitalism. The permanent arms budget is seen as a mechanism of raising demand and economic activity without adding to the capital stock (which would dampen investment), and

> the impact of arms expenditure on stability and investment is no less direct. It is heavily concentrated on the capital goods industries which are responsible for the big swings in the traditional business cycle. It provides a floor to the downswings and has, in the US, been deliberately used in this way. (Kidron, 1968)

The relevance of this argument here is that the State is seen as the servant of capital, and military expenditure is, for a number of reasons, a suitable means of securing profitability.[14]

The creation and maintenance of full employment are seen, following Kalecki (1943), to involve two areas of difficulties for capitalists. The first arises from the argument that prolonged full employment would not occur in *laissez-faire* capitalism. Government intervention is thus required if full employment is to be maintained. Thus the role of government activity would have to increase and encroach on the activities of the private sector. The second area of difficulty is that full employment changes the balance of power between workers and capitalists. This change in the balance of power may show itself in a loss of control by capitalists over the functioning of the labour process, through rising real wages and wage share, etc.

10.7 WELFARE STATE

A major development of the role of the State in industrialised capitalist economies in the past century or so has been the emergence and growth of the Welfare State. The Welfare State comprises the State provision of social services (basically social security, health, social welfare, education and training, and housing) and the State regulation of private activities which directly alter the immediate conditions of life of individuals and groups (based on Gough, 1979). One reason for considering the Welfare State is to illustrate some of the arguments discussed above.

How can this growth be explained? The notion of 'public goods' is not helpful in that most of the activities of the Welfare State are not non-excludable and non-rivalrous. It is clearly technically possible to exclude people from activities such as education, health care, income transfer payments, and it can also be seen that these activities are also ones in which one person's consumption is rivalrous with that of others.

One view (which has often been labelled Wagner's law) is that the growth of public expenditure comes from a growth of State activity, and that later growth is 'the inevitable accompaniment of social progress' (Peacock and Wiseman, 1961). Wagner identified three types of state activity, namely the maintenance of law and order (which would include laws to permit markets to operate), the production of a range of goods and services which the State can undertake but which the private sector for a variety of reasons cannot, and the provision of economic and social services such as education, a postal system. For our purposes, the important element of Wagner's law is that it could be seen as a technical explanation in the sense that it arises from an expansion in the demand for the goods and services which are best provided by the public sector.[15]

An explanation which places less emphasis on technical factors and more on more political economy aspects would focus on the class and political interests involved. One line of explanation would start from the observation that the political pressure for the introduction and development of the Welfare State came from trade unions, and left-of-centre political parties. It would be presumed from that observation that the Welfare State served the interests of labour, rather than that of capital. Hence, the evolution of the Welfare State would be linked to a rise in the political power of labour (associated with the extension of the franchise, organisation of trade unions, etc.)[16].

That explanation points towards increased power of labour. Another perspective is that the Welfare State operates in the interests of capital. The provision of pensions, education, health care, etc., help to remove agitation against capitalism. It links with the legitimisation role of the State. Further, some activities of the Welfare State reduce the cost of raising children (to the people directly involved), and thereby could be seen as cheapening the reproduction costs of labour.

It can also be argued that the Welfare State can be largely seen as an income transfer mechanism within the working class – the currently employed members pay taxes and social security contributions which finance payments to the currently unemployed and retired. Finally, the extent to which the Welfare State provides a better-educated, healthier working class means that it will produce a more productive working class. The advantages to capitalists of the Welfare State are particularly well-argued by O'Connor (1973). In connection with the social security system, he argues that it

> contributes to social and political stability by conservatizing unemployed and retired workers, the primary purpose of the system is to create a sense of economic security within the ranks of employed workers (especially workers in the monopoly sector) and thereby raise morale and reinforce discipline. This contributes to harmonious management–labor relations which are indispensable to capital accumulation and the growth of production. Thus the fundamental intent and effect of social security is to expand productivity, production and profits. *Seen in this way, social insurance is not primarily insurance for workers, but a kind of insurance for capitalists and corporations* (emphasis in original)

Further,

> organized labour is more or less satisfied [with the retirement pension system] because the system redistributes income in its favor. Monopoly capital is also relatively happy because the system insures comparative harmony with labor. If monopoly sector workers were compelled to contribute as much as they receive upon retirement, current money wages would have to be slashed sharply.

The Welfare State is situated within a capitalist economy, and that position places a series of constraints on its activities. The most obvious would include limits on the level of unemployment benefits and the type of education which can be provided. On the former, it is not only a matter that at some level of unemployment benefits relative to earnings, the labour force would be substantially reduced,[17] but also that with the existence of unemployment benefits (at a level which provides a decent standard of living), the power of workers is enhanced *vis-à-vis* capital. The financial consequences of dismissal from a job are reduced, which reduces the power of capital over labour in the workplace (cf. section 2.4). Unemployment benefits also undermine the work ethic and 'a "moral" principle of the highest importance is at stake. The fundamentals of capitalist ethics require that "you shall earn your bread in sweat – unless you happen to have private means' (Kalecki, 1971a).

In most industrialised economies, the State is heavily involved in the provision as well as the financing of education. Since education could be both privately provided and financed, the question arises as to why it is not generally so provided and financed, as indicated in the quote from Foley (1978) given above. Education serves many purposes. The requirements of the capitalist system could be seen as two-fold. First, education is part of the legitimisation process through which the values and aims of the capitalist system are transmitted to the next generation. Second, there is a requirement for the production of a skilled workforce. An individual capitalist firm often does not find it worth while to train its workforce in general skills (since the firm bears the costs but the workers can move to other firms whereby the firm loses the benefits of training). But collectively firms benefit from a skilled workforce, which leads to the public provision. However, this line of argument would point towards education being orientated towards skills which are useful in the work situation. But capitalism may require only that some of the workforce be skilled, and the remainder unskilled (cf. section

2.6). Further, the inculcation of obedience and acceptance of authority by workers would be advantageous for capitalists.

There are many other views on the purposes of education, and they are generally in conflict with the nature of education implied by the previous paragraph. These other views may be expressed in terms of the education of the 'whole person', 'education for life', etc., with education seen as a potentially liberating experience with the provision of a wide range of skills and knowledge. This view of education would stress education for all, a stress on originality and the questioning of authority which stand in contrast to the nature of education based on its legitimisation role discussed above. In general, these perspectives on education would be in conflict with one another. There may be occasions when they point in the same direction: for example, the teaching of literacy helps to provide necessary skills for the workforce and also is the basis of further enlightening education. But the more usual case is that of a conflict between the two.

These contradictory views on the purpose of education are reflected in many debates over the nature of education, and indeed the provision of education often incorporates elements both training geared towards work and 'education for life'. The contradictory pressures in the area of education provide an example of the contradictory position of the Welfare State within a capitalist economy. Within the Welfare State resources are allocated and decisions made on a different basis compared with market decisions. 'Social policy addresses itself to a whole range of needs – material, cultural emotional – outside the wide realm of satisfactions which can conveniently be left to the market' (Lafitte, 1973). Many advocates of the Welfare State would see the allocation of resources (to individuals) being based on need and rights than on the ability to pay. The Welfare State, for a variety of reasons, may not live up to these expectations (in a similar way the market may not operate as envisaged by pro-market advocates). But the point remains that the principles of allocation between individuals on which the Welfare State generally operates are different from the principles of allocation of the market system. An example of this can be given by the arrangements for retirement pensions. The market arrangements would link the pension paid to an individual with their ability to pay for that pension during their working life. There is a variety of principles which influence State provision (which leads to different structures of pension arrangements in different countries). One principle is that the State provision is rather like private provision, in which the pension finally paid is more or less closely linked to the contributions made during working life (and those contributions may be linked to earnings). An element of redistribution may be built in so that people on low earnings during their working life receive a pension which is greater than would be paid on an actuarial basis; and conversely those on high earnings receive a lower pension. Whilst many State pension arrangements have a strong insurance element, there are other principles at work as well. These include a minimum standard of living (or needs) principle and a citizenship right principle. The first of those would lead to a means-tested pension to seek to ensure that no one fell below a specified standard of living, whereas the second would pay a pension as of right to those living in a country for a particular period of time.

Much of the Welfare State is an income-transfer machine from, for example, the working to the non-working. There are other areas though, where the State is the producer: for example, in many countries education and health care are produced by State institutions. Even where not the producer, the State generally pays for much of education and health care. In the case of both education and health care, the basis on which they are allocated between individuals differs significantly from the ways in which they would be allocated by the market. For example, the British National Health Service is sometimes described as an 'island of socialism', and it can be viewed in that way. The allocation of health care resources is not determined by any market mechanism or ability to pay, and the principle of allocation is that of 'to each according to his or her need'.

On this view the Welfare State stands in opposition to the market mechanisms of capitalism. It is at the same time constrained by those market mechanisms, though the operation of markets is to some degree constrained by the Welfare State. An obvious example would be that the market for health insurance is heavily constrained by how extensive is the provision of health care by the State.

The second side is to see the Welfare State (and other parts of government provision) as providing the capitalist system with 'functions' which it cannot profitably provide itself and as reducing on the reproduction costs of labour. The inability of the capitalist system to profitably provide certain services (e.g. roads, education) is not dissimilar to the 'technical' explanation referred to above under Wagner's law, though it emphasises profit rather than technology (but a change in technology would change profit possibilities). The reproduction costs angle is more specifically Marxian. It may be recalled from above that the level of real wages in a Marxian analysis is linked to the reproduction costs of labour (and was a subsistence wage in that sense). The provision of 'free' education, child benefits, etc., has the effect of lowering the cost of raising children, and in that sense of reducing the reproduction costs of labour. On that basis, the Welfare State lowers wages as paid by the market.

This discussion of the Welfare State suggests two concluding remarks. First, a technical economistic analysis of the role of the Welfare State is insufficient, and the scale and nature of the Welfare State at any particular time in a particular country will reflect the outcome of the interaction of economic, political and social pressures. Second, many aspects of the Welfare State represent a replacement of the market and the market ethos (allocation according to the ability to pay) by non-market mechanisms and an ethos of allocation according to need. However, the Welfare State is heavily constrained by the capitalist economy. On one level these constraints would be such a limit to the scale of unemployment benefit if labour discipline and the workforce is to be maintained. At another level, the growth of the Welfare State and its associated ethos would undermine capitalism by the replacement of private provision by public provision and the diminution of belief in the capitalist ethos.

10.8 TAXATION

Up to this point, the discussion of the State has largely concerned the range of activities undertaken by the State. But in this section, the focus is on the revenue side, i.e. taxation. There is only space to consider taxation briefly, and most attention is given to the income distribution aspects of taxation. There are clearly a wide range of different taxes which are levied, ranging over income tax, profits tax, sales tax and property tax. Any particular tax may cause changes in people's behaviour (e.g. a tax on tobacco can be expected to reduce tobacco consumption). It has an impact on the distribution of income (as between people and as between different types of income) since no tax falls uniformly on everyone and every type of income. Finally, a tax has an impact on aggregate demand which thereby influences the level of economic activity. Thus, it would be expected that the level and structure of taxation would have implications for the distribution of income and for the level of economic activity. The discussion of taxation can conveniently be divided into two parts. The first is the general question of why certain types of taxation are used, and in whose benefit each type of tax operates. For example, it would be possible to say that profits tax impinges on profits (though to what extent is discussed further below), and hence the general trend in recent years to reduce the rate of profits tax would serve the interests of profit receivers. In turn, it might be possible to investigate the contribution of the decline in the rate of profit and the increased power of profit receivers.

The neo-classical approach focuses on the incentive effects of different forms of taxation. In some contrast, the radical political economy approach focuses on the distribution effects of different types of taxation. Take as an example the structure of income tax. Neo-classical economics would analyse the effects which income tax had on the trade-off between labour time and leisure time, and whether a change in the structure of income tax would increase or decrease the supply of labour time. The radical political economy approach would introduce two further considerations. First, for most workers the length of their working day (or week) is not a matter over which they have a great deal of control. Thus, any desire to change the number of hours worked as a response to a change in the structure of income tax is likely to be frustrated. Second, a change in the structure of income tax affects some income groups more than others, and hence such a change has an effect on the distribution of income. These distributional changes are important in their own right, and also for their possible impact on the level of aggregate demand. The second part of the discussion, which is given most attention here, is the technical analysis of the impact of a specified tax on income distribution and on the level of economic activity. For this purpose, a modified version of the macro-economic model which is further developed in the next chapter is employed. In effect this model draws upon two ideas which have been explored in the previous chapter. The first of these ideas is the basis of the Kaldorian theory of income distribution, expressed in terms of the equality between savings and investment, namely:

$$s_1 W + s_2 P = I \tag{10.1}$$

where W is wages, P profits, I investment and s_1, s_2 the propensities to save out of wages and profits respectively. This requires modification for government activity (and for simplicity the foreign sector is ignored) to read:

$$s_1 (1 - t_1) W + s_2 (1 - t_2) P + T = I + G \tag{10.2}$$

where t_1, t_2 are the rates of tax levied on wages, profits respectively, and T is total taxation (equal to $t_1 W + t_2 P$) and G is real government expenditure. Any transfer payment by government is represented here as negative taxation: thus t_1, for example, represents the balance between taxation on and transfer payments made to the working class. The tax rates on wages and profits have for simplicity been taken as constant. In the analysis below, again for reasons of simplicity, the government budget will be taken as balanced ($T = G$), and hence:

$$s_1 (1 - t_1) W + s_2 (1 - t_2) P = I \tag{10.3}$$

The second idea comes from the Kaleckian degree of monopoly, and this is expressed here as:

$$p = (1 + m) w/q \tag{10.4}$$

where p is price level, w wage rate, q labour productivity and m mark-up of price over unit cost. The mark-up itself may be influenced by the rate of profits tax. Multiplying equation (10.4) through by total output (Q), yields:

$$p Q = (1 + m) w L \tag{10.5}$$

Hence profits are mwL, wages wL. From equation (10.3) the following can be obtained:

$$w L = I/(u_1 + u_2 m) \tag{10.6}$$

$$P = m I/(u_1 + u_2 m) \tag{10.7}$$

$$p Q = (1 + m) I/(u_1 + u_2 m) \tag{10.8}$$

where u_i is $s_i (1 - t_i)$ ($i = 1,2$). There are many complexities which could be added to this simple model, notably investment which is taken here as exogenous could be related to profitability, etc., and the purpose here is simply to give a flavour of what could be called the post-Keynesian or Kaleckian analysis of taxation.[18] The post-tax wage and profits can be easily derived from equations (10.6) and (10.7) as $(1-t_1)\ I/(u_1 + u_2m)$ and $(1-t_2)\ m\ I/(u_1 + u_2m)$ respectively. The money wage is treated as constant and in effect acts as a numeraire. When the effect of a tax is analysed, in general prices will rise, so that some of the reported effect is a change in product prices, but in our analysis this would be a change relative to money wages. With that caveat in mind, it can be calculated from equation (10.8) that the effect of a tax change on national output (pQ) is given by:

$$d(pQ)/dt_1 = I\ s_1\ (1+m)/(u_1 + u_2m)^2 \geq 0 \qquad\qquad (10.9)$$

$$d(pQ)/dt_2 = I/(u_1 + u_2m)\ [s_2\ m\ (1+m) + dm/dt_2\ (1 - (1+m)\ u_2]\ (10.10)$$

Equation (10.9) implies that an increased tax on wages would raise national output (in both nominal and real terms as it is assumed that a change in wage tax does not affect the mark-up and hence does not affect product prices). The exception is when savings out of wages are zero $(s_1 = 0)$, when the tax change has no impact. It should be remembered here that a balanced government budget has been assumed, so that a rise in taxation is matched by an increase in government expenditure. The effect of a change of profits tax on national output is seen to depend on the response of the mark-up (m) to the tax change, and an increase in profits tax could reduce output if dm/dt_2 was sufficiently large. However, it could be argued that the upper limit to dm/dt_2 would arise when the mark-up rises to preserve post-tax profit margins,[19] and in that case, equation (10.10) simplifies to:

$$d(pQ)/dt_2 = m\ I/(u_1 + u_2m) \qquad\qquad (10.11)$$

which is clearly positive. However, the product price level has now changed so that the question arises as to whether real output has risen. In the case of the mark-up rising to preserve post-tax profit margins, then it can be shown that the price rise is such that real output declines despite the rise in nominal output.[20] The effect of tax changes on post-tax wages and profits can be calculated from the formulae given above. As would be anticipated, an increase in the tax on wages lowers the post-tax wages but raises the pre-tax wages. The effect of a change in the profits tax on post-tax profits is given by:

$$I/(u_1 + u_2\,m)^2\,[-m\,u_1 + (1-t_2)\,u_1\,dm/dt_2] \tag{10.12}$$

There are two special cases which are of interest. The first, which corresponds to the classical savings function, is where savings out of wages are zero and where all of profits are saved. The second case is where post-tax profit margins are preserved. In both cases, equation (10.12) simplifies to zero, i.e. post-tax profits are preserved in the face of an increase in profits tax.

This section has intended to give some indication of a post-Keynesian analysis of taxation. The emphasis is on the level of output and on the distribution of income. Clearly, a concrete situation would be much more complex than our simple analysis, but this analysis should serve to show that taxation has a range of effects which can be analysed within a post-Keynesian framework.

10.9 CONCLUDING REMARKS

The purpose of this chapter has been to explore in a rather general manner some features of the State and its activities, and the Marxian-inspired analysis has been to the fore. One aspect of a post-Keynesian analysis has been apparent in the previous section on taxation. In a more general sense, a post-Keynesian approach would see the government as a particularly important institution in a modern economy which has to be brought into economic analysis along with a range of institutions. Further, many post-Keynesians have emphasised the instability of a market economy, and the necessity for government intervention to help to stabilise such an economy. This instability can take the form of declining employment (as during the 1930s and much of the 1980s) for which expansionary government fiscal and monetary policies would be required.[21] Another source of instability can come from the monetary and financial system (as argued by Minsky, 1978, 1986). The threat of the collapse of the financial system (as occurred in 1929, and nearly happened in 1974) arising from financial fragility and a collapse of confidence may be averted by an injection of liquidity by the government, the rescue of failing financial institutions, etc.

One important aspect which has not been discussed is the international one, though to some degree this can be dealt with by extension of the arguments advanced above. The corporations of one country are involved in other countries in a variety of ways. They may seek the supply of important materials, they may produce overseas and they may export. In the promotion of these activities, business draws on the help of their government in many ways. This may range from lobbying other governments to provide access to their domestic markets through to military intervention. The support by one State of its own firms can clearly bring that State into conflict with other States who are supporting their own firms. Thus, relationships between States can be strongly influenced by the needs of the capitalist firms. But the growth of multinational firms has probably reduced those firms' dependency on 'their' government, and has increased the power of those firms *vis-à-vis* any national government (cf. section 6.7).

NOTES

1. In a number of European countries, parties which include 'Social Democratic' in their title would be associated with this political position. Corresponding parties exist in most other countries (e.g. the Labour Party in the UK). However, for much of the post-war period, the trend to the expansion of State activity with the State accepting a wide range of responsibilities (e.g. full employment, provision of pensions) formed the general consensus and was in practice accepted by many centre-right political parties.
2. Marquand (1988) in his chapter 4 on States and markets, argues that 'the state has played a central part in economic development in virtually all industrial societies, with the possible exception of early nineteenth-century Britain. Even in Britain, moreover, the state played an important facilitating role'. Further, 'Japan heads the list of developmental states, but it includes other striking examples as well'.
3. These definitions of the State draw heavily on Ham and Hill (1984).
4. The data on defence expenditure for the United States has been taken from the Statistical Abstract of the United States 1987 produced by the US Bureau of the Census.
5. For discussion on full employment as objective of economic policy see Tomlinson (1981, 1983, 1987).
6. For much more extensive discussion of the role of the Phillips curve in economics see Sawyer (1987).
7. See, for example, Sargent (1979), Minford (1983) and for a textbook

sympathetic to New Classical Macroeconomics, Parkin and Bade (1988).

8. There is an element though in this argument that people do not know what is good for them. When 'tough' policies are required, say, to reduce inflation, make industry more competitive, the electorate will blame politicians for the adverse effects of those tough policies without realising the long-term gains.

9. This line of argument corresponds to a monetarist analysis of the economy, heavily based on Friedman's work, whereby the initial response to a (monetary) stimulus is a rise in output but the final response is a rise in the price level with no long-run effect on output.

10. Amott (1984) argues that 'like the Thatcher government . . . , this [the Reagan] administration intervenes powerfully to restructure capital, alter the balance of labor–capital relationships and actively promote particular outcomes in the economy (and in the family) while simultaneously posing as the champion of state withdrawal from the economy'.

11. Jessop (1977) argues that '[a] Marxist theory of the capitalist state will be considered adequate to the extent that (a) it is founded on the specific qualities of capitalism as a mode of production, (b) it attributes a central role to class struggle in the process of capital accumulation, (c) it establishes the relations between the political and economic features of society, without reducing one to the other or treating them as totally independent and autonomous, (d) it allows for historical and national differences in the forms and functions of the state in capitalist societies, and (e) it allows for the influence of non-capitalist classes and non-class forces in determining the nature of the state and the exercise of state power'.

12. See, also, Miliband (1969, ch. 2) for an elaboration of this argument in the context of theories of the State.

13. Gough (1979) argues that his own approach is that 'it contains at any one time elements of both. In other words it is not the Marxist analysis of the welfare state that is contradictory, but the welfare state itself'.

14. Defence expenditure has often been viewed as supporting aggregate demand and profits. However, writing from a Marxian perspective, Smith (1977) argues that 'the empirical evidence suggests that military expenditure imposes a substantial burden. Among the advanced capitalist nations high military expenditure is associated with much lower investment, lower growth and higher rates of unemployment'.

15. For further discussion see Peacock and Wiseman (1961, pp. 16–20).

16. The rise in the political power of labour is not a continuous one, as can be seen by the experience of labour in the UK over the past fifteen years. It still remains that labour is much more powerful now than, say, a century ago.

17. This should not be taken to indicate that at the levels currently paid that unemployment benefits discourage work; but that it is a hypothetical possiblity. Indeed, such are the constraints on unemployment benefits that they are generally held at a low level.

18. Some initial work of this type is Kalecki (1937), with Asimakopolus and Burbridge (1974) being an extension.

19. One argument for the preservation of post-tax profit margins would be that those margins are set by the threat of entry into the industry. The condition for constant post-tax mark-up is $dm/dt_2 = m/(1-t_2)$.

20. The term $d(pQ)/dt_2$ can be expanded as $Q\, dp/dt_2 + p\, dQ/dt_2$. Now from equation (10.4), under the assumption of constant labour productivity, $dp/dt_2 = (w/q)\, dm/dt_2$, and hence $Q\, dp/dt_2 = (w\, Q/q)\, dm/dt_2$. The first term of this latter expression is equal to $w\, L$, itself equal to $I/(u_1 + u_2\, m)$, and dm/dt_2 is here equal to $m/(1-t_2)$. Combining those provides: $Q\, dp/dt_2 = m\, I/(1-t_2)\, (u_1 + u_2\, m)$. Since $d(pQ)/dt_2 = m\, I/(u_1 + u_2\, m)$, it is straightforward to derive that $p\, dQ/dt = m\, I\, (-t_2)/(1-t_2)\, (u_1 + u_2\, m)$, which is negative.

21. There are, though, examples of governments adopting deflationary policies in the face of mounting unemployment, often in the belief that the government budget should be balanced. Post-Keynesians would generally view this as folly brought about through government listening to anti-Keynesian economists such as monetarists.

Part Six

UNEMPLOYMENT, GROWTH AND DISPARITIES

Chapter 11

UNEMPLOYMENT AND INFLATION

11.1 INTRODUCTION

This chapter is concerned with the determination of capacity utilisation, unemployment and inflation in industrialised capitalist economies, which are broadly speaking the topics of short-run macroeconomic analysis. This will lead on to the next chapter, where growth and technical change are the topics dealt with. In turn, that chapter leads into Chapter 13 which examines the forces of cumulative change and the general idea that there are tendencies within the market mechanism for disparities (particularly those between regions and between countries) to widen over time. At the macroeconomic level, as at the microeconomic level, different types of economics need to be analysed in different ways, and hence the macroeconomic analysis given here is only intended to apply to industrialised capitalist economies.

Whilst it is possible to make a distinction between the microeconomic level and the macroeconomic one, it should be stressed that there is considerable interaction between them. The macroeconomic variables (particularly on unemployment, technical change) are important elements in the environment within which workers and firms operate. Similarly, the decisions which households and firms make build up to generate the aggregate outcomes. However, it is important to stress the two-way nature of the relationship between microeconomics and macroeconomics. The macro level influences the micro level and the micro decisions build up to the macro level. Further, there are relationships which are essentially macroeconomic in nature in the sense that they do not have a microeconomic counterpart.[1] The clearest example of this is (for a closed private economy) the requirement that actual savings equal actual investment expenditure and this does not have a counterpart at the individual level since an individual is not limited in this way.

There are many ways in which the approach adopted here differs from the Keynesian/monetarist orthodoxy, as will become apparent below. One general difference is that Keynesian/monetarist orthodoxy rests on a neo-classical model of the economy in which perfect competition reigns (and this is further argued in Sawyer, 1982a). There may be disputes about the speed with which such an economy will reach full employment and the role of imperfections in preventing full employment.[2] But an equilibrium position which involves full employment is taken to exist, to which the economy tends more or less quickly. The problem which arises within that framework is to explain divergences from full employment, and much of mainstream Keynesian economics has been devoted to such an exercise, invoking considerations such as trade unions, imperfect competition, lack of information and more recently efficiency wages and implicit contracts.[3] Thus the general vision here is that it is some form of 'imperfections' in the real world which prevents the achievement of full employment, with the implication that the removal of the imperfections would help to attain full employment.

In contrast, the approaches considered here conclude that balanced full employment of labour is a rare and fleeting occurrence.[4] This reflects, in part, the view that capitalist economies are subject to business cycles with employment and output continually changing so that a balanced equilibrium is never achieved. It will be seen below that the level of aggregate demand is an important determinant of the level of economic activity, and thereby of employment. Further, there is no reason to believe that aggregate demand will generally be at the level appropriate for full employment. Within the radical political economy approaches, two strands of thought can be distinguished. Some have argued that there will be a tendency for aggregate demand to be insufficient for full employment, and as a result for unemployment to be the usual occurrence. But others have argued that aggregate demand can often lead to a demand for labour in excess of the existing supply. However, the capitalist economy is only a part of the total and there are times when the labour force attached to the capitalist economy is fully employed and surplus labour is being drawn from the non-capitalist economies.

> Although not the case in the recent past, the historical tendency of capitalism has been to expand at a faster rate than natural reproduction would permit. The result is that the capitalist sector has had to draw on a succession of reserve armies. In the United States, for example, immigration was the main source of reserve labour until World War I temporarily, and post-war legislation permanently, reduced the flow of immigrants to a trickle. At that point, domestic agriculture became the main reserve army. (Marglin, 1984)

The capitalist industrialised sector of the economy in nineteenth-century Britain pulled in labour from the pre-capitalist agricultural sector (see Chapter 12). But whether there is unemployment within the capitalist economies or surplus labour without, in both cases there is an 'industrial reserve army' of the unemployed. The presence of this army will have the effect of restraining the power of the employed workforce.

The task which confronts the Keynesian/monetarist approach is the explanation of divergences from the presumed norm of full employment. In contrast, the approach adopted here views departures from full employment as the norm, and faces the task of explaining periods of full employment. Thus the starting point of the two approaches is quite different. It can also be mentioned that in a monetarist approach there would not be any restriction on the employment of labour arising from inadequate capital equipment. For if, for example, there was inadequate capital equipment the relative price of capital equipment would rise and the relative price of labour would fall. Firms would then substitute labour for capital equipment until both labour and capital equipment were fully utilised. In the radical political economy approach, as will be seen below, the under-utilisation of capital equipment and of the labour force is the usual state of affairs, and output could be expanded in response to an increase in demand. There may be occasions when aggregate demand is sufficient to employ the available labour but there is inadequate capital equipment, and others in which it is a shortage of labour which is the binding constraint. As explained below (section 12.2), within the radical political economy approach it is usually assumed that the possibilities of substitution between capital equipment and labour are extremely limited once the equipment is installed. The main point to be made here is that there is no particular reason to think that there will be the right 'balance' between capital equipment and the labour force, so that sometimes the inadequacy of capital equipment can prevent full employment of labour.

There are two themes which run through the explanations of the level of unemployment of labour in the radical political economy approach. The first is the importance of the level of aggregate demand in the determination of the level of unemployment. The second theme is that unemployment serves to restrain the labour force in its wage claims and to pressure workers to work hard and maintain productivity. The first part of this chapter is taken up with exploring the aggregate demand aspects, before moving on to the disciplining aspects.

The level of aggregate demand is in one respect an application of the idea of Keynes and Kalecki that the level of demand determines the level of output and thereby of employment. A central proposition of pre-Keynesian economics, which is reasserted in modern monetarism and new classical macroeconomics, is Say's law. This 'law' is often summarised as 'supply creates its own demand', so that, for example, the income which would be generated by the employment of potential supply of labour would all be spent. Thus, suppose that all potential employees were employed, and as a consequence a particular volume of wages and profits would be generated, provided that the output which was produced was actually sold. We label these wages and profits as W_f and P_f, and the net output produced as Y_f (where these variables are all measured at market prices). Then $Y_f = W_f + P_f$. The question arises whether the expenditure E out of these wages and profits will be exactly sufficient to buy the potential output. Say's law asserts that the expenditure will be, directly or indirectly, forthcoming. In such a case, there will always be sufficient demand (expenditure) to underpin full employment.

The approaches considered here implicitly or explicitly reject Say's law. There are a number of conditions under which Say's law would operate. The first would be if the propensity to consume out of all types of income was always unity, for then all income (whether wages or profits) would be spent. The second case would recognise that some people save, but this would not cause an insufficiency of demand provided that other people dissaved to the same degree. The third case, which is the one to which most attention is given, arises when any savings can always be channelled to finance investment expenditure. In these latter two cases, any income which arises is either directly spent (as consumer expenditure) or indirectly spent (by financing others' dissaving or investment). The interest rate has often been seen as the variable which would adjust to bring savings and investment into balance with one another. Thus, for example, if savings threatened to exceed investment, then the interest rate would fall which would encourage investment and discourage savings. In this way, savings and investment would be equated and ensure that potential full employment income was all spent (directly or indirectly). In contrast, the approaches of Keynes, Kalecki and others argue that Say's law does not operate, and that a discrepancy between potential savings and investment would be resolved through changes in the level of economic activity, rather than through changes in the rate of interest. In line with this tradition, our approach below will focus on the savings–investment relationship.

It is possible to look further at the components of aggregate demand, and these can be divided into consumer expenditure, investment expenditure, government expenditure and export demand. Those who have focused particularly on inadequacy of consumer demand have usually been labelled underconsumptionists (Bleaney, 1976). The inadequacy of consumer demand has often been attributed to the maldistribution of income. On the basis that the poorer members of society have a higher propensity to consume, a redistribution of income from rich to poor would be expected to raise the level of aggregate demand. Another slant on the same argument arises from the differential savings propensities thesis which was examined in connection with the distribution of income in Chapter 9. A further reason which arises in the next chapter (section 12.7) is an element of satiation of consumer demand in the absence of new products appearing on the market. The inadequacy of investment expenditure can arise from a shortage of investment opportunities (arising from, say, a slow-down of technical advance) and from low levels of profitability. These ideas are explored at length below.

If consumer and investment demand are inadequate to secure full employment, the question arises as to whether government expenditure can be used to generate sufficient aggregate demand. There may be some technical difficulties in doing so (e.g. finding the appropriate level of government expenditure, borrowing the required amounts) but there may be substantial social and political obstacles, and some of the political obstacles were explored in the previous chapter.

A firm faced by a lack of demand for its products may adopt a variety of strategies, ranging from reducing price, altering its products, moving into other markets, etc. However, many of those strategies would not be available to firms as a whole; for example, if all firms reduce prices there is little gained by the firms but they suffer reduced profits. But the firms of one country could seek to export to other countries. This search for export demand would lead to a search for overseas markets within and outside of the capitalist system. In the hands of authors such as Luxemburg (1913, 1963) this becomes a theory of imperialism with capitalist firms (supported by government) expanding into non-capitalist areas. On this line of argument, a tendency towards inadequate demand within capitalist economies would lead to capitalist firms seeking to expand into non-capitalist economies in the search for demand and for profits.

The second theme relates to the disciplinary nature of unemployment, as to some extent reflected in the term 'the industrial reserve army of the unemployed'. At least since the time of Marx, unemployment has been seen as 'the industrial reserve army [which] during the periods of stagnation and average prosperity weighs down the active army of workers; during the periods of over-production and feverish activity, it puts a curb on their pretensions' (Marx, 1976). Low levels of unemployment are seen to strengthen the position of labour, leading to some loss of discipline by capital over labour at the place of work and to upward pressure on wages (both money and real). The pressure on real wages may (at least eventually) depress profitability. The depression of profitability may lead to firms reducing employment and output and to cutting back on investment. Further, the decline in profitability may lead to pressure on government to restrain wages and to reduce the level of aggregate demand. All of these forces will help to undermine the low levels of unemployment.

We begin in the next section from a consideration of the relationship between savings and investment for the determination of the level of economic activity. This is followed by a section in which a more formal treatment of the savings–investment relationship is given, and the implications for excess capacity and unemployment are discussed in that and the following section. We then move on to consideration of the role of unemployment as a force for holding the claims of workers in check, which leads into our final main section dealing with inflation. The three main aspects of the analysis of inflation are the setting of prices, the determination of wages, and the nature of the monetary system, with these three aspects interacting to provide a conflict theory of inflation.

11.2 SAVINGS AND INVESTMENT

Kalecki and Keynes in their independent discovery of the importance of aggregate demand placed emphasis on the roles of savings and investment. The determinants of savings and investment and the ways by which they are brought into balance with each other are given a central role. For convenience we begin with a closed economy without a government so that the condition for equilibrium becomes *ex ante* savings equal *ex ante* investment, and then introduce government in a very simple way. Concerning this equilibrium condition, the contribution of Keynes (and also Kalecki) can be seen as two-fold. The first is the question of the mechanism by which savings and investment are brought into equality with one another. The pre-Keynesian view was that the rate of interest was the key variable which would adjust to bring desired savings and investment into equality. In contrast, Keynes saw the level of income as the crucial variable in this respect.[5] At one level this represents the replacement of price adjustment (via the rate of interest) with a quantity adjustment (via the level of income). In the simplest version, the level of income (and thereby output and employment) is determined by the savings–investment relationship.

The second contribution concerns the question of the *primacy* of investment or saving, which is the issue of whether it is predominantly investment decisions or savings decisions which are carried out, causing corresponding changes in savings or investment respectively. If only the equilibrium condition (desired savings equal desired investment) is considered, the question of primacy does not really arise. However, when disequilbria and movements between equilibria are considered, the question of primacy becomes relevant, even though it has been little discussed.

In the next section, the central equation in the analysis is the savings/investment equality (amended to allow for government activity). Similarly, the Kaldorian theory of income distribution (section 9.3) was centred on a comparable equation. In much of the discussion in the next two chapters, it is (often implicitly) assumed that investment decisions are the driving force to which savings are forced to adjust. For example, the discussion of long waves and technological change, the spur of new technology leads to investment plans which are fulfilled, without specific reference to savings.

The relative primacy of investment decisions over savings is a reflection of particular institutional arrangements.[6] In an economy which has not developed complex banking and financial arrangements, it is not possible for investment to have such importance. In a barter economy (i.e. an economy without money) the only way to save would be to the acquisition of real goods and services. Thus a desire to save would lead to a demand for some durable goods which could be used as a store of value. But the desire to save would thereby involve demand for goods and services. In such an economy, Say's law would operate, that is supply would create its own demand, in the sense that a person who had received an income would have to use that income to purchase goods and services even if the individual wished to store some of those goods and services.

Investment expenditure (like any other form of expenditure) has to be backed by money if it is to become effective in the market, that is, a desire to spend can only become a reality if backed by the possession of money. The firm (or individual) may finance the investment expenditure from its own resources (e.g. profits). When a firm (or individual) uses all their own savings to finance investment and no investment is undertaken without savings being made, then Say's law would still operate in that all income is spent either in the form of consumer goods and services or investment expenditure. In these circumstances, all savings are chanelled into investment.[7]

When the banking and financial systems are in their infancy, firms may be very limited in borrowing and largely dependent on their own resources for investment finance (cf. discussion above, section 6.4). However, as a financial system begins to develop it operates to channel savings (from 'surplus units') towards those firms which wish to invest in excess of their own funds ('deficit units'). So here savings retain their priority in the sense that savings have to occur *prior* to investment in order to provide the funds for that investment. In such circumstances, savings are necessary so far as the firm is concerned for investment to be able to occur. If there is a pent-up demand for investment held back by lack of funds, then an increase in savings will lead to an increase in investment.

The situation in industrialised capitalist economies is rather different with a highly developed banking system. A firm wishing to undertake investment expenditure can draw on its own resources or on borrowing through the non-banking financial system; in such cases the previous remarks are still relevant. But there is the option of borrowing from the banking system. A bank is defined here as an institution whose liabilities are regarded as part of the money supply (though banks may be defined in other ways for legal and control purposes). A deposit with a bank which is an asset for the depositor is a liability for the bank (since they have a commitment to repay the deposit at some stage). When a loan is granted by a bank, the immediate step is that the borrower has more funds in their bank account. The stock of money has increased by the amount of the loan. The bank has created as asset (the loan) and a liability (the deposit), and in the immediate sense is no better and no worse off (but will profit in the longer term by the interest payments on the loan). The borrower similarly has the same net wealth as before, though their liquidity position is improved so that they are in a position to spend. The loan permits the investment expenditure to take place. In national income accounting terms, any outturn investment and savings will actually be equal to one another (since we are here still dealing with the closed private-sector economy for simplicity). The investment expenditure actually takes place; as a consequence savings will occur. Some of that saving may be intentional, but in general some will be forced.[8] We will return to the subject of money below when inflation is discussed.

This discussion has assumed that the planned investment expenditure can take place provided that the finance is available. This is equivalent to assuming that there is spare capacity in the investment goods industries so that the supply can expand to meet the demand. Further, that expansion of supply does not take place at the expense of production in the consumer goods industries. In other words, it is assumed that there is some unemployment and excess capacity so that resources are available to be able to produce the investment goods which are demanded.

The practical relevance of this discussion can be seen from the following example. Suppose that a government wishes to encourage more capital formation (in the belief that this would increase economic growth). One route would be to encourage a higher level of savings in the belief that more savings lead to more investment and hence capital formation. This could happen, for example, by more desired savings leading to a fall in interest rate, which encourages investment. The view of Keynes and Kalecki is that this route is unlikely to lead to an increase in investment. The interest rate effects are rather small, but more importantly the increase in savings would occur initially at the expense of consumption. Aggregate demand would then fall, and investment is likely to be adversely affected by the fall in aggregate demand. The other route suggested by the approach of Kalecki and Keynes would be the direct encouragement of firms to increase investment (e.g. by subsidising investment). After the investment takes place, desired savings would rise through the impact of investment on income.

11.3 UNEMPLOYMENT AND EXCESS CAPACITY

This section draws on an amended version of a model presented by Steindl (1979) to explore the implications of aggregate demand (specifically the savings–investment relationship) for the analysis of both excess capacity and stagnation (slow growth). This analysis draws on a number of features which appear elsewhere in this book. It incorporates the differential savings hypothesis discussed in Chapter 9 and views profitability, capacity utilisation and technical change as the key determinants of investment, which is in line with the discussion in the next chapter. Further, the distribution of income between wages and profits is seen as important and determined by degree of monopoly considerations as in the theory of Kalecki also discussed in Chapter 9.

The analysis here begins with a closed economy where the government balances its budget, which enables some of the key issues to be examined without introducing the complications of an open economy and of government deficit or surplus. The focus is then on the savings–investment equation. From the condition for equilibrium of the equality between injections and leakages, we have savings plus taxation equals investment plus government expenditure, which with the assumed balanced government budget leads to an equality between savings and investment.

Savings are made up of savings out of post-tax wages (with

propensity to save s_1) and by savings out of post-tax profits net of depreciation (with a propensity of s_2) with s_1 significantly smaller than s_2. Thus planned savings S are $s_1 (1-t_1)W + s_2 (1-t_2) P$ (where W is pre-tax labour income, P is pre-tax profits net of depreciation and t_1, t_2 are the tax rates on wages and profits respectively). It is helpful for later purposes to express savings relative to full capacity output. The notation which we use is that Y is actual output while Y^* is capacity output. Wages relative to capacity output are equal to $(W/Y) (Y/Y^*)$, which is written as $l\, u\, (1-t_1)$ where l is labour (wage) share, u is degree of capacity utilisation and t_1 is tax rate on wages. Net profits are given as $(Y - W - D)$ where D is depreciation. The ratio of profits to capacity output, labelled $q(u)$, is then $u - l\, u - v\, d$ since $D/Y^* = (D/K) (K/Y^*)$ with K as a measure of the capital stock and d put equal to the rate of depreciation D/K and v as the capital–capacity output ratio. Bringing these various elements together yields the ratio of savings to capacity output as:

$$S/Y^* = s_2 q(u)(1-t_2) + s_1 l\, u\, (1 - t_1) \tag{11.1}$$

There is considerable agreement on the type of factors which influence investment, even though there is disagreement on the exact forms in which these factors influence investment. In the present discussion three groups of factors are identified (and the reasoning is elaborated in the next chapter). The first is the level of capacity utilisation on the basis that firms will invest to meet expected increases in demand only when their current capacity utilisation is high. The second is the level of internal finance (i.e. savings out of profits) on the basis that firms have a preference for internal finance (rather than external finance). The greater the availability of finance (particularly internal finance), the higher will be the level of investment. The final variable is technological opportunities. The idea here is that firms' investment is encouraged by the rate of technical change, and in particular the level of net investment would be zero in the absence of technical change. The reasoning behind the inclusion of each of these variables is discussed more fully in the next chapter. The investment equation in which investment is expressed relative to capacity output is then $g[u, s_2 q(u)(1-t_2),\ T]$, where T is some measure of technological opportunities.

This formulation differs from Steindl (1979) in that we have removed the lags between capacity utilisation and profitability and

investment. The influence of retained earnings on investment
expenditure should be noted, reflecting the view that firms have
preference for internal finance over external finance. An alternative
formulation would be the influence of the rate of profit on investment expenditure. In algebraic terms, the substitution of the rate of
profit for retained profits would have no impact on the results
obtained and discussed below.

The condition for equality between investment and savings (both
expressed here relative to capacity output) is:

$$g(u, s_2q(u), T) = s_2q(u) + s_1(l \, u - v \, d) \, (1 - t_1) \tag{11.2}$$

The distribution of income between wages and profits is indicated
by l, and this is determined by degree of monopoly considerations
(cf. section 9.2). In order to simplify matters, l is taken as constant
with respect to the level of output, etc., and we analyse the impact
of different levels of l.

Moving from one level of l to another would have a variety of
effects on the level of demand and capacity utilisation. A higher
value for l (labour share) would tend to stimulate aggregate demand
since there has been a shift away from profits towards wages, and
the propensity to spend out of wages is much higher than that out of
profits. This stimulating effect leads to a further effect, in that
higher aggregate demand leads to higher capacity utilisation, which
encourages a higher level of investment. However, profits (relative
to capacity output) would be depressed by the rise in l but raised by
the increase in capacity utilisation. To the extent to which profits
were increased, investment would further increase. Thus, it could
be anticipated that a higher labour share can often generate higher
aggregate demand and capacity utilisation.

The impact of changes in the exogenous variables on capacity
utilisation can be calculated from equation (11.2). An increase in
technological opportunities (rise in T) will lead to a rise in capacity
utilisation provided that $g_1 + s_2 (g_2 - 1) (1 - l) (1 - t_2) - s_1 l (1 - t_1)$ is
negative (where g_i denotes first derivative of g with respect to the ith
argument). This condition is equivalent to saying that savings
increase more than investment in response to an increase in capacity
utilisation; and we will assume that this condition does prevail. The
implication of this conclusion is that when conditions are favourable
for technical change, then the consequent stimulating effect on
investment will lead to both high levels of capacity utilisation and

also (since g is raised) the rate of growth of capacity and of output. Thus technical change appears to be good for capacity utilisation and for growth. It is not possible to say what the effect on employment will be, in that part of technical change is to reduce the amount of labour required to produce a particular level of output. This approach suggests that there is a favourable influence of technological change on investment, growth and capacity utilisation. In the next chapter there is some further discussion on variations over time in technological opportunities.

It can also be calculated for equation (11.2) that, under the conditions specified in the previous paragraph, the effects of a decrease in the degree of monopoly (a rise in l), an increase in profits tax and a decrease in s_2 are all predicted to be an increase in capacity utilisation. Each of these implications is of some significance, and they are discussed in turn.

A rise in the degree of monopoly by lowering labour's share is predicted to reduce capacity utilisation and the rate of growth of the capital stock and of output. Thus whilst a rise in the degree of monopoly would raise the share of profits, through a reduction in the volume of economic activity, it could lead to a fall in total profits. The alternative way of expressing this result is to say that lower real wages may lead to lower capacity utilisation and growth. The motivation of capitalists is the pursuit of profits, but the paradox arises that if the share of profits (degree of monopoly) is too high this will adversely affect the volume of profits. Wages play a dual role, for they are not only costs of production so far as the firms are concentrated but also a source of aggregate demand. A low level of wages may provide a high share of profits but a low volume of profits, and higher real wages may be beneficial for profits. There will be an upper limit to this effect such that real wages past some point will eat into total profits.

The reason why a rise in profits tax raises capacity utilisation is straightforward. The effect of a profits tax is to withdraw money from profits out of which there is a low propensity to spend and to use that money (under the assumption of a balanced budget) for government expenditure. Thus overall expenditure is raised, and this increases capacity utilisation.

A decrease in s_2 may simply reflect an increase in capitalists' propensity to consume, and it is not surprising that an increased propensity to spend raises capacity utilisation. But an increase in s_2

could also be used to reflect a diversion of surplus away from reported profits into expenditures such as advertising and managerial expenses. It may be recalled from Chapter 5 that the managers of a firm have some discretion in the uses of the excess of revenue over costs of a firm. Some of this excess will provide reported profits, but other parts may be used to finance managerial expenses, etc. The effect of a shift from reported profits to managerial expenses is to raise the proportion of profits (the difference between income and wages) which are spent, i.e. lowering s_2.

Equation (11.2) can be seen to provide an 'equilibrium' value for capacity utilisation (u). It is generally presumed that such a value of capacity utilisation will involve excess capacity (rather than firms producing output greater than the desired capacity). One line of argument to support this view was given by Kalecki (1945), who argued, in effect, that at full capacity there would be an excess of private saving over private investment. This can be indicated roughly as follows. Savings would be sY and with investment geared to growth of capital stock, and with a constant capital–output ratio, investment would be $dK = v\,dY = v\,(dY/Y)\,Y = vgY$ (where g is the growth rate of output). The growth of output (with a constant capital–output ratio) would be equal to the growth of employment plus the rate of technical progress. Kalecki argued, in effect, that the values of g, s and v were such that s was greater than gv. Thus there was a deflationary gap by which *ex ante* savings would exceed *ex ante* investment at full capacity, thereby creating excess capacity.

The level of employment of labour will depend on capacity utilisation (which in turn depends on the level of aggregate demand). In the approach discussed in this section, there is no reason to think that capacity utilisation will be at full capacity. Further, even if there is full capacity utilisation there will not necessarily be full employment of labour. In the approaches examined, there is no mechanism to ensure that there will be sufficient capital equipment to provide full employment of labour. Firms are interested in profits, and installed capital equipment and operate it in the search for profits. As such there is little reason to think that the amount of installed capacity will be just right for the provision of full employment.

11.4 MORE ON UNEMPLOYMENT AND EXCESS CAPACITY

The previous section has focused on the determination of excess capacity. The question to be addressed now is the relationship between excess capacity and unemployment. The general proposition remains, namely that the level of employment (as well as output and capacity utilisation) are effectively determined by the level of aggregate demand.

We begin from the observation that firms' decisions on the capacity to install depends on profitability, on the level of demand expected and the extent to which they are prepared to operate with excess capacity. It is generally assumed (cf. section 12.2) that installed capital equipment has a particular labour requirement and there are few opportunities for substitution between labour and capital equipment. The employment of more labour (whether more workers or longer hours being worked on average) involves the more intensive use of capital equipment, and in that way labour and capital equipment are more complementary than substitutes. In one direction, it may well be the case that the installed capital equipment is unable to provide employment for all those seeking work even if there were sufficient demand for the output. Kalecki (1976) identified the inadequacy of capital equipment as particularly a cause of unemployment in developing countries, whereas inadequacy of demand was generally the cause in industrialised countries. However, there may well be occasions (e.g. after a prolonged recession during which capital equipment was not fully replaced) when there is inadequate capacity in industrialised countries.

In the other direction, it is generally assumed that firms will operate with excess capacity, in part so that they can increase production to meet any increase in demand. However, the assumption of excess capacity is usually taken to involve firms being able to expand output at close to constant unit costs (or perhaps even declining unit costs). This would also mean that higher levels of output are more profitable for firms since with average direct costs constant or declining and average fixed costs declining, profits per unit of output would rise with output.

In the approach adopted here, the level of aggregate demand generates a particular level of output (assuming that the firms find it profitable to meet the aggregate demand), and a consequent level of employment. In a neo-classical approach, if that level of employment did not correspond to full employment, then it is argued that real wages would adjust within the labour market to bring demand and supply of labour into balance with one another. But in the approaches under review here that mechanism does not operate. Why not? The key point is the view (in the work of Keynes and Kalecki) that the activities in the labour market set *money* wages, but not real wages. It is commonplace to observe that unions and employers negotiate over money wages. The firms then set prices, based on the costs and demand which they face, in order to achieve their objectives (e.g. maximise profits). In the process of doing so each firm determines the relationship between the wage which it pays and the prices which it charges. So far as the individual firm is concerned it has set the real product wage for itself. The workers for that firm may have little interest in that real product wage, for simply they may buy little if anything of the output of the firm. But when account is taken of the prices set by all firms, then the firms collectively determine the real wage of the workers.

Real wages are the ratio between money wages and output prices. The money wages are settled in the labour market (with or without bargaining) whereas output prices are set by firms (or occasionally by the actions of an anonymous market). The orthodox view (cf. Friedman, 1968) has generally been that the real wage is effectively set in the labour market. The general post-Keynesian view (e.g. Weintraub, 1979b) is that money wages are set in the labour market but that real wages are set by the actions of firms in setting prices. In other words, in terms of market power, firms largely have the final say (though for modifications see Kalecki, 1971b), and the discussion below). There is then no reason why real wages which are set in this way would be appropriate for generating full employment in the labour markets.

11.5 UNEMPLOYMENT AND LABOUR MARKET DISCIPLINE

In the discussion in Chapter 2 on the labour process, the point was made that one of the factors influencing the power of employers over employees would be the state of the labour market including the level and rate of change of unemployment. In the context of the labour process, the relevance of unemployment is for the intensity of labour and thereby measured productivity. The other aspect, to which much more attention has been given, is the impact of unemployment on wage determination.

The effect of unemployment on wage determination is a familiar theme which is often discussed under the heading of the Phillips curve. It is necessary to distinguish two mutually exclusive approaches, both of which are often presented in the context of the Phillips curve.[9] The first approach, which has become the prevailing orthodoxy following Friedman (1968), views real wages as determined in the labour market, and the adjustment of real wages responding to the excess demand for labour. Unemployment is taken as a (negative) proxy for the excess demand for labour, and the rate of change of real wages decomposed into $\dot{w} - \dot{p}^e$ (i.e. rate of change of money wages minus expected price change). Rearrangement to provide a money wage change equation provides:

$$\dot{w} = f(U) + \dot{p}^e \tag{11.3}$$

The crucial part of this approach arises from a consideration of equilibrium where real wages are constant, i.e. when $\dot{w} = \dot{p}^e$. For then $f(U) = 0$, and the solution to that equation is generally labelled the 'natural' level of unemployment (denoted U_n). It corresponds to the excess demand for labour being zero, which means that the demand and supply of labour are in balance and this is essentially a position of full employment since the potential supply of labour at the going real wage is demanded and employed.

The second approach views unemployment as disciplining workers, so that, for example, the bargaining power of workers is enhanced by low levels of unemployment but reduced by high levels of unemployment. In the simplest case, the power of workers is taken as depending only (and inversely) on unemployment.[10] The ability of workers to push up wages ahead of prices is then related to unemployment. In this simple case, an equation which appears to be identical to equation (11.3) is obtained.[11] Further, it would again be possible to obtained a value of unemployment which would imply constant real wages (i.e the solution to $f(U) = 0$ which we label U_x). However, the interpretation placed on U_x is quite different from that placed on U_n. For U_x is simply the level of unemployment which constrains the power of labour such that real wages are held constant. It has no connotation of being 'natural', desirable or involving full employment.

A more general approach, which links unemployment and inflation, starts from the conflict over income shares as between labour and capital. On one side, unemployment (among other factors) holds back real wages. On the other side, the level of output helps to restrain price increases (relative to costs including wages). At high levels of employment and output, there would be an inflationary spiral as wages rose (with unemployment low) and prices rose (with demand high). The level of economic activity (including employment and output) is then seen as tending towards a level which will keep wages and prices in check. This view is further elaborated below.

The approach examined above explaining the level of employment does not predict that full employment will be a usual occurrence. Indeed, based on a combination of empirical observation and theory, the view is taken that unemployment is the norm (cf. note 4). An extension of this view is that the achievement of full employment is likely to require government intervention *and* socio-political changes to accommodate full employment. This line of thought is often associated with Kalecki (1943), although it has taken on renewed relevance in the post-1973 high levels of unemployment. When unemployment is seen as a disciplining force on the labour force, it follows that the labour force will be in a stronger position when there is full employment. The Phillips curve places emphasis on the role of variations in the level of unemployment on wage changes, which is one aspect of this line of argument. There are, however, two further aspects. The first arises from the observation that Phillips made his original estimates over the period 1861–1913 during which unemployment fluctuated, with periods of anything approaching full employment being rare. In particular, this was not an era of prolonged full employment. However, when there is something approaching full employment for a substantial period of time (such as the 1960s in many countries; cf. note 4), then inflationary pressures may build up. Money wages would be continually rising, and would be matched by rising prices both as a response to rising wages and also aided by strong demand for output. The second aspect is that prolonged full employment changes the nature of the relationship between employers and employees, and this has been touched on in a number of places above. The self-confidence and assertiveness of workers could be anticipated to increase under conditions of permanent full employment. This may involve a continuous upward pressure on wages, some of which firms find difficult to pass on as price increases. Within the workplace, the imposition of discipline becomes more difficult, since the consequences of loss of one job is much reduced when others are readily available.

One prediction which follows from this would be that periods of unemployment would generate greater factory discipline and labour intensity, and thereby higher levels of productivity. However, the impact of unemployment would depend on factors such as the nature of the social security system and industrial relations legislation. In countries where the social security system is highly developed, and in particular there is substantial provision for the unemployed, the effect of unemployment would be lessened. Weisskopf (1987) discusses this further, and finds empirical support from cross-country comparisons for this general view.

In this approach, government intervention is necessary to secure full employment, but such intervention meets resistance particularly from capitalists. This resistance can be discussed in terms of dislike of government intervention in general and dislike of specific forms of government activity, and this has been discussed in the previous chapter.

11.6 INFLATION

In the post-war world, inflation has become an almost continuous feature of industrialised capitalist economies. The rate at which prices have risen varies between countries and over time, but experience has been one of rising prices, with falls in the general price level being rare. For example, since 1950 the general price level has not fallen in any single year in the United Kingdom and most industrialised countries have recorded at most one or two years in which prices have fallen (see, for example, Budd and Dicks, 1982, Table 4.A3; and OECD *Economic Outlook*). This contrasts with the pre-war situation where there were periods of rising prices interspersed with periods of falling prices, and rapid inflation was generally associated with war or its immediate aftermath. Allsopp (1982) reports an average rate of inflation for a range of European economies of 0.2 per cent per annum over the period 1870–1913, and an average of 0.1 per cent per annum in the period 1920–39 with many individual countries reporting a negative average rate of inflation over this period. In contrast, the average over the period 1948–69 is 3.4 per cent per annum, rising to 9.1 per cent over the period 1969–79. In many industrialised countries, the rate of inflation peaked during the second half of the 1970s, but nevertheless averaged 8.3 per cent over the period 1979–87, though there was a downward trend in inflation such that the average rate in European countries declined in every year over this period. The persistence of inflation, without exploding into hyper-inflation, has been a general feature. At the same time, fear of inflation has often appeared as a major impediment on the reflation of an economy and lower unemployment. The approach adopted here seeks to explain the persistence of inflation and how it may form a barrier to full employment.

The discussion of inflation in this chapter has three major components. The first deals with the manner in which prices are determined, and draws on the distinction between cost-determined and demand-determined prices (Kalecki, 1971a). In each case, the description applied indicates the predominant determinant of prices and price changes (for further discussion see Sawyer, 1985b, pp. 20–3), and it can be recalled from Chapter 3 that one of the differences between the competitive and monopolistic regulation concerned price formation. Cost-determined prices are largely associated with modern industry, in which prices are set at a mark-up over costs (cf. Chapter 9).[12] Average costs as seen as approximately constant with respect to output, and the mark-up is similarly little effected by the level of demand. These ideas on pricing can be expressed as:

$$p = (1 + m)\ avc \tag{11.4}$$

with m as mark-up and avc as average variable costs. When the mark-up and average costs are constant with respect to output, price will rise in line with changes in the price of inputs (e.g. labour, raw materials). Price changes under these circumstances can then be described as predominantly cost-determined, for it can easily be seen that cost changes will lead to price changes. Further, changes in demand will have little impact on prices, though they would lead to changes in output. Cost-determined prices are associated with industrial, distribution and services sectors (rather than agriculture and mining sectors), where the condition that production can be easily expanded at close to constant costs is expected to be fulfilled.

Demand–determined prices, in contrast, are set by movements in demand and associated with agricultural and primary sectors of the economy. In those sectors, a fluctuation in demand cannot have an immediate impact on supply since agricultural products (whether crops or animals) cannot be immediately produced but require a considerable gestation period. Thus, in the short term, the major response to a change in demand is on price rather than on supply. The demand-determined prices are largely associated with atomistic competitive markets. Their direct relevance so far as developed industrialised countries are concerned is seen as small, for often even agricultural prices are set in those countries by government agencies (with price support programmes, etc.) rather than by an anonymous market.

When prices are set as a mark-up over costs, then the impact of demand on prices is seen as rather limited. Thus in particular, a lower level of demand would have little effect on the price–cost margins and would exert little downward pressure on prices. In turn, if prices did not fall, then there would also be considerable pressure by workers to prevent wages falling (as will be seen further below). These forces will operate to limit price reductions, and hence can be seen as part of the explanation for persistent inflation.

There is a rough correspondence between on the one hand cost-determined prices with oligopolistic conditions, and on the other between demand-determined prices with atomistic competitive conditions. Oligopolistic industries involve relatively few firms, often operating subject to constant unit costs with some control over their prices. In contrast, competitive industries involve many small firms with little control over their prices. Thus the general evolution of the economy from a competitive stage to an oligopolistic one may be linked with a change in the way in which prices are determined, and the responsiveness of prices to demand and cost changes.

The second element in the discussion of inflation refers to the nature of the money and the way in which it is created. For many centuries, money played a limited role in economic life (because exchange of goods and services was rather unimportant with people being largely self-sufficient). A physical commodity such as gold or shells would be used for money. Commodity money has three important features. First, it is valuable in its own right and not just because it is used as money. Second, it has a physical existence and third, additions to the stock of money can be made only slowly and at some appreciable cost (e.g. by mining more gold). From the perspective of inflation, it is this last feature which is particularly relevant. For the difficulties of producing money mean that the volume of money cannot be readily increased to underpin rapid upward movements in prices.

However, over the past two centuries or so the nature of money in developed capitalist economies has changed dramatically. There can be arguments over the precise definition of money, but a general feature of money as currently used is that it is credit money. Money is no longer a commodity but rather is created by an institution as a financial asset. So far as the holder of money is concerned it is a financial asset, though for the creator of money it constitutes a debt or liability. Cash issued by a central bank (which on most current definitions of money is only a small proportion of money) is a debt of the central bank and forms part of the National Debt. Money which is a balance with a bank constitutes a liability for the bank (since they are required to repay that balance within a specified time if requested to do so). Even if a rather narrow definition of money such as M1 (coins, bank notes, current account deposits with banks, etc.) is adopted, then in contrast with commodity money the following features are found to apply for the case of credit money. First, this money only has value to an individual because the social convention is that it is money, that is that it will be generally accepted in purchases of goods and services. Bank notes and coins have virtually no value as paper, and bank deposits only exist as entries in a computer memory.

The second feature is that most money has no physical existence. The fact that additions to the money stock can be easily made at low cost is the third feature. For bank notes and coins, it requires the Mint to produce more, which it can do at a resource cost which is trivial in comparison with the face value of the note or coin. Clearing banks can produce money by making loans. For loans to be extended requires both a demand and a supply of loans. Hence on the one side there have to be customers willing to take out loans. On the other side, it requires that the banks are willing and able to extend further loans. The willingness is likely to be related to the interest rate which they are able to charge on the loans (in combination with an assessment of the risk of making the loan) and the ability relates to the banks not being constrained by the available reserves and any reserve requirements which bind them. But the loans can be granted at virtually no resource cost.

A crucial feature of credit money in the discussion of inflation is that it is easily created and is largely done so by private banks outside of the immediate control of the central bank or government. For other purposes it is important that such money comes into existence alongside spending plans and that such money, being both an asset and a liability, does not constitute net worth.[13] The ease with which credit money can be expanded means that the volume of such money can be increased to accommodate a rise in prices. Thus central banks are seen as having considerable difficulties in controlling the stock of money, which is largely under the control of the private banking system.

The third element in the discussion is that inflation (and particularly upswings in the rate of inflation) arises from conflict over income shares.[14] In a perfectly competitive world, prices are presumed to adjust to achieve an equilibrium outcome. In such an outcome, each individual is achieving an optimum outcome given the constraints which they face. If they are dissatisfied with the outcome in some way (which would require some notion of a satisfactory outcome), there is nothing they can do about it. They are powerless to change price or anything else. The position is quite different when we consider a world in which firms set prices and workers and firms bargain over wages. In the real world of oligopolistic firms and of collective bargaining, firms and workers have some power to change prices and wages. Dissatisfaction with existing wages and prices may then lead to increases in those wages and prices. Further, if one group feels more powerful, they may raise their prices to which other groups may respond.

One aspect of the conflict between workers and firms can be seen from a rearrangement of the pricing equation given above. Average variable costs (*avc*) can be expanded into $(w L + n N)/Q$ (where w is wage, L labour input, n price of materials, N materials input and Q output). Then from equation (11.4), substituting for *avc* and rearranging one can obtain:

$$w/p = \{1/(1+m)\} \, Q/L - (n \, N/p \, L) \qquad (11.5)$$

This indicates the real product wage as determined by the pricing decisions of the firm. Similarly, the overall real wage in the economy will also be set by the pricing decisions of firms in total, and it will be assumed that a relationship rather like equation (11.5) will apply at the aggregate level (cf. discussion on the degree of monopoly in Chapter 9). The general proposition is that firms' pricing decisions collectively (in conjunction with productivity and the price of materials) set real wages. As far as the firms are concerned, the price set according to equation (11.4) and then by derivation the real wage set according to equation (11.5) are 'desired' outcomes. For example, the price may have been derived as a result of profit maximisation calculations.

A diagrammatic representation is given in Figure 11.1 where the p-curve corresponds to equation (11.5), providing a relationship between the real wage and employment. In terms of equation (11.5), it can be seen that the relationship between the real wage and employment depends on how labour productivity varies with employment (assuming for simplicity of exposition that the mark-up and N/L ratio are constant). For relatively low levels of employment, it has been assumed that labour productivity will rise with labour employment, which gives the initial upward slope on the p-curve. At relatively high levels of employment, labour productivity may fall with further employment, providing a downward slope on the p-curve. If the actual real wage/employment combination fell above the p-curve, then firms would be seeking to raise prices faster than wages in order to secure a lower real wage, and this is indicated on the diagram where $\dot{p}$ is the rate of price inflation and $\dot{w}$ the rate of wage inflation. But if the actual real wage/employment combination is below the p-curve, then prices will rise at a slower rate than wages, permitting real wages to rise (remembering that the real wage/employment combinations on the p-curve represent desired outcomes for the firms). In the discussion of prices and price changes, it has been implicitly assumed that there is no general trend in productivity, but this assumption was made to simplify the exposition. With a trend in labour productivity, then in terms of equation (11.5), there would be an upward trend in Q/L and thereby in w/p.

There is no reason to think that the real wage determined according to equation (11.5) would in any sense be regarded as satisfactory by the workers. They will have their own ideas on what constitutes

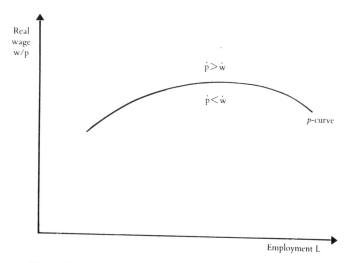

Figure 11.1 Real wage–employment relationship based on pricing.

an acceptable wage. For a group of workers, the relativity between their pay and that of groups with whom they like to compare themselves will be important. There will also be a strong element of real wage resistance, that is workers seeking to protect their previous standard of living.

This argument can be partially illustrated by the explicit introduction of the determination of money wages, though in circumstances where the conditions in the labour market have some influence (at least in the long run) on real wages. This can be achieved by use of a target real wage approach (Sargan, 1964; Henry, Sawyer and Smith, 1976; Sawyer, 1982a, 1982b) to money wage determination. The general idea here is that workers have a strong idea as to what constitutes a satisfactory wage, bearing in mind recent levels of their real wages, trends in productivity and the wages paid to groups with whom they like to compare themselves. In any particular year, the workers are seen to have a target for their money wages since it is money wages over which bargains are struck. But the target for money wages is influenced by their target real wages and by seeking to maintain their current level of real wages. The target money wage of workers (w^*) in their bargaining is expressed as the multiple of current money wages, expected prices (p^e) to actual prices and an element which reflects movement towards target real wage (T), i.e.:

$$w^*_t = w_{t-1} \left(p^e_t/p_{t-1}\right) \left(T/w_{t-1}/p_{t-1}\right)^{b_2} \tag{11.6}$$

The first part of the right-hand side of this equation indicates that the workers are seeking to maintain their current real wages in light of what they expect to happen to prices. The second part represents an attempt to shift real wages towards a target level.

There are many factors which help or hinder in the workers' pursuit of their target money wages, and by way of illustration we focus on the level of unemployment as a major influence. This can be represented by the following:

$$w_t = w^*_t f(U_{t-1}) \tag{11.7}$$

If the natural logarithm of variables in equation (11.7) is taken (with a substitution for w^* from equation (11.6), after rearrangement we have:

$$\ln w_t - \ln w_{t-1} = \ln p^e_t - \ln p_{t-1} + \ln f(U_{t-1}) + b_2 (\ln T - \ln(wt-1/pt-1)) \tag{11.8}$$

The term on the left-hand side is approximately the rate of change of money wages, whilst the first term on the right-hand side is the expected rate of inflation.[15] With those approximations and a linear function assumed for $\ln f(U_{t-1})$, we can arrive at:

$$\dot{w} = b_0 + \dot{p}^e + b_1 U_{t-1} + b_2 (\ln T - \ln w_{t-1}/p_{t-1}) \tag{11.9}$$

We can see that either $b_2 = 0$ or a target real wage which always quickly adjusts to the actual real wage (i.e. $T = w_{-1}/p_{-1}$) would allow equation (11.9) to simplify to an expectations-augmented Phillips curve.

A useful benchmark equation linking the real wage and unemployment level can be derived by taking the case where price expectations are fulfilled and wages rise in line with prices (where for simplicity a no productivity growth case is considered). This yields:

$$\ln (w/p) = c_0 + c_1 U + \ln T \tag{11.10}$$

where $c_0 = b_2^{-1}b_0$ and $c_1 = b_2^{-1}b_1$. From the inverse relationship between unemployment and employment, equation (11.10) can be interpreted as an equation in real wages and employment, and written as:

$$F(w/p, L, T) = 0 \tag{11.11}$$

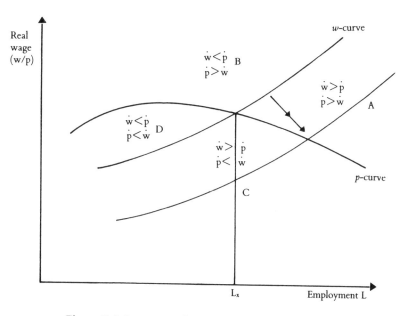

Figure 11.2 Interaction of wage and price determination.

This relationship between the real wage and employment is drawn in Figure 11.2 as the *w*-curve. This curve has been constructed so that for any point on the curve the real wage/employment combination is consistent with constant real wages so far as the forces at work in the labour market are concerned. Hence along the *w*-curve, money wages and prices would rise at the same rate. But for points below the *w*-curve, the process of collective bargaining would lead to wages rising faster than prices, whilst for points above the curve money wages would be rising less rapidly than prices.

In Figure 11.2, the implications of pricing and wage determination for the inflationary process are also indicated. In each zone, a pair of inequalities are shown. The first one indicates the relationship between wage inflation and price inflation from consideration of wage determination, whilst the second one indicate the relationship from the pricing process. Points in zone B, for example, are above the *w*-curve (hence wage inflation tends to be less than price inflation, $\dot{w} < \dot{p}$) and above the *p*-curve (hence price inflation tends to be more than wage inflation, $\dot{p} > \dot{w}$). In zones B and C, the two relationships between wage inflation and price inflation are mutually consistent, and in zone B real wages tend to fall and in zone C they tend to rise. However, in zone A, there is an inflationary spiral with wage bargaining pushing up wages faster than prices, and pricing decisions putting prices up faster than wages. In contrast, zone D would involve a dis-inflationary spiral.

A high level of demand, with high levels of output and employment, may place an economy in the equivalent of zone A. In such a case, the intereaction of aggregate demand and the conflict over income shares (as reflected in the wage-setting and price-formation processes) would lead to spiralling inflation. In this particular case, the conflict between workers and capitalists over the sharing out of national income (represented here by the conflict over real wages) generates inflation.

In the approach outlined here, the conflict over income shares could be resolved if there was some mechanism by which the economy could move to the point X. This point may well involve substantial unemployment (and also excess capacity) as ways of dampening down the demands on income shares from workers and from capitalists. Further, this resolution of the conflict over income shares does not mean that the income share which each side receives is in any sense satisfactory, but rather in the conditions of aggregate demand, etc., it is the best which they can achieve. The economy will, however, only reach point X if the level of aggregate demand is set accordingly to generate an employment of L_x. But if aggregate demand stays above this level, spiralling inflation would be the result and may involve substantial unemployment and excess capacity. There is nothing automatic in aggregate demand moving to provide an employment level of L_x, though a government which is concerned about inflation would deflate demand. It can be seen that employment below L_x will tend to reduce inflationary pressures.

Another method of 'reconciliation' would be to persuade one or other group that their claims are too high or excessive. The clearest example of this has been the use of incomes policies and other exhortation by governments to persuade or compel workers to accepting lower real wages. If, for example, workers could be persuaded to lower their target real wage, then the w-curve in Figure 11.2 would shift downwards, reducing the zone in which there is spiralling inflation and permitting a higher level of employment. Similarly, persuading firms to accept lower profits would shift the p-curve upwards, which would also lead to higher employment levels.

Workers and firms are not the only groups involved in the struggle over national income. The roles of government and the foreign sector are also relevant, and some of their impact can be illustrated by means of the approach developed above, and these are treated in turn. When the prices of imported goods and services rise, which is equivalent to real income being transferred from the domestic economy to the foreign sector, there is a direct impact on the rate of inflation. But such a rise by itself would provide a temporary boost to the rate of inflation. However, it can have a longer-lasting effect. A rise in the price of imported material can be seen by reference to equation (11.5) (i.e. a rise in n/p) to have the effect of reducing the level of real wages, and in terms of Figure 11.1 to shift the p-curve downwards. This is illustrated in Figure 11.2, where it can be seen that such a shift can set off an inflationary spiral. For example, if the employment level had been initially at L_x, a downward shift in the p-curve would now place the economy into the spiralling inflation zone.

An attempt by the government to increase its role in the economy (particularly when this involves raising taxation) can also be seen as inflationary. Consider, as an example, where the government increases the rate of income tax on wages. This may appear to have no effect on the rate of inflation. However, it does reduce the real take-home pay of workers. Assuming that the target post-tax real wages of the workers remain unchanged, then a higher pre-tax target real wage is now required. Thus in terms of the approach given above, this rise in income tax is equivalent to a rise in the target real wage. This would represented by a an upward shift in the w-curve in Figure 11.2, and once again it can be soon worked out that the economy may be thereby moved into the inflationary zone.

One sphere in which demand is particularly important is, not surprisingly, for demand-determined prices. We can approximately identify these prices with primary products.[16] The world level of demand is seen as particularly influential in this context. High levels of world demand (as in 1972/3) have a substantial effect on raising commodity prices, and conversely for low levels of demand.[17] It can be seen from Table 11.1 that the prices of primary products display wide swings, with rapid rises in some years and severe drops in others. The general trend of primary product prices relative to other prices will be discussed below (section 13.6), and our focus here is on the variability of these prices. In particular, it is notable that whereas the general price level of industrial products rarely falls, primary product prices frequently do fall. It was indicated above that the general trend in inflation in European countries had been downwards during the 1980s. The falls in primary product prices will raise the real living standards of the purchasers of those products (at the expense of the producers) and the decline in those prices would be a considerable help in the reduction of the rate of inflation. The figures in Table 11.1 could be held to support the view that one factor reducing inflation during the 1980s in the industrialised countries has been the general fall in commodity prices.

Table 11.1 Some statistics on primary product prices.

Year	Percentage change in (dollar) price indices for all commodities	all food
1969	+7.1	+7.1
1970	+3.1	+9.7
1971	−2.7	+0.6
1972	+13.0	+13.3
1973	+48.3	+39.5
1974	+33.2	+53.7
1975	−11.4	−10.3
1976	+9.4	+7.6
1977	+22.7	+37.2
1978	−7.7	−15.1
1979	+15.5	+7.8
1980	+13.4	+14.4
1981	−7.0	−17.1
1982	−15.1	−17.4
1983	+5.1	+6.6
1984	+1.2	−4.9
1985	−10.7	−12.9
1986	+5.3	+12.2

Note: Data up to and including 1976 based on National Institute of Economic and Social Research indices, whereas after 1976 data based on indices prepared by UNCTAD.
Sources: Calculated from *National Institute Economic Review*, various issues.

Primary commodities enter the industrial sector as inputs into the productive process (e.g. tin) or as consumption goods. A faster rise in commodity prices would in the former case lead to a rise in costs, which would be passed on to prices and directly to a rise in prices in the latter case where wages could be expected to respond. Thus faster rises in commodity prices would stimulate price inflation, and conversely lower rises (or falls) in commodity prices would dampen down price inflation. However, for many industrialised countries, primary products represent imported materials. The variations in primary product prices then appear to these industrialised economies as cost changes, and through the route of influencing costs and then output prices, primary product prices can affect the overall rate of inflation.

It is now possible to bring these elements together. The basic view of inflation here can be described as a conflict approach. Price and wage rises are initiated for a variety of reasons.[18] It may be a response to high levels of demand or to dissatisfaction with current wages and prices. A price rise will invoke two responses. First, those directly affected by the price rise will seek to offset it by raising their own prices. A rise in an input price would lead to an upward adjustment in the output price, and a rise in the price of consumption goods will provoke wage rises. There will be a strong element of cost-push inflation.

Second, the reaction of the money supply is particularly important (see, for example, Moore, 1979, 1988). The endogenous nature of credit money and the fact that production takes time and needs to be financed are the important facets here. When a firm increases expenditure on inputs, then that increased expenditure must be financed. The increased expenditure may arise from a desire to expand output which requires an increased volume of inputs, or from the requirements of paying higher prices for the inputs. In either case, the firm has to increase borrowing from banks or to run down their liquid assets to finance the increased expenditure. The use of the borrowing option would lead to increases in the money supply. In both cases, firms hope to reap higher revenue (whether from the sale of increased output or through charging higher prices) and from that extra revenue they will be able to continue to finance higher expenditure in the future. The increases in the money supply, in response to higher input prices, are a necessary feature of inflation (except in cases where there are 'excess' liquid assets, when effectively increased velocity of circulation can accommodate the increased prices) in permitting firms to make increased payments for inputs, which leads in turn to increased prices for output.

Thus, at the level of the firm, an increase in input prices may lead to an increased requirement for money to finance the purchase of the inputs. There are other ways, such as trade credit, by which the increase in input prices may be covered. Further, any requirement by the firm for more money is a short-term one in the sense that the firm seeks the money to finance expenditure, and hence soon parts with the money. If the increased stock of money or trade credit were not forthcoming, then some combination of reduced purchase of inputs and of lower (than otherwise) increases in input prices would be required. However, the view is taken here that it is usually the case that the funds are forthcoming, so that the money supply expands to underwrite inflation and allow it thereby to continue.

11.7 CONCLUDING REMARKS

The key features adopted in this chapter towards the explanation of unemployment and inflation are three-fold. First, there is a stress on the importance of effective demand and the related focus on the role of the savings–investment nexus. Second, the economy is envisaged as oligopolistic. Third, money is credit money created by the banking system, reflecting the institutional realities of developed capitalist economies.

NOTES

1. For further discussion see Pasinetti (1974, pp. 72–5 and pp. 118–20), Sawyer (1985b, pp. 269–71) and especially Skott (1983). For a counter-view see Weintraub (1979a).
2. For further elaboration see Eatwell and Milgate (1983b).
3. See, for example, Frank (1986).
4. 'A further exceptional and equally beneficial phenomenon was the achievement in the 1960s of full employment, at least in the north-western part of the area [Europe]. This was an unprecedented success for industrialised societies. Bouts of full employment for the urban labour force had occurred at cyclical peaks in the past, but a prolonged period of peace-time full employment, including the virtual disappearance of underemployment on the land, was something which the more

cyclically sensitive and agriculturally dependent pre-war economies had not experienced' (Boltho, 1982a).

5. Patinkin (1982) argues that the original feature of Keynes (1936) was a theory of effective demand which 'in more formal terms is concerned not only with the mathematical solution $F(Y)=Y$, but with demonstrating the stability of this equilibrium as determined by the dynamic adjustment equation $dY/dt = \phi[F(Y) - Y]$ where $\phi' < 0'$. In this quote Y stands for output and $F(Y)$ is the aggregate demand function. Thus, the focus is on the level of output adjusting rather than say the rate of interest.

6. This discussion is heavily influenced by Chick (1986), which should be referred to for further discussion.

7. In some post-Keynesian theories (e.g. Eichner, 1973), firms are postulated to set price in order to generate sufficient profits to largely finance their investment programme (for discussion see Chapter 6). When they succeed in entirely financing their investment out of retained profits, then all the firm's savings are channelled into its own investment. However, there may still be some external borrowing (which would depend on its cost relative to internal finance) and some savings by individuals. Thus the equality of desired savings and desired investment is not ensured.

8. For further discussion see Sawyer (1982a, 1985b).

9. For further discussion of the Phillips curve and an elaboration of the points made in the text see Sawyer (1987).

10. This is the simple case. In general, it would be expected that there are many other factors, such as rate of change of unemployment, bargaining stance of employers, which influence money wage determination.

11. Khan (1980) argues that the excess demand approach to the Phillips curve predicts that real wages move counter-cyclically, i.e. fall (relative to trend productivity) during business upswings and rise during downswings. In contrast, the bargaining approach views low levels of unemployment as strengthening the workers' position and raising real wages (again relative to trend productivity). He finds that his empirical evidence supports the bargaining approach.

12. For a full discussion on theories of pricing and the argument that they can be represented in terms of price as a mark-up over costs see Sawyer (1983, ch. 2).

13. This means that the stock of money in existence does not constitute net worth for the private sector. A fall in the price level makes borrowers worse off and lenders better off (in so far as debts are denominated in nominal terms), but with no change in net worth. Thus, the real balance or Pigou effect cannot operate to stimulate aggregate demand to move an economy out of a recession.

14. For a more formal analysis see Rowthorn (1977) and Sawyer (1982b).
15. For small values of x, the approximation $\ln(1 + x) = x$ can be utilised. Now $\ln w_t - \ln w_{t-1}$ can be written as $\ln(w_t/w_{t-1}) = \ln(1 + (w_t - w_{t-1})/w_{t-1})$ which is approximated by $(w_t - w_{t-1})/w_{t-1}$, that is the rate of change of wages.
16. For many primary products, the world price would be seen by most observers as essentially demand-determined (e.g. wheat). However, for some primary products, the price charged in a particular country may bear little relation with the world price; this would arise, for example, where the domestic producers are protected by tariffs or quotes as under the Common Agricultural Policy of the EC. For other primary products, with oil as the outstanding example, there has been a history of cartelisation and price setting. In those areas, the influence of demand is more debatable.
17. See, for example, Beckerman (1985), Beckerman and Jenkinson (1986).
18. An economy is moving through time, and there is rarely a time when there has been such stability in an economy that it is possible to say for sure what initiated any particular price or wage rise. It is more usually the case that any price or wage will be justified on the basis of some prior price or wage rise somewhere else in the economy. The 'story' told in the text is for purposes of illustration.

Chapter 12
INVESTMENT, GROWTH AND TECHNICAL CHANGE

12.1 INTRODUCTION

The macroeconomic experience of capitalist economies has generally involved cyclical ups and downs, growth and historically rapid technical change. The purpose of this chapter is to explore the relationships between those elements. One key element in the generation of business cycles, growth and technical change is investment in capital equipment. Further, investment itself is a central element of aggregate demand and thereby has a strong influence on the level of employment. The growth of capital equipment is necessary for growth of output and comes through new investment. But investment expenditure is liable to considerable fluctuation, leading to fluctuations in aggregate demand and in employment and output. Investment expenditure only continues through the prospect of profitable growth and from the spur of technical change. On the other side, investment in new machines is necessary for the implementation of new ideas. For example, a new production technique (say the use of robots in car production) generally requires investment in the appropriate capital equipment. But also a new production technique may involve changes in the organisation of work, the skills required and the relationship between employers and workers (cf. section 3.6).

This chapter begins with a discussion on the nature of capital equipment, which leads into a consideration of the determinants of investment expenditure. This is followed by an exploration of the two-way relationship between investment expenditure and profits. There is also a two-way relationship between investment and technical change, and the impact which the rate of technical change may have on investment and thereby on the rate of growth of economies is explored. Variations in the rate of technical change are likely to lead to variations in the rate of growth, etc. This is followed by discussion of the ways by which investment is necessary for technical change, and this also leads into a consideration of induced technical change. This discussion can then be drawn upon to provide a post-Keynesian perspective on growth and economic development. The chapter is completed by a discussion of the idea of long waves in economic activity driven by variations in the rate of technical change.

12.2 THE NATURE OF CAPITAL EQUIPMENT

It is useful to say something about how different approaches to economic analysis view the nature of capital equipment, as a background to the next section dealing with the determinants of investment expenditure, since views on the nature of capital equipment have a strong influence the factors which are thought to determine the demand for capital equipment. It is commonplace to say that theories must make assumptions, which will in some sense be a departure from reality, either in terms of directly contradicting reality or omitting some features of reality. When theorising about the demand for investment goods (or indeed any other type of good or service), it is necessary to make (often implicit) assumptions about the nature of investment goods. For example, it is necessary to make some assumption about the existence and efficiency of any second-hand market for such goods. When there is a highly organised second-hand market for, say, a particular type of machine, then the purchase of such a machine can easily be reversed by its sale. But if there is only a poorly organised second-hand market (or none at all), then the purchase of a particular machine is a long-term commitment which cannot be readily reversed.

A contrast can be drawn between the neo-classical picture of investment goods (and capital equipment) and the one implicit in the radical political economy approach. Authors within both the neo-classical and (more particularly) the radical political economy tradition vary to some degree in the way in which investment goods are modelled. The discussion in the text is intended to represent some consensus view within the radical political economy tradition.

The neo-classical view of capital equipment could be summarised by saying that such equipment is malleable and can be used in any desired ratio with labour and other inputs. Terms such as jelly or putty are often used to describe this approach, and analogies made with children's construction toys which can be assembled and re-assembled. The malleability of capital equipment taken literally would mean that capital equipment could take different physical forms and be used in different production processes. The substitutability means that the amount of labour which is combined with a particular amount of capital equipment can be varied, and, of course, as labour is varied so will the amount of output produced. This substitutability is a necessary assumption if the marginal product of labour is to have any meaning; for simply the marginal product of labour is the difference in output arising from a difference in labour usage on given capital equipment.

It is useful to distinguish between *ex ante* and *ex post* malleability and substitutability. The *ex ante* case arises when a firm is making plans for future production and the requirements for inputs. At this stage, there will usually be a range of possibilities over which capital equipment could be used and which types of labour. At the *ex ante* stage, the finance capital can be put to a number of alternative uses, and in that sense capital is malleable. Further, the ratio between expenditure on capital equipment and the labour to be employed on that equipment can vary to some degree, so that there is a degree of substitutability between labour and capital equipment. However, once capital equipment has been installed, it is difficult to change its form so that it is no longer malleable. Further, capital equipment is often designed to employ a particular amount of labour, and so substitution between capital equipment and labour is likely to be difficult.

A production function, such as $Y = f(L,K)$ where K is some measure of the stock of capital equipment, L a measure of labour input and Y of output, can be interpreted either in an *ex ante* or an *ex post* sense. The estimation of production functions based on observations of output and inputs assumes *ex post* malleability and substitutability. In the absence of malleability, the level of output would depend on the precise composition of the stock of capital equipment as well as its total. Further, an aggregate production function of this form is often used in neo-classical growth models (e.g. Solow, 1956, and discussed in texts on growth theory such as Hacche, 1979; Jones,

1975). However, this can be modified by the use of 'putty–clay' models in which there is *ex ante* malleability and substitutability but once the capital equipment has been installed there is not. When the production function is applied at an aggregate level, then the questions of measuring aggregate capital arise, and the difficulties of measuring aggregate capital were explored in Chapter 8.

The nature of the commitment which a firm makes when it purchases a piece of capital equipment depends on a variety of factors. The finance for that equipment may come from borrowing, in which case there is a financial commitment to meet the interest payments and to repay the loan. The malleability of the equipment would be one consideration, but the possibilities of physically changing equipment are usually very limited. For a single firm an important consideration would be the second-hand market for the equipment. Some capital equipment (e.g. road transport) may be traded in a second-hand market in which there are plenty of buyers and the loss on re-sale is relatively small. But for other specialised equipment there may be a poor second-hand market so that re-sale would represent considerable loss. Two further considerations arise. First, if a firm buys a piece of specialised equipment which turns out to be a mistake, then other firms are likely to realise that a mistake has been made and may also take the view that it would be a mistake for them to purchase this piece of specialised equipment. Hence, the re-sale price will be low. For general equipment with many alternative uses (e.g. a car), whilst its purchase may have been a mistake for a particular firm, there are many other firms in other industries which use cars. Second, this is a case where what may be true for the single agent (firm) is not true for the economy as a whole. A firm may be able to sell capital equipment and in that sense be able to unwind its commitment but the economy as a whole cannot do so for obviously there must be a buyer for that equipment if it is to be sold. The economy as a whole can destroy the equipment (or equivalently here leave it idle) but it has still expended resources in the building of that capital equipment which cannot be recouped unless sale of equipment overseas is a viable option.

The general view of capital equipment adopted within the radical political economy tradition has the following features. There is a need to distinguish between *ex ante* and *ex post* substitutability and malleability. In the *ex ante* case, there will be some possibilities of substitutability, though the extent of those possibilities is often overstated. There are few possibilities of substitution and manipulation *ex post*, and as a first approximation it can be assumed that there is none. Once a piece of capital machinery has been built, there will be variations in output (generally arising from fluctuations in demand) and in labour employed. Thus the capital equipment may be used more or less intensively (e.g. variations in the hours for which it is operated).

The view which is taken of the nature of capital equipment strongly influences discussion of the determinants of investment expenditure. Where capital equipment can be easily varied, both in terms of its type and quantity, then a firm does not need to pay much attention to future prospects. The firm can link its capital equipment to its current requirements, and expectations about the future are of little significance. In contrast, where capital equipment can only be changed with difficulty, then the firm has to pay much more attention to future prospects. Expectations and confidence about the future become much more important in the determination of the level of investment expenditure.

12.3 THE DETERMINANTS OF INVESTMENT EXPENDITURE

The main aim of this section is to consider the factors which determine the level of investment expenditure. The aggregate demand for investment goods is built up from the demand for investment goods of individual firms (see note 2 below). It is the interplay between four sets of factors which is analysed below. These factors are as follows:

1. The level of demand facing a firm relative to its current capacity.
2. Profitability and the availability of finance.
3. Expectations and confidence about the future.
4. The pace of technical change.

The first three factors are discussed in this section, and the influence of technical change is returned to below. The discussion here is limited to business investment, with the motives of the firms involved taken to be profit seeking, so that the basic reason for undertaking investment is to raise future profits. Other types of investment (e.g. public-sector investment) may be undertaken for different reasons, but space considerations do not permit discussion of other forms of investment.

This discussion of investment omits two important facets of the determinants of investment expenditure. The first one has to some extent been covered above (section 5.3) and this is the state of competition between firms. In the Marxian approach, there is an imperative on firms to invest in order to lower costs and to keep up with the opposition. This arises in conditions of competition and the imperative to invest may be reduced under conditions of oligopoly and monopoly. The second omission is any reference to social and political factors. The political factors would include the attitudes of government and firms towards each other. The election of a left-wing government perceived to be hostile to business and profits may through a variety of routes provoke an 'investment strike'. The social factors would include matters such as which spheres of activity are regarded as socially acceptable (and this can be reinforced by which forms of investment have proved profitable in the past). For example, a society in which land is regarded as a safe investment and where land ownership conveys status and prestige, and in which involvement with industry is given a low status (which some would broadly speaking describe as the British situation during much of the past two centuries) would tend to generate investment in land and property rather than in manufacturing industry. In turn, the directions in which investment flows help to determine the future structure and prospects for the economy.

Net investment is, by definition, an addition to the stock of capital equipment. A firm will seek further capital equipment in order to profitably increase output,[1] and hence net investment is linked to expected growth of output and this is the main idea behind the accelerator theory of investment, which can be expressed as follows. Consider a single firm which uses one type of capital equipment. Net investment is designed to raise the level of capital equipment towards the level desired by the firm. The rate of net investment during period t is I_t, which adds to the capital stock at the end of that time period. This investment will then aid production in time period $t + 1$, and the desired level of capital equipment in that period is taken as vY^e_{t+1}, where v is the desired capital–output ratio and Y^e is the expected level of output.[2] This can be written as:

$$I_t = k \left(vY^e_{t+1} - K_{t-1} \right) \tag{12.1}$$

where K_{t-1}, is the actual stock of capital equipment at the end of time period $t-1$, and k is the proportion of the desired change in the capital equipment which actually happens. The firm may be limited by financial constraints, availability of capital equipment, etc., from achieving the desired change in one time period.

This equation can be rewritten by explicitly introducing kvY_t (both positively and negatively) as:

$$I_t = kv(Y^e_{t+1} - Y_t) + k(vY_t - K_{t-1}) \tag{12.2}$$

This equation indicates that net investment is influenced by expected change in output (the first term on the right-hand side) and capacity utilisation (the second term which compares the capital equipment required for output, vY_t, with the actual capital equipment). The concern here is only with the influences on investment decisions, so it is not necessary to consider the conditions under which it would be possible to add together equations such as (12.2) to provide an aggregate investment equation (see note 2). Investment relative to output can be expressed as:

$$I_t/Y_t = kv(Y^e_{t+1} - Y_t)/Y_t + k(v - K_{t-1}/Y_t) \tag{12.3}$$

It can be seen from this equation that investment (relative to output) is influenced by expected growth (first term on right-hand side) and the difference between desired and actual capital–output ratio. This accelerator theory stresses the role of short-term changes in output for the determination of investment expenditure. However, when firms are operating with plenty of surplus capacity (which would be reflected in equation (12.3) by a large excess of actual capital–output ratio over the desired ratio), an expected change in output can be met by production with existing equipment and hence may not have any effect on investment plans. Firms may look further ahead when making investment decisions, and hence the longer-term prospects for growth of output could be relevant for investment decisions.

Profits influence investment decisions through a number of routes, direct and indirect. The direct and obvious route (though rather neglected in orthodox macroeconomics) is that since firms are profit-seeking organisations, they will only undertake investment if there is the prospect that it will add to their profits. It is then *expected* profitability of the investment project which is relevant. Expectations of future profitability will to some degree be influenced by current actual profitability. This would be particularly so when the level of investment in aggregate is considered for all firms, rather than when one specific project is being considered. However, the relationship between current and expected profitability may be only a loose one and there may be many factors which influence firms' views on future profitability. For some investment projects where there is both a long gestation period and a long period of operation (e.g. an electricity generating station) expectations on profitability have to be made over many decades into the future. The future profitability of a project will also depend on the demand which the firm expects to face and the consequent rate of capacity utilisation.

The indirect route through which profitability influences investment is that of the availability and cost of finance. In Chapter 5 the reasons were considered why firms would prefer to use internal finance rather than external finance on grounds of cost and of reducing outside intervention. The source of internal finance is largely profits, and hence the greater volume of profits encourages investment through the finance which those profits provide. Further, the availability and cost of external finance may be favourably affected by profitability.

It has been seen that expectations about the future (especially of demand and profitability) are important ingredients in the factors determining investment. The question arises as to how these expectations about the future are formed. Within the radical political economy tradition, at least two distinct strands of thought can be identified. The first strand would indicate the difficulties of foretelling the future so that views about future prospects are closely linked to current experience. For example, expectations concerning future profitability would be strongly influenced by current levels of profitability. In such a case, when current growth of output and level of profitability are relatively high, expectations of future growth and profitability may be thereby enhanced. Then, high growth of output would have an indirect influence on investment, via its impact on expectations of future growth (in addition to the direct influence).

The second strand of thought owes much to Keynes (1937), and stresses the unknowability and essential uncertainty of the future, to which some reference was made in Chapter 1. With the idea that views about the future are inevitably flimsily based, it would follow that views about the future may easily change. There can be waves of optimism and of pessimism about the future. In the context of investment, this would imply that when, for example, capitalists become pessimistic about the future, investment will decline (which leads to a depression of aggregate demand and growth, helping to confirm the pessimism). Further, such an onset of pessimism may be triggered by some major event, but is not closely linked to changes in the underlying economic situation for if it was then it would be an example of the first view outlined above.

The thrust of the discussion of this chapter is that growth and profitability, and in particular expectations on these two factors, will be important influences on investment. In the next section, the influence of investment on growth and change is investigated.

12.4 INVESTMENT, GROWTH AND BUSINESS CYCLES

Capitalist economies have generally experienced economic growth but not at a smooth and even pace. The view expressed here is that investment expenditure is intimately involved with growth and fluct-uations (business cycles), and in both cases there is a two-way relationship involved. The growth–investment connection is relative-ly straightforward. On the one side net investment, being an addition to the capitalist stock, will only proceed with the prospect of growth of demand for final output. A stationary economy would not require net additions to the capital stock, for the level of output is not expanding so that a constant level of the capital stock would be sufficient. On the other side, growth of output cannot in general occur unless the means of production are increased, which means here a growth of the stock of capital equipment, i.e. net investment. Thus growth requires that net investment actually happens. In effect, the linkages are that the expectation of growth leads to net investment, which permits the growth of output to occur.

The mechanism by which investment generates a business cycle can be described in the following way. An initial rise in expected output would lead to an increase in investment expenditure (cf. equation (12.2)). This increase in investment expenditure stimulates an increase in aggregate demand, and income has to rise such that the savings generated by the increase in income is equal to the rise in investment; that is the familiar multiplier mechanism at work. Thus there is a rise in output, which may generate expectations of further rises in output. If so, this would help to generate a further increase in investment expenditure. At the same time, capacity utilisation is rising and that stimulates investment expenditure further. This process can gather further momentum until the level of output and employment cannot expand further through supply constraints (e.g. there is a shortage of labour). At this point, the expectations on further output increases are much reduced, and it is then that investment expenditure begins to fall. The process of upswing is now thrown into reverse; the expectation of smaller increases in output than hitherto (or even decreases in output) reduces the demand for investment expenditure. This then leads to falls in demand and output, causing a further reduction in the rate of increase in output.

This explanation of the end of the upswing depends on supply constraints preventing a further expansion of output. Hence at the top of a business cycle, capital equipment and/or labour would be fully utilised. An alternative explanation to the end of the upswing focuses on profitability. It has been observed (e.g. Sherman, 1987a) that real wages and profitability fluctuate during the business cycle. In particular, it is observed that in the initial phases of an upswing profitability rises but tends to fall in the later stages, whereas increases in the share of wages largely occur at the top of the cycle. The rise in profitability can be accounted for by two factors. First, in the upswing of a trade cycle, capacity utilisation rises as does the more intensive use of the existing capital equipment and employed labour. The costs of the capital equipment and the fixed element of employed labour are now spread over a larger volume of output, leading to lower unit costs. Thus more output is produced at lower unit cost, leading to greater profits. Second, rising demand places firms in a stronger market position, allowing prices to rise (faster than wages), and this leads to an increase in profit margins. In the later stages of the upswing, unemployment has fallen which strengthens the position of workers, leading to rises in money wages. When money wages start to rise faster than prices, clearly profit margins tend to decline. Further, the firms may no longer be able to expand output at lower unit costs as they begin to run up against capacity constraints. These two combine to lead to falls in profitability. This decline in profitability would lead to firms cutting back on their investment plans (thereby cutting aggregate demand) and to a reluctance (and perhaps inability) to expand output since further expansion is less profitable than hitherto.

Sherman (1987a) provides the following description of the end of a business cycle upswing:

> To summarize the situation in the crisis, consumer demand is limited; it grows only minutely, as a result of the long previous fall in the average propensity to consume. At the same time, in the crisis, labour costs per unit are rising because productivity is falling faster than wages; raw material costs are rising faster than finished goods prices; and interest costs are rising. Hence the jaws of the nutcracker close, profits and profit rates are squeezed, and after a couple of quarters, production and investment decline, setting off a recession or depression.

An important element in this approach is that attention is paid to movements in aggregate demand (which in turn depend on, *inter alia*, the distribution of income) and in the distribution of income itself. The upswing of the business cycle comes to an end through a lack of increase in demand and because of the unprofitability of an expansion of production. Further, inability to expand production because of a shortage of capital equipment and of labour is seen to play a relatively small role.

The common feature of these views of the cycle mechanism is that they involve the decisions of firms on investment and production. Thus capitalists' decisions drive the business cycle. These theories relate to relatively short cycles (perhaps of the order of four to five years in length). Later, much longer cycles (of the order of forty to sixty years in length) are discussed. For both types of cycles and the explanations of them there are some common questions which arise. These include the following:

1. What brings a cyclical upswing to an end and what starts off a revival of economic activity?
2. How uniform are cycles and what is the role of 'exogenous' factors?

Each business cycle has some differences from any other cycle, but theories of cycles stress the similarity of different cycles. These questions are returned to below.

12.5 INVESTMENT AND PROFITS

In a capitalist economy, there is a two-way relationship between investment and profits, which can generate vicious and virtuous circles. The dependence of profits on investment arises from the Kaldorian theory of income distribution (cf. section 9.3). In its simplest form this provides the following equation for profits:

$$P = (I - s_1 \ Y)/(s_2 - s_1) \tag{12.4}$$

where P is profits, I investment, Y the level income and s_w, s_p the propensities to save out of wages and profits respectively. It can be seen that, according to this theory, profits would be negative unless investment is greater than $s_w \ Y$. In effect, profits only occur on condition that they are largely saved. The direction of causation in the approach of Kaldor runs from investment to profits so that higher investment stimulates higher profits. It should be noted that this relationship applies only at the macroeconomic level, and there is no corresponding micro-level relationship. However, in the approach of Eichner (1973, 1976), which was discussed in Chapter 6, there is a microeconomic link in that firms seek to generate sufficient profits to cover their investment needs. In other words, the investment requirements determine the profits of the firm to finance those investment expenditures.

The dependence of investment expenditure on profits has been discussed above, where it was argued that at the level of the firm there would be a positive relationship between planned investment expenditure and he volume of profits. In this case, the relationship is essentially a micro-level (i.e. firm level) one, though it can be aggregated up to the macroeconomic level. Thus, from equation (12.4) and the influence of profits on investment expenditure, a two-way relationship between investment and profits is achieved.

The interaction of investment and profits can generate a virtuous or vicious circle effect. A virtuous circle can operate from the expectations of high profitability which would encourage firms to undertake a high level of investment expenditure. The result of this high level of investment expenditure, as can be seen from equation (12.4), is a high level of profits. In some degree the expectations of high profitability which led to a high level of investment is justified by the actual outcome of high profits. The achievement of high profits may encourage anticipation of further increases of profitability, and also stimulate further investment. This would suggest that an economy can be launched onto a high profits/high investment path. But conversely, the expectation of low profitability depresses investment expenditure, which in turn leads to low profitability. A vicious circle is now in operation, launching an economy onto a low profitability/low investment path.

12.6 TECHNICAL CHANGE AND INVESTMENT

One influence on investment expenditure which has not so far been discussed is that of technical change. In this section, the two-way relationship between technical change and investment expenditure is explored. In one direction, the demand for investment expenditure is stimulated by technical change, and net investment would come to a halt in the absence of technical change. In the other direction, the implementation of technical change is seen to require gross investment so that new capital equipment is available to apply new technology and/or to produce a new range of products.

To see the first of those relationships, imagine a world in which technical change did not occur. Firms would continue to invest so long as their actual stock of capital equipment fell short of the desired level (so that they would find it profitable to extend their stock of capital equipment). But when that desired level of capital equipment has been achieved, net investment would fall to zero, with the only investment expenditure which takes place being to replace the capital equipment which had worn out. A growing labour force would require an increasing stock of capital equipment to match the increase in labour supply if the proportion in employment is to remain constant. But there is no guarantee that this requirement for investment would be translated into actual investment (and if it is not, then unemployment would rise). In the absence of technical change and population growth, the economy would move towards a stationary state in which the stock of capital equipment would have reached its desired level. There would be some gross investment to replace capital equipment as it wore out, but investment would be limited to this replacement level.

Technical change involves by definition new ideas, new products and new production processes. The production of a new product will generally require a new type of equipment. In other words, gross investment has to occur to permit the technical change to become a reality in the form of the production of a new product. At this point, it can be seen that the view taken of the nature of capital equipment (cf. section 12.2) becomes relevant. For if capital equipment is malleable then the existing capital equipment designed to produce an 'old' product could be transformed to provide capital equipment suitable for the production of the 'new' product. Similarly, for a new process of production to be introduced new types of capital equipment will usually be required. However, the view that capital equipment is generally not malleable would indicate that a new product or process would require new equipment. Thus gross investment has to take place in order that technical change (whether involving new products or processes) can be brought into effect.

One aspect of this argument has been stated as 'there cannot be capital deepening without some technical progress embodied in the new capital, and most new ideas need capital accumulation for their embodiment. Society's ability to absorb new knowledge depends on capital accumulation' (Thirlwall, 1987). Kaldor sought to express some of these ideas in the form of a technical progress function (Kaldor, 1957; Kaldor and Mirrlees, 1962), which relates the growth of productivity to growth of capital per worker. Its final formulation was described as giving

> explicit recognition to the fact that technical progress is infused into the economic system through the creation of new equipment, which depends on current (gross) investment expenditure. Hence the 'technical progress function' has been redefined so as to exhibit a relationship between the rate of change of gross (fixed) investment per operative and the rate of increase in labour productivity on *newly installed* equipment.

This line of argument would imply that the distinction between net investment and gross investment may be difficult to make in practice. A piece of new machinery can be introduced, which has the effect of replacing a previous piece of machinery in the sense that a similar product is made. But the production technique and/or the exact product produced may be different. Thus the extent to which the new machine replaces the old and the extent to which something new is involved would be difficult to determine. But on this view it is gross investment which is relevant in the sense that gross investment represents the sum of new machinery which is introduced.

Two important points arise out of this discussion. First, the pace of technical change could be expected to influence the volume of investment. Technical change opens up profitable opportunities for expansion (which would not be otherwise available). In the model presented in the previous chapter, the influence of technical change was included in a general way as an influence on the rate of investment which helped to determine the rate of growth and capacity utilisation. This would suggest that the rate of technical change would influence growth and capacity utilisation, an idea which is more fully explored below. Second, the implementation of technical change requires expenditure on investment, which itself depends on, as argued above, factors such as expectations of growth, profitability and confidence. Thus the general macroeconomic climate will through its effect on investment (especially gross investment) influence the effective rate of technical change. A faster pace of change will require more new capital equipment to implement the technical change, so that faster technical change relies on a higher rate of investment expenditure. When firms are reluctant to invest, then the actual pace of change will be slower than otherwise. New ideas and new products may be developed but not implemented through a lack of investment. There can be many new ideas for products and processes available (particularly for most countries who can draw on the ideas in use in the more technologically advanced countries) but their use in an economy still in practice depends on investment (which is discussed further in the next section).

12.7 THE NATURE OF TECHNICAL CHANGE

The changes which occur within the economy have many facets, though this section is devoted to those changes which fall under the heading of technical change. The discussion of technical change is limited to new products and new processes of production (whether those new products and processes represent minor or major changes over the previous ones). However, there are many other changes which to some degree accompany technical change and which are also important. The introduction of new products can have substantial impacts on the general lifestyle – an obvious example being the changes which have flowed from the invention of television. New processes of production may involve substantial changes in the organisation of work – an obvious example here being the implications of the introduction of mass-production techniques. There was some discussion on this point in Chapter 3. There are also a wide range of changes in ideas and attitudes of people as to how the economy works, and on the relationship between people and nature, etc. But these considerations would take us far afield, and the discussion is limited to the immediate impact of technical change involving new products and processes.

It is useful to make a number of distinctions within the broad category of technical change. The process of technical change has often been divided into invention and innovation or a roughly similar division into research and development. The basic distinction is between an invention which has been defined as 'an idea, a sketch or a model for a new or improved device, product, process or system' and 'an innovation in the economic sense [which] is accomplished only with the first *commercial* transaction involving the new product, process, system or device, although the word is used also to describe the whole process' (Freeman, 1982).

Thus, by definition, a successful innovation leads to a commercial application, and the development of an idea from the invention stage through to successful implementation is usually a costly and risky undertaking. Because innovation is the exploration of the unknown, the estimation of the costs and benefits involved is particularly difficult to make. Thus, firms may fall back on various 'rules of thumb' such as spend x per cent of sales revenue on research and development. In addition, 'there is a fundamental paradox in the determination of demand for information; its value for the purchaser is not known until he has the information; but then he has in effect acquired it without cost' (Arrow, 1962). For, as Kay (1984) argues, 'we need precise technical specifications of the R & D output as information to evaluate the R & D project; but such technical specifications are precisely the purpose of the project in the first place – if we had such blueprints, we would not need to conduct the R & D project'. Further, within a firm, some departments may favour research and development for reasons such as scientific prestige, the pursuit of knowledge for its own sake, or the fascination with a particular problem.

When research and development are undertaken by capitalist firms, it would be anticipated that they will be strongly influenced by considerations of profit. This will mean that the expectation of profit will be important for research and development, even though the expected profitability of research and development cannot be evaluated with much precision. Further, the direction which technical change takes will depend on these profit considerations. There will be times when a new discovery occurs which the firm had not been seeking, but generally firms will direct their research in directions which they believe will be profitable.

These remarks need to be modified to take account of other sources of invention. Research is undertaken in universities and other branches of higher education and in research institutes, and individual researchers motivated by curiosity rather than profit are still the source of some new ideas. The inventions from such research are usually available for implementation by the private sector. But so far as the profit-seeking firms are concerned these inventions occur exogenously, i.e. in ways which cannot be influenced by those firms. Further, it is often argued that basic research, which often has no apparent immediate application, will not be undertaken by profit-seeking firms as the pay-off from such research is subject to considerable uncertainty and time delay. But that basic research forms the basis of further advances in the future.

It is useful in the analysis of technical change to make the distinction between product and process innovation. The introduction of a new product by a firm poses a considerable threat to its competitors if the products of the competitors are thereby rendered obsolete. The demand facing the competitor firms would be dramatically reduced. The competitor firms would then be under considerable pressure to introduce their own new products to maintain their position in the market place. Indeed, competitor firms are likely to act to ensure that such a situation does not arise by undertaking their own research and development on new products. Thus the rivalry between firms will pressurise each firm into introducing new products and undertaking the necessary research.

The introduction of a new product may help stimulate the overall level of demand, although this would clearly depend on the nature of the new product. The initial introduction of television may help to stimulate demand, whereas the introduction of a slightly improved television when televisions are widely owned may have no impact on overall demand (even if it draws demand away from other television manufacturers). There is further discussion below on the impact on aggregate demand of the introduction of new products.

The introduction of a new process of production will often be undertaken to lower costs and increase profits, and in this case the firm introducing a process innovation would improve its cost and profit position (especially *vis-à-vis* their rivals). This does not immediately threaten the existence of their rivals, though there is a shift of profits towards the firm using the new process and away from its rivals. The innovating firm then has a greater pool of profits to finance investment (including research and development) and expansion and/or the potential to reduce prices to pressure its competitors. The pressure on competitors from process innovation still arises but operates over a longer time period than with product innovation.

It is also useful to make the distinction between cost-reduction and demand-creation effects of technical change, though in practice, any particular technical change is likely to involve elements of both demand creation and cost reduction. The stimulus of aggregate demand from technical change can arise through two routes. First, the introduction of a new product can stimulate consumer demand. It should be noted that this would not arise under the conventional theory of consumer demand (utility maximisation) unless one of two conditions were satisfied. If (some or all) consumers had reached satiation point with the existing products (i.e. do not wish to purchase more than the present level), then a new product would stimulate demand. Alternatively, a new product may lead consumers to have a stronger preference for consumption now over savings (and future consumption), again leading to an increase in aggregate demand. Indeed, following Schumpeter (1939), it can be argued that the introduction of new products is always at the initiative of the producers and not at the initiative of the consumers. Thus new products are introduced by firms to which consumers respond positively or negatively, but consumers are not in a position to propose that specific new products be introduced.

When a new product idea (e.g. television) is first introduced, it may initially face a relatively small demand, followed by a gradual build-up of demand, then a plateau or decline in demand. Hence the stimulating impact on aggregate demand from this product will eventually peter out. This can be seen by reference to the case of consumer durables. Consider a refrigerator as an example, and assume initially that there is an upper limit to the demand for refrigerators of one per household. The introduction of refrigerators leads to purchases of them, and the rate of purchase may increase as the idea of the benefits of a refrigerator becomes more widely accepted and income available to purchase them. However, after a time (perhaps many years), saturation point is approached, after which stage the demand for refrigerators falls close to replacement level. Improvements and design changes in refrigerators may shorten the life of existing refrigerators and raise replacement demand. But the general point remains that there would be an initial surge in demand which then flattens off.

The second aspect of demand-stimulating effects of technical change is the impact on investment expenditure (and this impact was included in the investment equation used in Chapter 11), and these effects on investment operate through two routes. The first one is that technical change opens up the prospects of higher profits, from a reduction in costs and from higher consumer demand, and the higher expected profits stimulate investment expenditure. The second route is the one discussed above, namely that the implementation of technical change requires investment.

The cost-reduction aspect of technical change does not only mean the production of existing products can be undertaken at a lower cost than previously. In practice, technical change which involves cost reduction is likely to involve other changes. The organisation of production is likely to change, and indeed as discussed above (section 2.6) technical change may be undertaken to enhance control of managers over labour. The relative demand for skilled and unskilled labour may also be changed. Firms incur costs to acquire or develop cost-reducing technical change and these costs are part of fixed costs. Technical change then alters the balance between variable (labour and material) costs and fixed (capital) costs and may also change the extent of economies of scale. The product being produced may be changed, which would make the measurement of cost reduction problematic. A crucial aspect of cost reduction is that employment of labour will usually be curtailed (per unit of output).[3] Thus the immediate impact of technical change, particularly the cost-reducing type, can be the creation of unemployment of labour. However, cost reduction may lead to price reduction and thereby increased demand, but that would depend on market conditions and degree of competition.

The implementation of cost-reducing innovation may require new equipment, and thereby in the short term there is a stimulus for investment. In turn this investment expenditure adds to aggregate demand, raising the level of economic activity and employment. There are, then, a variety of ways by which technical change affects the level of employment. The overall impact of technical change on employment will depend on the balance between the demand-creation aspects of technical change and the cost-reduction ones.

In the analysis of the process of technical change some authors have placed emphasis on the incremental nature of advances in knowledge. Each advance in knowledge builds on previous knowledge and represents only a small step forward, but the cumulative effects can be substantial. Another view places emphasis on the big step forward resulting from genius, by which a major new idea is developed. The further development of the 'big idea' requires many further smaller steps, but those subsequent steps can only take place after the major breakthrough has occurred. These two views on the advance of knowledge are not necessarily contradictory, and in particular the incremental advance of knowledge corresponds approximately to the practice of routine or normal science whilst the 'big idea' corresponds to paradigm shifts.

The incremental view is often associated with the idea that the process of technical change has now become a matter of routine, particularly for large companies. Each advance in knowledge is a small step forward, which prepares some of the ground for subsequent advances. However, the advance in knowledge often involves minor modifications to existing products or processes. Firms devote resources to research in much the same way that resources are devoted to other activities, and technical change is generated as a result.

One element of this incremental view of technical change is the notion of 'learning-by-doing'.[4] The basic argument, as indicated by the title, is that the proficiency with which a task is done improves the more the task is done. Better ways of performing the task, finding short-cuts and building up familiarity are among the reasons for this. The process of performing a task draws attention to difficulties and constraints, and people try to reduce the difficulties and overcome constraints. In doing so, further knowledge is gained which enables production to be undertaken at a lower cost or with less effort. Hence knowledge is gradually acquired, but the solution of one set of difficulties leads on to another set of difficulties. The idea of learning-by-doing can be applied to different groups (e.g. to an individual, to a firm) and at different levels (e.g. a simple task, a complex process). When an individual becomes more adept at a particular task (through learning-by-doing) then some of the knowledge which that individual has gained would be difficult to codify to pass on to others. But some of the knowledge can be passed on to others, and some of the learning-by-doing effects reside with the organisation rather than the individual.

It has been argued that many learning (or experience) effects can be summarised by an equation of the form log $UC = a + b$ log Q, where UC is the unit cost (of output produced to date) and Q the cumulative output with b expected to be negative. In this formulation, each successive proportionate increase of output has the same proportionate effect on unit cost. For example, a value of $b = -0.32$ indicates that for each doubling of output, unit costs decline by 20 per cent. This process of learning-by-doing and the speed with which improvements in productivity are spread and implemented can be quickened by the adoption of appropriate institutional arrangements. These could include specialist departments for the development and implementation of new ideas, or links between different departments to encourage transfer of information.

This general idea of gradual incremental technical change has been expressed as follows:

> The advance in scientific knowledge in physics cannot by itself secure the innumerable design improvements that result from the repeated application of particular engineering principles. The optimal design for the steam engine or the diesel engine or the sewing machine has only been achieved after many years or decades of experience. ... The gain in design through experience is even more important in the making of plant and equipment; hence the *annual* gain of productivity due to 'embodied technical progress' will tend to be all the greater the larger the number of plants constructed per year. (Kaldor, 1972)

An implication of the incremental view would appear to be that the pace of technical change will be reasonably constant since the overall pace of change is built on numerous small changes.

The notion of the relevance of the 'big idea' in the analysis of technical progress suggests that the rate of technical progress proceeds in fits and starts, and does not have the routine nature suggested by the incremental nature of knowledge approach discussed previously. However, a major breakthrough still requires implementation and also stimulates future developments. For example, the discovery of electricity would represent a major breakthrough, though such a discovery would stimulate many further small steps, and indeed may require those further steps before the discovery can be put into practical effect. There are some important implications arising from taking the 'big idea' view. First, major advances (e.g. electricity, steam as a means of propulsion, computers) lead to a wide variety of changes. To take the obvious example, the discovery of electricity provides the platform from which numerous uses of electricity are investigated and many types of electrical equipment are invented. New forms of entertainment were, for example, made possible (radio, television), and a whole range of activities become possible or a lot easier (e.g. preservation of food through refrigeration, heating). Second, the 'big idea' generates (as indicated) many further albeit small steps forward. Thus there is a stimulus to routine advances by opening up many new possibilities. Thus a 'big idea' stimulates the technological opportunities which can be followed up, and in the previous chapter this was represented by the variable T included in the investment equation. Third, big ideas occur relatively infrequently, and indeed would not really qualify as big ideas if they occurred regularly. The infrequency and more particularly the irregularity of new big ideas implies that the pace of technical change fluctuates considerably from era to era. When a new 'big idea' is first implemented, it has a significant impact on the economy, and that impact may gradually increase. The impact would include aggregate demand effects and changes in the organisation of production. However, the forces for change from the 'big idea' will gradually diminish. Growth and change which can be attributed to any particular big idea gradually die away. An important aspect of this argument, namely that there are long waves in economic activity with the higher levels of economic activity and growth being stimulated by the discovery and implementation of a 'big idea', is returned to below.

12.8 POST-KEYNESIAN PERSPECTIVE ON GROWTH AND TECHNICAL CHANGE

It can be readily observed that there are substantial differences in the growth experience of different countries. The explanation of those differences would constitute a major research programme. The objective of this section is more modest, namely to indicate the factors which a post-Keynesian perspective would suggest are important. It can also be observed that there are substantial variations in growth experience over time – for example, economic growth has generally been much lower in the period since 1973 than in the period 1950 to 1973. In the following section, discussion focuses on such variations of economic growth.

The previous sections have developed some of the basic concepts which underlie a post-Keynesian perspective on economic growth. In this section, we draw on the ideas of Kaldor[5] (but also see Cornwall, 1977, especially ch. 3) to provide a post-Keynesian treatment of growth. Three general ideas are given prominence, namely the relative roles of demand and supply and the interaction between them in the determination of the rate of growth; the nature of the technical conditions of production (e.g. whether there are increasing or decreasing returns to scale); and dynamic differences between major sectors of the economy (e.g. as between agriculture and manufacturing industries).

A major question in macroeconomics has been whether the level of economic activity (including the level of employment) is mainly determined on the supply side or the demand side. In the last chapter, it was seen that the Keynesian tradition has stressed the role of the level of aggregate demand in the determination of employment, etc., whereas the neo-classical tradition (and Say's law) has focused on the role of the supply side. A rather similar question arises in the context of economic growth and development. The neo-classical theory of growth (starting from Solow, 1956) would see economic growth as essentially determined by the growth of supply (to which the growth of demand adjusts) so that the rate of economic growth is given by the sum of the rate of growth of the labour force and of technical progress, where the growth rates of both labour and technical progress are essentially exogenously given. Further, the capital stock grows (in steady state) at the same rate as the labour force. There is no independent investment function, and the growth of savings is assumed to be matched by a growth of investment. At any point in time, production is undertaken subject to constant returns to scale; and over time technical change occurs like 'manna from heaven' (i.e. technical change is costless and proceeds at a constant rate). There are no essential differences between sectors of the economy, and equilibrium analysis requires that each sector grows at the same pace. In sum, the rate of economic growth is seen as determined by supply factors, and although the growth of demand is not usually explicitly mentioned this is assumed to passively adjust to support the growth of supply.

A post-Keynesian perspective does not make the sharp distinction between the forces of demand and those of supply which neoclassical economics makes, and see supply and demand as intertwined. However, there are (at least) two ways in which the post-Keynesian perspective could be said to stress demand factors rather than supply factors in the determination of the rate of economic growth. First, extending the idea that the employment of labour is demand-determined rather than supply-determined, the growth of employment is seen as strongly influenced by demand. It was seen above that unemployment and underemployment of labour were viewed as the norm. In particular, (as argued later in this section) dynamic sectors of the economy can draw on labour from the static sectors, so that growth in the dynamic sectors is not constrained by the supply of labour. Cornwall (1977) seeks 'to determine whether differences in employment patterns in the postwar period were primarily the result of demand or supply forces'. He concludes that

> for all practical purposes employment patterns were demand-determined in the various market economies in the postwar period. It is undoubtedly true that the supply of labour available for manufacturing was more elastic in some countries than others. But the evidence, however limited, consistently suggested that, when entrepreneurs in the manufacturing sectors of the different economies wanted labor, they found it one way or another. If not enough was available in the agricultural sector, then additional amounts were found by allocating a high proportion of, say, school-leavers or members of the secondary labor force to manufacturing and economising on what was allocated to the different service sectors.

Second, the growth of the capital stock depends on investment expenditure, which depends on profit and growth expectations, etc. There is no guarantee that the level of investment required to provide full employment will occur, as investment depends on factors such as expectations and availability of finance. However, a growth of demand will help to stimulate investment (as indicated above) and thereby the growth of the stock of capital equipment. Thus the growth of demand will help to stimulate the growth of supply, though there is no guarantee that supply will match demand.

In a Keynesian approach, aggregate demand is often split into the two components of endogenous or induced demand and of exogenous or autonomous demand. The general idea is that induced demand is a rather passive element of demand, and its level depends on the level of income. In the simplest Keynesian model, consumer expenditure depends on the level of income, and is an example of induced demand. In contrast, autonomous demand is not influenced by the level of income and is an active element of demand. Whereas induced demand depends on the level of income, the level of autonomous demand determines the level of income. At the level of the domestic economy, it can be argued that consumer expenditure, investment and government expenditure are largely induced demand, whereas exports constitute autonomous demand. In such a case, the growth of export demand would be the driving force behind the growth of demand and thereby of national income. A model which incorporates that idea is explored in the next chapter.

The importance of demand over supply does not mean that supply is unimportant, but rather that supply is generally able to adjust to demand. A high pressure of demand for output is seen to generate high demand for labour, which (as indicated above) can often be met by attracting workers from the countryside, out of the home and from other countries. Further, investment is encouraged by high demand and profits, and that eventually adds to the productive potential of the economy. It will also be argued below that a faster rate of growth of demand will stimulate a faster rate of technical change. But there is no automatic process by which demand is translated into supply. There are many ways by which there can be supply-side failures. For example, firms may fail to perceive the opportunities which are available. The financial system may fail to provide funds to enable investment to occur. In other words, the growth of demand provides the opportunities for growth of supply, but the growth of supply may not be forthcoming.

The post-Keynesian approach incorporates a dual economy approach (for further discussion see Cornwall, 1977, ch. 4; as well as later in this section), which can be contrasted with a neo–classical approach. In a neo–classical approach, any change in the composition of demand would provoke a change in relative prices and a supply adjustment; and also any change in the composition of supply would generate a relative price change and then a demand adjustment. In contrast, a post-Keynesian approach would stress the importance of demand and of quantity adjustment. An example of this will be given below when the relationship between agriculture and manufacture is discussed.

The technical conditions governing production are now considered, and these conditions have a number of dimensions. First, it is generally assumed that there are increasing returns to scale in many sectors of the economy, notably manufacturing. Second, the rate of technical progress is influenced by the actions of firms (e.g. by the rate of investment), and by the rate of growth (e.g. through learning-by-doing) so that in general it is endogenous rather than exogenous.

Kaldor along with many others argued that

> on an empirical level, nobody doubts that in any economic activity which involves the processing transformation of basic materials – in other words, in industry – increasing returns dominate the picture for the very reasons given by Adam Smith in the first chapter of the *Wealth of Nations:* reasons that are fundamental to the nature of technological processes and not to any particular technology. (Kaldor, 1972)

This argument can be backed up with an appeal to empirical evidence (e.g. Pratten, 1971), and also to some general arguments, which suggest a number of sources of decreasing costs, of which three are mentioned here. First, there is the 'principle of bulk transactions', which is that the costs associated with a purchase or sale do not rise proportionately with the scale of the transaction. Second, there are gains from specialisation and the division of labour. The relevance of gains from specialisation and division of labour here is the implication which the division of labour has for costs. The general consideration is that increasing division of labour leads to lower unit costs, and that the division of labour is enhanced by the scale of production. Hence unit costs decline with scale of production. But, further, these decreasing costs may operate not only at the level of the firm but also at the industry and economy level. For example, as an industry expands, specialist suppliers emerge who can themselves benefit from division of labour. The idea of learning-by-doing, discussed above, suggests that the rate of increase of output helps to generate productivity advances. The third source of decreasing unit costs arises from the relationship between area and volume. It can be argued that for many productive processes, the throughput depends on the volume of the pipes, tanks, etc., whilst the costs of the material used to make the pipes, tanks, etc., depends on the area of material used.

Neo-classical economics relies heavily on the idea that decreasing returns to scale set in at relatively small levels of output. Perfect competition is only viable under such conditions, for the existence of increasing returns would mean that any firm which for whatever reason is larger than others would have a cost advantage, which would generate higher profits and enable it to expand and reap further cost advantages. Pricing according to marginal costs would lead to losses since marginal costs would be below average costs under increasing returns to scale. Payment of factors according to marginal productivity would lead to over-exhaustion of the available product. However, the radical political economy approach is not constrained to have to assume constant or decreasing returns to scale, and indeed generally assumes (outside the primary sector) that production is undertaken subject to constant or decreasing costs. The term 'constant or decreasing costs' is used in preference to 'constant or increasing returns to scale' because the term 'returns to scale' is often taken to refer to situations where there is a proportionate increase in all inputs. But in reality such a proportionate increase (or decrease) rarely occurs; as the scale of production is changed, so does the proportion in which inputs are used and the nature of the inputs themselves. For example, the amount of capital equipment in use may double but this may involve twice as much use of the original type of equipment or it may involve different types of machinery being used which are appropriate to the larger scale of production.

A fast growth of demand, which is translated into a fast growth of supply, is seen to bring a rapid growth of productivity. This is viewed as applying particularly to the manufacturing sector, where 'the faster the rate of growth of manufacturing output, the faster will be the rate of growth of labour productivity in manufacturing owing to static and dynamic economies of scale, or increasing returns in the widest sense' (Thirlwall, 1983). Cornwall (1977) summarises this line of thought in the following manner:

> A dynamic economy of scale refers to a more or less continuous reduction in unit costs (and continuous increase in productivity) owing to continuous increases in the output of a firm, industry or economy over time. These economies are often described as learning

economies in that they are a function of cumulative output increases or cumulative gross investment and thus are partly a function of time itself. A well-known model used to test for the existence of economies of scale has come to be known as 'Verdoorn's Law'. The emphasis in this approach is on the importance of the rate of growth of output in determining the rate of growth of productivity, rather than the level of output determining the level of average productivity

A formal model incorporating Verdoorn's law (that the rate of growth of productivity depends on the rate of growth of output) is investigated in the next chapter.

The anticipation of growth of demand and of profits leads firms to increase investment and to hire more labour. The capital equipment thereby acquired will implement the most recent technology which will incorporate a higher level of productivity than available from the older technology. The more new capital equipment installed, the faster will be the growth of productivity. As argued above, the implementation of technological change requires new investment, and that investment only occurs under the stimulus of growing demand. When there is surplus labour elsewhere in the economy, firms find no particular difficulties in recruiting labour. Hence on the supply side, the inputs of capital equipment and labour (and also of any produced intermediate inputs) grow under the stimulus of growth of demand. Firms in the process of growing benefit from being able to reap further economies of scale and from learning-by-doing.

The final theme of the post-Keynesian perspective which we examine concerns the differences between the sectors of the economy. This is undertaken in two stages – by first looking at the relative importance of different sectors of the economy, and then at the differences of conditions of production.

The process of economic development can be portrayed in terms of changes in the relative importance of the primary sector (agriculture, mining), the secondary sector (manufacturing, energy, construction) and the tertiary sector (distribution and services). Economic development has been seen to be associated with a decline in the relative importance of the primary sector. Maddison (1982) states that 'in 1870 agriculture occupied half of the population of these sixteen non industrialised countries; in 1979, only 7.5 per cent'. There is generally a corresponding decline in the relative importance of the primary sector in terms of output. The initial stages of economic development are characterised by the process of industrialisation and the growth of the secondary sector. Employment and output of the secondary sector grows rapidly, but eventually the relative importance of the secondary sector levels out. Indeed, in the past twenty or thirty years, in a number of countries, the employment share of the secondary sector has begun to decline, and there has been much talk of the process of de-industrialisation. However, since labour productivity growth in the secondary sector tends to be faster than elsewhere, the employment decline is not necessarily matched by a decline in the relative importance of the output of the secondary sectors. The tertiary sector covers a wide range of activities under the heading of services and distribution. Some forms of employment in the tertiary sector tend to decline with economic development (e.g. domestic service), but many other forms of employment tend to increase (e.g. teachers, doctors). However, the evidence indicates a growth of the tertiary sector (especially in terms of employment), so that 'service employment now predominates, representing well over half of total employment' (Maddison, 1982).

The relationship between secondary sector (sometimes referred to below as the industrial sector) and the agricultural sector (which is an important part of the primary sectors) can be portrayed in terms of two historical phases. The initial phase (which still pertains in some countries) is where the agricultural sector is the dominant user of labour and the industrial sector is small and undeveloped. At this stage the agricultural sector is organsied on traditional lines, with heavy involvement of family labour, and productivity and growth are low. Production is largely undertaken to provide the means of subsistence for the (probably extended) family, with little production undertaken for sale to others and the available labour is not fully utilised. At this stage there is excess labour involved in the agricultural sector in the sense that a reduction in the labour force involved would not lead to a reduction in output, with those remaining in the agricultural sector working longer hours than before. The growth of industrial employment draws labour away from the agricultural sector (and also generally involves a shift from rural to urban living). Productivity is then enhanced by a shift from a low-productivity sector to a high-productivity one, and a rise in productivity in the agricultural sector (as employment declines). This rise in productivity is in terms of output per person involved in agriculture; those remaining in agriculture are likely to work longer hours to make up for those who have left agriculture. It is notable that much of the raising of productivity growth in agriculture at this stage comes from the reduction of employment and the reorganisation of production, rather than from technical progress.

At this stage of development, the agricultural sector has surplus labour, and the industrial sector can draw labour away from agriculture with little impact on agricultural production. The industrial sector is then not constrained by labour supply, since people move from agriculture to the industrial sector as employment becomes available in the industrial sector. Higher wages and employment prospects in the industrial sector may be sufficient to draw labour away from agriculture, though the conditions of work and living in the industrial sector and in the cities may still be poor. However, the development of the industrial sector can be constrained by the agricultural sector in the following way. Workers in industrial sectors need to be fed, so that the agricultural sector must be capable of producing a surplus of food over and above that required to feed the workers in agriculture. This surplus requires a relatively high level of productivity so that agricultural workers are able to produce more than they themselves need. But equally, the industrial sector can only develop when there is a demand for its production.

The second phase for agriculture (as displayed in a number of industrialised countries) occurs when agriculture is itself a high-productivity growth sector organised along capitalist lines similar to those in the industrial sector; in other words, when farming is organised along capitalist lines and able to implement technical change. At this stage, agriculture is capital-intensive with the use of much technically advanced equipment and the use of chemical fertilisers, etc. (which are themselves technical developments coming from the industrial sector). Surplus labour has been fully extracted from agriculture in the sense that output per person would not be further increased by labour leaving agriculture. However, technical change will lead to productivity growth, and a relatively slow growth in the demand for agricultural goods would lead to declining employment in agriculture. At this stage, manufacturing growth may become constrained by the availability of labour since further labour cannot easily be released from agriculture, and productivity levels in manufacturing and agriculture are comparable. However, labour has, when required, generally still been available from the household, by immigration and from the service sector.

The changing importance of the different sectors could be seen to be of some interest in describing the process of economic development, and may provide some guidance to currently Third World countries on the route to development. But some would see little significance for economic analysis. Over time, changes in the allocation of resources would take place, and in particular workers would have to move between industries, which may involve moving geographically as well. There will be some (temporary) unemployment as this allocation does not take place instantaneously; the extent of this unemployment will depend on the efficiency of the market mechanism and the extent of government intervention. However, the post-Keynesian view is that there are significant differences between the sectors in terms of their possibilities for growth, and it is to this aspect which we now turn.

Growth of the primary sectors is limited by the availability of natural resources (e.g. fertile land, fossil fuel). Although previously unutilised resources can be brought into use, these will often be of a lower quality (e.g. less fertile land, fossil fuels which are more difficult to obtain). Thus growth would involve higher unit costs and consequently higher prices. The features of the primary sectors are that production may be difficult to expand (because vital natural resources cannot be reproduced), and any expansion of output involves increasing unit costs. Further, there may be limited opportunities for technical progress to raise productivity. The evidence on the movements of the prices of primary products relative to those of manufactured products is discussed in the next chapter.

In contrast, the secondary sectors are not limited by natural resource availability, and the resources which it uses (e.g. machinery) can be readily supplemented. The expansion of production can at worst be achieved at approximately constant costs since the expansion of production can usually be achieved through duplication. That is to say, in order to double production a firm can exactly duplicate its current activities, although it may find better ways of doubling output and there may be additional costs of co-ordinating production in two factories. Further, the secondary sectors are particularly suitable for technological advance, and hence relatively rapid growth of labour productivity. Finally, the tertiary sector is labour-intensive and generally seen as having limited possibilities of productivity growth. In both the primary and tertiary sectors, productivity growth may rely on the secondary sector. For example, the application of fertilisers in agriculture to raise crop yields draws on the production of fertilisers by the manufacturing sector. This line of argument means that the growth of productivity in an economy depends on the balance between the three sectors. Thus, when an economy reaches a stage where the demand for manufactured goods tends to decline (relatively) and the demand for the output of the tertiary sector to increase, the economy will be faced with a slower growth of productivity. The implicit assumption is that the tertiary sector is unable to match the productivity record of the secondary sector.

This general line of argument has led some authors (notably Kaldor and Cornwall) to describe manufacturing as 'the engine of growth'. The manufacturing sector produces a substantial proportion of final demand.

> But in addition, a large part of the manufacturing sector is made up of industries that comprise [what could be termed] the technology sector. The technology sector develops inventions and innovations whose effects are later diffused throughout the entire economy. ...
> As a result, the manufacturing sector takes on importance as the sector propelling the rest of the economy not only because of the large number of backward linkages in the traditional input–output sense. (Cornwall, 1977)

This argument of Cornwall is rather similar to the first proposition of Kaldor's approach (see Thirlwall, 1983, 1987), namely that

> the faster the rate of growth of the manufacturing sector of an economy the faster will be the rate of growth of total output (GDP), not simply in a definitional sense that manufacturing output is a large component of total output, but for fundamental economic reasons connected with induced productivity growth inside and outside manufacturing. (Thirlwall, 1987)

Much of this discussion has proceeded as though an economy was operating in isolation from the rest of the world. The relationship in general terms between economies at different stages of economic development is discussed in the next chapter. To round off the present discussion, brief consideration is given to the differences in the technologies which different economies employ. These differences in technology would appear to mean that there can be opportunities for countries to import technology from the currently most advanced country or countries. For convenience the discussion here will be in terms of a single most advanced country, although in practice, which country is the leader may vary between industries. For most of this century, the USA has been the most advanced country in almost all industries, but this is no longer the case, with Japan being a leader in many industries. There may be restrictions on the import of technology and conditions attached to its transfer.

Suppose country A is technically advanced and country B relatively backward. It would be expected that the potential for technical advance would be greater for country B than for country A. The latter would only be able to advance by pushing back the technological frontier, whereas the former may to some degree by able to adopt ideas from country A. There may be many limitations on this process (e.g. the social arrangements in country B may not be conducive to new ideas). At a minimum, knowledge that something is possible would point the most likely directions for technical advance. But there are a variety of ways by which technology is transferred between economies. In effect, multinational enterprises transfer knowledge from one country to another when they apply ideas already tried and tested in one country in another country. There are also often possibilities of the purchase or licensing of technology by one country from another.

At the end of the Second World War, a considerable technological gap was generally considered to exist between the USA and the rest of the industrialised world. Measured in terms of GDP per person-hour, using figures from Maddison (1982, Table 5.2), in 1950 the average level of productivity in fifteen industrialised countries was 46 per cent of the US level, ranging from 14 per cent of the American level in Japan to 78 per cent in Canada. Western European countries in this group were operating at between 30 and 56 per cent of the American level. By 1973 for this group of countries the productivity gap had shrunk considerably so that productivity in the countries other than the USA was, on average, 69 per cent of the American level (and there was a further rise to 75 per cent by 1979). Throughout the long post-war boom (up to 1973) productivity grew noticeably faster in most of these industrialised countries (Australia and to a lesser extent the United Kingdom and Canada being the exceptions) than in the United States. For a variety of reasons the post-war period was particularly conducive to the transfer of technology, etc., from the USA to this particular group of countries. The closing of the productivity gap would suggest that for this group of countries future growth of productivity will be more difficult than it was prior to 1973. It is also the case that the growth of productivity in the USA itself slowed considerably after 1968.

The existence of a technological gap does not mean that a relatively technologically backward economy will necessarily catch up with the more advanced country. There are clearly many counter-examples to that proposition in the real world. Whilst a range of countries (e.g. many of the European Community countries, Japan) have during the post-war period closed much of the technological gap between the USA and themselves, there are many other countries which have not closed any of the gap. However, it can be argued that the most technologically advanced country at any particular time bears much of the costs of pushing back the technological frontier. Other countries can to some degree free-ride on the progress made by the technologically advanced country. However, the importing of technology is likely to require investment so that the technology is embodied in the requisite manner. Further, the economic, social and political organisation of the economy has to be conducive to technical change.

These arguments would appear to suggest that a relatively backward country could close the technological gap by adapting the latest technology provided that it can make sufficient investment and adopt the required forms of organisation. In the next chapter, some arguments which point in the opposite direction are considered, but they can be briefly mentioned here. There may be forces of cumulative causation which enable the originally more advanced countries to maintain or extend their technological and other advantages. Multinational enterprises, one of the routes by which technology is transferred, are likely to favour certain types of countries for the location of their operations. It would appear plausible that multinational enterprises will prefer countries where trade unions are weak, and where right-of-centre governments are entrenched (thereby reducing the threat of nationalisation or of restrictions on repatriation of profits). Finally, there may be forces at work which condemn relatively backward countries to remain in that position, and these are further examined below (section 13.5).

12.9 THE PACE OF TECHNICAL CHANGE AND LONG WAVES IN ECONOMIC ACTIVITY

Capitalist economies generally exhibit cycles of economic activity. The existence of business cycles with a length of the order of a few years has been widely recognised and has generated a literature seeking to explain them.[6] In the pre-war period, these cycles appeared to be of the order of eight years, but in the post-war period have tended to be more like four years in length. However Schumpeter (1939) argued for three types of business cycles. The shortest cycles were seen as averaging forty months in length, with further cycles having an average length of around eight to nine years. The longest cycles to which Schumpeter pointed were much longer ones of the order of forty to sixty years in duration. In this section, the focus is on the possibility of long waves in economic activity. It will be seen that the major concern is not so much with whether there is regular pattern of long waves, but rather with the view that different periods of time are distinguished by quite different levels of economic activity and growth.

The idea of long waves in economic activity is usually associated with the name of Kondratiev (1926),[7] who concluded that there had been three long waves in the industrial capitalist era. The first long wave started in 1780s/1790s reaching a peak in 1810/17 and its nadir in 1844/51. The second long wave peaked in 1870/5 and bottomed out in 1890/96. The third long wave, which was incomplete when Kondratiev was writing, had peaked in 1914/20. Schumpeter (1939) provided a rather similar dating and also labelled the waves. The first one, labelled the industrial revolution long wave, was associated with the rise of cotton textiles, iron and steam power, and was seen as covering the period 1787 to 1842. The second wave, labelled the bourgeois Kondratiev, lasted from 1843 to 1897, and was associated with the spread of the railways. The third, labelled the neoMercantilist, began in 1898 and was continuing when Schumpeter was writing; the key products of this wave were electricity, cars and chemicals.[8] This dating fitted with the prolonged recession of the 1930s as part of the downswing of the third long cycle. However, much of Kondratiev's data were price or price-related statistics rather than economic activity measures such as output and employment. It has often been assumed that prices and output both move together so that a cycle in a price variable would reflect a similar cycle in output variables, but the association may not be a close one. Further, the association is based on a competitive theory under which a high level of demand promotes a high level of output and rising prices, and that theory may prove unacceptable. It should finally be mentioned that there has been a continuing debate on the precise dating of the long waves (for further discussion see Maddison, 1982, pp. 67–73).

The questions which arise from the idea of long cycles (sometimes called Kondratiev cycles) are seen has as three-fold. First, there are statistical questions, such as which variables (e.g. prices, output, employment) relating to which countries should be used to try to identify the long waves. These problems are not insignificant but fall outside the province of this book. However, it should be noted that descriptions of these long cycles talk generally of economic activity usually without further precision. It would be expected that output and employment will move roughly together (especially over the long waves), but prices may not move in sympathy with output. The cycles relate to the developed capitalist world, and not only does the membership of that 'club' have to be identified, but the membership has expanded over time.

Second, provided that some long cycles can be observed, the question is where these are sufficiently regular to warrant a general expectation, rather than a specific explanation for each cycle. Since economic activity (however defined) varies from year to year, some apparent cycles could be generated by random movements. Thus there is the question of whether the discovery of a cycle in the statistics means that there is an underlying cycle or merely the observation of a random process. It has generally been felt that short cycles share sufficient common characteristics to warrant the search for a general explanation even if each cycle has some unique features. But in the case of long cycles at most four can be identified, so that there is plenty of room for debate as to whether they are sufficiently similar and whether explanations should be sought for cycles extending over two centuries. Some (e.g. Maddison, 1982) have used the term 'phases of capitalist development' to avoid the suggestion of regularity. Further, the use of a term such as cycle tends to imply not only regularity but also a uniformity whereby the upswing and downswing are of the same length (and Mandel, 1980, argues that the upswing tends to be about twice as long as the downswing).

Third, there are questions as to whether there are automatic forces which bring about recovery and limit expansion or whether the events occur by chance. As will be seen below, much emphasis is placed on major innovations. Some would argue that depression stimulates the search for new innovations, which thereby eventually bring about recovery (Mensch, 1979), and this argument is considered below. Others would argue that important new innovations which trigger off an economic recovery arise largely by chance, and each revival has its own peculiar explanation.

Many explanations have been advanced for fluctuations in economic activity, whether considered over a short period or over a long one. For example, in economies dominated by agriculture, the weather conditions are likely to play an important role which may generate year-to-year fluctuations and also longer movements if weather conditions move in long cycles. Others have pointed to specific happenings which stimulate or depress economic activity. As an example, consider the impact of the First World War. The build-up of military expenditure stimulated economic activity, and the ending of the war was followed by a short-lived post-war boom and inflation, and then by a widespread slump. The war also led to many important political changes, as the boundaries of nations and the power relationships between nations changed. All these events (as well as many others) have important economic impacts. Our discussion is limited to theories relevant to industrialised economies (in which factors like the weather and land availability are seen as of minor significance) and to systematic rather than exogenous or random factors.

Crucial inventions or discoveries do not occur frequently or regularly, and they bring many subsequent changes in their wake. Technical change will usually introduce new ways of production, generally involving lower costs and less employment of labour. It is likely to require different modes of work organisation (cf. section 3.6), and this will take time to recognise and organise. Further, technical change often involves new products which can help to stimulate the level of demand, and this would aid economic recovery.

The particular mechanism for the generation of waves, if not regular cycles, arises in this view from the process of technical change.[9] The proposition outlined here is based on Schumpeter (1939, chs 3 and 4). The process works roughly as follows. A seminal idea is discovered or invented (take as an example Watt's observation of the power of steam to raise a kettle lid).[10] At the time, the significance of the idea may not be realised and surely the future development of the idea can at most be only vaguely guessed at. After a time (which may stretch to many years), the significance of the discovery is realised, and steps are taken to build upon the idea. Ways have to be discovered on putting the idea into practice. In the example of steam, the significance of steam as a means of power had to be realised, and then steam engines developed as well as uses for such engines perceived. In the process problems arise which have to be resolved. Indeed this subsequent step will require the identification of uses for the new idea and the resources to overcome the problems in implementation. These applications generate (or unleash) new demands (e.g. rail travel) and also an investment boom (the building of the railways). The investment boom through the familiar multiplier process generates other demands. But eventually (and this may be measured in decades) the investment boom peters out (e.g. railways cover the country). The major new idea has many ramifications which it takes many years to realise. But eventually, the impact of that important new idea runs its course and in effect becomes virtually exhausted.

This process is by no means automatic. The original idea may occur by chance, but it requires that the knowledge of that idea be spread and that some people realise the significance of the idea. It may take years before the full significance is appreciated. The idea may require further development, and there may be a further range of technical problems to overcome before it can be put into effect. Many factors such as the availability of finance, the state of confidence, the degree of competition are likely to influence the speed with which an idea is adopted.

Schumpeter's argument rests on at least two propositions. First, there is the importance of the 'big idea' in the advance of knowledge, though this has to be followed by the implementation of that idea through many small steps. Second, the predominant effect of technical change is seen as demand creation. But the other side of much technical change is that it is cost reducing and labour replacing. To revert back to the steam engine example, it may help to create demand (and investment in the new steam-driven machinery). But the machinery may be instrumental in reducing the labour required to produce a given level of output. The demand creation of technical change (i.e. the introduction of new products for which there has been a latent demand, the investment stimulation) has to be counterbalanced against the labour-replacement aspect.

The long waves or phases of development which have been observed may have occurred largely by the effect of random (exogenous) factors in terms of economic analysis (though such factors may be explicable in terms of, say, political factors). For example, the end of the inter-war depression and the stimulation of the long post-war boom may have been due to the occurrence of the Second World War. At one level of economic analysis, the outbreak of war could be taken as an exogenous event for which an explanation from economic analysis is not sought, and hence within the context of the analysis occurs by chance. But at another level an explanation of the outbreak of war can be sought (drawing on, say, social and political factors as well as economic ones).

The regularity of the long waves is debatable, in part because there are at most four waves to be explored. There are many other important events (notably two world wars) which effect the level of economic activity, and more importantly here the pace of economic development. For example, war effort stimulates particular forms of research which may have substantial consequences for technical progress (e.g. the development of atomic and nuclear power was largely undertaken for military purposes during the Second World War; whether such developments represent progress is of course hotly disputed).

The analysis of Mensch (1979) has two elements of interest here. First, he argues that 'basic innovations occur in clusters'. He argues that

> the popular opinion that technical progress takes place during modern times in a continuous fashion (the continuity hypothesis) is inconsistent with reality. ... The changing tides, the ebb and flow of the stream of basic innovation explain economic change, that is, the difference in drive in growth and stagnation periods.

Thus booms occur following a spurt of new ideas, and conversely slumps follow a slow-down in new ideas ('technological stalemate'). Second, there are forces at work during the slump which stimulate the new ideas to underpin the next boom.

> The lack of basic innovations is clearly visible on the eve of every world economic crisis; it was apparent in the years before 1825,

before 1873, and before 1929. Then, under the pressure of those crises with the help of the government, the economy implemented a massive swell of basic innovations (new consumer goods, means of transportation, materials, and production processes) from which a number of new industries were created.

The arguments of Mensch have been challenged on two fronts. First, he presented evidence which suggested that during the 1930s (identified as a period of depression in terms of a long wave of economic activity), there was a faster rate of discovery of 'big' new ideas (than at other times) and that this was a result not of chance but of deliberate efforts by firms. A number of authors have challenged this evidence (e.g. Freeman, Clark and Soete, 1982; Solomou, 1986; van Duijn, 1983a,b).[11] Second, an alternative argument is that periods of economic depression with the associated lack of confidence, low levels of income, profits and demand are not conducive to undertaking risky activities such as research and development. Instead it could be argued that the signs of recovery would be more conducive to research and development. Thus the expectation of recovery stimulates research and investment, which helps to aid the recovery. However, that leads to the prior question of how the recovery occurs without the stimulus of new ideas and related investment. In the specific context of the 1930s there was a partial recovery in the second half of that decade, some of which may be ascribed to government expenditure on rearmament and some to replacement investment.

The interest in such long waves has revived recently associated with the suggestion that long post-war boom from roughly 1945 to 1973 was the upswing of such a cycle and the period since 1973 part of the subsequent downswing (as indicated above). It should be noted that according to the technical progress explanation of long waves outlined below, the downswing is a result of a slow-down in technical change. Thus the recession is seen as a consequence of slower technical change rather than the popular perception of more rapid change. However, the nature of technical developments may have changed, and become less demand-stimulating and most cost-reducing, which as argued above would mean the creation of unemployment as little extra demand is created but employment is reduced through the implementation of cost-reducing technical change. One way by which firms could confront labour is to seek to replace labour by machines, and thus direct efforts towards finding production techniques which are labour-replacing and cost-reducing.

The policy implications of the long-wave theories can now be briefly examined. The model examined in the previous chapter suggested that the pace of technical change, through its impact on investment and aggregate demand, could have a substantial impact on the levels of economic activity and employment. When the pace of technical change is relatively rapid with a high level of investment, then there may be little need for stimulating public expenditure. However, when the pace of technical change is relatively slow, full-capacity working and high level of employment may require a large government budget deficit (to offset the excess of private savings over private investment). But in such circumstances, the government may be unwilling or unable to run a large deficit (with consequent rising national debt and interest payments). Thus, government fiscal and monetary policies may be of limited relevance in setting the level of economic activity. If the analysis of Mensch is correct, then the role of government is largely limited to stimulating research and development; in particular, the government could support basic research from which it is hoped new 'big' ideas would arise. The public support of basic research would be reinforced by the long-term, risky nature of such expenditure and the widespread benefits arising which many have argued limit private involvement. However, if it is the sight of recovery that stimulates research and development, then there would be a further role for expansionary fiscal and monetary policy, which would not only expand economic activity but also stimulate technical change and encourage future expansion.

12.10 OTHER VIEWS ON LONG WAVES AND THEIR GENERATION

Mandel argues that

> the existence of these long waves in capitalist development can hardly be denied in the light of overwhelming evidence. All statistical data available clearly indicate that if we take as key indicators the growth of industrial output and the growth of world exports (of the world market), the periods 1826–1847, 1848–73, 1874–93, 1894–1913, 1914–

1939, 1940(48)–1967, and 1968–? are marked by striking fluctuations in these average rates of growth, with ups and downs between successive long waves ranging from 50 to 100 per cent. (Mandel, 1980; also see Mandel, 1975)

However, Mandel differs from many other writers in a number of key respects. First, he adopts a specifically Marxian approach, and argues that 'in reality, any Marxist theory of the long waves of capitalist development can only be an accumulation-of-capital theory or, if one wants to express the same idea in a different form, a *rate of profit theory*'.[12] Second, each long wave is different in basic ways from others, and the specific circumstances of each cycle needs to be examined. Long waves

> represent historical realities, segments of the overall history of the capitalist mode of production that have definitely distinguishable features. For that very same reason, they are of irregular duration. The Marxist explanation of these long waves, with its peculiar inter-weaving of internal economic factors, exogenous 'environmental' changes, and their mediation through sociopolitical developments (i.e. periodic changes in the overall balance of class forces and intercapitalist relationship of forces, the outcomes of momentous class struggles and of wars) gives this historical reality of the long wave an 'integrated' character. (Mandel, 1980)

Third, the discussion of long waves needs to be more extensive than solely to focus on the process of technical change and its effects. This is not to say that such change is not an important element. But, it is the impact of technical change on the rate of profit and thereby on the actions of capitalists which is important. There are further effects on factors such as the strength and actions of the working class which will also influence the workings of the long wave.

> The working class generally enters a long wave bearing the scars of long-term unemployment during the preceding period (reduced bargaining power and, in many cases, shaken self-confidence), so that it will not use the expansionist conditions (at least immediately) to catch up with the lowering of *relative* wages that had been one of the triggering factors for the upsurge in the rate of profit.

Thus in the early stages of an upswing of a long wave, workers are in a relatively weak position, which permits buoyant profits, and these profits may encourage firms to expand, etc., promoting the continuation of the upswing. Further, 'the general expansionist climate attracts huge migrations of underemployed labor and impoverished petty commodity producers from the periphery of industrial capitalism to the metropolitan centers' (Mandel, 1980).

Fourth, the long waves have broader effects than solely economic ones, for 'we can note a similar correspondence between the turn from one long wave to another, on the one hand, and the general ideological climate, by no means limited to economics on the other hand' (Mandel, 1980). Then, periods of economic prosperity will tend to generate (as for example happened in the 1950s) a socio-political climate favourable to capitalism, whereas periods of depression may have the reverse effect (as happened to some degree during the 1930s).[13]

Mandel predicted the end of the post-war boom (Mandel, 1964), at a time when virtually all economists accepted the view that Keynesian economics and other changes could ensure permanent high levels of employment and growth. He predicted the probable turning point around the late 1960s. Whilst 1973 is often seen as the watershed year, there are arguments that 1968/69 was the turning point marking the end of the long post-war boom, though to some extent masked by the temporary upswing of 1972.

The significance of this and the previous section is to stress that capitalism does not evolve in a smooth manner, and that there are substantial differences of economic experience between different eras. The recent experience provides a convenient example of this. The income of the OECD areas as a whole grew at an average annual rate of 4.5 per cent in the twenty years up to 1973 and the European economies averaged 4.8 per cent growth of income over the same period. In the period 1973 to 1987, these growth rates declined to 2.0 per cent and 2.1 per cent respectively.

The unevenness of growth and development in a capitalist economy over time is matched by an unevenness between different geographical areas (e.g. regions, nations), and this leads into the subject matter of the next chapter.

NOTES

1. The emphasis in the approaches to investment discussed here is on the role of economic activity specifically as reflected in the level and

change in output and profits. In particular, the role of relative factor prices which are important in the neo-classical theory of investment (see Jorgenson, 1963; Sawyer, 1982a, pp. 23–30, for further discussion) is ignored.

2. There are considerable difficulties of forming an aggregate investment equation which requires aggregation both across firms and across different capital goods (see Sawyer, 1982a, pp. 27–8). As discussed in Chapter 8, there are substantial difficulties in measuring capital, and those problems largely recur here. In particular, since net investment is the difference between gross investment and depreciation, it is necessary to measure depreciation, which is the change in value of the existing stock of capital equipment over the relevant time period. Gross investment can be taken as the market price of capital equipment purchased; there are difficulties in comparing the real value of gross investment over time.

3. It is conceivable that the technical change is capital-saving and labour-encouraging so that the cost reduction involves less capital and more labour. But that would appear to be an unusual occurrence, and anyway the capital equipment has to be produced by labour.

4. For a survey see Review of Monopolies and Mergers Policy (1978).

5. For discussion on Kaldor's contributions see the symposium in *Journal of Post Keynesian Economics*, Spring 1983, and Thirlwall, 1987, especially ch. 7). The text does not aim to be an authorative account of Kaldor's views but is rather loosely based on them.

6. The (broadly speaking) Keynesian approach to business cycles is discussed in, for example, Matthews (1959), Rau (1974). The new classical macroeconomics approach, which depends on 'surprises' (between expectations and outcomes) over prices is represented by, for example, Sargent (1979). For a discussion of Kalecki's approach to the business cycle see Sawyer (1985b). A radical political economy approach to business cycles is also given in Sherman (1989).

7. 'The Dutch economist J. van Geldern (writing under the pen-name J. Fedder) was the first author to draw attention to these wave-like movements. In the international literature the Russian economist N. D. Kondratiev is generally credited with the discovery of long waves. The register of Schumpeter's book does not even mention the names of Fedder or van Geldern. On the other hand, Wesley C. Mitchell gives full credit to van Geldern and A. de Wolff for their pioneering research into long waves' (Tinbergen, 1983).

8. This account is taken from Maddison (1982), who also provides his own periodisation. However, the phases identified by Maddison relate also to considerations such as government policy stance and the nature of international payments system (see his Table 4.11). The period

1950–73 is described as 'the golden era' and post-1973 as 'the phase of blurred objectives'. For a different periodisation and characterisation see Mandel (1980, pp. 105–6).

9. 'It is by no means far fetched or paradoxical to say that "progress" unstabilizes the economic world, or that it is by virtue of its mechanism *a cyclical process*. A theory of economic fluctuations running in terms of external factors plus innovations might be considered self-evident and only another way of stating that there would be no cycles in an undisturbed stationary, or growing, flow' (Schumpeter, 1939).

10. In empirical work, it may be difficult to identify the time and originator of the crucial idea. In part this is because the generation of any new idea depends on some preceding work, and hence each idea could be said to depend on some previous idea. 'Who was the "basic" inventor? Whoever he was, a long chain of previous inventions helped him. Take Faraday, whose demonstration to the Royal Society in London, anno 1831, is often taken as the birthday of the much later developed electricity industry. He could not have presented his theories without the outstanding achievements of scientists like Benjamin Franklin (1774), Galvani (1791), Volta (1800), Ampere (1822) and others. It was a long way – before Faraday and after him – to the large-scale electricity industry (Ray, 1983).

11. 'Mensch's results are faulted on a number of counts, the two most important being the use of unrepresentative innovation selection and the use of an inappropriate statistical test to distinguish Kondratieff waves' (Solomou, 1986).

12. Also, the 'expansive long waves are periods in which the forces counteracting the tendency of the average rate of profit to decline operate in a strong and synchronized way. Depressive long waves are periods in which the forces counteracting the tendency of the average rate of profit to decline are fewer, weaker, and decisively less synchronized. Why this occurs at certain turning points can be explained only in the light of concrete historical analysis of a given period of capitalist development leading up to such a turning point' (Mandel, 1980).

13. However, the second half of the 1960s (generally an era of prosperity) and the 1980s (an era of recession in many countries) would appear to not conform to that view. The intellectual climate of the late 1960s was generally rather hostile to capitalism, whilst that of the 1980s (at least in countries such as the UK and USA) has been much more favourable to capitalism.

Chapter 13
CUMULATIVE CAUSATION AND UNEQUAL DEVELOPMENT

13.1 INTRODUCTION

The organising theme of this chapter is that an outstanding feature of the real world is the existence and continuation of a variety of inequalities and disparities. The continuation and reproduction of these disparities are the central themes of this chapter, and it explores some theories which seek to explain and understand these disparities and their continuation, and also considers the policy implications of these theories.

Neo-classical economics and the equilibrium of perfect competition possess two properties particularly important here. First, in equilibrium, there is an equalisation of returns to each type of factor of production; e.g. anyone possessing a given bundle of skills and talents would receive the same wage (at least after adjustment for non-pecuniary returns). Second, there is no discrepancy of power between economic agents. This aspect has been extensively discussed in Chapters 2 and 3 in the context of power relationship between labour and capital. This notion of equilibrium and the forces leading to equilibrium have some powerful implications. It implies, for example, that there will be a tendency towards equality of return, at least for each particular factor of production. But, further, if a particular type of labour is receiving a high return (wage) then it would be anticipated that others will seek to train as that type of labour (if that is possible). The geographical aspect of this argument is also important. A depressed region would face a low demand for labour and would provide low wages as a consequence. The equilibrating mechanism would include the movement of labour out of the depressed region in search of high wages elsewhere and the inward movement of firms attracted by low cost of labour. These movements would be expected to continue until the wages were equalised across regions, and in effect full employment restored through wage flexibility and factor mobility.

This chapter examines a range of ideas which present a rather different view of how markets operate. These ideas suggest that there is not a movement towards a full-employment equilibrium, but rather that in addition to extensive unemployment there will be movements away from any kind of equilibrium. There are two central ideas which influence the discussion in a variety of ways. The first is the general idea of cumulative causation. This is the simple idea that there are ways by which success breeds success, and hence those (individuals, industries, regions, countries, etc.) who are initially successful and receive relatively high rewards will continue to gain at the expense of the initially unsuccessful. The second basic idea is that inequalities in economic terms (which are exacerbated by cumulative causation) generate inequalities of political power, cultural domination, etc. A region which is relatively rich does not only have more economic spending power but may be politically more powerful and exert cultural dominance over the less prosperous regions. It is then useful to think in terms of a division between the centre (core) and the periphery whereby the centre is not only economically successful but also is able to exercise political and cultural domination over the periphery. It is the economic relationship between the core and periphery which is the dominant theme of the latter half of this chapter.

The idea of vicious and virtuous circles is, as the phrase would suggest, that an economy (or region or firm) which is initially more successful will become even more successful, whilst the reverse is the case for the less successful. This general observation is most closely associated with the work of Myrdal (especially Myrdal, 1957, and used in Myrdal, 1944) and the terminology of cumulative causation, with an important contribution by Kaldor (1972).[1] One case of virtuous and vicious circles was seen in the previous chapter in the discussion of the relationship between profits and investment. In that case, the effect operated at the level of the economy since it was argued that economies could be launched onto high profit/high investment or low profit/low investment paths.

13.2 SUCCESS BREEDS SUCCESS, AND FAILURE BREEDS FAILURE

Many of the forces at work in the theory of cumulative causation can be encapsulated under the phrase 'success breeds success', and the often forgotten counterpart that 'failure breeds failure'. Cumulative causation is a very general notion and it can operate at different levels through a variety of routes. It is useful to make the broad distinction between those forces of cumulative causation which essentially operate at the level of the individual economic organisation (e.g. person or most usually firm[2]) and those which operate at a more aggregate level of a region or country.

The operation of cumulative causation at the level of the firm involves two related elements. These are the opportunities for re-investment of profits and increasing returns to scale (including dynamic returns). A firm which is relatively more profitable has a greater pool of finance at its disposal and that high profitability is likely to aid further borrowing (cf. section 6.4). The initially more profitable firm can thereby invest more and grow faster than the less profitable firms. This process would be nullified if there were decreasing returns, for that would mean that firms with larger output would incur higher unit costs. But increasing returns to scale will exacerbate the process, as indicated in Chapter 5.

However, the discussion of whether there are static decreasing or increasing returns to scale does not get to the heart of the matter here, which could be described as 'dynamic increasing returns' (cf. Kaldor, 1972). In the context of cumulative causation, etc., the following aspects of increasing returns can be usefully distinguished:

1. Adam Smith postulated that 'division of labour is limited by the extent of the market'. This would initially mean that there is a limit to how far the division of labour can be taken, with the limit formed by the size of the market. But the division of labour is usually seen to raise productivity and lower costs. Then as prices fall in line with costs, the demand for the product is expanded, and this extension of the market permits further division of labour. Thus there is a cumulative effect. Some of these cumulative effects may benefit the individual firm, whilst others may benefit the industry as a whole.

2. 'Learning by doing' widely interpreted. As discussed in the

previous chapter, the cumulative level of output influences the level of productivity. A firm with considerable experience benefits from higher levels of productivity, and is able to under-cut rivals (from lower costs) and/or earn higher profits. This firm is then able to expand further, and gain more experience and reap more productivity gains.

3. Each stage of technical advance builds on the earlier stages. The firm at the frontier of technical knowledge has the basis on which to build the next step forward, whereas a firm away from the frontier needs first to move to the frontier before being able to advance. Further, the firm at the frontier will have gained experience from the previous stages to help undertake the next stage.

At the aggregate level of a region or nation, Myrdal (1957) argued 'that the play of the forces in the market normally tends to increase, rather than to decrease, the inequalities between regions'. This arises from a combination of forces, although there may be some other counteracting forces at work. There will be a movement of labour and capital into the prospering regions and away from the depressed areas. This involves the movements of the factors of production into the prosperous region and away from the depressed region. It is the movement of the factors of production themselves, rather than the movement of their price. For in the neo-classical case, it would be expected that prices of factors would fall in the depressed region. The movement of labour exacerbates the inequality between region since 'migration is always selective, at least with respect to the migrant's age, this movement by itself tends to favour the rapidly growing communities and disfavour the others'. In general, it would be expected that migrants will be relatively young, enterprising, educated, etc.; in other words, migrants will generally have characteristics which make them more useful than average in production. The prosperous regions are likely to offer higher income, more attractive working conditions and also a wider range of cultural activities than the less prosperous regions. These features help the prosperous regions to attract more and better professional workers (e.g. medical practitioners, accountants, teachers). The level of services which are then provided in the prosperous regions would be better than those in the less prosperous regions. This will further reinforce the attraction of the prosperous regions and raise their competitive position (through better education, health, etc.).

However, it can be observed that much migration in the post-war era was from countries with low living standards to countries with higher levels of income. But much of the employment of the migrants was in low-prestige jobs with relatively low wages and poor working conditions. In terms of the segmented labour market theory (cf. Chapter 3), the immigrants were usually employed in the secondary labour sector. Even so, immigrant labour eased labour shortages in the relatively prosperous countries, and enabled their economic growth to continue. The low-status position of migrant labour in the receiving country often reflects discrimination against migrant labour. Finally, the country of origin of the migrant labour still lost an important part of their workforce in terms of age and education.

The movement of capital is seen to have a similar effect in moving from the less prosperous to the more prosperous areas. 'In the centres of expansion increased demand will spur investment, which in its turn will increase incomes and demand and cause a second round of investment, and so on' (Myrdal, 1957). The prosperous regions will offer a higher rate of profit than the depressed regions, which attracts capital from the depressed region into the prosperous regions. This inflow of capital permits further expansion of production and the reaping of further economies of scale, etc. Thus Myrdal (1957) concludes that 'capital movements will tend to have a similar effect of increasing inequality'.

A particularly important aspect of the idea of cumulative causation is its implications for the effects of the operation of unfettered markets. Myrdal (1957) argues that

> trade operates with the same fundamental bias in favour of the richer and progressive regions against other regions. The freeing and widening of the markets will often confer such competitive advantages on the industries in already established centres of expansion, which usually work under conditions of increasing returns, that even the handicrafts and industries existing earlier in the other regions are thwarted.

This general notion will recur below, and it should be noted that the implication of this line of argument is that relatively undeveloped regions or countries may have to withdraw from the general operation of the national or international market in order to be able to themselves develop their economy. Such a withdrawal would require the erection of some barriers to international trade and the flow of capital. For example, a policy of trade protection can be used as a means of partial withdrawal from the international economy whilst the domestic industries are built up.

The idea of cumulative causation is a general one in the sense that it can apply at different levels (e.g. firms, countries), but in each case the effects of the forces of cumulative causation are subject to some offsetting tendencies. To the extent to which cumulative causation works without offsetting tendencies, then growing disparities would be observed. Hence, when applied, for example, to regions of a country, growing disparities (of income, employment, etc.) arise between those regions. It could be argued that continually growing disparities are not generally observed (in this example between regions) but considerable and persistent disparities are observed. For example, Nicol and Yuill (1982) provide data on regional disparities within fifteen European countries. The degree of disparity varies between countries, in part depending on the size of the country and the number of separate regions identified within the country. However, for these fifteen countries in 1977 (or near date), on average, the most prosperous region has an income level nearly 50 per cent above the country's average level and over twice the level of the poorest region. Unemployment rates also display considerable disparity, with the ratio of highest unemployment rate to the lowest varying from just over a factor of two up to a factor six. For a sample of eight of these countries the trend over the period 1960 to 1977 is reported. In some countries there was a trend towards equality, but in others the reverse trend applied. For this sample as a whole, the average ratio of highest income per capita region to the lowest was 2.2 in 1960, 2.0 in 1970 and 2.1 in 1977, which suggests little trend in disparity despite regional policies in many countries designed to reduce regional disparities. In a similar vein, there has been a considerable persistence in the degree of inequality of income between individuals and between households (see, for example, Sawyer, 1976, 1982c).

The development of the British economy since the mid-nineteenth century both supports and undermines the cumulative causation idea.

> In the early nineteenth century, England and Ireland were both parts of the United Kingdom, and governed according to the same market-liberal principles. England had the most productive and innovative economy in the world. Most of Ireland remained poverty-striken and

backward, and her economy fell further behind England's than it had been before. (Marquand, 1988)

Thus there appeared to be cumulative causation forces at work as between one part of the United Kingdom (England) and another (Ireland). But the leading position of England in the world economy was gradually ceded as it was overtaken by the United States of America and then by Germany. Hence, the forces of cumulative causation did not serve to maintain the United Kingdom at the forefront, and indeed in the post-war world the British economy appeared to suffer from the adverse effects of cumulative causation as it declined relative to the rest of the world.[3] It may well have been that other countries were able to overtake the UK economy because of the adoption of deliberate government policies (see, for example, Marquand, 1988, especially chs 4 and 5).

The persistence of, but not usually increase of, disparities could be taken to indicate that there is some force in the idea of cumulative causation with some offsetting forces at work (as indicated in Myrdal, 1957). The offsetting forces can be divided into three groups. First, there can be factors at work which could be regarded as chance ones so far as systematic economic forces are concerned. For example, the discovery of a particular mineral in a region (country) or a large rise in the price of a primary product which the region (country) has in abundance will bring some prosperity to that region (country).

Second, relatively low prices of some factors of production (e.g. labour and land) in the unsuccessful regions may eventually operate to stimulate the growth of new industries. Firms (whether from within or from outside the region) seek to benefit from the lower costs of production in the depressed region. A limitation on this process will be that the market for the output produced may (at least initially) be in the more prosperous region, so that additional transport costs are incurred in transporting the output from the low-cost region of production to the high-income region. But it often happens that the exploitation of the relatively low costs of labour and land in the depressed regions is undertaken by firms which are based in the prosperous regions. For example, a prosperous firm may set up a branch factory in a depressed region, but the decision-making and other central functions remain located in the prosperous region. Thus the relationship between the depressed region and the prosperous ones has a strong element of inequality of power, with the economic power residing with prosperous region.

Third, deliberate political action may be taken to limit or overcome the disparities. In the case of regional disparities, this would be reflected in regional policies designed to reverse those inequalities. The purpose of regional policies is generally seen to be to move industry into the depressed regions, though the implementation of such policies requires that the depressed regions possess sufficient political power to bring the policies into effect.

Myrdal first applied the idea of cumulative causation in the context of discrimination against Negroes in the United States. He argued that

> white prejudice and discrimination keep the Negro low in standards of living, health, education, manners and morals. This, in turn, gives support to white prejudice. White prejudice and Negro standards thus mutually 'cause' each other. If things remain about as they are and have been, this means that the two forces happen to balance each other. Such a static 'accommodation' is, however, entirely accidental. If either of the factors changes, this will cause a change in the other factor too, and start a process of interaction where the change in one factor will continuously be supported by the reaction of the other factor. The whole system will be moving in the direction of the primary change, but much further. (Myrdal, 1944)

In this case economic and political discrimination are bound together, so that discrimination in one sphere will not generally be offset in the other. Thus deliberate political action such as measures of anti-discrimination legislation, affirmative action, etc., are unlikely to be readily adopted. There are plenty of examples (particularly in the sphere of racial and sexual inequality) where public action has reinforced those effects. Thus for a long time, the laws on segregation reinforced racial inequalities in the Southern States of the USA. But the clearest current example would be the South African apartheid laws. Indeed, one of the routes through which cumulative causation can work is that of political power, which includes enacting laws to favour the powerful at the expense of the weak.

There is, however, an optimistic side to the cumulative causation approach. It would mean that once some movement is made in the direction of reducing discrimination, the economic and political forces tend to reinforce that reduction.

If, for example, we assume that for some reason white prejudice could be decreased and discrimination mitigated, this is likely to cause a rise in Negro standards, which may decrease white prejudice still a little more, which would again allow Negro standards to rise, and so on through mutual interaction. . . . The principle of cumulative causation . . . promises final effects of greater magnitude than the efforts and costs of the reforms themselves. The low status of the Negro is tremendously wasteful all round – the low educational standard causes low earnings and health deficiencies, for example. . . . In the end, the cost of raising the status of the Negro may not involve any 'real costs' at all for society, but instead may result in great 'social gains' and actual savings for society. (Myrdal, 1944)

13.3 CENTRE AND PERIPHERY

Regions and countries interact with one another through trade, investment, migration, etc. The theory of cumulative causation helps to explain the persistence (and extension) of disparities between regions. But it is also necessary to consider the nature of the relations between the successful and the unsuccessful regions (countries). This leads to consideration of theories concerning the relationships between the centre (successful) and the periphery (unsuccessful).

The centre and the periphery idea, which clearly has spatial connotations, can be applied at a number of levels, of which the regional and national will be the two main ones discussed here. At a spatial level, there are other dimensions, and the division between rural and urban areas, and more recently between inner city areas and the suburbs would be an important ones. At another level, there are correspondences between the centre–periphery split and the dual labour market discussed in Chapter 3 in that there are substantial inequalities involved which the market mechanism exacerbates rather than relieves. There are many features of the spatial aspect of the centre–periphery concept and also different ways in which the broad concept can be interpreted (with some of the differences in interpretations ascribable to the different levels of application). Within a country, it can be applied to regional differences (including urban/rural and inner city/suburban ones). In the international context, it can be applied to differences between developed countries as well as to differences between industrialised and non-industrialised countries. The elements involved at the regional level and for differences between developed countries are rather similar, and are treated together. Later, attention is turned to the centre/periphery dichotomy applied to industrialised and non-industrialised countries.

The central area is more economically advanced than the periphery. But it is not just a matter that the centre has a higher income level than the periphery. The centre has economic power over the periphery, which may allow it, for example, to determine the relative prices at which trade between the centre and periphery takes place. The central area is economically and technically advanced as compared with the periphery. New ideas are developed and controlled by the centre, and production in the periphery may be controlled by the centre. Further, this economic power is allied with political and cultural power. The culture of the centre can to some degree be imposed on the periphery as a consequence of the economic power.

13.4 DISPARITIES WITHIN DEVELOPED ECONOMIES

The differences within and between industrialised economies draws heavily on the material which has already been discussed. From the previous chapter, the idea summarised in Verdoorn's law of dynamic increasing returns to scale within the industrialised sectors is important here (cf. section 12.8). The approach of Dixon and Thirlwall (1975) is used to illustrate some of the aspects of dynamic returns. For reasons which will become apparent below, the two areas referred to can be interpreted as two regions within a country or as two countries. After presentation of the model, the differences which arise depending on whether the model is interpreted at the inter-regional or the inter-national level are considered.

The model developed by Dixon and Thirlwall (1975) encapsulates a number of the key elements of the approach of Kaldor discussed above, and can be used to understand differences in growth rates between regions and between countries. The starting point is the post-Keynesian view that the growth of output depends on growth of demand. Many components of aggregate demand can be described as induced demand, i.e. they depend on the level of (domestic) income. The induced demand (which here include consumer and investment expenditure) depend on income, but the level of income itself depends on the level of autonomous demand. Hence the level of induced demand is ultimately derived from autonomous demand, and that autonomous demand can be identified with the demand for exports, as the only demand arising from outside the domestic economy. The model presented here is concerned with growth and all variables are expressed in rate-of-change form. On the demand side, the growth of output is governed by the growth of demand, and that growth is determined by the growth of exports. The demand side of the economy, which is the driving force in this model, is then represented in linear form as:

$$q = a\,x \tag{13.1}$$

where q is growth of output, and x growth of exports.

The demand for exports depends on the price of domestic goods relative to the price of foreign goods and on the level of world income. This can also be expressed in growth terms as:

$$x = c\,p_d + d\,p_f + e\,z \tag{13.2}$$

where p_d is the rate of change of a domestic price index, p_f is the rate of change of a foreign price index, z the growth of world income, and c, d, e the elasticities of export demand with respect to domestic prices, foreign prices and world income respectively. The domestic prices are based on a mark-up on average costs, and so the growth of domestic prices is given by:

$$p_d = w - g + t \tag{13.3}$$

where w is growth of money wage, g is growth of productivity of labour and t the rate of change of 1 plus the mark-up.

The production conditions are represented by Verdoorn's law (cf. section 12.8) according to which the growth of productivity depends on the growth of output, and in linear form this is:

$$g = b + f\,q \tag{13.4}$$

so that the growth of productivity of labour (g) depends on the growth of output (q), which in turn depends on the growth of demand. Productivity growth is a major component of technical progress, and equation (13.4) reflects the idea that technical progress is endogenous. Although there is no explicit mention of investment in this presentation, there is a significant role for investment. The growth of output requires investment to provide the capital equipment for increased production. Investment in new capital equipment (as argued in the previous chapter) is necessary for the implementation of technical change, and the more investment, the faster is technical change. Thus, investment is stimulated by expected growth of demand (leading to growth in output), and one of the effects of that investment is technical progress and productivity growth. Equation (13.4) (Verdoorn's law) also reflects 'learning-by-doing' (cf. section 12.7).

In equation (13.4), it is assumed that there are dynamic economies of scale, and hence in the linear form that f is greater than zero. An alternative presentation of equation (13.4) is:

$$e = -b + (1-f)\, q \tag{13.5}$$

where e is the growth of employment. The growth of employment is then a consequence of the growth of output (and of demand), and in general it is assumed that there is plentiful labour available (say from agricultural sector, other countries) to permit this demand-determined growth of employment to occur.

Equations (13.4) and (13.5) appear to be simple equations, which may or may not reflect some aspects of the real world. Looking at equation (13.5), it could be remarked that of course employment and output growth will be related to one another. However, equation (13.5) indicates that one per cent faster growth of output involves a less than one per cent faster growth of employment, whereas the neo-classical approach would suggest that the employment growth would be one per cent or more (with constant or decreasing returns to scale). The appendix to this chapter provides a detailed discussion of these equations, and the ways in which they reflect a post-Keynesian rather than a neo-classical view of the world.

The four equations (13.1) to (13.4) can be solved to provide a solution for the growth of output (with the other endogenous variables for which a solution can be obtained being p_d, q and x), which is:

$$q = a\, \{c(w - b + t) + dp_f + ez\}/(1 + acf) \tag{13.6}$$

(in this equation all the parameters are expected to be positive with the exception of c which is negative). It can be seen that differences in growth rates arise from two sources, namely differences in demand conditions and differences in productivity dynamism (i.e. Verdoorn's law). This would suggest, for example, that a region or country which was producing 'modern' goods and services for which there is a high income elasticity (high e above) would have a relatively high growth rate, since from equation (13.6) it can be calculated that dq/de is positive. This would imply that a country favoured by the demand for its production would enter into a virtuous circle, with the fast growth of demand stimulating growth of output, of productivity and a fall in prices. As an aside here it can be noted that the relative poor growth performance of, say, the British or American economies in the post-war period could be ascribed to the production of goods which have a low income elasticity of demand.

It should be noted that there is a fixed exchange rate assumption in the model outlined here, and it can also be seen that growth of output depends in part on the balance of growth of domestic prices (reflected in $c(w - b + t)$) and growth of foreign prices, and their relative impact on export demand. The fixed exchange rate assumption would be relevant for a model of differential growth between regions of a single country, between countries within a trading block where exchange rate movements are limited or in a world of fixed exchange rates.

This model clearly relates to possible differences in growth rates, and whether it leads to cumulative differences or diminishing differences (in level of output) would clearly depend on the values of the parameters involved. Cumulative differences could arise because, for example, a country facing favourable demand conditions (because of the structure of the commodities produced) combined with dynamism (reflected in relatively high values of b and/or f above) would have a higher growth rate than a country with unfavourable demand conditions and a lack of dynamism. If the favoured country already had a higher level of output than the unfavoured one, then this difference in output level would be magnified over time through the differences in growth rates. However, the important question in the context of cumulative causation is whether there are forces at work which lead to some systematic relationship between level of output and rate of growth. If, for example, a high level of output leads to a lack of dynamism, etc., then there would be a tendency towards convergence. In other words, high-output economies would tend to display slow growth, and low-output economies fast growth. Conversely, if a high level of output encourages faster growth, then there would be a process of cumulative causation and of widening gaps between high- and low-output economies.

This model does not explicitly mention savings, and it is driven by the growth of demand. It is implicitly assumed that investment in capital equipment takes place to underpin the growth of output, and that sufficient savings are forthcoming to finance that investment. But an economy (especially a low-output one) may not be capable of generating sufficient savings to finance investment. In such a case, the growth process described above could not take off, being constrained by the level of savings. There is a potential for growth which cannot immediately be realised owing to an inadequacy of savings.

13.5 DEVELOPMENT, UNDEVELOPMENT AND UNDERDEVELOPMENT

The coverage of this book has been limited to the operation of developed, industrialised capitalist economies. However, such economies trade with and invest in other economies, so that just from the narrow consideration of industrialised capitalist economies it is necessary to consider the relationship between those economies and the rest of the world. Further, there are good reasons to think (apart from empirical observation) that there are tendencies for the capitalist system to expand into non-capitalist areas. A crucial question which arises here is whether such expansion is beneficial for the previously non-capitalist areas, or whether the presence of industrialised capitalist economies prevents or distorts the development of the non-industrialised economies.

The relationship examined in the previous section has mainly been between regions which are industrialised (for this underpins the assumptions of dynamic increasing returns). The nature of the relationship between the regions was one of differences in economic performance, and within the model no attention was given to any consequent political relationships. For example, there was no discussion of the political dominance of the relatively prosperous region at the expense of the relatively depressed region. Apart from the obvious point that political influence in the wider world will often be related to material prosperity, the following can also be noted. The region with higher per capita income will generally be applying and developing the most recent technology (cf. section 12.8). The capitalists in the more prosperous region will generally have a higher volume of profits (if not a greater share of profits) which they will seek to invest. The less prosperous region may provide a profitable outlet for a firm's profits used for investment purposes in that the cost of labour will be lower there. However, the capitalists from the more advanced region will generally seek to employ the most recent technology (assumed to yield higher labour productivity) in conjunction with the employment of lower-cost labour.

This shift of production (via multinationals, for example) has the implication that some of the differences between the regions may be removed (though not all, for otherwise the capitalists would not find it worth while to shift production). Thus there are some forces at work which are reducing the differences between regions. However, these forces bring the 'branch factory' syndrome into operation. This arises when a firm whose headquarters are located in the central area establish a factory in the periphery to take advantage of cheaper labour and land. Although production takes place in the periphery, it is likely that crucial decisions (on prices, investment, etc.) are taken at the centre, and functions such as strategic planning and research and development are likely to be undertaken at the centre. In particular, decisions on expansion or contraction of employment in the factory located in the periphery are taken at the centre. The prosperity of whole communities is severely affected by factory closure, but the community itself has no influence in any decision on the future of the branch factory. The factory located in the periphery is not central to the operations of the firm, and can expanded or contracted to suit the profits of the firm.

In particular, when peripheral economies compete for the location of these factories (by, for example, the offer of subsidies), the continued operation of the factory may rest on its cost being lower than can be offered by the removal of that factory to another peripheral economy. Cowling and Sugden (1987b) argue that this power to shift production from one country to another enhances the position of capitalists via-à-vis labour. The bargaining power of labour is reduced by the activities of multinational enterprises. A multinational is able to co-ordinate its activities across countries and to move from one to another, whereas labour finds cross-country organisation difficult and is unable to move from one country to another.

Below the nature of the relationship between the industrialised capitalist economies and the non-industrialised economies is briefly considered, though the centrally planned economies are excluded from the discussion. The reason for this exclusion is that the scale of economic relations (e.g. trade) between capitalist economies and centrally planned economies is relatively small and subject to the control of the planning authorities. However, a major characteristic of centrally planned economies in respect of this discussion is that capitalist firms are not generally permitted to undertake production, and there is an absence of financial markets. A major concern below is the possible penetration of non-industrialised economies by capitalist firms, and the limitations of the development of such economies which is posed by the existence of industrialised economies.

However, the process of industrialisation, particularly during the nineteenth century, was often associated with the degradation of human labour. The thrust of Braverman's argument (cf. section 2.6) was, following Marx, that for many workers, industrialisation and technical change would reduce skills and increase alienation. Further, the culture of capitalism is materialistic, and its culture replaces other cultures when industrialisation and capitalism come together. Cultures in which, for example, spiritual values are emphasised and in which the pursuit of collective interests rather than individual interest will conflict with the materialistic self-interest culture of capitalism. Thus, the success of capitalism requires the destruction of those cultures which conflict with the capitalist culture.[4] Further, the spread of capitalism has historically been linked with the expansion of the capitalist firms of particular nations, which in recent times has been American capitalism. Thus the expansion of capitalism involves the replacement of indigenous cultures by American culture.

Although there are restrictions on trade and on movement of capital and labour between countries, it is reasonable to talk of a world market economy covering the developed capitalist economies and many of the developing economies as well. Some parts of the world are relatively untouched by capitalism and their economies organised on traditional lines. However, there is a strong possibility that such parts of the world will be invaded by capitalism, as capitalist firms pursue profits and markets. It will only be those countries where extensive barriers are erected against the rest of the world that can hope to operate outside the ambit of capitalism.

There are numerous historical examples of the more developed countries conquering less developed ones, though the relevant dimension of development may often have been in terms of the degree of sophistication of weapons (e.g. the Spanish conquest and exploitation of the Incas). Whilst attention is then directed at military conquest and at political domination, powerful economic forces are often involved. There were no doubt many motives behind the expansion of the British empire in the nineteenth century ranging from desire for adventure through to religious imperative to convert the heathen. But, at the same time, the conquest of Africa, for example, did provide raw materials for and make markets available to British capitalists.

The post-war period has seen the dissolving of the British, French, German, Dutch and Portuguese empires. It would appear, at least superficially, that there has been a substantial diminution of the military and political control of one country over another during this period. There are, of course, many examples of military involvement, particularly by the American government. Governments in many Latin American countries can only survive with at least the tacit agreement of the United States government. There are a variety of ways by which economic influence can be exercised by the economically powerful over the economically weak. The provision of aid and loans by the economically rich can be made conditional (explicitly or implicitly) on the pursuit of particular types of economic and political policies, involving austerity programmes of reduction in budget deficits, limits on money supply growth and currency devaluations. The nature of the relationship between the economically stronger and weaker nations is not historically fixed, and hence the analyses of such relations are historically specific. The broad discussion below is intended to apply to the post-Second World War situation. In this period the military dominance of one country by another has been reduced and replaced by a more subtle economic dominance.

> Broadly speaking, imperialism now means the domination by one
> country or group of people over others, in ways that benefit the

former usually at the expense of the latter. Capitalist imperialism, in particular, is the exercise of such domination by leading capitalist nations and their large private corporations, ordinarily over less-developed areas of the world. (Griffin and Gurley, 1985)

Within the radical political economy tradition, it is useful to distinguish two views (which may not be compatible with one another) on the consequences of developed capitalist economies for the underdeveloped, non-capitalist economies. The first, which is evident in the work of Marx, is that there is an inbuilt tendency for the capitalist system to expand as firms invade previously non-capitalist economies in the search for markets and for profits.[5] One essential part of this argument is that capitalist production is generally undertaken at lower cost (through the use of more advanced, capital-intensive techniques) than non-capitalist production.

> As long as machine production expands in a given branch of industry at the expense of the old handicrafts or of manufacture, the result is as certain as is the result of an encounter between an army with breach-loading rifles and one with bows and arrows. This first period, during which machinery conquers its fields of operations, is of decisive importance, owing to the extra-ordinary profits it helps to produce ... the cheapness of the articles produced by machinery and the revolution in the means of transport and communications provide the weapons for the conquest of foreign markets. By ruining hand-icraft production of finished articles in other countries, machinery forcibly converts them into fields for the production of its raw materials. (Marx, 1976)

A particular example given by Marx was the 'destruction of the Indian handicraft textile production by competition from the mechanised textile production of Lancashire' (Brewer, 1980). How-ever, this destruction did not arise only from undercutting of prices in the market because 'the producers control their own means of subsistence, and thus cannot be starved out by undercutting. It was only with the direct assistance of state power, then, that the destruc-tion of Indian textiles could occur, and even so it proceeded fairly slowly' (Brewer, 1980), for at the time in question India was part of the British empire. The expansion of the capitalist system was seen as progressive in that capitalism would replace feudalism, to be followed by its own replacement by socialism and communism. In the broad sweep of history, Marx foresaw the passage from feudalism through capitalism into socialism and finally communism. Hence, the growth of capitalism was progressive in being a step along the road to socialism.

The expansion of the capitalist system was seen as an aspect of the movement of capital into areas of potentially high profits. The initial replacement of pre-capitalist modes of production by capitalist modes would be highly profitable for the capitalists involved. But those capitalists would be followed by others, thereby bidding down the high rates of profit. Although this would be a long process, nevertheless there is a general presumption that capitalism will spread and eventually there would be some kind of uniformity. The tendency towards the equalisation of the rate of profit would be applied on a world scale. This general equalisation tendency stands in some contrast to the views discussed below where the emphasis is on the tendency for inequality to be reproduced.

A further tendency for the capitalist sectors to expand into the non-capitalist sectors comes from the following argument. In Chapters 9 and 12 some of the implications of differential savings propensities (out of wages and out of profits) were considered. However, profits will only continue at a particular level if there is expenditure elsewhere in the economy which matches the savings made out of profits (and also out of wages) (cf. section 9.3). It is necessary for the present discussion to allow for the role of foreign trade in the context of differential savings. Equations (9.6) and (9.7) can be modified to allow for foreign trade and government economic activity and combined to give:

$$s_2 P + s_1 W + T + M = I + G + X \tag{13.7}$$

where T is total taxation, M imports, G government expenditure, X exports. Rearrangement with national income $Y = W + P$ yields:

$$P = \{I + (G - T) + (X - M) - s_1 Y\}/(s_2 - s_1) \tag{13.8}$$

The implied causation of this equation has been discussed above (section 9.3). The strong implication of this equation is that investment, government budget deficit $(G - T)$, and export surplus $(X - M)$ all have the same impact on profits, whereas profits are diminished by workers' savings. Profits would increase if any item on the right-hand side is increased, provided that there is sufficient capital equipment and labour to produce the corresponding increase in output.

It has been argued by a number of radical political economists (e.g. Luxemburg, 1913, 1963; Kalecki, 1945; Baran and Sweezy, 1966) that there would be a tendency for the level of investment to be insufficient to support the maximum level of output and employment, so that output and profits will be less than they could be. Their arguments could be simply represented here by saying that a surplus of exports over imports or of government expenditure over taxation will help the realisation of profits. In particular here, the search by firms for overseas markets will aid the individual profits of the firms concerned and also the aggregate level of profits. The profits of capitalist firms in total (i.e. regardless of nationality of ownership) are enhanced by exports (over imports) outside of the capitalist economies. In other words, at the level of capitalist economies taken together, the level of profits is aided by the excess exports to the non-capitalist economies over imports from those countries. Baran and Sweezy (1966) concentrate on the methods of raising government expenditure which appear to be acceptable to capitalists, as has been discussed in Chapter 10. Luxemburg and others have stressed the search for overseas markets to stimulate exports and profits.

The second set of views within the radical political economy tradition finds expression in terms such as dependency, the generation of underdevelopment and the relationships between the centre and the periphery. The theories associated with these expressions differ in key respects. But they share the common feature of stressing the unevenness of development, and that the relationship between the more developed and the less developed is one of the dominance of the former over the latter. It is not just a matter that the more developed have higher income levels than the less developed, but rather also includes economic, political and cultural domination.

The tendency of the capitalist system to expand geographically and the disparities and inequalities which such a system generates are combined in the view of Harris (1978) when he argues that

> uneven and combined development is the specific form that accumulation takes in the capitalist economy. That is to say, the capitalist economy in the course of its expansion integrates or combines different spheres of economic life into one, global, and interdependent system. At the same time, development proceeds unevenly within the different spheres of that system. This is generally so between different

firms, industries, sectors, regions, and segments of the world economy. Underdevelopment is a particular manifestation of this process.

Whilst this view incorporates Marx's views of capitalism's growth and expansion tendencies, nevertheless 'the thrust of their argument, which turned Marx on his head, was that capitalism is a powerful engine of growth in the center, but in the peripheral countries it tends inevitably to produce underdevelopment and poverty (Griffin and Gurley, 1985).

Thus on this line of argument, unequal and uneven development and growth are an integral part of the capitalist system. This would mean that unbalanced rather than balanced growth occurs, and would reinforce the argument that capitalist economies cannot be usefully analysed using equilibrium techniques which search for balanced growth paths. It also would carry considerable implications for economic policy. For if uneven development is an integral part of capitalism, then a relatively backward country which remains within the capitalist system will suffer, and will find it very difficult or impossible to change their relative position.

The division of the world (capitalist) economies into (roughly) industrialised and primary producers could be argued to be an example of the principle of comparative advantage. Economies which are poor in terms of natural resources (whether for growing crops, mining, etc.) specialise in industrial products (where their comparative advantage is thought to lie) whereas economies which are rich in terms of natural resources specialise in primary products. Specialisation and trade are seen as increasing overall production and economic welfare. The rate at which different products exchange then determines how the gains of specialisation are shared out.

13.6 EXCHANGE RELATIONSHIPS BETWEEN INDUSTRIALISED AND NON-INDUSTRIALISED ECONOMIES

One aspect of the economic relationships between any two economies is the ratio at which the goods and services of economies exchange. There is an approximate (but not exact) correspondence between on the one hand developed, industrialised economies which produce industrial products, and on the other, developing non-industrialised economies which produce primary products (agricultural goods and minerals). Of particular relevance is the specialisation of these economies in terms of foreign trade. There are, of course, counter-examples. Industrialised economies continue to produce food, and some (e.g. the USA, Australia) to export primary products. Conversely, there is industrial production in the non-industrialised economies. However, there has been a continuing debate on the relationship between the general price level of industrial and primary products, which is seen as relevant for the relationship between developed and Third World countries.[6]

There may be a presumption in favour of the proposition that the prices of primary products would gradually *rise* relative to those of industrial products. The argument for this would be that the expansion of the production of primary products (to meet increased demand from rising income and population) would mean that less productive land and mines would have to be used, thereby raising the costs of production of primary products. Conversely, the production of industrial products often benefits from both economies of scale and technological advance, which tend to reduce costs of production. In so far as prices follow costs, this would lead to a rise in the relative price of primary products.

However, there has been much debate over the contrary proposition, namely that there is a tendency for the relative price of primary products to decline. An early expression of this view, and the implications for the development of the non-industrialised economies was given by Prebisch (1950) and Singer (1950). The idea that there was a general trend for the price of agricultural products to decline relative to the price of industrial products has generally been labelled the Prebisch–Singer thesis. The arguments in favour of this thesis are empirical and theoretical. The empirical argument is simply that it represents a generalisation of the empirical evidence (which is discussed below). One of the theoretical arguments is that the income and price elasticities of demand for agricultural products are rather low whilst those for industrial products are rather high. The demand for industrial products then tends to grow faster than the demand for agricultural products, tending to raise the price of industrial products relative to agricultural ones. Another theoretical argument draws on the structural differences between the two sectors. The industrial sector is seen as a modern capitalist sector in which producers and workers are well organised. This helps to ensure that as productivity rises, so do real wages in the industrial sector and the workers share in the technical progress in the industrial sector. In the agricultural sector, the presence of surplus labour prevents wages rising, thereby allowing production to continue in the face of low prices. Indeed, Prebisch (1950) links together the tendency of the terms of trade between agricultural products and industrial products to decline with the centre–periphery distinction introduced above. The agricultural production takes place largely in the periphery whilst industrial production takes place at the centre. Prebisch saw a growing gap between centre and periphery with persistent unemployment in the periphery exacerbated by the tendency of the terms of trade of the periphery to decline.

The terms of trade between the industrialised products and the primary products can be seen as set in an unfair manner, though that requires some criteria of fairness. This argument, which is examined below, has usually been advanced in terms of the industrialised countries exploiting the producers of primary products (which could be interpreted either in terms of the price of primary products being 'too low' or the price of industrialised products being 'too high').

A range of recent studies have confirmed the essence of the Prebisch–Singer thesis. Sarkar (1986), for example, concludes that

> there has been a secular decline in the terms of trade of primary products in relation to manufactures; that declining trend continued even in the post-Second World War years. ... Concurrently, the terms of trade of the developing region *vis-à-vis* the developed region also deteriorated.

However, the picture is obscured by the dramatic oil price rises of the 1970s, and the trend may not continue into the future as the exports of manufactures by the developing region increase.

Another author concludes that

> the evidence points to a deteriorating trend in the relative price of primary products. Given the reservations which must be made about the quality of the evidence, there can be no finality about this conclusion, but it has been reached by examining one by one the main points adduced to question the inference of the deterioration and

finding that they are contradicted or not confirmed by relevant material [e.g. falling transport costs]. (Spraos, 1983)

Further,

> the relative price of the developing countries' primary products has had its ups and downs since the war, it has on average done quite well by the standards of the pre-war decades, even when petroleum is excluded (as a special case) since 1973.... The middle years of this decade [the 1980s] will go down in economic history as a period when primary producers hit rock bottom, whatever method is used to illustrate their real value or purchasing power. There have been hardly any exceptions to this general decline. (Ray, 1987)

Spraos (1983) also uses double factorial terms of trade (DFTT), which is net barter terms of trade (NBTT) adjusted for productivity changes, and also employment-corrected weighted DFTT (ECWDFTT). If p is NBTT, DFTT is $p\ qc/qm$ where qc is productivity in primary production and qm is industrial production, and ECWDFTT is $p\ qc\ Nc/qm$ where Nc is employment in primary product production in developing countries. He then concludes that 'viewing jointly the evidence for minerals and agricultural products the conclusion must be that the ECWDFTT for the entire commodity-producing sector of developing countries were effectively deteriorating over the period of the data'.

The reliance of the periphery on agricultural products, with a tendency for the relative prices of those products to decline, raises questions on how economies in the periphery can develop. The declining agricultural prices would suggest seeking to move away from agricultural production, even though their current comparative advantage may appear to lie with agricultural production. However, the question arises as to whether the relationship between industrialised centre and the periphery within a world economy is such that the industrialisation of the periphery is heavily constrained or even totally prevented. If the answer to that question is yes, then the development of non-industrialised countries is inhibited by their participation in the world economy, which assigns those countries to being dependent on the industrialised countries, with the policy implication of (partial or total) withdrawal from the world economy. This withdrawal could range from restrictions on trade (imports) and on the activities of multinational enterprises through to a 'siege' economy (in which the economy seeks to withdraw from as much contact with other economies as possible).

Those economies which are now industrialised capitalist ones have clearly evolved from a non-industrialised, non-capitalist phase. The question arises whether economies which are currently non-industrialised and/or non-capitalist would be able to evolve in a similar manner in light of the presence of the already industrialised economies. In other words, do the operations of industrialised countries hinder or prevent the industrialisation of other countries? The currently non-industrialised economies would appear to have the advantage of being able to learn from the experience and mistakes of the first countries to industrialise and to be able to draw on the production techniques, capital equipment, managerial experience, etc., which the industrialised economies possess. However, the first economies to industrialise did not have to overcome the economic dominance and technological superiority of other industrialised economies. The crucial question is then whether the industrialised economies operate in ways which prevent the full development of the non-industrialised economies.

This can be expressed by drawing a distinction between *un*development and *under*development. The state of undevelopment could be taken as in an absolute sense, i.e. the absence of industrialisation but with time and the right policies, etc., the undeveloped economy can evolve into a developed economy in ways similar to those followed by the currently developed economies. In contrast, the state of underdevelopment is a relative one in that an underdeveloped economy may be able to industrialise but it will do so in a way which is dictated by the already developed economies and will remain behind those economies. For example, the developed economies (and particularly the capitalist firms) may find it advantageous to locate some types of industrial production in previously non-industrialised economies, for this would enable those firms to gain from the lower labour costs of those economies. This has happened in industries such as electrical goods where much production is now located in countries such as Taiwan and Singapore, which are given the label of New Industrialised Countries (though we could also note that the number of such countries is small relative to the number of non-industrialised countries).

The view that there is a tendency for the (relative) price of primary products to decline over time leads to (at least) two policy conclusions. The first would be to seek ways of reversing such a trend. This would include policies such as the formation of cartels of primary producers (of which OPEC is the best-known example) to bolster up primary product prices, and an appeal to the richer industrialised countries to support a variety of policies to maintain primary product prices. The second would be attempts by agriculture-based economies to industrialise. This raises two considerations.

The first consideration is that industrialisation would require the rejection of the essentially static neo-classical argument for specialisation according to comparative advantage. One statement of a successful rejection of this argument is as follows:

> Should Japan have entrusted its future, according to the theory of comparative advantage, to those industries characterised by intensive use of labour? [With a population of 100 million] had [Japan] chosen to specialise in this kind of industry, it would almost permanently have been unable to break away from the Asian pattern of stagnation and poverty ... The Ministry of International Trade and Industry decided to establish industries which require intensive employment of capital and technology, such as steel, oil refining, petrochemicals, automobiles, aircraft, industrial machinery of all sorts, and later electronics, including electronic computers. From a short-run, static viewpoint, encouragement of such industries would seem to conflict with economic rationalism. But, from a long-range point of view, these are precisely the industries where income elasticity of demand is high, technological process is rapid and labour productivity rises fast. It was clear that without these industries it would be difficult to raise our standard of living to that of Europe and America; whether right or wrong, Japan had to have these heavy and chemical industries. ('the words of a high-level MITI official': quoted by Scott, 1984, from OECD, 1972)

The second consideration is the nature of the relationship between industrialised economies and the Third World economies. Prebisch's concern was particularly directed towards the relationship between the United States and the Latin American countries, and the policy implication drawn was import substitution. This was directed towards a policy of industrialisation with an element of trade protection. The general idea was that a country could to some degree manufacture goods for its own consumption in place of imports. The protection would be required at least in the initial stages to help the domestic industry overcome the advantages of foreign producers acquired through, for example, economies of scale, learning by doing, etc.[7]

Whilst the Prebisch–Singer thesis has often been discussed as an empirical matter, namely whether or not there has been a tendency for the terms of trade for primary producers to deteriorate, it could be seen as part of a much wider question, namely the distribution of the gains from trade. A rather different approach to this question is contained in Emmanuel (1972), the title of which points to its line of argument, *Unequal Exchange*. Any idea of unfair exchange requires, of course, a benchmark of fair exchange. The contrast is drawn between high-wage and low-wage countries. The unequal exchange arises when 'the products of the high-wage country are dearer and the products of the low-wage cheaper *than they would have been if wages were the same in the two countries*' (Brewer, 1980). The determination of prices is based on a Sraffian approach (cf. Chapter 8 and also see Brewer, 1980, ch. 9). Another expression of this is that 'poor nations trade products containing more for less labour-hours from rich nations' (Griffin and Gurley, 1985).

There are two central assumptions in Emmanuel's approach. First, capital is internationally mobile (and will move in pursuit of profits) whereas labour is not usually mobile. Thus there are substantial limitations on the migration of labour, particularly from low-income to high-income countries. In contrast, there are fewer limits on the movement of capital (and those countries which exclude foreign capital would be outside the world capitalist economy). The mobility of capital helps to generate a tendency towards the equalisation of the rate of profits across the capitalist world (cf. section 5.5).

Second, the ratio of wages to the productivity of labour is taken to be lower in poor countries than in rich ones. There is not mobility of labour to reduce the discrepancy of wages between countries. This assumption means that the wage rate in the developing countries is lower than in developed countries, which is a reflection of the differences in the labour market and other economic conditions in the two sets of countries. In particular, real wages are in each case set at a subsistence level but that level is not necessarily a physical subsistence level (cf. section 7.4), but rather contains, in the words of Marx, an 'historic and moral' element.

Another important line of argument can be expressed by the 'dependency leading to underdevelopment' (e.g. Frank, 1969; Baran, 1957). For present purposes two elements of the dependency school are highlighted. The first is that the nature of the relationship between industrialised and non-industrialised is one of dependency of the latter on the former. Thus the nature of the power relationship is for power to reside with the industrialised countries.

The second element could be seen as the segmented labour market approach (section 3.3) extended to the whole of the market system viewed world-wide. The capitalist economic system is seen as covering much of the globe (with the considerable exception of the socialist countries). There may be limitations (national barriers to trade, for example) on the degree to which all these economies are integrated into the world capitalist economy. The crucial point is that the world capitalist economy operates to generate and to reinforce inequalities between the advanced economies and the less advanced.

13.7 CONCLUDING CONSIDERATIONS

There are two related themes running through this chapter, and which have echoes throughout the book. These themes are the general notion of cumulative causation and that unfettered market forces work for the benefit of the economically strong and to the detriment of the economically weak. These themes have considerable implications for economic policy and for economic theory, and in this final section some of these implications are considered.

In the area of public policy, the question arises as to the effects of the operation of unfettered market forces on human welfare and the development of economies. There are numerous inequalities and disparities between people, sexes, classes, regions and countries. The key question is seen to be whether market forces tend to eliminate or exacerbate those inequalities. As seen above (section 3.8), the neo-classical view is that market forces (especially competition) will tend to reduce inequalities (other than those which could in some sense be said to be economically justified). The discussion on the labour market in Chapter 3 and in this chapter has indicated that there are many alternative arguments to the effect that market forces tend to exacerbate disparities. The evidence produced above has also suggested the persistence of economic disparities.

The implications for economic policy considered here arise when markets are seen to perpetuate inequalities (between nations,

regions or individuals). Then any aid or protection for the economically weak has to come from outside of the operation of markets. The
public policy implication is some form of intervention by government in or withdrawal from the market mechanism. At the national
level (as indicated above in the discussion of the import substitution
policy) this is likely to involve some form of trade protection and/or
limits on inward movement of capital. At the regional or individual
level, concerted action by the relevant government is likely to be
required to move resources in the direction of the economically
weak. But the clear difficulty at this level is that the economically
weak are likely to also be politically weak, and hence unable to
obtain policies which benefit them.

The implications for the construction of economic theory are
severalfold, of which seven are highlighted here.[8] The first is that
much of the cumulative causation argument relies on some degree of
increasing returns to scale, whether dynamic or static. A great deal
of the neo-classical literature, especially on perfect competition,
gains from trade, etc., rests on the rejection of any assumption of
increasing returns to scale. In particular, it has been well known
since at least Sraffa (1926) that perfect competition is not viable
under increasing returns (cf. section 12.8). Thus, the view that
increasing returns are present in a significant number of industries
would lead to the rejection of perfect competition as a useful
method of analysis since the structure of perfect competition would
not be viable with increasing returns to scale. Further, under
increasing returns to scale, the firm is provided with an incentive to
expand output (to reap lower costs). Thus, whereas with the
decreasing returns case, it could be said that the technical factors (as
reflected in the cost conditions) limit the expansion of the firm, that
is not the case with increasing returns. Hence, in so far as there are
limits on the size of firms, they would arise from demand and
finance factors rather than cost conditions.

The second implication is that the technical possibilities for production are gradually discovered and enhanced by firms as production takes place, and this was reflected in the idea of learning-by-
doing. This means that it cannot be readily assumed that firms have
full knowledge of the technical possibilities, and that their current
knowledge has been built up by past experience and experimenta-
tion. Thus the past behaviour of a firm is relevant for its current
position. But, further, 'the fact that exogenous production possibility

sets are unknown and unknowable implies that notions of Pareto-*optimality* and intertemporal *efficiency* becomes meaningless' (Skott, 1983).

The third implication is a related one, which is the use of historical rather than logical time. Historical time corresponds to our usual understanding of time, namely that time only moves forward. Starting from position A yesterday and moving to position B today is not necessarily reversible. In moving from A to B and from yesterday to today, experience has been acquired, commitments may have been made, etc., which mean that the move back from B to A may not be possible. The more usual approach in neo-classical economics (which is reflected in all comparative static exercises, for example) is to use logical time. In such a case it may be convenient to talk of A as occurring at time $t-1$ and B at time t, but in discussion of the move from A to B, the passage of time does not enter in any essential way. Indeed it would not make any difference to the analysis whether the time period was a microsecond or several years, and the move from A to B can easily be reversed and would be merely the negative of the original move. This notion of the importance of historical over logical time can be seen to link to one of the important themes of post-Keynesian economics (cf. section 1.2).

The fourth implication concerns the allocation and reallocation of resources between sectors and between industries. In the post-Keynesian view of growth and development discussed in the previous chapter, the allocation of resources between sectors is seen as largely a reflection of the demand for resources, which in turn is a reflection of the demand for the output of the sectors. the reallocation of resources (including labour and capital equipment) between sectors would be largely determined by shifts in demand, and little affected by changes in relative prices. Labour moves between different industries more in response to job opportunities than to movements in relative wages. The approach of Kaldor and others on this has been explicit, with sectors such as agriculture viewed as being able to release labour to other sectors with little impact on output. Thus employment in the industrial sector is then determined by the demands of the industrial sector. Employment in the agricultural sector is in a sense historically and socially determined, depending on the degree of industrialisation.

The neo-classical process focuses on the idea of substitution at the margin, with for example, a firm able to substitute between different factor inputs in response to relative prices. Although it has not been explicit in this discussion, the possibilities of substitution are viewed as limited and insignificant, with much more importance given to the complementarity of inputs.

> The problem of replacing substitution effects with income effects is, of course, that there are no neat equilibrium solutions, but this cannot be justification for elevating the principle of substitution to the centre of the economic stage. It is misleading because it ignores the important complementarities that exist in the real world between the demand for products; the demand for factors of production, and between activities in general. For example, capital and labour are for the most part complementary in the production process. (Thirlwall, 1987)

Whilst the precise combination of capital equipment and labour employed may be influenced by their relative price, nevertheless an important consideration is that the use of capital equipment requires people (labour) to work it.

> The demand for labour (employment) is determined by the rate of accumulation. Similarly, economic activities should be thought of as expanding together. ... The supply of one activity establishes the demand for others; the expansion of one sector stimulates the demand for others, and in the process of expansion resources are generated. (Thirlwall, 1987)

This leads on to the fifth implication, namely the relevance of the creation of resources rather than their allocation. In the very short run, the existing amount of factors and the known production possibilities may form a binding constraint on the level and composition of production, though even then there is usually some unemployed labour and capital equipment. But in any other time span, the approaches discussed in this book would generally argue that any such constraints can gradually be pushed back. Capital equipment can be built, labour drawn from households, from other countries, etc., and knowledge advanced. But these do not happen automatically. They rely on the stimulus of demand, on supporting social and political arrangements (so that, for example, new productive resources are created rather than the modern equivalent of the pyramids built) and the ability of an economy to generate and utilise the necessary surplus.

The sixth implication is rather fundamental in that the usefulness of equilibrium analysis is undermined. This undermining takes a number of forms. One view is that the real economies exhibit disparities and inequalities which cannot easily be comprehended by (neo-classical) equilibrium analysis. As Skott (1983) argues, 'one may choose to ascribe the lack of convergence to the effects of exogenous shocks, but it would seem more promising to examine the possibility that there exist endogenous economic forces which tend to cause income levels to diverge between regions and countries'. Another view is that in the presence of cumulative causation, it is fruitless to seek for equilibrium solutions, and that the requirement on analysis that it must produce equilibrium solutions prevents much useful analysis. Since most economic analysis (including the Sraffian approach discussed in Chapter 8) makes heavy use of equilibrium analysis, the implication of this line of argument would be a call for a drastic change in the dominant mode of economic analysis.

The final implication relates to the analysis of markets, and the nature of the competitive process. This is in a number of respects a theme which has run through this book, and the comments made here reflect that. The market mechanism can be seen as one among a number of institutional arrangements through which resources are allocated. It has been seen that even in economies which are labelled market economies, many resources are allocated within firms, others are allocated by governments and yet others by a variety of means (e.g. charity). Any particular market mechanism operates within a body of law and with a specific set of political and social arrangements which influence how that market mechanism actually operates.

In the neo-classical approach, resources are viewed as moving in response to price signals, with resources moving into areas of high rewards and away from areas of low rewards. In contrast, the radical political economy views resources as moving in response to the level of demand, and in particular that workers tend to move according to the availability of work. Further, output prices may be seen as set in the Sraffian approach by the costs of production (with an equalised rate of profit) or as in the Kaleckian approach (section 9.2) by the market power of the firms involved. Neo-classical economic analysis also strongly suggests that with price flexibility a (competitive) market economy would operate in an efficient manner with the full employment of resources including labour.

The radical political economy approaches have argued that modern capitalist economies do not conform to perfect competition. More importantly, full employment is not a usual outcome from the operation of markets (cf. section 11.4).

The competitive process is not one of atomistic competition, but rather is a mixture of rivalry and co-operation in a situation of oligopoly. Atomistic competition is destroyed by the process of competition in the face of increasing returns with resulting concentration. The nature of competition under these circumstances has been extensively discussed in Chapters 5 and 6. Two additional points are made here. First, whereas the analysis of perfect competition focuses on relative prices and the allocation of resources, the analysis of radical political economy is concerned not only with price formation, but also with the utilisation of resources (e.g. whether there tends to be excess capacity), the creation of resources, and decisions over the labour process. Second, it is difficult (if not impossible) to evaluate the benefits and costs of competition (whereas in contrast the perfect competitive approach is simply evaluated in terms of the Pareto criterion). This in part reflects that there are numerous dimensions to the effects of competition, and that there are several meanings attached to the term 'competition'.

Firms are generally organised on a hierarchical basis with the owners and managers exercising control over the workforce. Thus within each firm decisions are taken in the interests of the owners and managers, rather than of the workers. The existing market mechanisms (especially but not only those based on capitalist ownership) make substantial use of control by managers over workers. Production is organised in a way which raises profitability and aids control over the workforce, rather than on the basis of efficiency and the welfare of the workers involved.

Finally, there is not an antinomy between government and markets even though that is how the relationship is often portrayed. It is rather that how markets operate depends on the role of government, which may range from the legal framework for contracts through to the adoption of a developmental role by the government. Industrialisation has often been strongly aided by the State (as indicated in Chapter 10), though the adoption of the wrong policies has on other occasions held back or prevented industrialisation. But interventions in the economy by the State are responses to a host of social and political pressures. On occasions, interventions may speed up economic growth and industrialisation but on other occasions slow it down: there are no uniform linkages on the relationship between government intervention and the pace and nature of economic change. Government intervention often takes the form of changing the structure of the market concerned. This can involve the restructuring of industry (e.g. encouraging mergers, promoting reduction of capacity), changing the balance of power between the two sides of the market (as often occurs in the labour market where industrial relations legislation, willingness of government to intervene in industrial disputes, etc., help to determine the power balance) and in many other ways. In modern industrial societies, the question is not whether government should be involved in the economy, but rather how and in whose interests governments intervene.

APPENDIX

In Chapter 12, there was discussion of Verdoorn's law, and in Chapter 13 this idea was formally expressed by a simple equation (equation (13.4)). The purpose of this appendix is to provide some detailed discussion on the implications of Verdoorn's law and also to say a little on the idea of a technical progress function (Kaldor, 1957; Kaldor and Mirrlees, 1962).

Equation (13.4) in the text is:

$$g = b + f q \qquad (A13.1)$$

where g is the rate of growth of output per employee (labour productivity), and q is the growth of output, from which:

$$e = -b + (1-f) q \qquad (A13.2)$$

can be easily derived, with e the rate of growth of employment.

Before discussing the implications of these equations, it is useful to briefly consider a production function approach. For simplicity, a Cobb–Douglas production function is used of the form:

$$Q = L^a K^b e^{ct} \qquad (A13.3)$$

where c is the rate of (exogenous) technical change. By differentiation we obtain:

$$q = a e + b k + c \qquad (A13.4)$$

where k is the rate of growth of capital equipment. This equation can be rearranged to read:

$$e = (1/a) \, q - (b/a) \, k - (c/a) \tag{A13.5}$$

In equation (A13.3), since the production function represents part of a neo-classical approach, the rate of technical progress (c) is exogenously given, and ($a + b$) would normally be taken equal to unity to indicate constant returns to scale. There are a number of notable features of this equation and approach. If the production function is used within a neo-classical approach and marginal productivity theory it is required that $a + b$ add up to unity. It would then be expected that the coefficient $(1/a)$ in equation (A13.5) would be greater than unity according to that approach. Further, the production function approach separates the rate of technical progress from the rate of investment (growth of capital equipment). Finally, note that the growth of employment is negatively related to the rate of technical progress.

In one sense equation (A13.2) appears to be a simplified version of equation (A13.5) with the k term omitted. Indeed, if it is assumed that the growth of stock of capital equipment is related to growth of output then equation (A13.5) could simplify down to equation (A13.2). To illustrate, suppose that $k = x \, q$, then we have:

$$e = q \, (1 - x \, b)/a - (c/a) \tag{A13.6}$$

Is it to be concluded that equation (A13.2) is merely a naive version of a conventional production function approach? The algebraic similarity is misleading for the derivation of the two equations has been quite different. The views taken of technical change and knowledge of the available production possibilities are quite different. In the neo-classical case, technical change occurs at a predetermined rate with production possibilities known to the firms. In the approach of Kaldor, the rate of technical change is endogenously determined (by learning-by-doing, rate of investment, etc.) and production possibilities are only gradually discovered and extended. The coefficient on q in equation (A13.1) would be predicted by Kaldor and others to be less than unity (reflecting dynamic scale economies). In contrast, in equation (A13.6) the coefficient would be unity if $x = 1$ (for then the coefficient on q becomes $(1-b)/a$ which with constant returns to scale is equal to 1 since $a + b = 1$), and less than unity to the extent to which k exceeds q.

It is necessary to consider the causation involved in the relationship between output and employment. It could be considered that firms make decisions on output and employment simultaneously in response to the market conditions which they face. For a perfectly competitive firm, output and employment decided upon would depend on the relative prices which the firm faced. In imperfectly competitive cases, firms can be seen as making a number of decisions simultaneously, and of particular relevance here is that such firms would be deciding upon both output and employment at the same time in response to the demand and other conditions which they face. In that case, it would not matter whether the output–employment relationship was estimated in terms of equation (A13.5) or equation (A13.6). However, at the macro level what interpretation should be placed on an output–employment relationship? If there is always full employment, then employment is predetermined and output arises as a consequence of that level of employment. Conversely, when there is unemployment then the causation is reversed and is seen by Keynesians to run from aggregate demand through output to employment. In the context of growth, this would mean that equations (A13.1) or (A13.2) would be appropriate for econometric estimation in the sense that causation is treated as running from right to left, but equation (A13.4) would not in the sense that this equation treats employment growth as exogenous and as determining growth of output.

The idea of a technical progress function relates the growth of labour productivity to the growth of capital per worker, e.g. in a linear form:

$$g = m + n\,(k - e) \tag{A13.7}$$

with $n < 1$, and this can be rewritten as:

$$q = m + n\,k + (1-n)\,e \tag{A13.8}$$

This can be seen as rather similar to equation (A13.4). The important differences of interpretation are as follows:

1. In the technical progress function case, the driving force is the growth of demand which stimulates investment (reflected in k) and also provides the market for the resulting output. In the case of equation (A13.4), supply is the driving force, with the growth of inputs leading to growth of output without any direct concern as to whether that growth of supply can actually be sold.

2. In the technical progress function approach, the level of output achievable at a particular time depends on the past history of the economy, for that will have determined the growth of labour, capital equipment and technical knowledge. The use of production function (as in equation (A13.3)) leaves aside any discussion of how the existing levels of labour, capital equipment and knowledge came into being.

NOTES

1. For an extensive discussion on the ideas of cumulative causation see Skott (1985).
2. The discussion below is confined to the firm rather than the individual. However, the following is a case where it applies to an individual. 'For example, a poor man may not have enough to eat; being undernourished, his health may be weak; being physically weak, his working capacity may be low, which means that he is poor, which in turn means that he will not have enough to eat; and so on. A situation of this sort, applying to a country as a whole, can be summed up in the trite proposition: "a country is poor because it is poor"' (Nurkse, 1952).
3. See Stafford (1983) for some further discussion on the difficulties which a cumulative causation explanation of British economic decline faces. The basic difficulty is that in the nineteenth century, Britain was the leading industrial nation, and the idea of cumulative causation would indicate that their lead would be retained and perhaps extended.
4. An early statement of this general notion is in Tawney (1926).
5. For further discussion see Brewer (1980, ch. 2).
6. 'As in the pre-war period, a major proportion (averaging 82% during 1953–81) of the primary product exports of the developed countries were directed to other developed countries. On the other hand, about 80% of the total primary product exports of the developing region were directed to the countries of the developed region. Furthermore primary products constituted 83% of the total flow of commodities from the developing region to the developed one during 1953–81; the share would be 69% if we excluded fuels from the total flow. Meanwhile, the average share of manufactures in the total exports of the developed region towards the developing one stood at 78% and 80% (including and excluding fuels respectively) during the same period. So an observed decline (or improvement) in the NBTT [net barter terms of trade] of primary products must be expected to imply a similar trend in the terms of trade of the developing region vis-à-vis the developed region' (Sarkar, 1986).

7. See Pollin and Alarcon (1988) for a recent evaluation of the import substitution policies.
8. For discussion which has influenced this section see Skott (1985), Thirlwall (1987, ch. 13) and Kaldor (1985).

BIBLIOGRAPHY

Aaronovitch, S. (1977) 'The firm and concentration', in F. Green and P. Nore (eds), *Economics: An Anti-text* (Macmillan).

Aaronovitch, S. and Smith, R. (1981) *The Political Economy of British Capitalism* (McGraw-Hill).

Aglietta, M. (1979) *A Theory of Capitalist Regulation: The US Experience*, (trans D. Fernbach) (New Left Books).

Alchian, A. A. and Demsetz, H. (1972) 'Production, information costs, and economic organizations', *American Economic Review*, vol. 62.

Allen, S. G. (1988) 'Productivity levels and productivity change under unionism', *Industrial Relations*, vol. 27.

Allsopp, C. (1982) 'Inflation', in A. Boltho (ed.), *The European Economy: Growth and Crisis* (Oxford University Press).

Amott, T. (1984) 'The politics of Reagonomics', in E. Nell (ed.), *Free Market Conservatism: A Critique of Theory and Practice* (Allen and Unwin).

Archibald, G. C. (1971) 'Introduction', in G. C. Archibald (ed.), *The Theory of the Firm* (Penguin Books).

Armstrong P., Glyn, A., and Harrison, J. (1984) *Capitalism Since World War II* (Fontana).

Arrow, K. J. (1951) *Social Choice and Individual Values*, Cowles Foundation Monograph no. 17 (Wiley).

Arrow, K. J. (1962) 'Economic welfare and the allocation of resources for invention', in *The Rate and Direction of Inventive Activity: Economic and Social Aspects* (National Bureau for Economic Research, Princeton University Press).

Asimakopulos, A. and Burbridge, J. B. (1974) 'The short period incidence of taxation', *Economic Journal*, vol. 84.

Auerbach, P. (1988) *Competition: The Economics of Industrial Change* (Blackwell).

Auerbach, P. and Skott, P. (1988) 'Concentration, competition and distribution: A critique of theories of monopoly capitalism', *International Review of Applied Economics*, vol. 2.

Baran, P. (1957) *The Political Economy of Growth* (Monthly Review) (and with introduction by R. B. Sutcliffe, Penguin Books, 1973).

Baran, P. and Sweezy, P. (1966) *Monopoly Capital* (Monthly Review Press).

Baranzini, M. and Scazzieri, R. (1986a) 'Knowledge in economics: A framework', in M. Baranzini and R. Scazzieri (eds), *Foundations of Economics: Structure of Inquiry and Economic Theory* (Blackwell).

Baranzini, M. and Scazzieri, R. (eds) (1986b) *Foundations of Economics: Structure of Inquiry and Economic Theory* (Blackwell).

Bauer, P. (1942) 'A note on monopoly', *Economica*, vol. 8.

Baumol, W. J. (1959) *Business Behaviour, Value and Growth* (Macmillan).

Becker, G. (1957) *The Economics of Discrimination* (University of Chicago Press).

Becker, G. (1966) 'Crime and punishment: an economic analysis', *Journal of Political Economy*, vol. 74.

Becker, G. S. (1973), 'The theory of marriage, part 1', *Journal of Political Economy*, vol. 81.

Becker, G. and Landes, W. M. (eds) (1974) *Essays in the Economics of Crime and Punishment* (Columbia University Press).

Becker, G. S., Landes, E. and Michael, R. T. (1977) 'An economic analysis of marital instability', *Journal of Political Economy*, vol. 85.

Beckerman, W. (1985) 'How the battle against inflation was really won', *Lloyds Bank Review*, January.

Beckerman, W. and Jenkinson, T. (1986) 'What stopped the inflation? Unemployment or commodity prices?', *Economic Journal*, vol. 96.

Berle, A. A. and Means, G. C. (1932) *The Modern Corporation and Private Property* (Macmillan).

Bhaduri, A. and Steindl, J. (1983) 'The rise of monetarism as a social doctrine', *Thames Papers in Political Economy*, Autumn.

Bleaney, M. (1976) *Underconsumption Theories* (Lawrence & Wishart).

Blumberg, P. (1968) *Industrial Democracy: The Sociology of Participation* (Constable).

Boadway, R. and Bruce, N. (1984) *Welfare Economics* (Blackwell).

Bohm-Bawerk, E. von (1975) *Karl Marx and the Close of His System* (Merlin) (first published 1896).

Boltho, A. (1982a) 'Growth', in A. Boltho (ed.), *The European Economy: Growth and Crisis* (Oxford University Press).

Boltho, A. (ed.) (1982b) *The European Economy: Growth and Crisis* (Oxford University Press).

Borts, G. (1981) 'Report of Managing Editor', *American Economic Review*, vol. 71, no. 2.

Bowles, S. (1985) 'The production process in a competitive economy: Walrasian, neo-Hobbesian and Marxian models', *American Economic Review*, vol. 75.

Bowles, S. and Edwards, R. (1985) *Understanding Capitalism* (Harper & Row).

Bowles, S. and Edwards, R. (eds) (1989) *Radical Political Economy* (2 vols) (Edward Elgar).

Bowles, S., Gordon, D. M., and Weisskopf, T. (1986) 'Power and profits: The social structure of accumulation and the profit ability of the postwar U.S. economy', *Review of Radical Political Economies*, vol. 18.

Boyer, R. (1979) 'Wage formation in historical perspective', *Cambridge Journal of Economics*, vol. 3.

Bradley, I. and Howard, M. (eds) (1982a) *Classical and Marxian Political Economy: Essays in Honour of Ronald Meek* (Macmillan).

Bradley, I. and Howard, M. (1982b) 'Piero Sraffa's "Production of Commodities by means of Commodities" and the rehabilitation of classical and Marxian political economy', in I. Bradley and M. Howard (eds), *Classical and Marxian Political Economy* (Macmillan).

Braverman, H. (1974) *Labor and Monopoly Capital* (Monthly Review Press).

Brewer, A. (1980) *Marxist Theories of Imperialism* (Routledge & Kegan Paul).

Budd, A. and Dicks, G. (1982) 'Inflation – a monetarist perspective', in A. Boltho (ed.), *The European Economy: Growth and Crisis* (Oxford University Press).

Burch, P. H. (1972) *The Managerial Revolution Reassessed* (Lexington Books).

Burkitt, B. (1984) *Radical Political Economy* (Harvester Wheatsheaf).

Burnham, J. (1941) *The Managerial Revolution: What is Happening in the World* (John Day).

Canterbery, E. R. and Burkhardt, R. J. (1983) 'What do we mean by asking whether economics is a science', in A. S. Eichner (ed.) *Why Economics is not yet a Science* (Macmillan).

Catephores, G. (1987) 'Alienation', in J. Eatwell, M. Millgate and J. Newman (eds), *The New Palgrave* (Macmillan).

Chandler, A. (1977) *The Visible Hand: The Managerial Revolution in America* (Harvard University Press).

Chick, V. (1986) 'The evolution of the banking system and the theory of saving, investment and interest', *Economics et Societes* (Cahiers de l'ISMEA Serie Monnaie et Production, no. 3).

Clifton, J. (1977) 'Competition and the evolution of the capitalist mode of production', *Cambridge Journal of Economics*, vol. 1.

Coase, R. (1937), 'The nature of the firm', *Economica*, vol. 4.

Cole, K., Cameron, J. and Edwards, C. (1983) *Why Economists Disagree* (Longman).

Cornwall, J. (1977) *Modern Capitalism: Its Growth and Transformation* (M. E. Sharpe).

Cosh, A. and Hughes, A. (1987) 'The anatomy of corporate control: directors, shareholders and executive renumeration in giant US and UK corporations', *Cambridge Journal of Economics*, vol. 11.

Cowling, K. (1981) 'Oligopoly, distribution and the rate of profit', *European Economic Review*, vol. 15.

Cowling, K. (1982), *Monopoly Capitalism* (Macmillan).

Cowling, K. (1983) 'Excess capacity and the degree of collusion: oligopoly behaviour in the slump', *Manchester School*, vol. 51.

Cowling, K. (1985), 'Economic obstacles to democracy', in R.C.O. Matthews (ed.), *Economy and Democracy* (Macmillan).

Cowling, K. and Sugden, R. (1987a), 'Market exchange and the concept of a transnational corporation: Analysing the nature of the firm', *British Review of Economic Issues*, vol. 9.

Cowling, K. and Sugden, R. (1987b) *Transnational Monopoly Capitalism* (Harvester Wheatsheaf).

Cowling, K. and Waterson, M. (1976) 'Price–cost margins and market structure', *Economica*, vol. 43.

Crompton, R. and Reid, S. (1982) 'The deskilling of clerical work', in S. Wood (ed.), *The Degradation of Work* (Hutchinson).

Cross, R. (1982) 'The Duhem–Quine thesis, Lakatos and the appraisal of the theories of macroeconomics', *Economic Journal*, vol. 92.

Cutler, A. (1978) 'The romance of labour', *Economy and Society*, vol. 7.

Cyert, R. M. and March, J. G. (1963) *Behavioural Theory of the Firm* (Prentice Hall).

Davidson, P. (1981) 'Post Keynesian economics', in D. Bell and I. Kristol (eds), *The Crisis in Economic Theory* (Basic Books).

Deacon, A. (1981) 'Unemployment and policies in Britain since 1945' in B. Showler and A. Sinfield (eds), *The Workless State* (Martin Robertson).

Deane, P. (1978) *The Evolution of Economic Ideas* (Cambridge University Press).

Department of Employment (1985) *Employment: The Challenge for the Nation*, Cmnd. 9474 (HMSO).

deVroey, M. (1975) 'The separation of ownership and control in large corporations', *Review of Radical Political Economics*, vol. 7.

deVroey, M. (1984) 'A regulation approach interpretation of contemporary crises', *Capital and Class*, no. 23 (Summer).

Dixon, R. J. and Thirlwall, A. (1975) 'A model of regional growth rate differences on Kaldorian lines', *Oxford Economic Papers*, vol. 27.

Dobb, M. (1973) *Theories of Value and Distribution Since Adam Smith* (Cambridge University Press).

Doeringer, P. B. and Piore, M. J. (1971) *Internal Labor Markets and Manpower Analysis* (Heath Lexington Books).

Drago, R. (1984) 'New use of an old technology: the growth of worker participation', *Journal of Post Keynesian Economics*, vol. 7.

Dugger, W. M. (1983), 'The transactions cost analysis of Oliver E. Williamson: A new synthesis ?', *Journal of Economic Issues*, vol. 17.

Duhem, P. (1906) *The Aim and Structure of Physical Theory* (trans P. Wiener, Princeton University Press, 1954).

Dumenil, G., Glick, M. and Rangel, J. (1987) 'The rate of profit in the United States', *Cambridge Journal of Economics*, vol. 11.

Eatwell, J. (1982) 'Competition', in I. Bradley and M. Howard (eds), *Classical and Marxian Economy* (Macmillan).

Eatwell, J. (1987a) 'Competition: classical concepts', in J. Eatwell, M. Millgate and J. Newman (eds), *The New Palgrave* (Macmillan).

Eatwell, J. (1987b) 'The standard commodity', in J. Eatwell, M. Millgate and J. Newman (eds), *The New Palgrave* (Macmillan).

Eatwell, J. (1987c) 'Import substitution and export-led growth', in J. Eatwell, M. Millgate and J. Newman (eds), *The New Palgrave* (Macmillan).

Eatwell, J. and Milgate, M. (eds) (1983a) *Keynes's Economics and the Theory of Value and Distribution* (Duckworth).

Eatwell, J. and Milgate, M. (1983b) 'Introduction', in J. Eatwell and M. Milgate (eds),

Keynes's Economics and the Theory of Value and Distribution (Duckworth).

Edwards, R. (1979) *Contested Terrain* (Heinemann).

Ehrlich, I. (1973) 'Participation in illegitimate activities: theoretical and empirical investigation', *Journal of Political Economy*, vol. 81.

Eichner, A. S. (1973) 'A theory of the determination of the mark-up under oligopoly', *Economic Journal*, vol. 83.

Eichner, A. S. (1976) *The Megacorp and Oligopoly, Micro-foundations of Macro Dynamics* (Cambridge University Press).

Eichner, A. S. (ed.) (1979) *A Guide to Post-Keynesian Economics* (M. E. Sharpe, and Macmillan).

Eichner, A. S. (1983a) 'Why economics is not yet a science', in A. S. Eichner (ed.), *Why Economics is not yet a Science* (Macmillan).

Eichner, A. S. (ed.) (1983b) *Why Economics is not yet a Science* (Macmillan).

Eichner, A. S. (1985) *Towards a New Economics* (M. E. Sharpe; also published by Macmillan, 1986).

Eichner, A. S. (1987), *The Macrodynamics of Advanced Market Economies* (M. E. Sharpe).

Elbaum, M., Lazonick, W., Wilkinson, F. and Zeitlin, J. (1979) 'The labour process, market structure and Marxist theory', *Cambridge Journal of Economics*, vol. 3.

Elger, A. (1979) 'Valorisation and deskilling – a critique of Braverman, *Capital and Class*, vol. 7.

Elger, T. (1982) 'Braverman, capital accumulation and deskilling, in S. Wood (ed.), *The Degradation of Work?* (Hutchinson).

Emmanuel, A. (1972) *Unequal Exchange: A Study of the Imperialism of Trade* (New Left Books).

Ferber, M. A., Green, C. A. and Spaeth, J. L. (1986) 'Work, power and earnings of women and men', *American Economic Review*, vol. 76.

Ferguson, C. E. (1969) *The Neo-classical Theory of Production and Distribution* (Cambridge University Press).

Fine, B. and Harris, L. (1979) *Rereading Capital* (Macmillan).

Fine, B. and Murfin, A. (1984a) *Macroeconomics and Monopoly Capitalism* (Harvester Wheatsheaf).

Fine, B. and Murfin, A. (1984b) 'The political economy of monopoly and competition', *International Journal of Industrial Organisation*, vol. 2.

Foley, D. (1978) 'State expenditure from a Marxist perspective', *Journal of Public Economics*, vol. 9.

Francis, A. (1980) 'Company objectives, managerial motivations and the behaviour of large firms: an empirical test of the theory of "managerial" capitalism', *Cambridge Journal of Economics*, vol. 4.

Francis, A., Turk, J. and Willman, P. (eds) (1983) *Power, Efficiency and Institutions* (Heinemann).

Frank, A. G. (1969) *Capitalism and Underdevelopment in Latin America* (rev. edn) (Modern Reader Paperbacks).

Frank, J. F. (1986) *The New Keynesian Economics* (Harvester Wheatsheaf).

Freeman, C. (1982) *The Economics of Industrial Innovation* (2nd edn) (Frances Pinter).

Freeman, C. (ed.) (1983) *Long Waves in the World Economy* (Butterworth).

Freeman, C., Clark, J. and Soete, L. (1982) *Unemployment and Technical Innovation* (Frances Pinter).

Freeman, R. B. and Medoff, J. L. (1984) *What do Unions Do?* (Basic Books).

Friedman, A. (1977) *Industry and Labour: Class Struggle at Work and Monopoly Capitalism* (Macmillan).

Friedman, M. (1953) *Essays in Positive Economics* (University of Chicago Press).

Friedman, M. (1962) *Capitalism and Freedom* (University of Chicago Press).

Friedman, M. (1968) 'The role of monetary policy', *American Economic Review*, vol. 58.

Galbraith, J. K. (1967) *The New Industrial State* (Hamish Hamilton).

Gerdes, C. (1977) 'The fundamental contradiction in the neo-classical theory of income distribution', *Review of Radical Political Economics*, vol. 9.

Gintis, H. (1976) 'The nature of labor exchange and the theory of capitalist production', *Review of Radical Political Economics*, vol. 8.

Glyn, A. and Sutcliffe, R. (1972) *British Capitalism, Workers and the Profit Squeeze* (Penguin Books).

Gordon, D. M., Edwards, R. and Reich, M. (1982) *Segmented Work, Divided Workers* (Cambridge University Press).

Gough, I. (1979) *The Political Economy of the Welfare State* (Macmillan).

Green, F. (1984) 'A critique of the neo-Fisherian consumption function', *Review of Radical Political Economy*, vol. 16.

Green, F. and Nore, P. (eds) (1979) *Issues in Political Economy* (Macmillan).

Green, F. and Sutcliff, B. (1987) *The Profit System: Economics of Capitalism* (Pelican Books).

Greenway, D. and Shaw, G. K. (1988) *Macro-economics* (2nd edn) (Blackwell).

Griffin, K. and Gurley, J. (1985) 'Radical analyses of imperialism, the third world, and the transition to socialism: a survey article', *Journal of Economic Literature*, vol. 23.

Hacche, G. (1979) *The Theory of Economic Growth: An Introduction* (Macmillan).

Hahn, F. (1982) 'The neo-Ricardians', *Cambridge Journal of Economics*, vol. 6.

Ham, C. and Hill, M. (1984) *The Policy Process in the Modern Capitalist State* (Harvester Wheatsheaf).

Hannah, L. (1983) *The Rise of the Corporate Economy* (2nd edn) (Methuen).

Hannah, L. and Kay, K. (1977) *Concentration in Modern Industry* (Macmillan).

Harcourt, G. C. (1972) *Some Cambridge Controversies in the Theory of Capital* (Cambridge University Press).

Harcourt, G. C. (1982) 'The Sraffian contribution: an evaluation', in I. Bradley and M. Howard (eds), *Classical and Marxian Political Economy* (Macmillan).

Harcourt, G. C. and Kenyon, P. (1976) 'Pricing and the investment decision', *Kyklos*, vol. 29.

Harris, D. (1978) *Capital Accumulation and Income Distribution* (Routledge & Kegan Paul).

Hayek, F. (1944) *The Road to Serfdom* (Routledge & Kegan Paul).

Henderson, J. M. and Quandt, R. E. (1971) *Microeconomic Theory: A Mathematical Approach* (McGraw-Hill).

Henley, A. (1987) 'Trade unions, market concentration and income distribution in United States manufacturing industry', *International Journal of Industrial Organisation*, vol. 5.

Henley, A. (1988) 'Political aspects of full employment: a reassessment of Kalecki', *Political Quarterly*, vol. 59.

Henry, S. G. B., Sawyer, M. and Smith, P. (1976) 'Models of inflation in the U.K.: an evaluation', *National Institute Economic Review*, no. 76.

Hicks, J. (1976) 'Revolutions in economics', in S. J. Latsis (ed.), *Method and Appraisal in Economics* (Cambridge University Press).

Hilferding, R. (1981) *Finance Capital* (based on translations by M. Watnick and S. Gordon, edited with an introduction by T. Bottomore) (Routledge & Kegan Paul) (originally published in German, 1910).

Himmelweit, S. (1979) 'Growth and reproduction', in F. Green and P. Nore (eds), *Issues in Political Economy* (Macmillan).

Hirschman, A. O. (1970) *Exit, Voice and Loyalty* (Harvard University Press).

Hodgson, G. (1982a) 'Theoretical and policy implications of variable productivity', *Cambridge Journal of Economics*, vol. 6.

Hodgson, G. (1982b) 'Worker participation and macroeconomic efficiency', *Journal of Post Keynesian Economics*, vol. 5.

Hodgson, G. (1982c) *Capitalism, Value and Exploitation* (Martin Robertson).

Hodgson, G. (1988) *Economics and Institutions* (Polity Press).

Hollis, J. M. and Nell, E. J. (1974) *Rational Economic Man* (Cambridge University Press).

Howard, M. (1983) *Profits in Economic Theory* (Macmillan).

Howard, M. (1987) 'Economics on a Sraffian foundation: a critical analysis of neo-Ricardian theory', *Economy and Society*, vol. 16.

Jessop, R. (1977) 'Recent theories of the state', *Cambridge Journal of Economics*, vol. 1.

Jessop, R. (1982) *The Capitalist State: Marxist Theories and Methods* (Martin Robertson).

Jevons, W. (1871) *Theory of Political Economy* (Macmillan).

Jorgenson, D. (1963) 'Capital theory and investment behaviour', *American Economic Review*, vol. 53.

Jones, D. C. and Svejnar, J. (eds) (1982a) *Participatory and Self-managed Firms* (Lexington Books).

Jones, D. C. and Svejnar, J. (1982b) 'The economic performance of participatory and self-managed firms: a historical perspective and review', in D. C. Jones and J. Svejnar (eds), *Participatory and Self-managed Firms* (Lexington Books).

Jones, E. (1983) 'Industrial structure and labour force segmentation', *Review of Radical Political Economy*, vol. 15.

Jones, H. G. (1975) *An Introduction to Modern Theories of Economic Growth* (Macmillan).

Junankar, P. N. (1982) *Marx's Economics* (Philip Allan).

Kaldor, N. (1955) 'Alternative theories of distribution', *Review of Economic Studies*, vol. 23.

Kaldor, N. (1957) 'A model of economic growth', *Economic Journal*, vol. 67.

Kaldor, N. (1961) 'Increasing returns and economic progress: a comment on Professor Hicks' article', *Oxford Economic Papers*, vol. 13.

Kaldor, N. (1966) *Causes of the Slow Rate of Economic Growth of the United Kingdom* (Cambridge University Press).

Kaldor, N. (1972) 'The irrelevance of equilibrium economics', *Economic Journal*, vol. 82.

Kaldor, N. (1985) *Economics without Equilibrium* (University College Cardiff Press).

Kaldor, N. and Mirrlees, J. (1962) 'A new model of economic growth', *Review of Economic Studies*, vol. 29.

Kalecki, M. (1937) 'A theory of commodity, income and capital taxation', *Economic Journal*, vol. 47.

Kalecki, M. (1938) 'The determinants of the distribution of national income', *Econometrica*, vol. 6.

Kalecki, M. (1943) 'Political aspects of full employment', *Political Quarterly*, vol. 14.

Kalecki, M. (1945) 'Full employment by stimulating private investment?', *Oxford Economic Papers*, no. 7.

Kalecki, M. (1970) 'Theories of growth in different social systems', *Scientia*, no. 5–6.

Kalecki, M. (1971a) *Selected Essays on the Dynamics of the Capitalist Economy* (Cambridge University Press).

Kalecki, M. (1971b) 'The class struggle and the distribution of national income', *Kyklos*, vol. 24.

Kalecki, M. (1972) *The Last Phase in the Transformation of Capitalism* (Monthly Review Press).

Kalecki, M. (1976) *Essays on Developing Economies* (Harvester Wheatsheaf).

Kamenka, E. and Neale, R. S. (1975) (eds) *Feudalism, Capitalism and Beyond* (Arnold).

Katouzian, H. (1980) *Ideology and Method in Economics* (Macmillan).

Kay, N. M. (1984) *The Emergent Firm* (Macmillan).

Keynes, J. M. (1936) *The General Theory of Employment, Interest and Money* (Macmillan).

Keynes, J. M. (1937) 'The General Theory of Employment', *Quarterly Journal of Economics*, vol. 51.

Khan, L. H. (1980) 'Bargaining power, search theory and the Phillips curve', *Cambridge Journal of Economics*, vol. 4.

Kidron, M. (1968) *Western Capitalism Since the War* (Weidenfeld and Nicolson).

King, J. E. (ed.) (1989) *Marxian Economics* (3 vols) (Edward Elgar).

Kondratieff, N. D. (1926) 'Die langen Wellen der Konjunktur', *Archiv fuer Sozialwissenschaft und Sozialpolitik*, December.

Kraft, P. and Dubnoff, S. (1986) 'Job content, fragmentation, and control in computer software work', *Industrial Relations*, vol. 25.

Kriesler, P. (1987) *Kalecki's Microanalysis* (Cambridge University Press).

Krueger, A. (1963) 'The economics of discrimination', *Journal of Political Economy*, vol. 71.

Lafitte, F. (1973) 'Social policy in a free society', reprinted in W. Birrell *et al.* (eds),

Social Administration: Readings in Applied Social Science (Penguin Books).

Lange, O. (1937) 'On the economic theory of socialism', *Review of Economic Studies*, vol. 4.

Larner, R. (1966) 'Ownership and control in the 200 largest non-financial corporations, 1929 and 1963', *American Economic Review*, vol. 56.

Layard, P. R. G. and Walters, A. A. (1978) *Microeconomic Theory* (McGraw-Hill).

Lazonick, W. (1979) 'Industrial relations and technical change: the case of the self-acting mule', *Cambridge Journal of Economics*, vol. 4.

Leech, D. (1987) 'Corporate ownership and control: a new look at the evidence of Berle and Means', *Oxford Economic Papers*, vol. 39.

Leibenstein, H. (1966) 'Allocative efficiency vs. X-efficiency', *American Economic Review*, vol. 56.

Leibenstein, H. (1976) *Beyond Economic Man* (Harvard University Press).

Lenin, V. I. (1916), *Imperialism: The Highest Stage of Capitalism*, in V. I. Lenin, *Selected works*, Vol. 5 (Lawrence & Wishart, 1936).

Lichenstein, P. M. (1983) *An Introduction to Post-Keynesian and Marxian Theories of Value and Price* (Macmillan).

Lippit, V. D. (1985) 'The concept of the surplus in economic development', *Review of Radical Political Economics*, vol. 17.

Littlechild, S. C. (ed.) (1989) *Austrian Economics* (2 vols) (Edward Elgar).

Littler, C. R. and Salaman, G. (1982) 'Bravermania and beyond: recent theories of the labour process', *Sociology*, vol. 16.

Llewellen, W. G. (1969) 'Management and ownership in the large firm', *Journal of Finance*, vol. 24.

Llewllen, W. G. (1971) *Ownership Income of Management* (N.B.E.R.).

Lord, S. (1979) 'Neo-classical theories of discrimination: a critique', in F. Green and P. Nore (eds), *Issues in Political Economy* (Macmillan).

Luxemburg, R. (1963) *Accumulation of Capital* (Routledge & Kegan Paul), (first published 1913).

McCloskey, D. N. (1986) *The Rhetoric of Economics*, (Harvester Wheatsheaf).

McCombie, J. S. L. (1983) 'Kaldor's laws in retrospect', *Journal of Post Keynesian Economics*, vol. 5.

McKenzie, R. and Tullock, G. (1981) *The New World of Economics* (3rd edn) (Irwin).

McNulty, P. J. (1987) 'Competition: Austrian concepts', in J. Eatwell, M. Millgate, and J. Newman, (eds), *The New Palgrave* (Macmillan).

Machlup, F. (1967) 'Theories of the firm: marginalist, behavioural, managerial', *American Economic Review*, vol. 57.

Maddison, A. (1982) *Phases of Capitalist Development* (Oxford University Press).

Mainwaring, L. (1984) *Value and Distribution in Capitalist Economies: An Introduction to Sraffian Economics* (Cambridge University Press).

Mandel, E. (1964) 'The economics of neo-capitalism', *Socialist Register, 1964*.

Mandel, E. (1968) *Marxist Economic Theory* (Merlin Press).

Mandel, E. (1975) *Late Capitalism* (New Left Review Press).

Mandel, E. (1980) *Long Waves of Capitalist Development* (Cambridge University Press).

Manning, A. (1987) 'Trade union power and jobs: theory and policy', *International Review of Applied Economics*, vol. 1.

Manwaring, T. (1984) 'The extended internal labour market', *Cambridge Journal of Economic*, vol. 8.

Marglin, S. (1974) 'What do bosses do?' *Review of Radical Political Economy*, vol. 6.

Marglin, S. (1984) 'Growth, distribution and inflation: a centennial synthesis', *Cambridge Journal of Economics*, vol. 8.

Marquand, D. (1988) *The Unprincipled Society* (Fontana Press).

Marris, R. (1964) *The Economic Theory of 'Managerial' Capitalism* (Macmillan).

Marshall, A. (1919) *Industry and Trade* (Macmillan).

Marshall, A. (1920) *Principles of Economics* (8th edn) (Macmillan).

Marshall, R. (1974) 'The economics of racial discrimination: a survey', *Journal of Economic Literature*, vol. 12.

Marx, K. (1976) *Capital*, vol. 1 (trans. B. Fowkes) (Penguin Books).

Marx, K. (1978) *Capital*, vol. 2 (trans. D. Fernbach) (Penguin Books).

Marx, K. (1981) *Capital*, vol. 3 (trans. D. Fernbach) (Penguin Books).

Mason, E. (1958) 'The apologetics of managerialism', *The Journal of Business*, vol. 31.

Matthews, R. C. O. (1959) *Trade Cycle* (Cambridge University Press).

Meek, R. (1967) *Economics and Ideology, and Other Essays* (Chapman & Hall).

Meek, R. (1973) *Studies in the Labour Theory of Value* (Lawrence & Wishart).

Menger, C. (1951) *Principles of Economics* (trans. J. Dingwall and B. Hoseliz) (Free Press).

Mensch, G. (1979) *Stalemate in Technology: Innovations Overcome the Depression* (Bellinger).

Miliband, R. (1969) *The State in Capitalist Society* (Weidenfeld and Nicolson).

Minford, P. (1983) *Rational Expectations and the New Macroeconomics* (Martin Robertson).

Ministry of Reconstruction (1944) *Employment Policy*, Cmd. 6527 (HMSO).

Minsky, H. P. (1978) 'The financial instability hypothesis: a restatement', *Thames Papers in Political Economy*, Autumn.

Minsky, H. (1986) *Inflation, Recession and Economic Policy* (Harvester Wheatsheaf).

Mises, L. von (1949) *Human Action: A Treatise on Economics* (Hodge).

Moore, B. (1979) 'The endogenous money stock', *Journal of Post Keynesian Economics*, vol. 2.

Moore, B. (1988) *Horizontalists and Verticalists: The Macroeconomics of Credit Money* (Cambridge University Press).

Morishima, M. (1973) *Marx's Economics* (Cambridge University Press).

Morishima, M. and Catephores, G. (1978) *Value, Exploitation and Growth* (McGraw-Hill).

Mueser, P. (1987) 'Discrimination', in J. Eatwell, M. Milligate and J. Newman (eds), *The New Palgrave* (Macmillan).

Murray, R. (1985) 'Benetton Britain: the new economic order', *Marxism Today*, November.

Myrdal, G. (1944) *The American Dilemma: The Negro Problem and Modern Democracy* (Harper & Row).

Myrdal, G. (1957) *Economic Theory and Underdeveloped Regions* (Duckworth).

Naples, M. E. (1986) 'The unravelling of the union-capital truce and the U.S. industrial productivity crisis', *Review of Radical Political Economics*, vol. 18.

Ng, Y. K. (1983) *Welfare Economics* (Macmillan).

Nichols, T. (1969) *Ownership, Control and Ideology* (Allen and Unwin).

Nichols, T. (1986) *The British Worker Question* (Routledge & Kegan Paul).

Nicol, W. and Yuill, D. (1982) 'Regional problems and policy', in A. Boltho (ed.), *The European Economy: Growth and Crisis* (Oxford University Press).

Nolan, P. and Edwards, P. K. (1984) 'Homogenise, divide and rule: an essay on *Segmented work, divided workers*', *Cambridge Journal of Economics*, vol. 8.

Nolan, P. and O'Donnell, K. (1987) 'Taming the market economy? A critical assessment of the GLC experiment in restructuring for Labour', *Cambridge Journal of Economics*, vol. 11.

Nove, A. (1972) *An Economic History of the U.S.S.R* (Penguin Books).

Nurkse, R. (1952) *Some Aspects of Capital Accumulation in Underdeveloped Countries* (Cairo).

Nyman, S. and Silberston, A. (1978) 'The ownership and control of industry', *Oxford Economic Papers*, vol. 30.

O'Connor, J. (1973) *The Fiscal Crisis of the State* (St Martin's Press).

OECD (1972) *Industrial Policy of Japan* (Paris).

Ollman, B. (1976) *Alienation: Marx's Conception of Man in a Capitalist Society* (Cambridge University Press).

Ong, N-P., (1981) 'Target pricing, competition and growth', *Journal of Post Keynesian Economics*, vol. 4.

Oster, G. (1979) 'A factor analytic test of the theory of the dual economy', *Review of Economics and Statistics*, vol. 61.

Parkin, J. M. and Bade, R. (1988) *Modern Macroeconomics* (2nd edn) (Philip Allan).

Pasinetti, L. (1974) *Growth and Income Distribution* (Cambridge University Press).

Pasinetti, L. L. (1977) *Lectures on the Theory of Production* (Macmillan).

Patinkin, D. (1982) *Anticipations of the General Theory* (Blackwell).

Peacock, A. and Wiseman, J. (1961) *Growth of Public Expenditure in the United Kingdom* (Allen and Unwin).

Pheby, J. (1988) *Methodology and Economics* (Macmillan).

Piore, M. J. (1973) 'Notes for a theory of labour market stratification', in R. Edwards, M. Reich and D. Gordon (eds), *Labor Market Segmentation* (Lexington Books).

Piore, M. and Sabel, C. T. (1984) *The Second Industrial Divide: Possibilities of Prosperity* (Basic Books).

Pollard, S. (1968) *The Genesis of Modern Management* (Penguin Books).

Pollin, R. and Alarcon, D. (1988) 'Debt crisis, accumulation crisis and economic restructuring in Latin America', *International Review of Applied Economics*, vol. 2.

Poulantzas, N. (1973) *Political Power and Social Classes* (New Left Books).

Poulantzas, N. (1977) *Crisis of the State* (New Left Books).

Poulantzas, N. (1978) *State, Power and Socialism* (New Left Books).

Pratten, C. K. (1971) *Economies of Scale in Manufacturing Industry* (Cambridge University Press).

Prebisch, R. (1950) *The Economic Development of Latin America and its Principal Problems* (UN Economic Commission for Latin America).

Purdy, D. (1988) *Social Power and the Labour Market* (Macmillan).

Quine, W. van O. (1951) 'Two dogmas of empiricism', *Philosophical Review*, vol. 60.

Rau, N. (1974) *Trade Cycles* (Macmillan).

Ray, G. F. (1983) 'Innovations and long-term growth', in C. Freeman (ed.), *Long Waves in the World Economy* (Butterworth).

Ray, G. (1987) 'The decline of primary producer power', *National Institute Economic Review*, no. 121.

Rcati, A. (1986) 'The rate of profit and the organic composition of capital in West German industry from 1960 to 1981', *Review of Radical Political Economics*, vol. 18.

Reich, M. (1981) *Radical Inequality: A Political-economic analysis* (Princeton University Press).

Reich, M. (1984) 'Segmented labour: time series hypothesis and evidence', *Cambridge Journal of Economics*, vol. 8.

Review of Monopolies and Mergers Policy (1978) *A Consultative Document*, Cmnd. 7198 (HMSO).

Reynolds, P. (1984) 'An empirical analysis of the degree of monopoly theory of distribution', *Bulletin of Economic Research*, vol. 36.

Reynolds, P. (1987) *Political Economy: A Synthesis of Kaleckian and Post Keynesian Economics* (Harvester Wheatsheaf).

Ricardo, D. (1951) *The Principles of Political Economy and Taxation* (Cambridge University Press) (first published 1817).

Robbins, L. (1932) *An essay on the Nature and Significance of Economic Science* (Macmillan).

Robinson, J. (1956) *The Accumulation of Capital* (Macmillan).

Robinson, J. (1962) *Economic Philosophy* (Watts).

Robinson, J. (1971) 'The second crisis of economic theory', *American Economic Review*, vol. 61.

Rosenberg, N. and Frischtak, C. R. (1984) 'Technological innovation and long waves', *Cambridge Journal of Economics*, vol. 8.

Rosenberg, S. (1983) 'Reagan's social policy and labour force restructuring', *Cambridge Journal of Economics*, vol. 7.

Rosenberg, S. and Weisskopf, T. E. (1981) 'A conflict theory approach to inflation in the post war U.S. economy', *American Economic Review*, vol. 71.

Rothschild, K. W. (1947) 'Price theory and oligopoly', *Economic Journal*, vol. 67.

Rothschild, K. (ed.) (1971) *Power in Economics* (Penguin Books).

Rowthorn, R. (1974) 'Neo-Classicism, neo-Ricardianism and Marxism', *New Left Review* (reprinted in Rowthorn, 1980).

Rowthorn, R. (1977) 'Conflict, inflation and money', *Cambridge Journal of Economics*, vol. 1 (reprinted in Rowthorn, 1980).

Rowthorn, R. (1980) *Capitalism, Conflict and Inflation* (Lawrence & Wishart).

Rumberger, R. W. and Carnoy, M. (1980) 'Segmentation in the US labour market: its effects on the mobility and earnings of whites and blacks', *Cambridge Journal of Economics*, vol. 4.

Ryan, P. (1981) 'Segmentation, duality and the internal labour market', in F. Wilkinson (ed.), *The Dynamics of Labour Market Segmentation* (Academic Press).

Samuels, W. J. (1987) 'Institutional economics', in J. Eatwell, M. Millgate and J. Newman (eds), *The New Palgrave* (Macmillan).

Samuels, W. J. (ed.) (1988) *Institutional Economics* (3 vols) (Edward Elgar).

Samuelson, P. A. (1957) 'Wage and interest: A modern dissection of Marxian economic models', *American Economic Review*, vol. 47.

Sargan, J. D. (1964) 'Wages and prices in the United Kingdom', in P. E. Hart, G. Mill and J. K. Whittaker (eds), *Econometric Analysis for National Economic Planning* (Butterworth).

Sargent, T. (1979) *Macroeconomic Theory* (Academic Press).

Sarkar, P. (1986) 'The Singer–Prebisch hypothesis: a statistical evaluation', *Cambridge Journal of Economics*, vol. 10.

Sawyer, M. (1976) 'Income distribution in OECD countries', *OECD Economic Outlook, Occasional Studies*, July.

Sawyer, M. (1979) *Theories of the Firm* (Weidenfeld and Nicolson).

Sawyer, M. (1982a) *Macro-economics in Question* (Harvester Wheatsheaf).

Sawyer, M. (1982b) 'Collective bargaining, oligopoly and macro-economics', *Oxford Economic Papers*, vol. 34.

Sawyer, M. (1982c) 'Income distribution and the welfare state', in A. Boltho (ed.), *The European Economy: Growth and Crisis* (Oxford University Press).

Sawyer, M. (1983) *Business Pricing and Inflation* (Macmillan).

Sawyer, M. (1985a) *Economics of Industries and Firms* (2nd edn) (Croom Helm).

Sawyer, M. (1985b) *The Economics of Michal Kalecki* (Macmillan).

Sawyer, M. (1987) 'The political economy of the Phillips curve', *Thames Papers in Political Economy*, Summer.

Sawyer, M. (1988) 'Theories of monopoly capitalism: a survey', *Journal of Economic Surveys*, vol. 2.

Sawyer, M. (ed.) (1989) *Post Keynesian Economics* (Edward Elgar).

Sawyer, M. (1990) *Economic Analysis of Firms* (Routledge).

Schumpeter, J. (1939) *Business Cycles, a Theoretical, Historical and Statistical Analysis of the Capitalist Process* (McGraw-Hill).

Scitovsky, T. (1943) 'A note on profit maximization', *Review of Economic Studies*, vol. 11.

Scott, B. R. (1984) 'National strategy for stronger US competitiveness', *Harvard Business Review*, vol. 82.

Semmler, W. (1981) 'Competition, monopoly and differentials of profit rates: theoretical considerations and empirical evidence', *Review of Radical Political Economy*, vol. 13.

Semmler, W. (1983) 'Competition, monopoly and differentials of profit rates: a reply', *Review of Radical Political Economy*, vol. 15.

Semmler, W. (1987) 'Competition: Marxian concepts', in J. Eatwell, M. Millgate and J. Newman (eds), *The New Palgrave* (Macmillan).

Sen, A. K. (1978) 'On the labour theory of value: some methodological issues', *Cambridge Journal of Economics*, vol. 2.

Shaiken, H., Herzenberg, S. and Kuhn, S. (1986) 'The work process under flexible production', *Industrial Relations*, vol. 25.

Shand, A. (1984) *The Capitalist Alternative: An Introduction to Neo-Austrian Economics* (Harvester Wheatsheaf).

Shapiro, N. (1981) 'Pricing and the growth of the firm', *Journal of Post Keynesian Economics*, vol. 4.

Sherman, H. J. (1986) 'Changes in the character of the US business cycle', *Review of Radical Political Economics*, vol. 18.

Sherman, H. J. (1987a) 'The business cycles of capitalism', *International Review of Applied Economics*, vol. 1.

Sherman, H. J. (1987b) *Foundations of Radical Political Economy* (M. E. Sharpe).

Sherman, H. J. (1989) *Business Cycles* (forthcoming).

Simon, H. A., (1959) 'Theories of decision-making in economics and behavioural science', *American Economic Review*, vol. 49.

Singer, H. (1950) 'The distribution of gains between investing and borrowing countries', *American Economic Review*, vol. 40.

Skott, P. (1983) 'An esssay on Keynes and general equilibrium theory', *Thames Papers in Political Economy*, Summer.

Skott, P. (1985) 'Vicious circles and cumulative causation', *Thames Papers in Political Economy*, Summer.

Smith, A. (1904) *An Inquiry into the Nature and Causes of the Wealth of Nations* (Metheun) (first published 1776).

Smith, R. (1977) 'Military expenditure and capitalism', *Cambridge Journal of Economics*, vol. 1.

Solomou, S. (1986) 'Innovation clusters and Kondratieff long waves in economic growth', *Cambridge Journal of Economics*, vol. 10.

Solow, R. (1956) 'A contribution to the theory of economic growth', *Quarterly Journal of Economics*, vol. 70.

Spraos, J. (1983) *Inequalising Trade?* (Clarendon Press).

Sraffa, P. (1926) 'The laws of return under competitive conditions', *Economic Journal*, vol. 36.

Sraffa, P. (1960) *The Production of Commodities by Means of Commodities* (Cambridge University Press).

Stafford, G. B. (1983) 'The class struggle, the multiplier and the alternative economic strategy', in M. Sawyer and K. Schott (eds), *Socialist Economic Review, 1983* (Merlin Press).

Steedman, I. (1975) 'Positive profits with negative surplus value', *Economic Journal*, vol. 85.

Steedman, I. (1977) *Marx after Sraffa* (New Left Books).

Steedman, I. (1981) 'Ricardo, Marx and Sraffa', in I. Steedman *et al.* (eds), *The Value Controversy* (Verso).

Steedman, I. (1985) 'On "input" demand curves', *Cambridge Journal of Economics*, vol. 9.

Steedman, I. (ed.) (1989) *Sraffian Economics* (2 vols) (Edward Elgar).

Steedman, I. *et al.* (1981) *The Value Controversy* (Verso).

Steindl, J. (1952) *Maturity and Stagnation in American Capitalism* (Blackwell) (re-issued with new introduction by Monthly Review Press, 1976).

Steindl, J. (1979) 'Stagnation theory and stagnation policy', *Cambridge Journal of Economics*, vol. 3.

Stigler, G. (1958) 'Ricardo and the 93% labor theory of value', *American Economic Review*, vol. 48.

Stopford, J. M. and Dunning, J. H. (1983) *Multinationals: Company Performance and Global Trends* (Macmillan).

Sweezy, P. (1939) 'Demand under conditions of oligopoly', *Journal of Political Economy*, vol. 47.

Sweezy, P. (1981) 'Marxian value theory and crises', in I. Steedman *et al.* (eds), *The Value Controversy* (Verso).

Tarling, R. and Wilkinson, F. (1977) 'The social contract: post-war incomes policies and their inflationary impact', *Cambridge Journal of Economics*, vol. 1.

Tawney, R. H. (1926) *Religion and the Rise of Capitalism* (John Murray).

Thirlwall, A. P. (1983) 'A plain man's guide to Kaldor's growth laws', *Journal of Post Keynesian Economics*, vol. 5.

Thirlwall, A. P. (1987) *Nicholas Kaldor* (Harvester Wheatsheaf).

Thompson, K. (ed.) (1984) *Work, Employment and Unemployment* (Open University Press).

Thompson, P. (1983) *The Nature of Work* (Macmillan).

Thurlow, L. (1969) *Poverty and Discrimination* (Brookings Institution).

Tinbergen, J. (1952) *On the Theory of Economic Policy* (North-Holland).

Tinbergen, J. (1983) 'Kondratiev cycles and so-called long waves. The Early Research', in C. Freeman (ed.), *Long Waves in the World Economy* (Butterworth).

Tobin, J. (1980) 'Are new classical models plausible enough to guide policy?', *Journal of Money, Credit and Banking*, vol. 12.

Tomlinson, J. (1981) 'Why was there never a "Keynesian revolution" in economic policy', *Economy and Society*, vol. 10.

Tomlinson, J. (1983) 'Where do economic policy objectives come from? The case of full employment', *Economy and Society*, vol. 12.

Tomlinson, J. (1987) *Employment Policy: The Crucial Years* (Oxford University Press).

van Duijn, J. J. (1983a) *The Long Wave in Economic Life* (Allen and Unwin).

van Duijn, J. J. (1983b) 'Fluctuations in innovations over time', in C. Freeman (ed.), *Long Waves in the World Economy* (Butterworth).

Vane, H. and Thompson, J. (1985) *An Introduction to Macroeconomic Policy* (Harvester Wheatsheaf).

Verdoorn, P. J. (1949) 'Fattori che regolano lo sviluppo della produttivita del lavoro', *L'Industria*, 1949.

Walras, L. (1954) *Elements of Pure Economics* (trans. W. Jaffe) (Allen and Unwin).

Webber, M. J. and Rigby, D. L. (1986) 'The rate of profit in Canadian manufacturing, 1950–1981', *Review of Radical Political Economics*, vol. 18.

Weintraub, E. R. (1979a) *Microeconomic Foundations – the Compatibility of Microeconomics and Macroeconomics* (Cambridge University Press).

Weintraub, S. (1979b) 'The missing theory of money wages', *Journal of Post Keynesian Economics*, vol. 1.

Weiss, L. (1971) 'Quantitative studies of industrial organisation', in M. Intriligator (ed.), *Frontiers of economics* (North-Holland).

Weisskopf, T. E. (1979) 'Marxian crisis theory and the rate of profit in the post war U.S. economy', *Cambridge Journal of Economics*, vol. 3.

Weisskopf, T. E. (1987) 'The effect of unemployment on labour productivity: an international comparative analysis', *International Review of Applied Economics*, vol. 1.

Weisskopf, T. E., Bowles, S. and Gordon, D. M. (1983) 'Hearts and minds: a social model of U.S. productivity growth', *Brookings Papers on Economic Activity*, 1983.

Williamson, O. E. (1964) *The Economics of Discretionary Behavior: Managerial Objectives in a Theory of the Firm* (Prentice Hall).

Williamson, O. E. (1975) *Markets and Hierarchies: Analysis and Antitrust Implications* (Free Press).

Williamson, O. E. (1981) 'The modern corporation: origins, evolution, attributes', *Journal of Economic Literature*, vol. 19.

Williamson, O. E. (1985) *Economic Institutions of Capitalism* (Collier-Macmillan).

Williamson, O. E. (1986) *Economic Organisation: Firms, Markets and Policy Controls* (Harvester Wheatsheaf).

Winter, S. G. (1964) 'Economic natural selection', *Yale Economic Essays*, Spring.

Wolff, E. N. (1986) 'The productivity slowdown and the fall in the U.S. rate of profit, 1947–76', *Review of Radical Political Economics*, vol. 18.

Wood, A. (1975) *A Theory of Profits* (Cambridge University Press).

Wood, S. (ed.) (1982a) *The Degradation of Work?: Skill, Deskilling and the Labour Process* (Hutchinson).

Wood, S. (1982b) 'Introduction', in S. Wood (ed.), *The Degradation of Work?* (Hutchinson).

Wood, S. (1985) 'The labour process', Unit 9 of The Open University, *Labour: Processes and Control* (part of Work and Society course) (Open University Press).

Wood, S. and Kelly, J. (1982) 'Taylorism, responsible autonomy and management Strategy', in S. Wood (ed.), *The Degradation of Work?* (Hutchinson).

Woods, J. E. (1987) 'Invariable standards of value', in J. Eatwell, M. Millgate and J. Newman (eds), *The New Palgrave* (Macmillan).

Work Relations Group (1978) 'Uncovering the hidden history of the American workplace', *Review of Radical Political Economics*, vol. 10.

Zeitlin, M. (1974) 'Corporate ownership and control', *American Journal of Sociology*, vol. 79.

Zimbalist, A. (ed.) (1979a) *Case Studies in the Labor Process* (Monthly Review Press).

Zimbalist, A. (1979b) 'Introduction' to A. Zimbalist (ed.), *Case Studies in the Labor Process* (Monthly Review Press).

SUBJECT INDEX